Impact of War on
Federal Personnel Administration
1939-1945

GLADYS M. KAMMERER

Impact of War on Federal Personnel Administration 1939-1945

UNIVERSITY OF KENTUCKY PRESS

LEXINGTON

*Publication of this book is possible partly
by reason of a grant from the
Margaret Voorhies Haggin Trust
Established in memory of her husband
James Ben Ali Haggin*

COPYRIGHT, 1951

UNIVERSITY OF KENTUCKY PRESS

PRINTED AT THE UNIVERSITY OF KENTUCKY BY THE
KERNEL PRESS AND BOUND BY KINGSPORT PRESS, INC.

To My Brother Bill

Glossary of Specialized Names and Symbols

AAF	Army Air Forces
ASF	Army Service Forces
CSC	Civil Service Commission
FEPC	Committee on Fair Employment Practice
JIT	Job Instruction Training
JMT	Job Methods Training
JRT	Job Relations Training
NRPB	National Resources Planning Board
OCD	Office of Civilian Defense
OEM	Office of Emergency Management
OPA	Office of Price Administration
OPM	Office of Production Management
Roster	National Roster of Scientific and Specialized Personnel
SECP	Shore Establishments and Civilian Personnel (Navy Department)
USES	United States Employment Service
WLB	War Labor Board
WMC	War Manpower Commission
WPB	War Production Board
IVb	A classification of clerical positions in the Navy Department

Preface

The impressive military record of the United States in World War II was due in no small measure to the high levels of effectiveness attained by the administrative management of the Federal government. The move for administrative reform launched in the thirties bore fruit in many of the changes instituted in 1939-1940 which helped to set the stage for building a war organization which met the pragmatic test.

No less important than the structural changes effected for the improvement of wartime administration was the staffing of the vast Federal organization. The concentration of authority and responsibility for civilian recruitment in the Civil Service Commission during the defense period made that agency the focal point for pressures both for deterioration and improvement of the service. For personnel administration, as for other functions of public administration, the war furnished both a prolonged crisis and an unparalleled opportunity. The challenge to improve recruitment methods was inescapable, and, on the whole, a new partnership was forged between the Civil Service Commission and the employing agencies. The personnel function assumed increased importance in virtually all agencies. In-service training and employee relations were similarly areas of progress in many departments. Adjustment to crisis conditions provoked a new flexibility in Federal personnel administration which not only preserved the merit system but provided a new point of departure for the merit system in the postwar period.

During the war years I found it possible in 1944 and 1945 to study the operations of the Civil Service Commission and of four departments of special significance: the War Department, the Navy Department, the Office of Price Administration, and the Department of Agriculture. Both the War and Navy departments, as industrial producers, had become the principal government employers and perforce were compelled to adopt personnel programs of a scope unparalleled elsewhere. OPA, a new war agency, was faced with some of the most difficult and novel operating problems of the war years and developed a distinctive approach to personnel problems. The Department of Agriculture, widely known in the prewar years for its well-managed personnel office, demonstrated the adjustment of an "old line" agency to the new problems of the period. Through the generous cooperation of Commissioner Arthur S. Flemming, all records and materials within the Civil Service Commission library and statistical office were made available. In addition, I was able to interview a number of staff members who were most helpful in furnishing additional data. All material from the four departments mentioned above was gathered by interview. Mr. Lee P. Brown of the Office of the Secretary of War was most helpful in his suggestions and generous in the time given to directing contacts within the War Department, as was Mrs. Astrid K. Kraus, of the same office. Commander S. L. Owen, Director of the Training Branch in the Shore Establishments and Civilian Personnel, Navy Department, also gave invaluable assistance in arranging interviews and furnishing material in his office.

The completion of this study was made possible by the American Association of University Women, through the Kathryn McHale fellowship for 1945-1946.

Acknowledgement is also extended to the editors of the *Journal of Politics* for the permission they gave to use in the last chapter material which originally appeared as an article in the February, 1948, number of the *Journal*.

To the Civil Service Commission library staff and especially Miss Rose Saidman, law librarian, Mr. John W. Mitchell, chief, Federal Employment Statistics Staff, the many training and employee relations officers in the four departments I visited, and many other Federal officers who so generously gave of their time to furnish information, I am deeply indebted. I wish to express sincere appreciation to Professor Leonard D. White of the University of Chicago for his counsel, constructive criticism, patience, and encouragement. I should like to extend thanks and appreciation to Professors Floyd W. Reeves and C. Herman Pritchett, also of the University of Chicago, who likewise read this manuscript, for their helpful suggestions. And, last but not least, the services of Miss Irene Haynie in typing this manuscript with great accuracy and dispatch were invaluable.

GLADYS M. KAMMERER

Table of Contents

	Page
Preface	vii
List of Tables	x
List of Illustrations	xi

Chapter
- I. Introduction: Statement of the Problem 1
- II. Centralization of the Responsibility for Recruitment . . 12
- III. A New Aggressive Approach to Recruitment 43
- IV. Application of the New Aggressive Approach to Particular Occupational Groups 64
- V. The Deterioration in Standards for Selection 88
- VI. The New Emphasis on Loyalty 117
- VII. Development of Training Policies and Organization . . . 135
- VIII. Development of Training Programs 154
- IX. Increased Mobility Within the Service 185
- X. Intensification of Pressures for Higher Pay: Statutory Adjustments 215
- XI. Intensification of Pressures for Higher Pay: On the Classification Act and Wage Administration 235
- XII. Controls on Federal Employment 254
- XIII. Broadening Employee Relations Programs 283
- XIV. Administrative Changes and Reorganization of the Civil Service Commission 321
- XV. An Evaluation of Wartime Personnel Administration . . 342

List of Tables

Table		Page
1.	Growth in Federal Civilian Employment, Selected Months, 1939-45	17
2.	Turnover in the Federal Service, Selected Months, April, 1943-April, 1945	18
3.	Expansion of Civil Service Commission Staff, Selected Months, 1939-45	19
4.	Expansion of Staff and Volume of Work of the Seventh Civil Service Regional Office at Chicago, June, 1939-June, 1944	20
5.	Employment and Unemployment in the United States, Selected Months, 1939-45	25
6.	Women Employees in the Federal Service and in the United States, Selected Months, July, 1940-July, 1945	51
7.	Percentage of Negro Classified Workers in Various Services by Agency Groups, March 31, 1944	54
8.	Distribution of Total and Negro Federal Workers Within Major Agency Groups, March 31, 1944	56
9.	Cases Docketed by FEPC Against Federal Agencies	57
10.	Dollar-a-Year Men and WOCS in War Production Board, Selected Months, 1943-1945	66
11.	Distribution of Employees in the War and Navy Departments, June 30, 1944	84
12.	Increases in Selected Salary Rates Under the Pay Act of 1945 as Compared with Rates Effective Through June 30, 1945	233
13.	Reasons for Turnover, Federal Departmental Service, October Through December, 1942	296
14.	Participation in War Department Civilian Suggestion Program, April, 1945	306

List of Illustrations

Figure   Page

1. Percentage Distribution of Paid Civilian Employment in the Executive Branch of the Federal Government by Agency: Semiannual, 1920-1938; Monthly, 1939 to 1945   9

2. Distribution of Paid Civilian Employment in the Executive Branch of the Federal Government by Agency: Semiannual, 1920-1938; Monthly, 1939 to 1945   10

3. Chart Showing Relationship of Recruiting Representatives to Liaison Representatives and Examiners   23

4. Chart Showing the Relationships Between the Civil Service Commission and the War Manpower Commission   28

5. Organization of the Civil Service Commission in 1939. . 323

6. Chart Showing Organization of the Civil Service Commission in 1944 328

7. Organization of the Regional Offices of the Civil Service Commission 336

CHAPTER ONE

Introduction: Statement of the Problem

FROM THE vantage point of 1948, the six war years from 1939 to 1945 emerge as a period furnishing the greatest test public administration has faced in this country. Almost beyond comprehension is the magnitude of organizing industrial production for modern mechanized warfare in a global conflict, sustaining and controlling the civilian economy to prevent both privation and inflation, and shifting millions of persons into new occupations and localities. Federal personnel administration was as profoundly affected as any of the other phases of administration by the variety and complexity of novel war programs. New and unforeseen demands for personnel accumulated under the pressure of defense preparation and, later, of total war. These demands caused radical adaptations in, and departures from, principles and procedures hallowed by nearly sixty years of practice. Complacency was rudely shaken as administrators and personnel technicians had to bethink themselves of ways and means to mobilize and keep the vast army of civilian employees on the job to fulfill the government's responsibilities in directing the war effort and actually producing some of the material of war.

The threefold expansion of the Federal civil service was not alone the greatest factor for change. That expansion must be considered within the frame of reference of a rapidly expanding economy and growth of our armed forces. The competition of the military and industry for manpower created an ever tighter labor market within which the Federal government had to compete, in contrast to the situation in 1939 when the unemployed exceeded nine millions. The usual government advantages in employment were inoperative under conditions of labor scarcity. The labor force, suddenly more mobile, moved from job to job searching for the best-paid work with the most attractive perquisites. Controls over the movement of labor had to be devised to assure supply to essential activities.

Another factor of importance was the peculiar urgency of World War II which compelled rapidity of adjustment. The ruthless nature of the Axis enemies, the way in which the United States was suddenly swept into the conflict, the world-wide battlefronts, all barred compromise with the usual. The alarm that swept the United States in May, 1940, never abated but intensified even as late as December, 1944, when sudden reverses in the Ardennes seemed to shake out of our hands the victory that had been deemed so close. Fear of "too little and too late," the cartoonists' and editorialists' *bête noire,* emboldened the administrator. As the nation moved through one crisis to another, now military, now economic, even personnel administrators needed imagination, foresight, and boldness to try the new and to improvise when there were no guidelines.

To the student of geology, time, change, and conflict are the great natural forces shaping the material world. To the student of war administration, they also appear valid except that he sees time in inverse proportions to the view the geologist cultivates. Instead of endless eons, the student of war administration sees the telescoping of time through conflict. Changes that ordinarily take years to effect are adopted in a few days or months as tradition distintegrates temporarily.

First of all, in this examination of the trends in personnel administration under the impact of World War II the wartime setting will be briefly recounted. The principal military and economic events which created crisis administration and labor scarcity will be pointed out briefly as signposts for the story. Secondly, the wartime adaptations of personnel administration to a new set of demands will be indicated. Each major change wrought in personnel administration will be treated separately in one or more chapters which follow. Finally, an evaluation of wartime personnel administration will be made to point out the areas of weakness and strength and the conclusions to be drawn from our wartime experiences in this field.

The Wartime Setting

1. From the Invasion of Poland to Pearl Harbor

From the day Germany attacked Poland, September 1, 1939, and France and Britain were drawn into the war, it was clear that the United States would sooner or later feel the repercussions of the cataclysm abroad. But for over six months the effects were slight. The most notable event in this early period was the declaration of a limited national emergency on September 8, 1939. Thus a basis was provided for a new executive order authorizing the first emergency appointments in the Federal service a few days later. A few industries began to feel the stimulus of war orders as British and French purchasing missions sought to buy planes in the United States. The aviation industry was still so small, however, that months of preparation were needed to gear plants to the modest orders received.

All the greater, therefore, after the *Sitzkrieg* phase of the war in the first eight months, came the shock of the German invasion of the Low Countries and France on May 10, 1940, and the fall of France by June 17, 1940. The United States was rudely jarred into feverish defense planning. President Roosevelt called upon Congress for 50,000 planes and a two-ocean navy on May 16, 1940. The President created a place for the administration of the many new defense functions foreseen by an administrative order establishing an Office of Emergency Management in the Executive Office on May 25, 1940.[1] Through the resurrection of the National Defense Act of 1916, an Advisory Commission to the Council of National Defense was appointed May 29, 1940, to plan the defense program and get it under way. Out of the Advisory Commission evolved in the next two years all the major war agencies, such as the War Production Board, the Office of Price Administration, the War Manpower Commission, the Office of Civilian Defense, and the rest. The Civil Service Commission reached a principal milestone in May, 1940, when Congress delegated responsibility to it for the recruitment of all Federal employees needed in the new defense program.

During the summer of 1940, sentiment was mobilized in favor of our first peacetime conscription by the alarm felt here over the isolation of Great Britain after Dunkirk and the air *blitz* which started in August, 1940. The Selective Training and Service Act was passed on September 16, 1940. Induction of the first draftees began about six weeks later, when National Guard inductions also started, and the first draining of the most employable part of the nation's labor force began. From the loose organization of the Advisory Commission defense production was reorganized

[1] 3 *CFR, Cumulative Supp.* 1320.

under a new Office of Production Management, located within the Office of Emergency Management, on January 7, 1941.[2] The "tooling up" process was speeded materially in 1941 through this reorganization. The determination to aid Britain culminated in the Lend-Lease Act of March 1, 1941, which furnished a powerful stimulus to production and hence to employment by compounding our government's purchases with those for our friends resisting aggression.

The German invasion of Yugoslavia and Greece on April 6, 1941, sounded new alarms. President Roosevelt declared a state of unlimited national emergency on May 27, 1941. German consulates were closed by order of the President on June 16, 1941. The German attack on Russia on June 22, 1941, increased American fear as grave misgivings were expressed regarding Russia's ability to withstand the advancing *Wehrmacht*. Many persons expressed the fear that time seemed to be running out for American preparations. That feeling was heightened by the sinking of the American destroyer *Reuben James* by German submarine action off the coast of Iceland on October 31, 1941. By that time a diplomatic crisis with Japan was at hand.

Area labor shortages had begun to appear in some regions as a result of increased defense production in certain industries. One of the first industries to suffer a shortage was West Coast shipbuilding, for which the first stabilization agreement for employment was approved by OPM on April 11, 1941. Materials, however, were in 1941 a more critical item than labor, for priorities had to be developed beginning in March, 1941, and OPM called for increased production of steel plate for defense purposes as well as curtailment for nondefense uses in June, 1941. For the most part, the country had been passing through the preparatory stage, and labor shortages were primarily in skilled-labor brackets.

2. PEARL HARBOR TO V-J DAY

Immediately following the disaster at Pearl Harbor on December 7, 1941, the sights were raised out of all prior range with respect to military, industrial, and governmental manpower needs. The age limits for draft registration were changed to a range from eighteen to sixty-four years of age on December 20, 1941. By the end of February, 1942, the army was reorganized into three

[2] Executive Order 8629.

principal branches: ground forces, air forces, and service forces. The first War Powers Act permitting presidential creation and reorganization of executive agencies was passed on December 18, 1941, with a second War Powers Act following on March 27, 1942. An Emergency Price Control Act had been passed January 30, 1942, granting power to enforce priorities and rationing. In one of the major reorganizations of 1942 the War Production Board superseded OPM on January 16, 1942,[3] and the War Labor Board was created January 12, 1942.[4] The War Manpower Commission was set up April 18, 1942.[5] A "war production drive" was opened by the new WPB chairman, Donald M. Nelson, on March 9, 1942.

A manpower shortage began developing in the spring of 1942, as one disaster followed another from the fall of Bataan in April to Rommel's capture of Tobruk in June, and the tempo of production and conscription had perforce quickened. The War Manpower Commission announced its first policies to prevent labor pirating in July, 1942. By September the federalized United States Employment Service was transferred to WMC for the duration. Through this transfer WMC gained a more effective control over the movement and assignment of the nation's labor force. The reduction of the age for military induction to eighteen in November, 1942, cut deeper into the available labor supply, and as a result the campaign to enlist women, minority groups, the aged, and the school-age youth gained momentum. At the same time the armed forces likewise sought women for the newly authorized women's reserve corps, beginning with the Women's Army Auxiliary Corps in May, 1942. Gold mining was one of the nonessential occupations halted for the duration in October, 1942.

On the economic front the battle opened when the President issued his "hold-the-line" order in April, 1942, with a seven-point program to check inflation. Major points in that program were the tying of wages to prices and provision for the control of wage rises by the War Labor Board. In July, 1942, the War Labor Board laid down the line it followed for the duration, in the so-called "Little Steel formula," which provided a yardstick for determining permissible increases in base pay. In the meantime the Office of Price Administration, in April, 1942, issued its general maximum-price regulations, establishing the ceiling at the

[3] Executive Order 9024.   [4] Executive Order 9017.   [5] Executive Order 9139.

March, 1942, level. Congress, after prodding from the President in the form of a forceful talk to the nation, passed the Cost of Living Stabilization Act on October 3, 1942, to authorize price ceilings on foods and rents. Justice James F. Byrnes was immediately appointed to the post of Director of Economic Stabilization. By his "wage-freeze" order in October, 1942, President Roosevelt ordered all wage increases to be based on the "Little Steel formula" thenceforth.

The mounting of offensives from the remote islands of the Pacific to the desert of North Africa, together with the planning for other greater campaigns against the German and Japanese home bastions, forced production up continuously. The production goals WPB announced for 1943 were double those of 1942 and included production of 100,000 planes. A great steel production drive was started in June, 1943. The armed forces planned for 15,000,000 men and women in uniform. The President established the Office of War Mobilization under James F. Byrnes on May 27, 1943, to unify the various programs and activities of Federal agencies for mobilization of natural, human, and industrial resources.

Invasion was wasteful of weapons, chewing up equipment as soon as it came from America. The pressure for production was actually intensified rather than lessened by the opening of the second front in 1944. Heavier offensives were the order of the day in the Pacific also when the American Army returned to the Philippines in October, 1944. With Allied reverses in the Battle of the Bulge in December, 1944, cries grew louder for increasing amounts of weapons. But the climax came in Europe on V-E Day, May 8, 1945. The two bombs which fell early in August, 1945, one on Hiroshima and the other on Nagasaki, not only helped to end the war in the Pacific but rang down the curtain on one age of history and ushered in a new one. V-J Day came on August 14, 1945, after six years of world-wide tension and terror and nearly five of prodigious American production.

Federal employment rose from less than a million at the outbreak of the war in 1939 to over three million in 1943. But the labor force of the nation had expanded by some 10,000,000 persons during the same period as unemployment reached an irreducible minimum. The rise in the number of employed persons to 54,000,000 in July, 1944, was achieved despite the 1944 military strength of over 12,000,000 men and women in all branches. Employment in all types of manufacturing had risen from 10,000,000 persons to 16,000,000 while production of goods and services had increased 60 per cent from 1940 to 1944.[6] Shipyard employment had increased fifteen times and aircraft and aircraft parts employment twenty times over 1940 levels by 1944. The War and Navy departments' civilian employment totals reached all-time peaks of 1,615,896 and 766,150 respectively in February, 1945. The extraordinary growth of those departments in relation to the rest of the service and in relation to total Federal expansion is shown in Figures 1 and 2, where it can be seen that they comprised close to 70 per cent of all Federal employment in contrast to 20 per cent in 1939.

Principal Changes in Personnel Administration, 1939-45

The sudden expansion of the Federal service under the irresistible pressure of all-out war and worsening manpower shortages wrought changes of a fundamental character in personnel administration. Continuation of the old ways and patterns would have been disastrous to the conduct of the war. Change came gradually after the launching of the defense program in May, 1940, for labor shortages were local and sporadic at first. The great change, providing for the abandonment of most prewar civil service procedures and standards, came with the war service regulations, adopted in February, 1942, at the very time industry was abandoning civilian goods manufacture for all-out war production. Shortly thereafter the War Manpower Commission was established, and gradually it superimposed a network of manpower controls upon the framework of the streamlined war service regulations. Government manpower requirements thereby came within the purview of total manpower requirements for a war economy and had to be reconciled with the needs of war industries and the demands of the armed forces.

The principal changes of the war years were ten in number. They were: (1) the centralization of responsibility for recruitment in the Civil Service Commission; (2) the adoption of a new aggressive approach to recruitment; (3) the deterioration in qualifications standards for employment; (4) a new emphasis on

[6] Donald H. Davenport, Charles D. Stewart, and Hugh B. Killough, "Impact of War Upon Employment," *Public Personnel Review*, V (1944), 140-45.

loyalty as other standards fell; (5) the development of training programs; (6) increased mobility within the service; (7) the intensification of pressures for higher pay; (8) control over the volume of Federal employment; (9) the evolution of employee-relations programs; and (10) reorganization of the Civil Service Commission for improved personnel management. Although there were other changes within the same period by reason of new legislation, such as the Ramspeck Act of 1940, the Ramspeck-Mead Act of 1941, and the establishment of a merit system for Federal lawyers under the Board of Legal Examiners, they were merely a continuation of the trend started in the late 1930's for the improvement and rationalization of public administration. Other changes during the war years, such as the enactment of more favorable veterans' preference legislation and the promulgation of elaborate reduction-in-force procedures, were in actuality within the context of demobilization and postwar plans rather than an integral part of wartime development.

The Federal civil service changed profoundly under the impact of war. Emphasis was laid on speed and positive service by the Civil Service Commission. The Commission itself gained new power through its control of recruitment into the war agencies as well as its increased jurisdiction over the permanent civil service. Unprecedented responsibility rested upon it in staffing the greatest civilian army of employees in our history. The problem involved in this study is to determine whether with its new power and shift of emphasis it met the demands of wartime administration adequately. It is also important to discover whether wartime experience contained any lessons of value for the postwar era.

Competition for manpower among the armed forces, industry, and government became so intense that controls had to be imposed by a specially created manpower agency. A problem to be considered is whether or not our Federal personnel system possessed sufficient flexibility to operate successfully in a tight labor market under manpower controls imposed upon virtually all employers and workers. Related to that question is another: Could the basic principles of the merit system survive when entrance standards were deteriorated by the scarcity of manpower?

The phenomenal development of in-service training and employee-relations services during the war years raises further questions. What training needs were disclosed by the war and

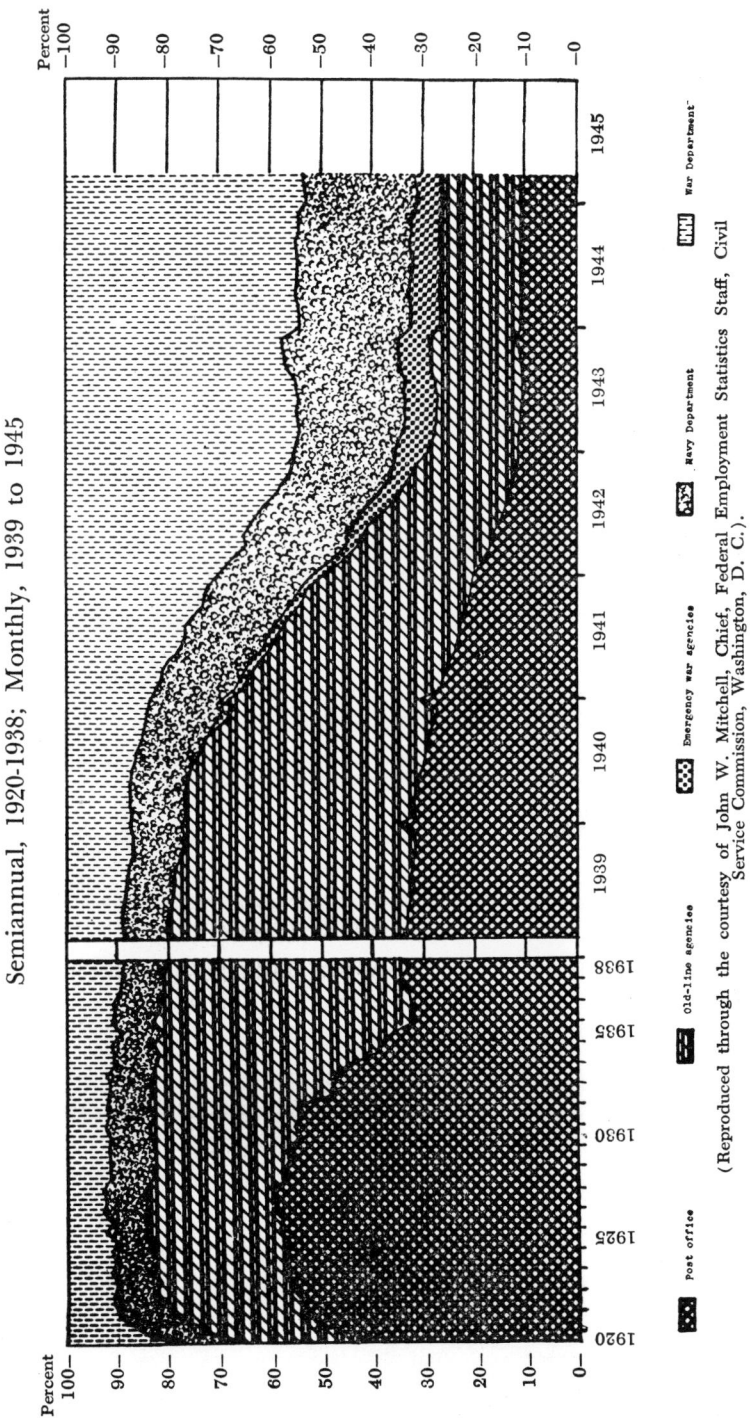

Fig. 1–Percentage Distribution of Paid Civilian Employment in the Executive Branch of the Federal Government by Agency (including outside continental U. S.) Semiannual, 1920-1938; Monthly, 1939 to 1945

(Reproduced through the courtesy of John W. Mitchell, Chief, Federal Employment Statistics Staff, Civil Service Commission, Washington, D. C.).

10 IMPACT OF WAR ON FEDERAL PERSONNEL

Fig. 2–Distribution of Paid Civilian Employment in the Executive Branch of the Federal Government by Agency (including outside continental U. S.) Semiannual, 1920-1938; Monthly, 1939 to 1945

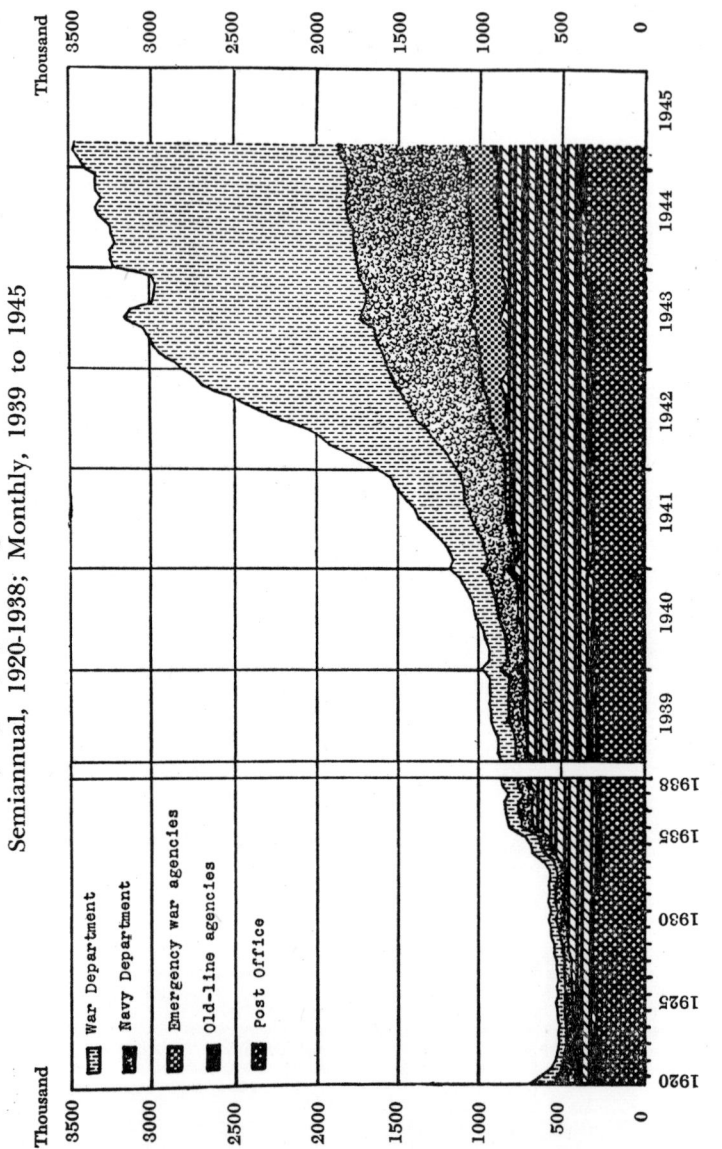

(Reproduced through the courtesy of John W. Mitchell, Chief, Federal Employment Statistics Staff, Civil Service Commission, Washington, D. C. The section of the chart for the years 1939-1945 was published in *Federal Employment Statistics Bulletin*, February, 1945).

how effectively were they met? What lessons for the future can be found in the agencies' experience with training and with employee relations?

The injection of the loyalty issue created problems concerning employee rights in war and in peace and the dangers inherent in direct congressional interference with the enforcement of the loyalty qualification. In addition, there is the problem of legislative usurpation of executive authority.

The effectiveness of congressional control over personnel administration is brought under question by an examination of the attempt to control volume of employment in wartime. If Congress cannot control numbers in the Federal service, the question is pertinent as to whether the Bureau of the Budget is able to do so. There is the further problem of where control should be lodged.

The handling of the pay problem raised issues regarding the entire salary structure under the Classification Act and as to whether or not statutory rigidity of salaries actually impaired the purpose for which the law was passed. If not, what changes could be made to remedy wartime shortcomings?

Of importance, too, is a glance at the profession of personnel administration. What was the significance of the new responsibilities and expansion of programs to the profession? Were advances built upon a solid foundation for future growth?

Finally, it is necessary to try to read the direction taken by the Civil Service Commission to determine to what extent it broke with the past. Did it have a clear concept of where it was headed? What clarification did the war furnish of Commission relationships with the agency personnel offices? Only a clear answer to the question of the direction taken by the Commission will furnish a clue as to whether or not the lessons etched by war experience have furnished the starting point for future progress or have been discarded as hastily as possible in favor of a return to pre-1939 outlook and procedures.

CHAPTER TWO

Centralization of the Responsibility for Recruitment

JUST AS the first real impact of the war in Europe was not felt in the United States until the Low Countries were overrun and France was clearly doomed, so the field of public management here experienced few repercussions of war until the nation had once resolved to launch a gigantic rearmament program. Many of the measures of 1939 and 1940, helpful as they were to sound war administration, were the outgrowth of the Report of the President's Committee on Administrative Management in the mid-thirties and were unrelated to war. From May, 1940, however, when President Roosevelt called for 50,000 planes, a new current was set in motion. Most important, for the purposes of this study, was the effect the emergency had upon personnel administration, namely, the ineluctable imperative to recruit at a speed and volume unparalleled by any "depression" experiences of the preceding decade. The fear of "too little and too late" was omnipresent. We were in the grip of crisis administration.

Of major significance was the decision to centralize responsibility for that vast recruitment in the Civil Service Commission. There was, however, nothing inevitable about that decision. No pattern or tradition for that move was offered by World War I, which had been waged successfully on the civilian side by considerable staffing outside the merit system. Nor did the depression years of 1933 and 1934 offer any helpful precedent inasmuch as the vast majority of the New Deal agencies had been manned by political recruits entirely outside Civil Service Act coverage. In World War II, therefore, new ground was broken for the Civil Service Commission by charging it with the obligation of finding what proved to be the many millions of civilian employees required by the Federal government during the next five years.

As a matter of fact, the Commission was in an incomparably stronger position to assume the added burdens of World War II recruitment than it would have been in 1917 or 1933 to receive similar responsibility. It had as its most important asset vigorous leadership at the top in the person of the minority member, Arthur S. Flemming. As further advantages it had a close link to the White House through the new Liaison Officer for Personnel Administration, William McReynolds, himself an old civil servant; some powerful advocates in Congress led by Robert Ramspeck, who in 1942 became Democratic whip; and the new personnel fraternity in the agencies as well as the new Council of Personnel Administration upon which to rely for co-operation. The hearings and debates on the Ramspeck Act showed that the prevailing winds of congressional and informed public opinion blew in the direction of expanding, not contracting, the coverage of the merit system. The advice given in 1937 by the President's Committee on Administrative Management to expend merit system coverage "upward, downward, and outward" had obviously not fallen on deaf ears.

Congress took two significant steps to centralize responsibility for recruitment, and the President—by executive order—a third. The first step was the determination that all defense recruitment should be under the civil service rules. This decision was reached in May, 1940, when the first large defense appropriations were made by Congress. The second step came a few months later with the enactment of the Ramspeck Act, extending the coverage of the Civil Service Act to virtually all regular permanent positions hitherto exempt. By these two steps, responsibility for recruitment of at least 95 per cent of all Federal employees was placed in the Civil Service Commission during the war in contrast to the coverage of 67 per cent it possessed in 1939. By the executive order creating the War Manpower Commission and making the Civil Service Commission subject to it, centralization of authority over recruitment was powerfully underlined for all Federal agencies. The Federal government was viewed as a single employer by the War Manpower Commission, and its sole authorized spokesman on recruitment, both as to numbers and policy, was the Civil Service Commission. Any other approach to the problem of placing this responsibility would have entailed chaos within the government on recruitment and would undoubtedly have resulted in inability to reconcile public with private requirements.

EXTENSION OF THE JURISDICTION OF THE COMMISSION OVER THE NEW DEFENSE AND WAR POSITIONS AND AGENCIES

1. THE DECISION OF 1940 AND ITS SCOPE

How, one may well ask, was the initial decision made in 1940 to assign the responsibility for all recruitment to the Commission? Not without a struggle against tradition and only by dint of forceful argument did the Commission secure its gigantic assignment, one which, it should be noted, it sought deliberately. In fact, the House Military Affairs Committee had already placed the customary exemption from the Civil Service Act in a proposed rearmament measure in May, 1940. The committee was not predisposed to take a bright view of the Commission's ability to act with dispatch in the crisis. As a matter of fact, committee members felt not only that there was excessive rigidity to the merit system, but also that the Commission was hopelessly enmeshed in its own red tape. They were on fairly solid ground in the latter conclusion inasmuch as the Commission, starved for years, had been pleading with the Appropriations Committees for more funds to extricate itself from its backlog of work. Had any members of the Military Affairs Committee taken the trouble to read the House Appropriations Committee hearings, they could scarcely have been reassured to learn that the Commission had been nine months in arrears as of June 30, 1939,[1] and that during the early months of fiscal 1940, 3,313 registers were four or more years old and thus entirely valueless.[2]

Therefore, it is all the more remarkable that Commissioner Flemming's assurances that Commission procedure would not be allowed to impede the urgencies of recruitment and that all deadlines would be met convinced Congress that it should delegate control of emergency recruitment to the Commission.[3] He had argued that uncontrolled interagency competition for manpower would obstruct the entire government program and increase confusion in a labor market destined to contract.[4] The extension of

[1] U.S. Congress, House, Hearing on *Independent Offices Appropriation Bill*, 1941, 76th Cong., 3d Sess., December 12, 1939, p. 683.

[2] U.S. Congress, House, Hearing on *First Deficiency Appropriation Bill*, 1940, 76th Cong., 3d Sess., February 7, 1940, p. 65.

[3] U.S. Congress, House, Committee on the Civil Service, Hearing on *Investigation of Civilian Employment*, 78th Cong., 1st Sess., pursuant to H.R. 16, Part I, March 10, 1943, p. 21. Hereafter cited as *Investigation of Civilian Employment*.

[4] Leonard D. White, "The Scope and Nature of the Problem," in *Civil Service in Wartime*, ed. by L. D. White (Chicago, 1945), 11.

civil service coverage in 1940 created the precedent for later statutory and executive order agencies. From that moment, Commissioner Flemming looked upon his promise as a solemn contract to deliver the employees requisitioned in the number, to the place, and at the time required by all agencies directly involved in the war program.[5]

As War Department establishments sprang up around the country, Navy yards expanded and resounded with activity, and one after another of the defense and war agencies made its appearance, the number of Federal employees increased by leaps and bounds. It is, however, deceptive to think of recruitment merely in terms of the original staffing of some three million positions. Some positions had to be filled over and over again as turnover soared to a maximum average rate of 5 per cent per month during fiscal 1944.[6] At times the turnover rate was as high as 7 per cent per month, which, if constant at that figure, would have averaged almost 85 per cent per year. In the achievement of the impressive net growth shown in Table 1, the salient fact is that approximately 7,750,000 persons were appointed to all departments and agencies in the period from June 1, 1940, to December 31, 1944, about 5,250,000 of whom were placed in the War and Navy departments.[7]

A glance at Table 1 shows the fact that the trebling of the Federal civil service in size during the course of the war is no more significant than the phenomenal growth of the War and Navy departments to their peak strength of 1,615,896 and 766,150 respectively in February, 1945. Expressed in other terms, the War Department showed a thirteenfold expansion in the number of civilian employees and the Navy Department an eightfold expansion; at top strength the War Department was 170 per cent larger than the entire Federal civil service in 1939 while the Navy Department reached 80 per cent of the total Federal employment as of the outbreak of hostilities in Europe. It is mere anticlimax to point out that by 1945, 172,552 employees were attached to agencies nonexistent in September, 1939, and that even the so-called "old line" agencies grew by some 115,644 employees during the same period.

[5] Arthur S. Flemming, "The Mobilization of Personnel for the Field Establishments of the War and Navy Departments," *ibid.*, 120-25.
[6] Unpublished data from the office of John W. Mitchell, Chief, Federal Employment Statistics Staff, Office of the Chief of Administrative Services, U.S. Civil Service Commission. See Table 2.
[7] Flemming, in *Civil Service in Wartime*, 118.

At the very time Congress saw fit to place the wartime burden of recruitment exclusively upon the Civil Service Commission, it was in the act of bringing to final passage a piece of legislation which did much to broaden the range and types of positions under Commission jurisdiction during the early years of its recruitment drive—the Ramspeck Act of November 26, 1940.[8] Ultimately nearly 200,000 positions were "blanketed in" under the competitive classified civil service by the various executive orders issued under the authority of that statute.[9] During 1941 and 1942 a series of complex rules was evolved from the executive orders to cover all the various kinds of employees and former employees who could be recommended for status by agency heads during the calendar year 1942. In this manner the Commission was faced with the responsibility for filling a considerable block of positions hitherto outside the range of its jurisdiction at the same time that its defense load was growing by leaps and bounds. Thus, its jurisdiction covered the entire normal total of the Federal civil service and, if one includes all the positions created for the duration of the war, 95 per cent of the wartime service.[10]

2. EFFECT ON THE COMMISSION'S FIELD STAFF

By the very magnitude of its task, the Civil Service Commission was forced to expand its own field staff, to decentralize its work to an increasing extent to its regional offices, and to establish techniques for expediting its own procedures. Table 3 shows the striking expansion in the Commission's field staff which grew from a mere 21.5 per cent of the entire Commission staff in June, 1939, to 53.5 per cent of the entire staff in June, 1945. In other words, while the total Commission staff expanded nearly fourfold, the field staff grew nearly tenfold. Table 4 illustrates the growth of the Chicago field office as a typical example.

The Commission's regional directors were in a much stronger position than the central office of that agency to develop "custom-made" recruiting programs to meet the emergency. Because of

[8] 54 *U.S. Statutes* 1216 (1940).

[9] Executive Orders 8743, 8744, 8894, 8940, 9259, and 9506.

[10] In addition, the state employment services were federalized in the United States Employment Service for the duration of the war at President Roosevelt's request in December, 1941, shortly after Pearl Harbor, first under the Federal Security Agency and then by Executive Order 9247 of September 17, 1942, under the War Manpower Commission. Upon the Civil Service Commission thereby devolved the duty of manning the USES positions when state registers were exhausted.

TABLE 1
GROWTH IN FEDERAL CIVILIAN EMPLOYMENT, SELECTED MONTHS, 1939-45[a]

Month	Total Number of Federal Employees	Employees in Washington, D.C.	Field Service Employees	Employees Outside Continental U.S.	War Department Employees	Navy Department Employees	All Others (except P.O. and emergency war agencies)	Emergency War Agencies
September, 1939	940,133	126,063	814,070	b	122,595	91,637	426,180	....
January, 1940	939,296	127,520	811,776	44,966	128,293	101,131	419,735	....
July, 1940	1,026,572	138,471	888,101	89,297	142,649	126,211	452,805	....
January, 1941	1,151,148	158,587	992,561	b	205,555	176,231	447,175	16,614
July, 1941	1,391,689	185,182	1,206,507	b	328,219	235,467	489,712	20,628
January, 1942	1,703,099	223,483	1,479,616	b	530,487	327,905	492,439	29,784
July, 1942	2,327,932	274,001	2,053,931	b	912,378	475,683	523,347	96,957
January, 1943	2,864,021	284,643	2,579,378	b	1,285,364	580,213	501,970	172,736
July, 1943	3,126,216	279,261	2,692,455	154,500	1,403,793	673,987	549,667	182,688
January, 1944	3,015,336[c]	263,126	2,752,210	415,766	1,481,110	714,071	507,076	183,723
July, 1944	2,941,209[c]	270,501	2,670,708	393,969	1,506,795	758,915	526,392	181,614
January, 1945	2,889,000[c]	256,497	2,632,503	552,618	1,614,542	760,525	520,654	172,399
July, 1945	2,899,621[c]	255,454	2,644,167	854,170	1,138,285[c]	698,451[c]	b	160,302

[a] Statistics furnished by John W. Mitchell, Chief, Federal Employment Statistics Staff, Office of Chief of Administrative Services, U.S. Civil Service Commission, Washington, D. C.
[b] Not available.
[c] Does not include any employees outside continental United States.

marked sectional differences in the proportion and types of labor available for recruitment as well as in the kinds and degree of industrial concentration, they were closer to changes in the manpower situation from day to day. Thus they could serve the War and Navy departments' great expansion in their field establishments through a realistic knowledge of local problems and re-

TABLE 2

TURNOVER IN THE FEDERAL SERVICE, SELECTED MONTHS, APRIL, 1943–APRIL, 1945[a]

Month	Replacement-Turnover Rate[b] D. C. Area	Replacement-Turnover Rate[b] Entire Service	Separation Rate Entire Service	Accession Rate Entire Service
	%	%	%	%
April, 1943[c]	2.8	5.0	5.3	5.9
July, 1943	3.7	5.7	7.0	6.3
January, 1944	2.7	4.3	4.4	4.8
Average for fiscal 1944	3.0	5.0	....	....
July, 1944	3.4	5.1	5.2	5.5
January, 1945	2.8	4.4	4.5	5.4
April, 1945	2.5	4.1	4.8	4.2
Average for fiscal 1945	2.8	4.0	....	....

[a] Statistics furnished by John W. Mitchell, Chief, Federal Employment Statistics Staff, Office of Chief of Administrative Services, U. S. Civil Service Commission, Washington, D. C.

[b] Replacement-turnover represents the total volume of additions required to replace separations other than separations for curtailment of the work force. Individual agency figures on turnover are totaled and then divided by the average Federal employment for the month under consideration.

[c] No statistics available in the Civil Service Commission prior to April, 1943.

sources. Realizing this early, the Commissioners, in the words of Arthur S. Flemming, made this kind of delegation:

> You are the Commission, as far as your district is concerned. If the War or Navy Department wants two or three hundred men put on the job within 72 hours and you know you can get those men on the job in 72 hours, but there is some minute, some memorandum of the Commission standing in your way we want you to get the men on the job and tell us how you did it afterward; because maybe you have stumbled into a minute or a memorandum that ought to have been wiped off of the books anyhow.[11]

[11] U.S. Congress, House, Hearing on *Independent Offices Appropriation Bill*, 1942, 77th Cong., 1st Sess., December 12, 1940, p. 530.

In time, to serve the War and Navy departments more speedily the regional directors were requested to station rating-examiners and rating-board inspectors at local board establishments with full authority to pass upon all matters hitherto referred to the regional or central Commission offices for final decision.[12] It was left within the discretion of the regional managers to determine where

TABLE 3

EXPANSION OF CIVIL SERVICE COMMISSION STAFF, SELECTED MONTHS, 1939–45[a]

Date	Total Number of Employees	Total Number of Employees in Washington, D. C., Metropolitan Area[b]	Field Service Employees Outside of Washington, D. C., Metropolitan Area	Per Cent of Total Employees in Field
June, 1939	1,768	1,387	381	21.5
December, 1939	1,829	1,417	412	22.5
June, 1940	2,780	1,909	871	31.3
December, 1940	3,980	2,863	1,117	28.0
June, 1941	6,709	4,292	2,417	36.0
December, 1941	5,014	3,219	1,795	35.7
June, 1942	7,832	4,486	3,346	42.7
December, 1942	7,349	3,817	3,532	48.0
June, 1943	7,218	3,328	3,890	53.8
December, 1943	6,334	3,155	3,179	50.1
June, 1944	6,887	3,325	3,562	51.7
December, 1944	6,889	3,299	3,590	52.1
June, 1945	6,819	3,167	3,652	53.5

[a] Statistics furnished by John W. Mitchell, Chief, Federal Employment Statistics Staff, Office of Chief of Administrative Services, U. S. Civil Service Commission, Washington, D. C.

[b] There is a small field staff in the Fourth Region Branch Office in Washington, D. C., which is included in the total for metropolitan Washington.

such rating boards were necessary.[13] Soon permanent recruiting representatives, specializing in that activity alone, were stationed by the regional directors at centers of intensifying defense activity, while other recruiting specialists were moved from place to place as the exigencies of mobilization demanded.[14] Thus, while it was left to Commission representatives on the spot to devise the ways and means of enlisting the requisite personnel, either from eligible registers or on exhaustion of the latter from outside the

[12] Civil Service Commission, *Fifty-seventh Annual Report*, 2.
[13] CSC, *Circular Letter No. 2925*, June 21, 1941.
[14] *Ibid.*, No. 3006, Supp. No. 1, September 28, 1940.

registers, they were under the imperative necessity of providing the War and Navy departments on twenty-four-hour notice exactly the quota requisitioned. No leeway of one or two less than the quota was tolerated.[15]

Pearl Harbor merely served to multiply and accentuate the pressures on the recruiting representatives, who were forced to sit down with the regional directors to plot new drives and techniques to "beat the bushes" for recruits for novel programs. For example, it fell to the regional offices to produce clerical personnel for 7,500 to 10,000 tire-rationing boards within three weeks when the initial OPA rationing program was launched early in 1942.[16] The mandatory assignment of quotas for critical programs to the various regional offices located full responsibility for performance on each regional director and placed a premium on his ingenuity. When one regional director developed a suc-

TABLE 4

EXPANSION OF STAFF AND VOLUME OF WORK OF THE SEVENTH CIVIL SERVICE REGIONAL OFFICE AT CHICAGO, JUNE, 1939–JUNE, 1944[a]

Staff and Activity	Fiscal Year Ending June 30, 1939	Fiscal Year Ending June 30, 1943	Fiscal Year Ending June 30, 1944
Number of staff	33	364	321
Applications received	23,816	412,520	205,330
Placements	3,703	203,381	110,173
Visitors	50,577	882,730	516,681
Outgoing mail	60,672	1,838,876	1,306,858

[a] Data furnished by Seventh Regional Office, United States Civil Service Commission, Chicago, Illinois.

cessful technique, he shared it with the others through regional directors' conferences or by means of suggestions from the Chief of Field Operations through the regular circular letters of the Commission.

Early in the defense period the Commission found it necessary to station liaison officers in the operating agencies in the departmental service to expedite Commission action on all matters where final decision rested with the central personnel agency.[17] They were also to secure advance information on personnel needs to

[15] *Ibid., No. 3045*, September 26, 1940. [16] *Ibid., No. 3565*, January 30, 1942.
[17] CSC, *Fifty-seventh Annual Report*, xi.

enable the Commission staff at headquarters to do such advance planning as was possible. A Liaison Section was organized in the Examining and Personnel Utilization Division, and the executive branch was divided into zones, each with a zone office under a civil service representative-in-charge, from which various representatives worked. One liaison officer or representative might serve several departments or one; for example, the War Department alone constituted almost all of one zone with several representatives handling cases from two or three branches thereof.[18] Their authority included power of final approval for the Commission on all emergency personnel transactions except transfers, classification matters, retirement, and the establishment of qualifications. Nonemergency cases went to the relevant division of the Commission for decision.[19]

In similar fashion, liaison representatives, or expediters, were placed in the larger War and Navy field establishments by the regional offices of the Commission.[20] Their authority was similar to that of the liaison representatives in the departmental service except that they were responsible to the regional directors. To avoid jurisdictional disputes when Army Corps Area boundaries did not coincide with Civil Service regions, field liaison representatives were ordered to handle every case referred to them regardless of Civil Service regional boundaries.

Frequently, recruiting representatives were assigned to various agencies with a dual responsibility: to the Commission's liaison officer for completion of the recruiting assignment and to the recruiting representative's immediate technical supervisor, usually an examiner, in the central or regional Commission office, as the case might be, on the manner of handling his assignment.[21] Recruiting representatives had an administrative responsibility to the examiners and a staff responsibility to the liaison officers. These relationships may be seen in Figure 3. The exact frame of authority within which each recruiting representative worked was

[18] CSC, *Directory of Liaison Section*, June 21, 1944.
[19] CSC, "Outline of Authority and Responsibilities of Civil Service Representatives," June 1, 1944. (Mimeographed.) For example, liaison officers could authorize such emergency appointments for the immediate dispatching of persons overseas on a government mission.
[20] CSC, *Departmental Circular No. 257*, Letter of February 15, 1941, to the War Department.
[21] CSC, *Circular Letter No. 3824*, September 24, 1942.

defined by the examiner supervising recruitment in a particular occupational field or by a regional director. Moreover, the avowed objective of the Commission was to delegate the maximum authority commensurate with the recruiting representative's ability and experience.[22]

Thus the Civil Service Commission extended itself outward through an expansion of its field staff and through liaison officers in the operating agencies in order to meet mounting recruitment pressures. Likewise, more authority had to be delegated to these two categories of Commission employees correlative with their recruitment responsibilities. These extensions outward were made to obviate the danger of the Commission becoming a bottleneck in the staffing process.

THE DEVELOPMENT AND SIGNIFICANCE OF THE MANPOWER CONTROLS

1. NECESSITY OF ESTABLISHING MANPOWER CONTROLS

Defense production coupled with the Selective Service Act and the "all-out" pressures of war revolutionized the American labor market and created a manpower situation in 1942 that clearly called for controls. When the decision had been made to centralize Federal recruitment for defense, the labor market was still very "easy"; that is, the unemployed numbered more than 9,000,000. Within a few months, however, the Selective Training and Service Act was passed with the effect of drawing off at first only a small but highly employable part of the country's labor force; later, of course, it drew off huge numbers. Then, too, as industry began the gradual process of retooling for conversion to war production at about the same time, the demand for skilled workers early reached an acute stage. With the actual declaration of war, government and private industry soon found themselves in sharp competition as the armed forces drained off more and more of the nation's available manpower. Table 5 illustrates what happened to the labor force during the war years. Unemployment almost disappeared as the number of employed persons rose by about ten millions from September, 1939, to July, 1945, and the number of unemployed declined by 8,500,000 to but 950,000 at the latter date. In addition to the competition between

---

[22] *Ibid.* See also Flemming, "Emergency Aspects of Civil Service," *Public Administration Review*, I (1940-41), 27.

CENTRALIZATION OF RESPONSIBILITY 23

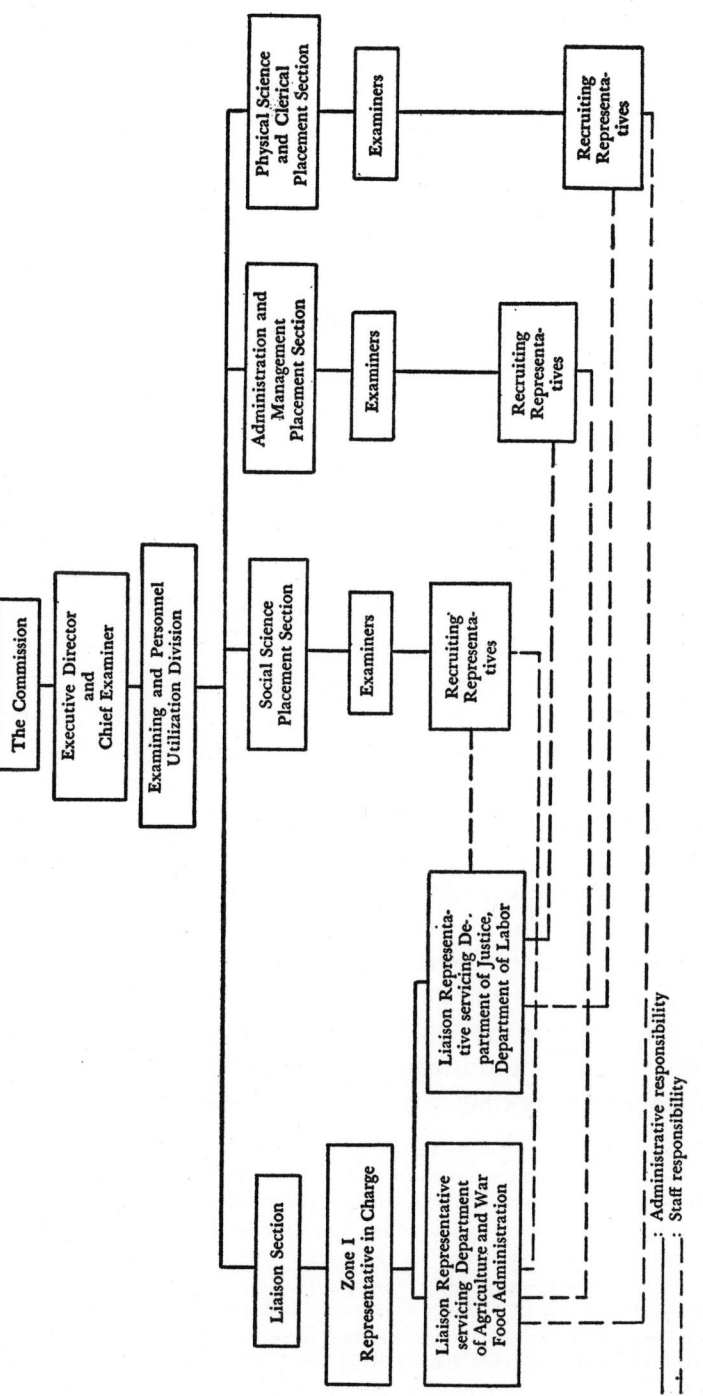

Fig. 3.—Chart showing relationship of recruiting representatives to liaison representatives and examiners.

government and business, intense intragovernmental competition for manpower had developed. The legal centralization of recruitment for the Federal service was destined to run into headlong collision with the overriding necessity the operating agencies faced to secure personnel where and as they could.

(a) *Reason for treating government as a single employer.*—Had one government agency been permitted to scramble competitively with another for available manpower—as, for example, the War Department with the Department of Agriculture—workers might have been enlisted for the less essential, rather than the more critical, tasks. If hiring policies differed as between establishments of the governmental employer, than it behooved the manpower organization to bring about uniformity, both for internal and external consistency.[23] Workers would undoubtedly have gone to those agencies that had the most aggressive recruitment techniques and were most reckless in "blowing up" positions to obtain higher-grade allocations and therefore higher salaries. Not only would the more daring or less conservative departments have secured the best personnel available outside the government, but they would have been drawing employees already in the service away from their competitor agencies to less vital work in many instances. The cost to the taxpayer, not merely in money but in energy, time, and talent dissipated in devising clever tactics of intramural competition instead of being devoted to the main objective of successful prosecution of the war, would have been far greater than what was actually so wasted.

On the other hand, in weighing claims for manpower as between industry and the Federal government, considerations of equity dictated that both should subscribe to the same recruitment policies because the principal efforts of both were dedicated to military victory. Industry could scarcely have been asked to conform to policies not honored by government in all its parts.

[23] Even the governmental demands for military manpower were for a time brought under manpower controls by Executive Order 9279 of December 5, 1942, until congressional pressure, stirred up by the furore over deferment on an occupational instead of family-dependency basis, caused the separation of the Selective Service System from the jurisdiction of the War Manpower Chairman by Executive Orders 9409 and 9410 of December 23, 1943. Certain disastrous repercussions upon labor supply followed separation. Skilled mechanics, irreplaceable because of their long, intensive training, were drafted into the armed forces from private and Navy shipyards, aircraft plants, and other hard-pressed war production establishments by a decentralized organization with no clear and uniform national policy.

(b) *Role of the Civil Service Commission in the development and enforcement of manpower policies.*—From May, 1940, the Commission had anticipated labor shortages in certain occupations or localities and had acted on the theory that as the authorized representative of the government in its capacity of employer it must furnish a model of conformance to local or national rules on manpower allocation.[24] Long before there was an apparent

TABLE 5

EMPLOYMENT AND UNEMPLOYMENT IN THE UNITED STATES, SELECTED MONTHS, 1939-45[a]

Month	Number of Employed Persons	Number of Unemployed Persons
September, 1939	44,121,990[b]	9,450,556
April, 1940	45,100,000	8,800,000
July, 1940	47,700,000[c]	9,300,000
January, 1941	45,200,000	7,600,000
July, 1941	50,400,000	5,600,000
January, 1942	49,700,000	4,500,000
July, 1942	54,500,000	2,800,000
January, 1943	51,800,000	1,600,000
July, 1943	54,600,000	1,400,000
January, 1944	50,400,000	1,100,000
July, 1944	54,000,000	1,000,000
January, 1945	50,120,000	840,000[d]
July, 1945	54,270,000	950,000

[a] All data except for the month of September, 1939, obtained from *Monthly Labor Review* reports entitled "Unemployment in the United States."
[b] *American Federationist*, XLVI, Part II (1939), 1360.
[c] Summer employment figures customarily show a marked rise as a result of vacation employment of the school population and seasonal employment in agriculture.
[d] A wartime low of 630,000 was reported in October, 1944.

national labor shortage, certain industries which required skilled labor experienced difficulties in recruitment. Local employers found it expedient to enter agreements against "labor pirating" or "scamping," as it was called in shipyard argot, from vital defense production. In keeping with agreements of that kind, the Civil Service Commission in 1941 instructed its regional directors to refuse to recruit eligibles already engaged in vital defense work.[25] The Navy Department, accused of some pirating on its

[24] Flemming, in *Civil Service in Wartime*, 131.
[25] CSC, *Circular Letter No. 3433*, September 29, 1941.

part, finally issued orders to cancel tenders of appointment to defense workers unless they had secured the consent of their employers to the change[26] or Navy work would more fully utilize their skills.[27] The Commission, however, did not feel impelled to originate a policy of its own of generally requiring a release from the last employer of an eligible who had taken a civil service examination or who had applied after the issuance of a Commission announcement.

President Roosevelt brought a semblance of order out of a deteriorating situation by creating in 1942 the War Manpower Commission, which was given power to adopt a uniform national manpower policy to apply with equal force to government and private enterprise.[28] Originally conceived as a policy-making body rather than one with an operational program, the War Manpower Commission was given authority to prescribe policy over the Federal government's manpower requirements with responsibility for enforcement delegated to the Civil Service Commission throughout the war. Thereby the WMC directives were applied to Federal departments and agencies engaged in recruitment. Thus, the Commission was recognized by WMC as alone authorized to recruit for Federal positions subject to the Civil Service Act and to represent the government as an employer, subject to substantially the same regulations as was private industry.[29]

Certain agencies of the government concerned with manpower allocation were authorized to act in an advisory capacity to the chairman of the War Manpower Commission. Among them was the Civil Service Commission, represented by Commissioner Flemming. That he should present Civil Service Commission views was entirely consistent with the fact that his fellow commissioners had earlier delegated to him responsibility for all national defense activities of the Commission. Within the Bureau of Placement of the War Manpower Commission a government employment division headed by a Civil Service Commission division chief was set up to secure conformity between Commission and WMC policy and rules. Actually the WMC division was not a new organizational unit but simply a division of the Civil Service Commission shown in WMC organization. The same identity

[26] *Ibid.*, No. *3467*, November 7, 1941. [27] *Ibid., Supp. No. 1,* January 7, 1942.
[28] Executive Order 9139.
[29] CSC, *Departmental Circular No. 407,* February 5, 1943.

of organization was to be found in the WMC Bureau of Manpower Utilization, which had a division of governmental agencies headed by the Civil Service Commission's section chief for personnel utilization. At the regional level Civil Service Commission regional directors paralleled Commissioner Flemming's national role as advisers to the WMC regional directors. (See Fig. 4.)

The significance of the controls developed by the War Manpower Commission, in so far as government employment was concerned, was to underline the central authority of the Civil Service Commission over the employing agencies by forcing them to recognize the Commission as the WMC enforcement agency over them. All official agency claims to personnel, therefore, had to be viewed within that frame of reference and had to be resolved in a manner beneficial to the government's war program as a whole. Priorities were established by the War Manpower Commission among agency claimants for the manpower available. In the total field of war production activities government was but one claimant among many and could speak authoritatively on its own manpower problems only through the Civil Service Commission. Scarcely less impressive was the fact that for the first time in our history government and private industry found themselves operating under the same legal restrictions in so far as hiring controls were concerned. That is not to say that industry could not easily outbid government, for the "fringe" adjustments allowed by the War Labor Board—such as bonuses, incentive payments, and provisions for upgrading—enabled it to do just that. Nevertheless, it had to conform to all the restrictions on clearances, referrals, recruitment campaigns, and publicity just as did government establishments.

In order to enforce manpower policies and at the same time effectuate centralization of recruitment responsibility, the Civil Service Commission equated violations of WMC regulations with violation of the Civil Service rules. Removal from office was in order for anyone appointed in violation of either set of regulations.[30] The sanction for failure to remove anyone appointed in violation was a request by the Commission to the General Accounting Office to withhold salary payments to the employee involved.[31]

[30] *Ibid., No. 419,* April 19, 1943, and *No. 441,* October 29, 1943.
[31] *Ibid., No. 419.* The channel for communication and appeal to WMC by the

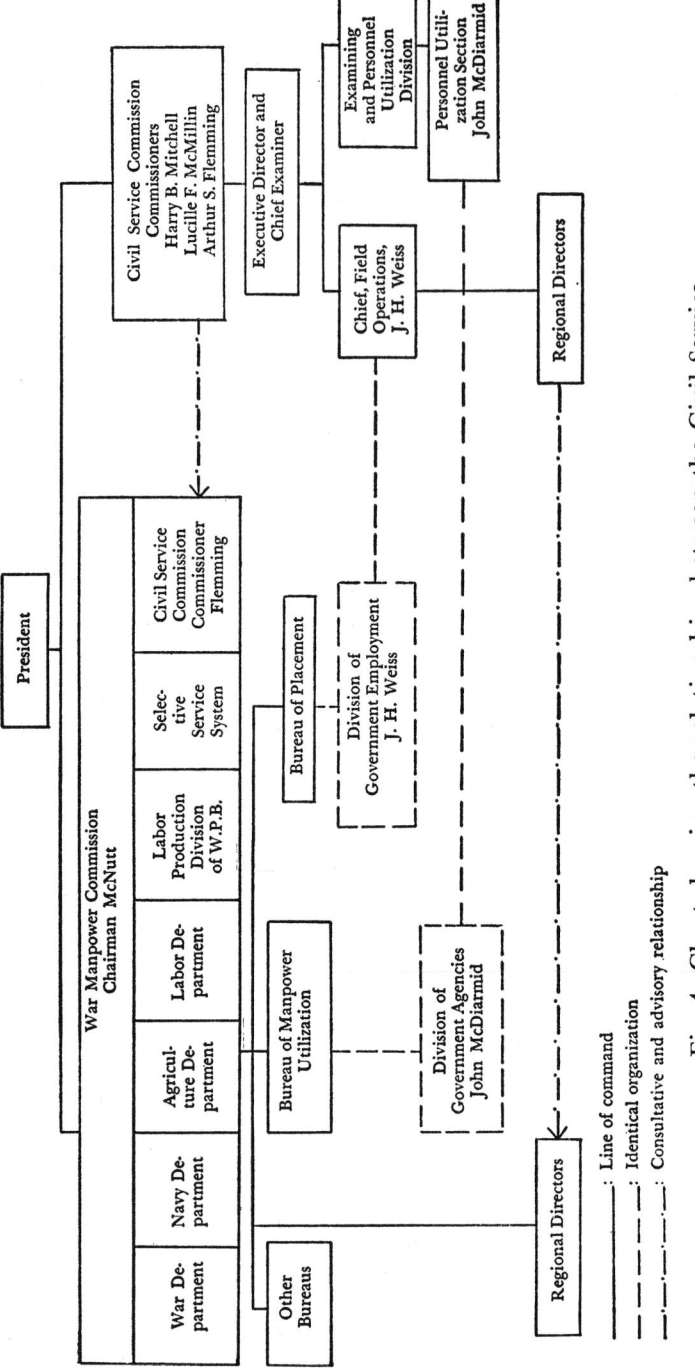

Fig. 4—Chart showing the relationships between the Civil Service Commission and the War Manpower Commission

One of the most effective means for centralizing Civil Service Commission control of recruitment was the series of WMC limitations placed on interregional recruitment. For small needs Civil Service regional directors could make arrangements with each other, as always, without recourse to the United States Employment Service.[32] But for large needs, clearance was more complex, requiring first, agreement between Civil Service and War Manpower regional directors on the impossibility of filling the quotas within the War Manpower region, then reference to the Civil Service Commission in Washington. In no event were agencies to bypass the Commission by direct presentation to the War Manpower Commission. Upon the Civil Service Commission's decision to request interregional clearance, the matter was presented to the War Manpower Commission for determination. If the latter approved, it allocated quotas to the appropriate War Manpower regions with positive orders to fill the quotas. Then only were Civil Service regional directors notified by Washington to effect arrangements with the War Manpower regional directors for positive recruiting programs.[33] As the sole authorized representative before WMC of government needs for interregional recruitment, the Commission found its control over the employing agencies maximized by their very dependence upon it as their spokesman.

The United States Employment Service had become, after its transfer to the War Manpower Commission in September, 1942,[34] the most important constituent part of the latter's organization both for control purposes and for assistance in Federal and private recruitment. When the unemployed had numbered many millions at the beginning of the defense period and had formed

---

employing agencies was through the Commission, by its central office for the departmental service, or through its regional directors for the field service.

[32] CSC, *Circular Letter No. 4013,* June 7, 1943.

[33] When the question arose of application to Schedules A & B positions (excepted from the Civil Service Act and Rules), it was decided that arrangements for interarea and interregional clearance must be essentially the same as for other positions to be arranged by the Civil Service Commission through WMC. CSC, *Departmental Circular No. 442, Supp. No. 4,* May 25, 1944. This was consistent with the WMC view of government as one employer and made mandatory a coordination in recruiting nonexistent before the war. Purely local recruiting for Schedules A and B positions required no Commission clearance; agencies could go directly to the USES for assistance.

[34] Executive Order 9247.

the vast majority of USES registrants, that agency had operated under the stigma of placing so-called "reliefers" only and had been shunned in so far as possible by both labor and management. But the sharp contraction of the labor market, especially with respect to skilled labor, forced employers to turn to USES increasingly as the only remaining large source of labor supply. Thus as improved employment opportunities became available through USES, labor more readily registered with it. The cumulative effect was that it could provide helpful facilities for recruitment to all employers, including the Federal government. Individuals registered themselves with USES who had never anticipated acceptance of public employment and were not in the habit of reading recruiting circulars.

The wartime use of USES to fill government job orders served to augment Commission control over Federal recruitment. As early as the summer of 1940 the Commission turned to the USES as one of its most important sources for recruiting laborers in government establishments. But all negotiations between Federal agencies and USES had to move through the Civil Service Commission regional offices.[35] During 1941 officials of the Commission and USES studied ways in which the government could best avail itself of the extensive recruiting resources of USES.[36] After USES came under WMC, Federal agencies were more strongly compelled by that transfer to channel job orders through the Civil Service Commission because the Commission was their sole negotiator with all parts of WMC. The Civil Service Commission was in an incomparably stronger position than any department, after government use of USES increased, to demand for the employing agencies a fair share of the flow of workers through USES. WMC, through USES, actively assisted the Commission in meeting its recruiting quotas.

2. THE NATURE OF THE MANPOWER CONTROLS

The objective of the manpower controls was, in short, to direct the available labor supply of the nation into employment essential to the war program by preventing pirating of workers among employers and unnecessary "milling around" from job to job by employees. The evolving manpower program limited recruit-

---

[35] CSC, *Circular Letter No. 2927*, July 23, 1940.
[36] Flemming, in *Civil Service in Wartime*, 133.

ment, both Federal and private, by three principal controls: determination of geographic areas for recruitment, limitation of the occupational classes which could be drawn upon, and the establishment of priorities for supplying employers, both public and private, as well as between Federal agencies. Of political necessity the manpower controls were voluntary and essentially local with double lines of control: over employers and over workers, to deal with both demand and supply. The development of manpower policies remained hesitant, as was natural so long as it was based upon voluntarism, and highly empirical. The basic philosophy, if any, was to avoid a "labor draft," for controls were largely improvised. If, after a timid trial in one area, a program met the pragmatic test, then it was more widely urged by the War Manpower Commission. Although eventually a set of minimum controls was promulgated by the chairman of the War Manpower Commission, each area or region could adopt such additional regulations as were required by local shortages. Each successive tightening of WMC controls strengthened the grip of the Civil Service Commission over government hiring practices.

(a) *Controls over employers, both public and private.*—Control over employers as to area, occupation, and priority of labor recruitment was subject to four progressively more stringent types of manpower controls: (1) the establishment of employment stabilization plans; (2) the development of controlled referral, later called priority referral; (3) the setting of employment ceilings for individual employers; and (4) the use of manpower priority ratings to allocate the available labor supply. In objective, the four types of controls were similar, but not until employment ceilings and manpower priorities had been adopted was an effective system evolved to channel labor where it was most urgently required.

The first of these controls, *employment stabilization agreements*, constituted the earliest WMC method of control, adopted in July, 1942. Employment stabilization agreements were local plans, adopted by WMC area- or regional-directors after consultation with their Management-Labor committees, to eliminate reprehensible hiring practices in a critical labor area devoted to essential war production activities.[37] The effect of these agreements

[37] War Manpower Regulations, July 16, 1942, 7 *FR* 5500, July 17, 1942. *A critical labor shortage area* was one characterized by a concentration of essential war produc-

was to channelize all soliciting and hiring of workers in critical occupations through the USES to bring such hiring into accord with a co-operative plan worked out for the area. Civil Service regional offices were accordingly instructed to get whom they could from their own available lists when recruiting orders were placed with them; if they found themselves unable thereby to fill their quotas, they were to place orders with the nearest USES office.[38] Industrial hiring at the gate was still the order of the day, and there was no restriction on the hiring of workers engaged in activities other than essential war production activity if the worker could show a release from his last employer. The first critical labor shortage areas were agreed upon and announced by the War Manpower Commission and critical occupations designated in September, 1942.[39] Restrictions, therefore, became both geographic and occupational since limitations applied to the recruitment of workers from one critical area into another as well as from employment in a critical occupation.

The need for stricter control over all employers early in 1943, underlined by growing area labor shortages and stepped-up military inductions, led to the next innovation, the adoption of *controlled referral*, in February, 1943. The objective of controlled referral was to refer workers to jobs according to the relative importance of the work to the war effort. Controlled referral, adopted in thirty-two critical labor shortage areas, was designed to accomplish two things: one, to compel the conduct of all hiring, rehiring, solicitation, and recruitment of workers through the USES alone; and two, to secure the referral by USES of recruits obtained by *any* employer to another deemed to be in more

---

tion, a shortage of workers in designated critical occupations, and an excessive rate of turnover among such workers or a migration of workers in critical occupations to other areas. *The criteria of essentiality of occupation* were: (a) the fulfillment of government war contracts, (b) the performance of government services directly promoting war production, (c) the maintenance of indispensable civilian activities, health, safety, welfare, or security, (d) the supplying of material under subcontracts for any of the foregoing activities, (e) the production of raw materials, manufactured supplies or equipment, or performance of services necessary for the fulfillment of war or essential civilian activity contracts. *Critical occupations* were those specifically designated by WMC in war production activities. CSC, *Departmental Cirular No. 376,* September 23, 1942.

[38] CSC, *Circular Letter No. 3766,* August 8, 1942.
[39] CSC, *Departmental Circular No. 376,* September 23, 1942.

CENTRALIZATION OF RESPONSIBILITY 33

urgent need, subject, of course, to appeal up the hierarchy in WMC.[40]

Through controlled referral Commission authority over recruitment was intensified, in that it could compel one Federal agency to relinquish a recruit it had found to another Federal agency or to a private employer in more urgent need of workers. Urgency of need rather than ranked priority of program as among essential employers was still the governing factor in manpower allocation. Government agencies were reminded that the Civil Service Commission was alone authorized to recruit for all Federal positions under the Civil Service Act.[41] Publicity for openings in the Federal service, as well as recruiting within a critical labor shortage area for placement either within or outside the area, required clearance with the USES.[42] It devolved upon the Civil Service regional directors to present to the manpower offices the urgency of recruitment for positions to which the Commission had assigned top priority.

The establishment of twelve regional employment stabilization plans for both the Federal government and private employers created a set of minimum controls over interregional recruitment in the various area plans. Aside from certain relaxations for the District of Columbia pertaining to departmental service recruitment,[43] interregional recruiting in the field service was contingent upon ten conditions, some of which were revolutionary for Federal employment,[44] and it had to be requested through the chan-

[40] WMC Directive, *General Order No. 3*, February 2, 1943.
[41] CSC, *Departmental Circular No. 407*, February 5, 1943.
[42] WMC forbade publicity if the USES was able to furnish an adequate number of applicants at the time they were needed, while clearance with the local USES office was required if the latter was unable to furnish applicants from a covered area for positions outside the area. Also, because of serious housing and transportation complications in most critical labor-shortage areas by 1943, the stabilization plans usually included an in-migrant clause requiring clearance with the USES prior to hiring non-residents of the area. Clearance of in-migrants for Federal employment devolved upon the Civil Service Commission to compel a more thorough search for labor and a shifting of labor from nonessential to essential activity before resorting to outside recruitment. CSC, *Circular Letter No. 3691*, February 20, 1943.
[43] CSC, *Departmental Circular No. 420, Supp. No. 4*, May 29, 1943.
[44] (1) Full utilization by the employer of his present labor force; (2) exhaustion of all local sources of labor supply; (3) danger of impediment to war production through lack of working force; (4) embodiment of minimum needs in the number to be recruited; (5) indication of wage rate ranges and minimum specifications for job performance; (6) agreement to follow a positive recruitment itinerary arranged and supervised by USES or agreement to delegate hiring commitments to USES;

nels heretofore described.[45] Pooled interviews were arranged by USES for Commission representatives and private employers when eligibles were secured in surplus labor areas who were willing to accept employment in private industry outside the region or at a Federal establishment within the region. Only when Federal local establishments' needs were especially urgent were regional manpower directors ordered to fill them ahead of private employers granted a priority for interregional clearance in that region.

A new controlled referral plan was devised after serious difficulty was encountered in the tight West Coast region during the summer of 1943.[46] Through USES alone could those persons last employed in a critical occupation be employed unless the area stabilization plan provided a variant. The hiring of in-migrants in Federal field establishments had to comply with two stabilization programs: that of the area whence the person came and that of the area to which he had gone for employment.[47]

Further contraction of the labor market in 1944 led to the coordination of manpower and production needs by the establishment of *employment ceilings* and *manpower priority ratings*. For the first time allocation of workers by USES was based upon urgency of the types of production activity rather than the urgency of need for workers. Many nonindustrial government establishments, of course, fell in priority under the new arrangements. Employment ceilings or manpower allowances constituted a state-

---

(7) administration of medical examinations at the place of recruitment and at the employer's expense (except when stipulated otherwise, as for Federal employment); (8) provision by the employer of transportation from the point of recruitment to the job location if necessary; (9) transportation back if the employee for any reason did not accept the job; (10) available housing facilities for workers on arrival at the job location.

[45] *See above,* p. 29.

[46] Bernard M. Baruch was sent to the West Coast to investigate the problem for James F. Byrnes, Director of the Office of War Mobilization. His report, postulated on the belief that there was available manpower which could be channeled where needed by means of a community "labor budget," recommended power in WMC to make labor utilization surveys. This power was never granted. See *New York Times,* September 18, 1943, for text of the Baruch report.

[47] Although not required to do so, the Civil Service Commission adopted the policy of requiring releases from state, county, and municipal governments before hiring any of their employees, despite the fact that many of these units of government were not parties to employment stabilization agreements and recruitment of any of their employees denied a release would have been legitimate.

ment of the minimum number of employees needed to meet production or program requirements after the relative urgency of area activities had been determined by an Area War Production Urgency Committee under War Production Board chairmanship.[48] Each major type of employer in a community was represented on the Production Urgency committees through a relevant government agency. Thus the War and Navy departments represented their contractors; the Office of Defense Transportation, the transportation companies; War Food Administration, the food processors; and the Civil Service Commission, the Federal agencies, if they constituted a significant part of area employment. Employment ceilings, as well as manpower priority ratings, were fixed by Area Manpower Priorities Committees under WMC chairmanship. Like Production Urgency committees, they were composed of representatives of government agencies. Usually to be found were representatives of WMC, WPB, the War and Navy departments, Aircraft Resources Control Office, Selective Service System, Smaller War Plants Corporation, Maritime Commission, ODT, and the Civil Service Commission.[49] For Federal establishments, Bureau of the Budget personnel ceilings were accepted as employment ceilings by WMC.

Manpower priority ratings determined the order of referral of available labor to local employers on the basis of their urgency and the employment ceilings established for them. Establishments filling pressing war orders received the same kind of priority over referral of personnel to them that they possessed from the War Production Board with respect to materials. All male workers were referred to jobs in employment stabilization areas after July 1, 1944, on the basis of the relative urgency of the jobs open in war production. Women were similarly referred in areas suffering a shortage of women workers.[50] The War Manpower Commission promulgated a rating scale to classify on the basis of urgency both interregional and local recruiting orders and to integrate the two.[51]

The turn of the year brought a more refined assignment of priority categories and restricted their use to the chairman of the

[48] CSC, *Circular Letter No. 4169,* June 17, 1944.   [49] *Ibid.*
[50] CSC, *Departmental Circular No. 442, Supp. No. 7,* August 26, 1944.
[51] Federal departmental recruiting received a "C" rating, which gave it middle standing after AA, A, and B interregional orders and first-rank local priority orders. CSC, *Circular Letter No. 4169, Supp. No. 1,* August 8, 1944. Recruiting for the field

36   IMPACT OF WAR ON FEDERAL PERSONNEL

National Manpower Priorities Committee for top priority and to the Area Manpower Director for second priority.[52] The notable point about new categories was that top priority was open invariably for one kind of establishment which, as might be guessed, was that of the Manhattan District Project; at all times orders from Manhattan District Project establishments were offered first to qualified applicants. Thus did atomic bomb production find recognition in WMC controls. Simultaneously an attempt was made to tighten the regulations for interregional recruitment on proof that it had been used too freely and that intraregional recruitment had not been conducted with sufficient intensity.[53] By reserving interregional recruitment for a kind of *in extremis* treatment, WMC virtually foreclosed the possibility of its use by USES on behalf of the Civil Service Commission.[54] But with the rapid advance to a climax of the war in Europe, relaxation of the regulations governing interregional recruitment followed within a few months.[55]

Victory in Europe soon scrapped the national controls, for a little over a month after V-E Day the War Manpower Commission, by rescission of most of its general orders and directives as of June 13, 1945, removed the minimum controls and restored programs to a purely local or regional basis.[56] In areas freed from manpower controls, the Federal government was, like any other employer, free for the first time since 1942 to hire any and all eligibles for the departmental service without any clearances. Where manpower controls remained in effect in the field, the onus

---

service could fall into any category, as each establishment and agency fitted into the rating scale on the basis of production urgency. There was, moreover, the contingency of a higher rating for departmental recruiting for a particular program requirement.

[52] CSC, *Circular Letter No. 4169, Supp. No. 1, Revised,* January 5, 1945.

[53] WMC, Field Instruction No. 571, Revised, Bureau of Placement No. 230, December 2, 1944, attached to *ibid.*

[54] Because recruiting for the departmental service was assigned to a very low rating.

[55] More categories of priority were developed and were open for submission to the National Manpower Priorities Committee, which undertook to judge each individual case primarily on the basis of the type of labor required as compared with its availability in other regions. CSC, *Circular Letter No. 4169, Supp. No. 1, Revision No. 2,* April 13, 1945.

[56] Rescission of all directives except Directives X, XII, and XVI, which affected government establishments, 10 *FR* 8801, July 14, 1945.

of responsibility for seeing that a clearance was in order fell upon the employee, not the employer.[57]

(b) *Control over employees.*—To turn back at this point to trace the control projected over workers, we find a much simpler pattern than that over employers and, on the whole, a much less effective one. It was never really difficult for a worker to leave any job, regardless of essentiality, inside or outside of government, in order to accept another possibly less essential but more lucrative. Labor remained quite free throughout the war and highly mobile.

The principal means devised to attempt to prevent workers in essential and critical occupations, which included government, from continually changing jobs for higher compensation was the requirement of a USES statement of availability or a release from the last employer. There was at first no attempt to restrict the hiring of workers in other categories. When controlled referral was adopted in 1943, a standard requirement was included in employment stabilization plans that workers could not accept new employment within thirty days of a change of job unless they had secured a statement of availability.[58] In effect, this requirement penalized workers thirty days' pay for unauthorized employment transfers. In controlled areas the rule applied even to the placement of persons previously engaged in occupations not subject to controlled hiring. After the Baruch report later in 1943 controls were tightened by raising the thirty-day period to sixty days.[59] The difficulty was that USES accepted as legitimate a number of reasons for granting referral to war work on the ground of existence of a compelling reason for a change of jobs. Most employees possessed of any ingenuity found it a simple matter to invent personal hardship reasons or to create enough irritations to provoke their discharge.

Over male workers of draft age the threat of induction into military service was imposed as a sanction for "job-jumping," inasmuch as clearance with the Selective Service System was required for a change in employment from a position that carried occupa-

[57] CSC, *Departmental Circular No. 442, Supp. No. 11,* July 25, 1945.
[58] CSC, *Circular Letter No. 3961,* February 20, 1943.
[59] CSC, *Departmental Circular No. 442,* October 19, 1943. For Federal employees this period commenced when they went off active duty rather than at the expiration of accumulated annual leave.

tional deferment.⁶⁰ Workers in that category were made liable for immediate induction unless cleared. The employer could, however, hire them if they were armed with the necessary WMC clearances, provided he was willing to assume the risk of their departure through impending induction. This control was obviously not very effective in a tight labor market.

3. EFFECT ON GOVERNMENT AGENCIES OF PRIORITIES MANPOWER

An examination of the facts brought to light through congressional hearings seems to indicate that there were at least two effects upon government agencies from the priorities for manpower developed by the manpower controls. One result was that low priority agencies chafed under their inability either to engage in recruiting themselves or to secure clerical personnel in sufficient numbers through the Commission for the departmental service. The General Accounting Office voiced its dissatisfaction to the Ramspeck Committee with the prior claim the war agencies had on recruits obtained by the Commission.⁶¹ Not only did that agency receive few recruits, but the quality of those sent it alleged to be so poor they were incapable of training. The Commission was, therefore, unrealistically stigmatized for a failure to produce employable personnel, despite labor-market conditions and the more pressing need of other parts of the government. For example, the Comptroller General accused the Civil Service Commission of a complete collapse under the impact of war on the ground the Commission was incapable of furnishing "proper personnel." He alleged that the General Accounting Office could itself obtain superior types of recruits in its field service for transfer to Washington but was estopped by the Commission from making such transfers. When the Commission itself obtained such persons, he charged, it assigned them to the war agency offices in Washington first.⁶²

In the second place, agency priorities, as well as the labor shortage and establishment of employment ceilings by the Bureau of the Budget, which will be discussed later in another connection, eventually forced the attention of the Civil Service Commission to the need for manpower utilization within the Federal service. When it was impossible to secure low-grade clerical workers in the

---

⁶⁰ *Ibid., No. 516,* January 25, 1945.
⁶¹ *Investigation of Civilian Employment,* Part II, June 3, 1943, pp. 454-55.
⁶² *Ibid.*

CENTRALIZATION OF RESPONSIBILITY 39

numbers requisitioned, the need for attention to the training, use of skills, and intelligent placement of employees already on the payroll was inescapable. Although the personnel utilization program of the Civil Service Commission, which was launched in 1944, was primarily an aspect of employment control (discussed in Chapter XII), it was not unrelated to the priorities problem.

THE PROBLEM OF UNAUTHORIZED AGENCY RECRUITING

The declaration of the Comptroller General in 1943 that his agency could enlist a level of recruits the Commission was unable to furnish expresses succinctly one of the principal reasons for the persistence of unauthorized agency-recruiting. Many administrators, especially in low-priority agencies, shared Mr. Warren's feeling of dissatisfaction with the quality of Commission recruits. That unauthorized recruiting was of considerable proportions the Ramspeck Committee learned in its investigation of civilian employment during the war years. In the six months from September 1, 1942, to February 28, 1943, out of a total of 1,300,000 appointments audited by the Commission, 102,000 were made as a result of unauthorized recruiting.[63] Of the 102,000, 14 per cent were rejected as not meeting qualifications standards, but the work load of the Commission prevented more than a mere paper check. The Commission in 1944 was forced to warn departments against enlisting private employment agencies to assist in recruitment.[64] Certain specific cases of small-scale abuse in recruitment were unearthed by the Ramspeck Committee, one case being the Army-Navy Electronics Production Agency, of which the Committee concluded:

> Recruiting appeared to be on a personal basis rather than in accordance with civil-service regulations. Former business associates, friends, and other considerations influenced the selection of departmental and field staffs. Falsification of qualifying experience, improper classification of positions, and clique control were prevalent.[65]

The seriousness of this charge from a committee headed by as staunch a friend of the merit system as Robert Ramspeck cannot

---

[63] *Ibid.,* Part I, March 11, 1943, pp. 35-36.
[64] CSC, *Departmental Circular No. 481,* May 16, 1944.
[65] U.S. Congress, House, Committee on the Civil Service, *Investigation of Civilian Employment,* House Report 2084, 78th Cong., 1st and 2nd Sess., 5-6.

be lightly brushed aside. Moreover, to eliminate loopholes the Civil Service Commission took the measure of canceling, in 1943, all joint recruiting programs, under the broad authority of which unauthorized recruiting had usually been conducted, and further ruled that it was not obliged to certify agency nominations unless they were the best qualified and available persons known to the Commission.[66] Under joint recruiting, a direct type conducted by the agencies under agreement with the Civil Service Commission, the agency retained the power of appointment. Under direct recruitment, as ordinarily meant, the power of appointment was delegated to the Commission by the employing agency. Inasmuch as agencies often utilized the delegation granted by the Commission to recruit one group of employees to cover a search for others, not actually authorized, the grant of power had to be revoked and limited to special cases.

Because the power of appointment was retained when unauthorized recruiting was employed, the reluctance of agencies to abandon their circumvention of Commission and WMC rules is comprehensible, if not justifiable. Agency responsibility for internal management and program operations superseded the observance of rules with which lower-priority agencies, at least, were none too sympathetic. Poor placement by a central personnel agency in the more important administrative positions held dire consequences for operating success, for which the central personnel agency in no way held itself accountable.[67] The right to appoint personnel, traditionally that of the employing agencies, the latter clung to tenaciously and jealously.

Despite Commission orders, departments, therefore, continued to engage in *sub rosa* recruiting activities, holding to the applications they received only to submit them almost as a *fait accompli* for the last step in formal approval of appointment. Intragovernmental competition was thus never really eliminated, and, to the end, government agencies were as stubbornly engaged in a covert struggle with each other and with the Commission as they were with industry for personnel. The Civil Service Commission was unable to command their confidence to rely upon it as sole sup-

[66] CSC, *Memorandum to the Heads of All Departments from the Commissioners as to Federal Recruiting Policies,* February 8, 1943.

[67] George C. S. Benson, "Central Control Agencies with Special Reference to Personnel," *Personnel Administration,* V (October, 1942), 7-9.

plier of personnel because they ascribed its failure to fill quotas to ineptitude and disadvantageous manpower restrictions instead of to the major reasons: labor market conditions and military urgency. So long as they conducted recruiting forays of their own, they rendered the task of the Commission proportionately more difficult. As the Comptroller General put it, "That is just another one of those circles we are in around here in this war."

Conclusions

Unique as were the WMC controls in and of themselves, an important consequence is worth noting. They subjected one Federal agency, created by statute, to the directives of another, created by executive order, not a state of affairs much to the taste of the legislative branch of government.[68] The power of the President, under Section 1753 of the Revised Statutes, to issue regulations on the entry of personnel into the executive branch actually eliminated any possibility of legal conflict between the War Manpower Commission and the Civil Service Commission. But it was, nonetheless, the first time in its sixty-year life span that the Civil Service Commission had been brought under another executive agency's controls. Administrative friction was avoided by giving the Civil Service Commission representation in the War Manpower Commission and thus a voice in its policy formulation and also by delegating to the former the enforcement of the latter's controls over government employment.

Another unusual aspect of the coverage of the WMC controls was that for the first time since the creation of the Civil Service Commission nongovernmental recruiting had to be conducted under some of the same legal restrictions as government recruitment. Not that the control of industrial personnel ever approached in completeness control of governmental personnel, but the very fact that the two were in many areas brought under a common roof of restrictions subjecting them to almost identical standards was revolutionary.

Never entirely effective by their very nature, the WMC controls,

[68] Said Representative Miller of Connecticut, in the course of the struggle in 1943 and 1944 in Congress to deny funds to executive order agencies, "Oh, for the day when once again we can truthfully say that we live under a government by congressional legislative enactment and not a government by Executive order." 90 *Cong. Record* 2067, February 25, 1944.

projected almost timidly and with continual adaptation and variation to rapidly changing conditions, were still a pillar of strength to the Civil Service Commission as well as a formidable barrier to free action in Federal recruitment. They underscored the congressional action of 1940 in making the Civil Service Commission responsible for all defense recruitment and in extending the normal coverage of Commission authority through the Ramspeck Act. Actually they were a limitation probably of more value to government as an employer than to industry operating under cost-plus contracts for the most part. In their absence it would have been even more difficult to compel the government agencies to recognize the congressional mandate for centralized recruitment through the Civil Service Commission.

With the end of the war these limitations were sloughed off, and the permanent gain during the period was clearly the vast extension of coverage of the Civil Service Act through the congressional decision in 1940 against exemption of the temporary war agencies and of expansion in the War and Navy departments. Despite the fact that war agencies have disappeared as independent entities, the transfer of certain surviving functions into "old line" departments and agencies and the increased size of the civilian complement in the military departments for some time to come have resulted in a Federal service more than double that of 1939. A battle to extend the Civil Service Act such as that engendered by the Ramspeck Act has been obviated. A major precedent has been established for emergency recruitment in war or peace.

CHAPTER THREE

A New Aggressive Approach to Recruitment

THE FACTOR of urgency implicit in the centralization of responsibility for Federal recruitment in 1940 revolutionized the approach to the task of mobilizing the army of civilian employees. War and preparation for war are crises which demand precedent-shattering measures. Mountains of red tape must be cut. Institutional adaptation must be effected with an alacrity shocking in normal times, or the institution is likely to be superseded or bypassed. Commissioner Flemming had promised on behalf of the Civil Service Commission in 1940 to furnish the manpower for the emergency, even on twenty-four hours' notice, and he had no intention of failing and thereby allowing the Commission to be thrown into the discard for the duration. It was clearly a case of "sink or swim," and he who would swim in rapidly shifting currents must quicken and strengthen his stroke.

The old passive "civil service as usual" attitude of waiting idly in the hope that enough people with the "right" qualifications would read unattractive announcements buried on postoffice bulletin boards and go through the many motions to apply for positions had to yield to speed, certainty, and relentless activity. Nothing could be left to chance, especially as the slack in unemployment was taken up by the armed forces and competing private enterprise. The fewer left to be recruited, the bolder and more enterprising the recruiter had to become. Ingenuity and persistence were essential qualities in a recruiter.

The new aggressive approach to recruitment manifested itself in three ways. One was the development of new and radically different techniques for reaching and enlisting the employable public. Another was the active development of new sources of supply from among neglected sectors of the population, particularly minority groups. Lastly, programs had to be adapted in "custom-built" style to particular occupational groups and rapidly changing conditions.

The wartime revolution in attitudes and techniques of recruitment did not occur in entirety hard on the heels of congressional centralization of defense recruitment in the Civil Service Commission in 1940. It was only as the production and program pressures developed and multiplied and the labor market was metamorphosed, as shown in Table 5 of the preceding chapter,[1] that changes appeared. Changes came slowly and gradually but in increasing tempo until after Pearl Harbor, when they came with a rush. From the beginning of 1942 until the end of the war the Civil Service Commission largely abandoned its prewar negativism in favor of positive service in recruitment through as many rapid and radically new adjustments as appeared to be necessary.

New Techniques and Relationships in Recruitment

An active relentless search for available or potential recruits in the highly competitive wartime labor market broke the "cake of custom" in civil service recruiting techniques. Passivity and negativism were as out of date as the Victorian broughams of 1883. The job titles of "recruiting representative" and "liaison officer" were revolutionary innovations and connote the psychological distance between 1939 and 1940. Government was forced by circumstances to adopt methods that had been employed successfully by private enterprise to a greater or lesser degree, depending upon the state of the local labor market, for many generations. Just how positive and unremitting government had to make its search can be deduced, in part, from the story Table 5 of the preceding chapter tells of employment and unemployment during the war years.[2] No hamlet in the hill country, no lonely Dakota farm, no isolated country schoolhouse could, at least in theory, be considered too remote or too insignificant to be overlooked. If life in Washington or in a large industrial center was painted in roseate hues instead of the dull gray of reality, and a long journey at government expense extolled as high adventure to the isolated rustic, one has to remember that such ruses have ever been the way of the recruiters since colonial trading companies beat the drums for their land schemes in the wilderness of North America. The only difference is that during the war years government was doing a "selling job" as aggressively as any entrepreneur.

[1] See above, p. 25. [2] Ibid.

The lines of development in devising new techniques were really two, from an earlier emphasis on positive recruitment, applied extensively and intensively, to a shift of emphasis to direct recruitment. Positive recruitment may be defined as an active campaign to attract qualified applicants through the media of publicity and salesmanship best adapted to the occupational group sought. Direct recruitment, on the other hand, may be defined simply as telescoping recruitment, examination, certification, and selection in the hands of a recruiter who seeks out eligibles and has the power to make hiring commitments. The usual method of examination in direct recruitment is by interview. The Commission recruiting representative was the recipient of a double delegation: from the Civil Service Commission to examine and certify, and from the employing agency of the power to appoint. For a time in 1942 and 1943 joint recruitment was used commonly as a variant of the latter method, whereby agency representatives in the company of Commission recruiters made direct offers of employment. The Civil Service Commission urged direct recruitment more and more forcefully upon the employing agencies as the labor market grew tighter, but the latter only reluctantly agreed to its adoption inasmuch as it involved the relinquishing of their traditional and sacrosanct prerogative of the appointing power to the Commission.

Positive recruitment received its impetus in May, 1940, as a result of the decision to initiate an active search for skilled labor. The devices used were nation-wide publicity about job openings through "spot" announcements over national radio chains, press releases, and cultivation of co-operation with state employment services and the Railroad Retirement Board to obtain lists of unemployed workers. Regional directors started canvassing their areas for prospective employees and supplemented national publicity with their own local press and radio announcements.[3] The Commission for a time tried publicizing a Consolidated List of all field office vacancies everywhere in the country.

"An aggressive selling attitude" keynoted the new Commission policy recommended by the regional directors themselves. Publicity was broadened to include community contacts with such organizations as labor unions, units of local government, fraternal

[3] CSC, *Circular Letters No. 2898, Supp. No. 2,* May 31, 1940, and *No. 3116,* December 27, 1940.

bodies, veterans' organizations, alumni associations as well as educational institutions, public assistance offices, and even manufacturing plants which retained lists of applicants for employment. Applicants themselves were regarded as a source of supply for others and were requested to give pertinent information about their friends and acquaintances in the course of interviews or when returning application forms. Efforts were made to keep in touch with defense construction workers and contractors employed on work nearing completion in order to reach another group of potential applicants.[4]

Direct recruitment superseded positive recruitment in importance and volume after Pearl Harbor when government production perforce leaped forward and wartime regulatory agencies proliferated from the Office of Emergency Management in all directions. Direct recruiting during the war years often involved traveling a planned circuit around a district to address organized groups, to visit schools, and even to canvass from house to house or by the telephone in times of stress. Commission representatives were placed in USES offices in the large industrial cities where government establishments were major claimants.[5] A representative's imagination and ingenuity placed the only limitations on the sources to which he might turn, for instructions to the regional directors were that they were to exhaust every possible source of personnel to fill positions essential to the war program even to the extent of going to private employers to obtain voluntary transfers to government establishments of those essential to the war program.[6] Efforts were even made to secure data from local Selective Service System boards on IV-F cases, deferred from military service, and on men over thirty-eight years of age released for physical reasons.[7] The Commission also turned to the officer procurement branches of the Army and Navy and the women's service recruitment offices for information about applicants not accepted for military service. Rejected FBI applicants were similarly regarded as potential recruits. Early in 1942 the Commission sent letters to national trade associations, selected retail trade associations, national highway users' organizations, purchasing agents, university professors of industrial management,

[4] *Ibid.*, No. *3181*, February 10, 1941, and No. *3203*, March 13, 1941.
[5] *Ibid.*, No. *3601*, February 26, 1942.   [6] *Ibid.*, No. *3552*, January 20, 1942.
[7] *Ibid.*, No. *4002*, May 12, 1942.

persons prominent in the management field whose names were provided by university alumni offices, city managers, state leagues of municipalities, and names furnished by the Civil Service Assembly and the Society for the Advancement of Management to enlist their interest in employment opportunities offered by the Federal government.

It would, moreover, be a mistake to assume that direct recruitment was limited to lower-grade CAF and labor positions, for "key" individuals with wide business and professional acquaintance were often employed as dollar-a-year men to recruit professional and administrative personnel.[8] Special arrangements were made to deputize members of the National Civil Service League to enlist business executives in the recruitment of executives. Individual recruiting circulars designed in more attractive format than the traditional announcements were devised for specialized positions, sent out to members of pertinent organizations, and followed up within several days by telephone or personal calls from Commission representatives.[9] The Commission also secured names of eligibles for administrative positions from the New York State Department of Civil Service, the United States Chamber of Commerce, and the personnel offices of some of the larger corporations.

Competition with private employers who provided transportation for industrial labor and clerical workers to the place of employment forced government to undertake similar provisions for lower-grade positions.[10] As part of the consideration, every worker so recruited was required to sign a formal agreement to reimburse the department or agency for his travel costs if he resigned voluntarily before the completion of six months of employment in that agency. The Navy Department was the first to receive travel authorization, with funds from the President's Emergency Fund, for recruitment for its critical field shore establishments on the West Coast.[11] Later the same authority was

[8] *Ibid.*, No. *3808*, September 11, 1942.   [9] *Ibid.*, No. *3629*, March 24, 1942.
[10] The payment of traveling expenses by the employing agency was conditioned on inability by the labor board to recruit locally, the existence of similar provision by other principal local employers, and the arrangement of suitable housing accommodations for recruits on the day of their arrival. Thus the number of units of housing available served as a brake on the number of persons who could be recruited.
[11] CSC, *Circular Letter No. 4058*, August 20, 1943.

48   IMPACT OF WAR ON FEDERAL PERSONNEL

extended to the War Department and a few other agencies, but never to all.[12]

THE CULTIVATION OF NEW SOURCES OF SUPPLY

Government, as well as industry, had to discover and develop new sources of supply for the labor market as 12,000,000 persons were withdrawn from the nation's labor force into military service. That the total labor force increased by some six millions (see Table 5) during the war years indicates a notable success in that endeavor. The obvious solution which seemed readiest at hand, once hiring officials were convinced that white male workers were unobtainable in the numbers desired, was to promote the recruitment of women. There were millions of housewives, domestic workers, and part-time employees who might be enlisted by attractive wages and working conditions. The Negro offered another fertile source to be tapped if the barriers of racial prejudice could be broken down. To a lesser extent school youth, the aged, the physically handicapped, and racial minorities like the Nisei and Filipinos, all became, in turn, potential recruits for the government service. The significant fact about the development of these hitherto neglected sectors of the population is that their utilization required not so much the debasing of relative qualifications standards as the eradication of reprehensible mental attitudes of appointing officers and workers.

1. WOMEN

The Federal government was relatively slow to realize the potentialities of women workers, especially for laborer positions. Despite the fact that it was probably simpler in the long run to induce the appointment of women in lieu of men than to push the employment of other minority groups, appointing officers held back in many cases until driven by sheer desperation. It was with naive surprise that many supervisors in the War Department establishments and Navy yards learned that women could be trained to do almost any of the rough, heavy work always before considered exclusively masculine, whether it be welding or running a fork-lift truck. The Commission tried to encourage exploration of the possibility of utilizing women workers in 1941, when skilled labor was already hard to recruit, with a warning

[12] *Ibid.,* No. 4096, December 31, 1943.

that the widespread use of older men would not make up the deficiency created by conscription and defense production.[13] Stress was laid on the obvious need for in-service training programs if women were to be utilized, a need which should not have served as a deterrent to their employment inasmuch as the employment of males available during the war required identical programs.

Certain field establishments such as War Department arsenals had, however, as early as 1941 hired increasing numbers of women not merely to replace male workers but to work side by side with them as the civilian labor force increased. Edgewood Arsenal, for example, had 2,513 women employees in April, 1941, as compared with a mere 181 before the emergency.[14] In the War Department as a whole the number of women employees jumped by 51,320 and in the Navy Department by 8,652 in the first year of defense activity, fiscal 1941.[15] By the end of another fiscal year the number of women employees had trebled the 1941 totals in the two named departments, in the total civil service and in the field service. But the proportion of increase was less for the departmental service. The great majority who accepted laborer positions entered by way of recruitment as female trainees and found their way into such varied jobs as sheet-metal workers, crane operators, turret lathe operators, shipfitters, munitions handlers, instrument and radio repairmen, draftsmen, and engineering aides.[16]

The basic WMC policy was to adhere to equality of the sexes when referring unemployed persons to training or job openings, with due regard to the physical and other requirements of the work.[17] But it was also that agency's policy to refrain from recruiting younger women with small children until all other sources of the local labor supply had been exhausted; and if it was found necessary to enlist such women, then adequate day-care facilities for their children had to be provided by the community, not by employers or by unions. Women were likewise admitted to pre-employment training courses conducted by public vocational schools on a basis of equality with men, and employers were asked to encourage them to take supplementary in-plant training for

[13] CSC, *Departmental Circular No. 266,* June 16, 1941.
[14] Lucille Foster McMillin, *The First Year* (Washington, 1941), 15.
[15] *Ibid.,* 25.
[16] Lucille Foster McMillin, *The Second Year* (Washington, 1943), *passim.*
[17] 8 *FR* 1867, February 11, 1943.

up-grading. Both management and labor were requested to remove all occupational barriers in any trade for which women could be fitted, to promote their acceptance in the shop, and to base wage rates for all workers on the work performed irrespective of sex.

The fact is that women furnished the greatest single source for recruitment into government service as well as into industry. The telling point with respect to recruitment of any minority group is not what policy statements were issued by the Commission and what rules formulated, but how the civil service actually did change with respect to such groups. Table 6 shows that the number of women employees rose from 186,000 in 1940 to 1,106,000 in 1944 and that the proportion of women in the Federal service rose from 18 per cent in 1940 to 37 per cent by July, 1944, their date of top strength. To put it another way, there were at the latter date 100,000 more women in the Federal service than the entire service numbered in 1939. Simultaneously the proportion of women in the nation's labor force increased by almost the same figure. An interesting point is that many of the women recruited into the Federal service were Negroes, a fact that leads up to a consideration of that source of labor supply.

2. NEGROES

Negro employment, which probably would have increased somewhat in the government service because of the manpower shortage, received a stimulus through the positive efforts exerted by President Roosevelt to obtain equal opportunity for all Americans in the war effort. While Rule I of the Civil Service Rules has long operated against racial discrimination in Federal civil service appointments,[18] the practice of such discrimination was often far too subtle to be corrected by legal mandates without special enforcement machinery.[19]

The real landmark in employment policy came with President

---

[18] CSC, *Civil Service Act, Rules and Regulations Annotated* (Washington, 1943), 216.

[19] Early in 1941 the Commission had deleted from applications all reference to race and ceased to require photographs. CSC, *Departmental Circular No. 248*, January 10, 1941. The photographs formerly required had been protested for years by Negro organizations and by some Congressmen. Yet as late as the summer of 1945 the State Department still demanded photographs of its applicants for the departmental service despite a Commission reminder to the departments to abandon that practice. *Ibid., No. 449*, November 10, 1943.

Roosevelt's Executive Order No. 8802 of June 25, 1941, which contained a categorical prohibition against discrimination because of race, color, creed, or national origin in Federal employment as well as in private employment for defense. That policy he implemented by establishing the Committee on Fair Employment Practice in the Office of Production Management to investigate complaints, redress valid grievances, and make recommendations

TABLE 6

WOMEN EMPLOYEES IN THE FEDERAL SERVICE AND IN THE UNITED STATES, SELECTED MONTHS, JULY, 1940–JULY, 1945

Month	Women Employed in the Federal Government[a]	Women Employed in the United States[b]
July, 1940	186,210[c]	10,800,000
January, 1941	227,377[d]	10,200,000
July, 1941	266,407[d]	12,000,000
January, 1942	....	12,700,000
July, 1942	558,279[e]	14,700,000
January, 1943	....	15,700,000
July, 1943	998,519[f]	17,900,000
January, 1944	975,491	16,400,000
July, 1944	1,106,132	18,590,000
January, 1945	1,064,798	16,690,000
July, 1945	1,082,338	19,810,000

[a] Figures not regularly reported by sex by the Civil Service Commission until 1943.
[b] *Monthly Labor Review* for all figures in this column. Found in the monthly report entitled "Unemployment in the United States."
[c] Civil Service Commission, *Fifty-seventh Annual Report*, 35.
[d] Lucille Foster McMillin, *The First Year*, 25.
[e] McMillin, *The Second Year*, 3.
[f] Figures for 1943 and subsequent years from Civil Service Commission, *Monthly Report of Employment, Executive Branch of the Federal Government* (multilithed).

to the President. A letter from the President to all department heads drew their attention to the existing lack of uniformity and lack of sympathy toward the employment and assignment of Negroes in the Federal service.[20] He, therefore, reiterated the basic principle of equal opportunity set forth in Executive Order 8802 and called for a thorough examination of personnel policies. The Commission took up the cudgels by emphasizing its central responsibility in enforcing the Civil Service Act and Rules, especially Rule I in this connection, and its intention of correct-

[20] CSC, *Circular Letter No. 3418*, September 18, 1941.

ing alleged discrimination by the departments.[21] The Commission agreed to turn over all its complaints to the FEPC and required that they be submitted in writing.

A definite policy was adopted by the Commission of placing at the head of a register the name of any eligible passed over by an appointing officer because of race, creed, color, or national origin and keeping that name in top position until the individual had received a number of considerations equal to those lost because of discrimination.[22] The discovery of such discrimination was admittedly difficult, for the allegations of those discriminated against were hard to support with facts. The number of considerations lost by reason of discrimination was virtually beyond proof. Therefore, although this policy seemed praiseworthy, it was well-nigh valueless. Under the Civil Service rules submission of the name was not made, however, to the guilty agency if the register was active and there was assurance of opportunities elsewhere in the service, for the ostensible reason that resubmission could scarcely benefit the individual before prejudiced persons. Yet with perfect inconsistency, it was stated by the Commission that if the policy of discrimination was deliberate the name of the eligible should be resubmitted even though other eligibles were available. It is hard to see how an appointment forced upon a consciously bigoted appointing officer would help the person deliberately passed over. The Commission discountenanced a policy of hiring by racial quotas as a justifiable reason for passing over eligibles.[23]

Once direct recruiting was widely used, it was possible for the Commission to implement its nondiscrimination policy more effectively. For example, recruiting representatives were ordered not to furnish additional eligibles or undertake positive recruiting if they had previously furnished an adequate number of names of qualified eligibles which had been returned without selection but with a request for more names.[24] Since joint recruiting by the departments was being discouraged in 1943, when this policy was

[21] *Ibid.* [22] *Ibid., No. 3805,* September 9, 1942.
[23] *Ibid., No. 3936, Supp. No. 3,* October 19, 1943. After the Commission received complaints of discrimination by the War Department against the hiring of Negro nurses at Letterman General Hospital, it ruled that names passed over because of race, creed, color, or national origin must be immediately resubmitted to the same appointing officer with a notation of the finding of discrimination.
[24] *Ibid., No. 4026,* June 24, 1943.

enunciated, it behooved the departments to comply with the President's policy.

How did national defense and war affect Negro employment in the Federal government? Comparison with 1938 shows great gains for the Negro. In that year only 8.4 per cent of the Federal employees in the departmental service were Negroes with about the same proportion in the field service.[25] Of all the departments the Navy at the beginning of the national defense program showed the most liberal hiring policy toward Negroes since it employed between 5,000 and 6,000 skilled and semiskilled Negroes in the Navy yards in September, 1940.[26] The Social Security Board had this to say of the government's policy: "Outside of Navy yards the practice of government establishments appears to be little better than that of many private establishments."[27] By March, 1944, the percentage of Negroes in the departmental service had risen to 19.2, in the field service to 11.2, and to 12 for the service as a whole.[28]

Much more significant than mere numbers had been the shift in grades of Negro employment. In contrast to 1938 when 90 per cent of the Negroes in the departmental service were in the custodial service and only 10 per cent in all other services, only 50 per cent of Negro departmental service employees were custodial employees in 1944 whereas 36 per cent were in the CAF and professional services. (See Table 7.) However, FEPC remarked the fact that the overwhelming proportion of Negro employment, 70 per cent, was industrial—in the ASF and Navy shore establishments—and that of the 30 per cent in the classified service 57.7 per cent was to be found in the ephemeral war agencies, presumably as war service appointees. The greater range of occupations for Negroes could be attributed in part to the appointment of Negro women as stenographers, typists, and clerks.[29] One might, therefore, question what permanent gains the war brought the Negro in employment opportunities. Table 7 reveals that 60 per

[25] Fair Employment Practice Committee, *First Report, July 1943-December 1944* (Washington, 1945), 92.

[26] Federal Security Agency, Social Security Board, Bureau of Employment Security, Division of Research and Statistics, *Negro Workers and the National Defense Program* (Washington, 1941), 12. (Mimeographed.)

[27] *Ibid.*   [28] FEPC. *First Report,* 92.

[29] President's Committee on Fair Employment Practice, War Manpower Commission, *The Employment of Negroes in the Federal Government,* prepared by Elmer W. Henderson (mimeographed), 3.

TABLE 7

PERCENTAGE OF NEGRO CLASSIFIED WORKERS IN VARIOUS SERVICES BY AGENCY GROUPS, MARCH 31, 1944[a]

Agency Groups	CAF Service	Professional Service	Subprofessional Service	Crafts, Protective and Custodial Service	Clerical-Mechanical Service	Executive Order Employees[b]	Total All Services
Bureau of the Budget	8.3	....	....	91.7	....	....	100.0
War Agencies	59.5	0.7	2.4	36.1	....	1.3	100.0
Executive Departments	40.7	0.2	1.5	29.2	28.1	0.3	100.0
Independent Agencies	17.9	0.5	14.4	66.6	....	0.6	100.0
Total All Agencies	35.7	0.7	7.8	49.6	6.2	....	100.0

[a] From Fair Employment Practice Committee, Division of Review and Analysis, *The Wartime Employment of Negroes in the Federal Government*, prepared by Cornelius L. Golightly with the assistance of India W. Hemphill (Washington: mimeographed, January, 1945), 3, and Tables XII-A, XIII-A, XIV-A, and XV-A.

[b] Executive order employees are those who are not under the Classification Act but whose salary scales are fixed by Executive Order 6746 of June 21, 1934.

cent of the Negro employees in the war agencies were in the CAF and professional services in contrast to the 18 per cent in the independent agencies in those two services.[30] The independent agencies, on the other hand, had 66.6 per cent of their Negro employees in the Crafts, Protective and Custodial Service.

The results of an FEPC study released in 1945 are summarized in Tables 7 and 8. Table 8 reveals that the Negroes enjoyed somewhat better opportunities in the departmental service in all agencies except in the emergency war agencies, where the proportion of field service employees and Negro employees in the field service was almost identical. The older executive departments reveal a poor record with 81.1 per cent of their Negro employees in the departmental service although they employed only 32.9 per cent of their total personnel in the departmental service. This fact seems to indicate that a considerable time must elapse before changed attitudes and policies permeate the field service.

One last point before leaving the question of Negro employment: What Federal agencies were involved in charges of alleged racial discrimination? Table 9 summarizes this information with respect to discrimination in hiring practices as apart from discriminatory working conditions and other types of unfairness. FEPC statistics reveal that of all types of complaints registered with it refusal to hire constituted 46.6 per cent of the total and 48.8 per cent of all complaints based on racial discrimination alone.[31] This proportion probably held good for government agencies, which seemed to be no better and no worse than their counterparts in private enterprise.

3. YOUTHS

Youths from fourteen to eighteen years of age were another fertile area for recruitment, supplying more than 3,000,000 extra workers on the labor force.[32] With respect to this group the Civil Service Commission had to sound certain warnings, such as reference to local District of Columbia limitations on night work and

---

[30] "Independent agencies" as used by FEPC in its reports covers the usual independent regulatory commissions, Civil Service Commission, and others not considered among the ten executive departments or the war agencies.

[31] FEPC, *First Report*, Table 8, p. 132.

[32] "Sources of Wartime Labor Supply in the United States," *Monthly Labor Review*, LIX (1944), 264.

TABLE 8

DISTRIBUTION OF TOTAL AND NEGRO FEDERAL WORKERS WITHIN MAJOR AGENCY GROUPS, MARCH 31, 1944[a]

Agency: Total and Negro	Total and Negro Federal Workers Reported			Total Classified Federal and Negro Workers Reported		
	In Numbers	Percent in Dept. Service	Percent in Field Service	In Numbers	Percent Dept. Service	Percent Field Service
All Agencies Total	2,295,614	9.4	90.6	1,178,413	17.0	83.0
Negro	273,971	15.2	84.8	82,183	44.8	55.2
Bureau of the Budget	548	97.6	2.4	526	97.5	2.5
Negro	24	100.0	0.0	24	100.0	0.0
War Agencies Total	1,928,216	4.5	95.5	866,826	9.8	90.2
Negro	231,458	6.0	94.0	47,452	29.2	70.8
Executive Departments	168,631	32.9	67.1	140,631	35.0	65.0
Negro	15,593	81.1[b]	18.9	13,011	84.3[b]	15.7
Independent Agencies	198,219	37.4	62.6	170,420	38.3	61.7
Negro	26,896	55.7	44.3	21,696	55.2	44.8

[a] From Fair Employment Practice Committee, Division of Review and Analysis, *The Wartime Employment of Negroes in the Federal Government*, prepared by Cornelius L. Golightly with the assistance of India W. Hemphill (Washington: mimeographed, January, 1945), 30-31. Not all agencies reported to FEPC. For example, for this report, Agriculture, Justice, and Labor departments did not report, and the Post Office Department found it impossible to report for their field service.

[b] Note the fact that the field employment of Negroes by these agencies was very poor as reflected in this distribution.

compliance under WMC policies with school attendance and child labor laws. Youths had to be paid at the same rates as adults for similar work according to WMC rules. Civil Service regional directors were early authorized to lower the minimum age for

TABLE 9

CASES DOCKETED BY FEPC AGAINST FEDERAL AGENCIES[a]

Agencies	Total No. of Complaints	Complaints of Racial Discrimination
War Department	341	287
Navy Department[b]	213	169
USES	96	78
Executive Office of the Pres.[c]	77	61
Civil Service Commission[d]	53	47
Post Office Department	35	29
Treasury Department	20	15
Veterans' Administration	14	10
Department of Agriculture	11	7
Department of Commerce	10	9
Maritime Commission	9	8
Federal Works Agency	4	4
State Department	2	2
Government corporation	2	2
Department of Justice	1	1
Other government agencies	35	31
Grand total from all parties public and private	4,081	3,298

[a] Fair Employment Practice Committee, *First Report, July 1943-December 1944*, Table 11, pp. 134-35.
[b] Proportionately a worse record than that of the War Department as the latter employed twice as many persons. One would, however, expect the concentration of complaints against these two departments which had about 80 per cent of the Federal employees.
[c] Includes all OEM agencies.
[d] No particular significance is to be attached to the large number of complaints against the Civil Service Commission and USES. Many who felt discriminated against had their only direct dealings with one or the other of these agencies and thus lodged complaints against them instead of against the department or employer which probably was the real offender.

stenographers and typists to sixteen when necessary to attract eligibles.[33] Some instances of careless recruitment of the very young for Navy yard work came to light and necessitated Commission insistence that sixteen was the absolute minimum age for

[33] CSC, *Circular Letter No. 3295,* June 21, 1941.

that kind of labor and that proof of age as well as evidence of parental consent to employment were mandatory conditions of eligibility.[34] The Post Office Department was permitted fourteen-year-olds for part-time work during the Christmas rush season.[35]

4. THE AGED

The aged also constituted a group of some importance for original recruitment, aside from the fact that many employees who reached superannuation were asked to remain in their positions during the emergency.[36] The Bureau of Old Age and Survivors' Insurance in the Social Security Board assisted industry and government by sending appeals to recipients of monthly checks to apply to their nearest USES office to inquire about opportunities for employment in either industry or government.[37] Retired Federal employees were frequently invited to return to the service and were given temporary or war-service appointments. Reemployment of this group was permitted by legislative action.[38]

5. THE HANDICAPPED

The physically handicapped were a group which the Commission sought strenuously to persuade appointing officers to accept. To a large extent, however, placement of handicapped persons was beyond Commission control in that physical qualifications standards for any position are determined in the last analysis by the employing agency which has program responsibility. But departments were reminded of satisfactory service that such employees as blind dictating machine operators had rendered where already employed.[39] To promote better understanding of how the handicapped could be utilized and to co-ordinate the efforts of the Civil Service regional offices and the State Rehabilitation Services, standing ready to supply recruits, a permanent joint committee was established on which were represented the Commission, the Office of Vocational Rehabilitation in the Federal Security Agency, the Veterans Administration, the Veterans Employment Service of the War Manpower Commission, and the

[34] *Ibid., No. 3997,* May 3, 1943.
[35] *Ibid., No. 4048,* November 15, 1943.
[36] CSC, *Departmental Circular No. 400,* December 31, 1942. Executive Order 9047, January 30, 1942, permitted retention indefinitely of those exempted by law of January 24, 1942, from retirement.
[37] CSC, *Circular Letter No. 4083,* November 12, 1943.
[38] 54 *U.S. Statutes* 678 (1940) and 56 *U.S. Statutes* 13 (1942).
[39] CSC, *Departmental Circular No. 354,* July 7, 1942.

Council of Personnel Administration. A booklet entitled *Untapped Manpower,* together with the Commission's *Manual for Placement of the Physically Handicapped,* was sent to Federal appointing officers in 1942. State Rehabilitation Services were requested to submit to recruiting representatives, not to appointing officers, the names of qualified handicapped persons, and in turn the Commission informed the Vocational Rehabilitation Office in the Federal Security Agency of employment needs and opportunities.[40] More than 30,000 severely handicapped persons were placed in Federal industrial establishments alone by 1944.[41]

The placement of disabled veterans was a natural concomitant of this program, and in 1942 the Commission ordered its regional directors to undertake a positive program to inform disabled veterans of opportunities.[42] Arrangements were effected with the appointing agencies and the armed forces or Veterans Administration to consummate placements before the medical discharge of the veterans. The Regional Offices were asked to work with State Rehabilitation Services to help veterans who needed retraining to develop new skills and to co-operate with USES to secure those already available for employment. In 1944 the Commission established local boards of Civil Service examiners at Army hospitals to issue accurate information to disabled hospitalized veterans, receive direct recruiting orders, and administer and rate tests on the spot.[43] The program was curtailed in 1945 by a cut in Commission appropriations.

6. ORIENTALS

Although he represented a numerically less significant minority group than the Negro, the Oriental faced the same problem and enjoyed the same advantage from the tight labor market. Filipinos were under a lesser onus of discrimination than American-born Japanese, as was natural. The resistance of the Filipinos to Japanese invasion caused a reversal of feeling for the beleaguered wards of this country and led Congress to remove the statutory prohibition against their employment because of noncitizenship.[44] But even with respect to the Japanese a reversal of the arbitrary

[40] CSC, *Circular Letter No. 3907,* December 14, 1942.
[41] CSC, *Departmental Circular No. 323, Revised, Supp. No. 28,* June 30, 1944.
[42] CSC, *Circular Letter No. 3964,* March 1, 1943.
[43] *Ibid.,* No. 4131, March 9, 1944.
[44] 56 *U.S. Statutes* 266 (1942).

bar to employment came in 1943. Regional directors were, therefore, asked to send well-qualified recruiting representatives to the various relocation centers to get applications into the hands of Japanese-Americans who had already been cleared by the War Relocation Authority to leave the center and who happened to possess skills in shortage occupations.[45] Even those not yet cleared were allowed to apply through the War Relocation Authority. Employment was predicated on agreements with the various agencies as to the specific number of cleared, qualified, and available Nisei who were desired in the departmental and field service with the understanding that appointment was unconditional upon their arrival at the place of employment. The Navy, however, entered a blanket objection to all persons of Japanese origin for employment at the Pearl Harbor Navy Yard as well as at all naval establishments on the West Coast, regardless of whether the Nisei were veterans of the present war or nonveterans.[46] Navy objection for Pearl Harbor employment, in fact, extended to all persons of the Oriental race except American or Hawaiian-born Chinese, who could be considered after a determination of suitability by the Commission. Moreover, no certification was permitted for any Japanese to any position in the War Department.[47] A rational man might well question the necessity of a policy as harsh as that of the War and Navy departments, based as it was on the nebulous sophistry of "security," of which the military in time of war is customarily presumed to be the sole judge and from which the mere civilian has no appeal. One must remember Nisei were inducted into our army at the time they were barred from civilian positions in the War Department. War Department policy, therefore, toward the Japanese-Americans was in part ambivalent and irrational.

7. PART-TIME EMPLOYEES

As a means of tapping an unwonted source for recruitment, arrangements were made to give part-time employment in such critical occupations as stenographer, typist, tabulating machine operator, and telephone operator to those gainfully employed full-time in private industry.[48] This practice of hiring employees of

[45] CSC, *Circular Letter No. 3982,* March 27, 1943.
[46] CSC, *Circular Letter, Inter-Regional Recruiting Series No. 10* (undated).
[47] CSC, *Circular Letter No. 4025,* June 23, 1943.
[48] CSC, *Departmental Circular No. 398, Supp. No. 1,* January 25, 1943.

others to supplement one's own staff in part-time capacity was not uncommon in industry in 1943. For government, this was a unique way of relieving the labor shortage by bringing in persons who might not have considered a full-time government position. Part-time employment of farmers and businessmen at government industrial establishments to fill special rush orders was adopted at some War Department installations.[49]

8. VETERANS

Before leaving the subject of development of new sources, mention must be made in passing of the recruitment of men over thirty-eight years of age for whom the Army signified its readiness to discharge to civilian employment.[50] Release from the Army was contingent on actual employment offers in essential occupations, a condition which precluded the Civil Service Commission from deluging the Army with recruiting circulars and raiding it for recruitment purposes. Operating agencies, however, were permitted to write directly to over-age soldiers to offer re-employment in a former position.

Veterans' Placement Representatives, later called Veterans' Federal Employment Representatives, were established in all Commission regional offices to keep in touch with all discharged veterans in their district in order to offer Federal employment to those qualified.[51] Early in 1944 President Roosevelt wrote to the heads of all departments and agencies requesting a delegation of direct recruiting authority for all veteran placement to the Commission as "his" representative.[52] Civil Service recruiting representatives, preferably veterans themselves, were assigned to all Army separation centers to effectuate recruitment as the military discharge rate accelerated in 1945.[53] Although this program was primarily related to the implementation of the Starnes Act of 1944 for veterans' preference, it was also in a secondary sense related to the determination to overlook no potential or actual areas for recruitment during the manpower shortage.

---

[49] Marian Drake Hall, "Personnel Administration at a Government War Plant—A Case Study," *Public Personnel Review*, V (October, 1944), 228.
[50] CSC, *Circular Letter No. 3998*, May 4, 1943.
[51] CSC, *Personnel Series No. 32*, April 15, 1944.
[52] Letter of President Roosevelt to Heads of All Executive Departments and Agencies, February 26, 1944.
[53] CSC, *Circular Letter No. 4243*, January 30, 1945.

Conclusions

Crises often liquidate attitudes of mind as well as the paper procedures which are, after all, merely a reflection of fixed ideas. That the approach to recruitment was revolutionized by the national emergency prevailing from the inception of defense measures in 1940 is apparent from the foregoing account. Abandoning the negative and passive philosophy, feasible, even if not desirable, in a labor market flooded with millions of unemployed persons, the United States Civil Service Commission embarked on a positive and persuasive program to seek actively for the best and induce them to accept Federal employment. Nothing could have been more antithetical to the old "keep the rascals out" rationale, for what ensued was a gigantic sales campaign to reach the American public and enlist it for the duration.

The narrowing margin between the total labor force available and that part gainfully employed induced an increasingly intensive and extensive search. New modes of publicity were designed for all categories and levels of employment while traveling recruiters stalked their prey from house to house, village to village, school to school. Many thousands of those persons found acceptable were bundled off for a free ride at government expense to remote parts of the country.

A certain amount of education of appointing officers and supervisors was necessary as well as a frank campaign to "sell" government employment to those previously neither preferred by the government nor themselves attracted to it. Women as the largest minority group furnished the greatest supply, rising to a total greater than the entire service in the prewar years. Other minorities found comparable opportunities during the shortage.

The result of all this activity in recruitment has not been wholly beneficial to postwar recruitment to the Federal service. Although many persons became aware for the first time of employment opportunities in the government service, many thousands of others were unhappy and frustrated in routine jobs or in positions which had great potentialities, as in scientific research, never realized. This latter group acutely felt the frustrating weight of bureaucracy and red tapism holding them down. Small wonder then that two sharp cries of protest were heard when it appeared that the old passivity and bureaucratic delays of civil service procedures might return at the end of the war.[54]

The answer of the Commission, announced in its postwar program, was its determination to continue its close wartime cooperation with the employing agencies in recruitment, training, and improvement of employee relations. Significantly the Commission stressed that in working with the agencies on many joint programs it had learned to accelerate its work without sacrificing the merit system and that it would be remiss not to profit by the lessons of the war. It set as goals the elimination of all unnecessary paper work, making the agencies partners in the performance of such service functions as examination and classification, with the further delegation of authority to the agencies to take personnel actions subject only to adherence to established standards. Thus the war experience of the Civil Service Commission seems to have ushered in a permanent reorientation of policy for positive service and speed in performance.[55]

[54] Floyd W. Reeves, "Civil Service as Usual," *Public Administration Review*, IV (1944), 327-40; John Fischer, "Let's Go Back to the Spoils System," *Harper's Magazine*, CXCI (1945), 362-68.

[55] CSC, *Sixty-Second Annual Report* (Washington, 1946), *passim*.

CHAPTER FOUR

Application of the New Aggressive Approach to Particular Occupational Groups

IN MOVING from the general to the particular in an investigation of recruitment techniques some arresting wartime developments are encountered. Over at least one vital area, the recruitment of executives, the conduct of the Civil Service Commission necessarily remained incomplete in fact, despite all that has been said of centralization of responsibility for recruitment. Yet that very incompleteness of control was an advantage and not a handicap. By allowing freedom where it was not equipped by experience to render first-rate service immediately and where it would have been immensely difficult to serve well during the learning process, the Commission wisely gave those in charge of operating responsibilities freedom in getting men and women who could most effectively carry out their program. What may be just as valuable from the standpoint of administration, persons who believed in the objectives of a program could be recruited under that freedom. In addition, a new device for listing talents for ready reference in an emergency was evolved.

The selection of the four occupational groups to which aggressive recruitment policies were applied has been to a certain extent arbitrary. The fields to be examined in turn are the recruitment of executives, both dollar-a-year men and salaried administrators, the mobilization of scientists and professional personnel, the obtaining of stenographers and typists, and the enlistment of labor, both skilled and unskilled. That is not to say that other groups were insignificant but merely that these were more significant. No program as vast as our wartime administration could have succeeded without the importation into government service of a great influx of top-flight administrative talent from private enterprise. A program usually stands or falls on the kind of leadership and sense of direction imparted by policy-making administrators to their routine employees. For that reason, if no other, it is essential to examine briefly the way in which the government augmented its executive force by "raiding" industry and borrowing on a virtually uncompensated basis what talent it could secure. Secondly, modern war is a battle of scientists and technicians in great degree, regardless of the demand for such professional persons as the lawyers spinning out a web of regulations, directives, and orders over the civilian economy. And what machine is more important to the accomplishment of the objectives of government than the everyday typewriter? Without the girl to operate that machine, the finest organization extant would be stalled. Lastly, the overwhelming proportion the blue-collar worker assumed to total Federal employment during the war made him as much a producer of the weapons—whose output the executive directed and regulated, the scientist designed, and the typist described in specifications—as his counterpart in any privately owned industrial plant. In a war of machines he was a vital cog.

The Recruitment of Executives: Dollar-a-Year Men and Salaried Administrators[1]

1. DOLLAR-A-YEAR MEN

The mobilization of top administrative talent was dramatically highlighted by the stream of dollar-a-year men moving into Washington by 1941 and 1942 entirely outside the civil service system of recruitment. They often entered the government with a fanfare and in the white light of publicity, a glare from which they never escaped. Congressional misgivings at their utilization were expressed almost unremittingly, and they were subject to the continuous probing of the Truman Committee. As a matter of fact, Senator Harry S. Truman freely expressed disapproval of the loan of these men by companies with a large stake in the defense program and suggested that all should disassociate themselves from their corporations and salaries for the duration and become regular government employees. This was the tenor of congressional remarks about their use.[2]

Why then were so many business executives and industrial managers recruited as dollar-a-year men instead of as salaried full-time government employees through the Civil Service Commis-

[1] See Herbert Emmerich, "The Search for Executive Talent," in *Civil Service in Wartime*, 22-46.
[2] 88 *Cong. Record* 381-82, January 15, 1942.

66 IMPACT OF WAR ON FEDERAL PERSONNEL

sion? In the early days of defense, that is, of the National Defense Advisory Commission, later the Office of Production Management, it was both expedient and necessary to resort to dollar-a-year men to obtain the talent and experience requisite to direct our industrial capacity into the new channels of "tooling up" for war production. Since the dollar-a-year men possessed an unrivaled *expertise* in the field of industrial production, they were indispensable to the planning and organization of defense and war production. As corporation executives, they were neither interested in

TABLE 10

DOLLAR-A-YEAR MEN AND WOCS IN WAR PRODUCTION BOARD, SELECTED MONTHS, 1943–1945[a]

Month	Number
June, 1943	865
September, 1943	857
December, 1943	796
July, 1944	686
January, 1945	522
April, 1945	626
July, 1945	498

[a] Civil Service Commission, *Monthly Report of Employment Executive Branch of the Federal Government* (multilithed). No statistics were maintained before 1943 on this category of employees. While many agencies have used dollar-a-year men and WOCS (without compensation), their employment has not been in major executive positions as in WPB but rather as occasional consultants or emergency recruits like the epidemiologists in the Public Health Service.

nor attracted by the usual civil service recruitment methods nor could they have been expected to manifest interest in regular Federal employment. Equally important, government salaries were inadequate to compensate corporation executives who normally earned many times the top salary for government administrators—$8,000 per annum. Congressional authorization was, therefore, secured for their enlistment.[3] There was, after all, the precedent of their utilization by the Council of National Defense and the War Industries Board in World War I. Later, after Pearl Harbor and the creation of the War Production Board, recruitment of dollar-a-year men was accelerated over that in the defense period. No statistics were maintained on their employment until 1943, but in that year they probably reached their peak and con-

[3] 54 *U.S. Statutes* 599 (1940).

stituted 78 per cent of the executive force of WPB.[4] The number of dollar-a-year men declined gradually by 1945 to 56 per cent of the 1943 total in the War Production Board, as shown in Table 10.

One significant reason for the use of dollar-a-year men, not without validity, was the vital need in OPM and WPB for enlisting the confidence of that part of our many-sided public with which those agencies had to deal. It must be remembered that the typical business and industrial executive was for some few years before the war antigovernment and antiadministration. In the light of that hard fact, only a member of the business fraternity could work effectively through government to recruit businessmen or to win their co-operation with agency programs. Their use was actually one of the ways of winning consent so essential in a democracy. This was no secret to President Roosevelt; he knew only too well that the success of the war program depended on enlisting the services of those to whom he was anathema.[5]

In truth, the arrangement of the classification system in the higher levels of the Federal service, particularly grades CAF-13 through CAF-15, augmented the difficulty of recruiting administrators from business on a salaried basis. There were too few classification grades in that range, a condition which engendered the tendency to classify too many positions at the CAF-14 grade, at $6,500, or even at CAF-15, at $8,000 per year. Herbert Emmerich, when Executive Secretary of OPM, testified before the House Civil Service Committee: "In part at least we are compelled to go to industry with our hats in hand and ask them to pay men while they are working for the Government because of the fact that in these higher grades the present arrangement of pay rates is less flexible than in industry."[6] It was his opinion that the engineering and technical personnel paid by industry at scales ranging from $6,000 to $9,000 per year might have been secured as regular civil servants had the government salary scale been more flexible.

Many business executives who would have spurned a civil service appointment felt they could afford to contribute their services to the war effort if they could remain on their company payrolls

[4] Emmerich in *Civil Service in Wartime*, 37.
[5] Interview with Herbert Emmerich, August 28, 1945.
[6] U.S. Congress, House, Committee on the Civil Service, Hearings on *A Bill to Amend Section 13 of the Classification Act of 1923, as Amended,* 77th Cong., 1st Sess., 31.

and return to their permanent positions at any time. It would be a mistake, however, to regard their government compensation as merely the nominal sum they received, for they were allowed traveling expenses and often the usual per diem allowance for living expenses, which was tax free. The latter was an item of some consequence to many of the lesser executives in a period of what seemed like oppressive taxation to many Americans.[7]

Some who have deplored the use of dollar-a-year men have said that government itself should have developed a sufficient number of persons with broad managerial ability to direct the various production activities of WPB. But that argument loses all validity when we realize that many business executives of broad managerial experience but without a knowledge of technical operations were useless in solving production problems. For example, WPB solved the steel production problem only after it had obtained the services of the president of one of the smaller steel companies who knew thoroughly the technical side of his industry.[8]

Dollar-a-year men were recruited by OPM and WPB without the assistance of the Civil Service Commission. That the usual Commission channels would have been wholly incapable of recruiting corporation executives and production specialists was the prevalent feeling among the top-flight Washington administrators responsible for the war program.[9] This attitude did not reflect dislike of the Commission but a frank recognition that the latter had never developed any contacts with that stratum of American economic life needed to direct industrial controls. Indeed, it had never been required to do so. Civil Service examiners were not expected to know the identity of the leading technical specialists in copper mining, nylon manufacture, or the production of steel forgings. Nor did the examiners enjoy a personal acquaintance with business and industrial executives on which to base a cogent appeal to borrow their services or the services of their assistants.

The recruitment of dollar-a-year men was conducted on a highly personalized basis through such "key" men as Sidney Weinberg, assistant to the chairman of OPM and WPB, who through his work as an investment banker had a wide acquaintance in busi-

---

[7] Interview with Frederick Roe of Chicago, November 2, 1945.   [8] *Ibid.*
[9] Interview with Emmerich, August 28, 1945, and Roe, November 2, 1945.

APPLICATION TO PARTICULAR OCCUPATIONS 69

ness and industrial circles. He was, in fact, one of the most famous of the "body snatchers," as these recruiters of dollar-a-year men were called.[10] Through face-to-face talks and by means of long-distance calls the "body snatchers" appealed successfully to countless corporation executives to come to Washington as dollar-a-year men.

Chaos, too, may be said to have characterized their recruitment activities, especially in the early days. There were, as a rule, three kinds of agents for recruitment: (1) men like Weinberg, who knew the top-flight industrialists, (2) the division chiefs brought in by the former and who knew the lesser people in their own industry, particularly technical specialists, and (3) industry representatives who made nominations at industry meetings called by OPM and later WPB.[11] Those in the second group, the division chiefs or their section chiefs, were often carried away by their own enthusiasm for a projected program and indulged in hectic and successful recruitment before final determination had been made to proceed with the program. Those who were left stranded in some neglected organizational nook of OPM or WPB have been aptly called "forgotten battalions" by Emmerich.[12] Telephone calls were put through hastily to the persons suggested and appeals made to their patriotism, with a "build-up" stressing the importance of the position to be filled and the stature of the man to whom the appeal was directed. Often different divisions within WPB were calling the same men and the same corporations in their competitive scramble for personnel. Once the individual agreed to come to Washington, calls had to be made to his company officers or the directors to negotiate the loan of that person. But WPB was hard pressed to compete with the armed forces inasmuch as many potential recruits often rejected civilian service for the glamor of a colonel's eagles or a commander's stripes, either of which lent a certain aura of distinction and seemed to connote more essential war service than civilian employment. The "Wall Street colonels and commanders" became commonplace around Washington.

Getting able executives to Washington often necessitated some deception, which in turn created organizational difficulties, espe-

[10] Interview with Roe, November 2, 1945. [11] *Ibid.*
[12] Emmerich in *Civil Service in Wartime*, 43.

cially in the early days of OPM. Director William S. Knudsen, himself an uncompensated employee, allowed division executives to recruit whom and where they would without previous position and organizational analysis to determine the exact assignment of functions and responsibilities.[13] It is not surprising, therefore, that jurisdictional disputes plagued OPM and many uncompensated employees left Washington in a "huff" as rapidly as they entered. Many had been engaged so quickly they had had no time to decide whether they were on the rolls of OPM or were lobbying for their company.

By the time WPB was established some of the more egregious blunders in the recruitment of dollar-a-year men had been isolated and obviated. One of the first steps taken by Donald M. Nelson, as chairman, was to require position analysis and adherence to a personnel policy initiated early in 1942 through the efforts of Herbert Emmerich, then Executive Secretary. One of the basic principles in that policy was that the agency personnel director and the assistant to the chairman had to agree before any person was employed. Eventually definite recruitment standards were evolved to govern the appointment of dollar-a-year men and WOCs (without compensation).[14] These standards made it mandatory that any such appointee had been paid at least $5,600 per annum before his appointment, that it had been impossible to find a well-qualified person to serve as a regular salaried employee, and that the dollar-a-year man had refused to serve on a regular salaried basis. Those who were categorically barred from dollar-a-year or WOC status were: (a) lawyers, (b) trade association employees or paid consultants, (c) members of WPB Industry Advisory Committees within the preceding twelve months, (d) private consultants, (e) those who had within the preceding year served as regular salaried Federal employees, changed their nongovernmental status materially, or had been convicted of monopolistic practices, (f) those engaged in private activities that would constitute violations of the Hatch Act if carried on by salaried government employees, and (g) those who as WPB employees would be required to make decisions affecting their own or com-

---

[13] Interview with Emmerich, August 28, 1945.
[14] War Production Board, Manual of Policy and Organization, *General Administrative Order No. 2-4* (amended), August 22, 1944.

APPLICATION TO PARTICULAR OCCUPATIONS 71

petitors' companies.[15] All appointments were subject to a complete investigation by WPB.[16]

Dollar-a-year men were for the most part loyal, however undisciplined may have been their behavior and despite the difficulties they encountered in learning to adjust their thinking to the "public interest." This was the considered opinion of those who observed them closely[17] in contrast to the criticism, often lurid, voiced in the press and in Congress of the role the dollar-a-year men played. The Truman Committee said in 1942 in an investigation it had made of charges that certain dollar-a-year men had slowed down war conversion:

> In his testimony before the committee, Mr. Knowlson expressed the opinion that the employment of dollar-a-year men was a matter of the personal integrity of the individual. The committee does not wholly concur in this conclusion. It belives that the Guthrie case points to the conclusion that certain dollar-a-year men within the Bureau of Industry Branches are unable to divorce themselves from their subconscious gravitation to their own industries. . . .
>
> The committee believes that most dollar-a-year and without-compensation men are honest and conscientious, and that they would not intentionally favor big business. However, it is not their intentional acts that the committee fears but their subconscious tendency, without which they would hardly be human, to judge all matters before them in the light of their past experiences and convictions.[18]

The committee, therefore, thought that dollar-a-year men should be used in an industry branch associated with a field other

[15] The disqualification of lawyers was adopted at the insistence of John Lord O'Brian, general counsel of OPM and WPB, in order to achieve loyal and disinterested service from attorneys. O'Brian is generally credited with having maintained a reasonable degree of purity in the employment of dollar-a-year men. Through some unhappy experiences with trade association representatives, it was revealed that they were desperately opposed to expansion in their own fields, served as tale-bearers, and generally inhibited industry people. (Interview with Roe, November 2, 1945.)

[16] At first the names of dollar-a-year men, when appointed, were presented to President Roosevelt for his personal approval, but after Pearl Harbor that power was delegated to agency heads. At no time did the President disapprove any appointee on political grounds. See Emmerich in *Civil Service in Wartime*, 39.

[17] Herbert Emmerich, Frederick Roe, Donald M. Nelson, and Lyle Belsley. The latter was Emmerich's successor as Executive Secretary of WPB.

[18] 88 *Cong. Record* 5325, June 18, 1942.

than that which employed them. The following exchange on the floor of the Senate explains the committee attitude:

> *Senator Truman.* No dollar-a-year man should be allowed to have control over the industry with which he is connected and from which he is receiving a salary. . . . the people who have no financial interest in industry are anxious to see the war effort go forward a little more rapidly than are those still connected with industry.
>
> *Senator Lucas.* From that statement, am I to understand that the committee of which the distinguished Senator is chairman would advocate the elimination of all dollar-a-year men?
>
> *Senator Truman.* We made a very strong statement on that subject on January 15, and Mr. Nelson came to the committee and discussed the matter with us, and told us that he thought he could not possibly organize the Office of Production Management into the War Production Board unless he could make use of the dollar-a-year men. We told him we would go along with him to the best of our ability, but we still held to the conclusion that a man's heart is where his pocketbook is. . . .
>
> *Senator Burton.* . . . It is the opinion of the committee that in securing the services of these men for the Government, if they are unable to sever their private connections, their services should be rendered to the Government either in an advisory capacity or in a capacity in which they will be administering someone else's orders. They should not be in positions where they will make the final decisions on questions of policy, and they should not make decisions for the Government in connection with their own industries.[19]

The difficulty with the Truman Committee suggestion was that the principal value of the dollar-a-year men to the Board was their knowledge of the industry whence they came. However, most dollar-a-year men stood in awe of the Truman Committee and strove hard to avoid the implication of sharp practice on behalf of their companies. Further, those from the larger corporations were much too sophisticated about the role of public relations in modern economic life to risk any steps that would have reflected unfavorably on them or their companies.[20] It required patience and tact and more organizing ability than many possessed to con-

[19] *Ibid.*, 5325-26.
[20] Interview with Emmerich, August 28, 1945.

APPLICATION TO PARTICULAR OCCUPATIONS 73

struct an organization and effect its smooth operation. Not all the ablest came from the largest companies by any means.[21]

2. SALARIED EXECUTIVES

The war offered the first opportunity to the Civil Service Commission to recruit for regular salaried executive positions in the Federal service. Thus, before the war it was a rare occurrence to hold examinations for $4,600 and $5,600 positions, not to mention positions above those levels, because of the normal feasibility of promotion from within and, not to be overlooked, the exception of many such positions from the merit system before the passage of the Ramspeck Act.[22] Even Commissioner Flemming confessed, "When we first started recruiting for those jobs we had a great deal to learn."[23]

While the Commission was learning, it delegated to the operating agencies a large measure of freedom in the mobilization of administrators, a delegation viewed as "wise" by Emmerich.[24] As Commissioner Flemming put it, the difficulty in channeling all recruitment centrally for the higher administrative personnel was the lack of agreement on what qualities and capacities make the "good" administrator. Even if agreed upon, they were frequently too elusive to show in a paper record of qualifications.[25] The war agencies, therefore, had to procure many of their administrators through their own top-flight officers who had a wide acquaintance in government or academic circles and knew, as a result, where to turn. They employed much the same personalized appeal as was utilized to induce businessmen to become dollar-a-year men.

It would be misleading to leave the impression that the Civil Service Commission even in its "learning" period abandoned the field of higher civil service recruitment to the appointing agencies. One of the most important steps taken by the Commission was the creation of the Committee on Administrative Personnel on December 13, 1941. The committee was composed of leading representatives from government, industry, and academic circles and acted in an advisory capacity to the Commission.[26] The ob-

[21] Companies often did not feel they could spare their best talent and sent "second raters" or "lame ducks." See Emmerich in *Civil Service in Wartime*, 39.
[22] *Investigation of Civilian Employment*, Part I, March 19, 1943, p. 103.
[23] *Ibid.*
[24] Emmerich in *Civil Service in Wartime*, 41.
[25] *Investigation of Civilian Employment*, Part I, March 19, 1943, p. 103.
[26] Summary of meeting of the Committee on Administrative Personnel, June 20,

jectives of the committee, as the members stated them, were to recommend policies for the recruitment, selection, placement, and development of administrative personnel.[27] The chairman of the committee was the operating chief of the new Administrative and Management Placement Section in the Civil Service Commission, which included the Administrative Examining Unit set up in 1941.

The Committee on Administrative Personnel made many recommendations calculated to assist both the Commission and the agencies in their administrative recruitment problems. For example, they recommended an immediate enlargement of the examining staff with a number of individuals competent to recruit, evaluate, review, negotiate, and arrange for the placement of administrative personnel.[28] From the first the committee recognized the need for an administrative training program and the value of extending the usefulness of the National Roster of Scientific and Specialized Personnel into the administrative field.[29] It proposed an interagency transfer program of administrative personnel actively promoted by the Commission to assist the war agencies and the staffing of the Commission with higher-grade personnel representatives to negotiate transfers into the war agencies.[30] It pointed out the need for adequate publicity on openings and demands in the service for administrators, central interviewing, a standard application form, and a special executive roster in the Commission.[31] Later in 1944 the committee recommended the establishment of regional advisory committees of persons of outstanding administrative competence to parallel the

---

1944. The original members of the Committee on Administrative Personnel included Emery E. Olson of the Commission staff as chairman; William L. Batt, Sr., of the War Production Board; James V. Bennett, director of the Bureau of Prisons; Frederick M. Davenport, chairman of the Council of Personnel Administration; Robert L. Johnson, president of Temple University; Guy Moffett, consultant, Liaison Office for Personnel Management; Donald C. Stone, Assistant Director of the Bureau of the Budget in charge of the Division of Administrative Management; and Leonard D. White, professor of public administration at the University of Chicago and former Civil Service Commissioner. Later Alvin E. Dodd, president of the American Management Association, and Howard Coonley, director of the Conservation Division of WPB, were added.

[27] Minutes of the Committee on Administrative Personnel, December 20, 1941.
[28] *Ibid.*   [29] *Ibid.*, January 3, 1942.
[30] *Ibid.*, February 14, 1942, and March 21, 1942.   [31] *Ibid.*, February 14, 1942.

APPLICATION TO PARTICULAR OCCUPATIONS 75

work of the national committee in the regional Commission offices.[32]

For certain of the war agencies, such as OPA, WPB, WMC, and OCD, in addition to the Commission itself, special recruiting circulars and announcements were designed for higher-level administrative and professional positions, and such positions were widely advertised for open competition.[33] The Commission's regional offices employed prominent local persons with extensive community contacts on a dollar-a-year basis to recruit individuals of demonstrated administrative capacities required for special assignments in either the field or departmental service. In some cases employees from the appointing agencies were detailed to the Commission for special recruiting assignments.[34] A unique advertising and publicity campaign was employed successfully in the New York City newspapers to fill the post of regional OPA director in 1943.[35] When victory came within sight, the problem arose of securing administrators for the reconversion program; to assist in this task each regional director of the Commission was asked to furnish a minimum of ten names of especially able administrators in the month of September, 1944.[36]

Needless to say, Congress viewed personalized recruitment with dismay, not out of deep devotion to the merit system, but rather out of loving attachment to the spoils system. Senators were chagrined to find spoils going to "bureaucrats" building up personal machines which should normally have been theirs under the old rules. Senator Francis Maloney of Connecticut summarized prevailing congressional opinion of agency recruitment in commenting on the selection of "fraternity brothers, corporate politicians, and industrial refugees."[37] Led by the veteran spoilsman of the Senate, Kenneth McKellar, Congress launched its attack in the fall of 1942 against the War Manpower Commission by means of an amendment to its deficiency appropriation which was pushed through without a record vote.[38] The amendment required sena-

[32] *Ibid.*, January 19, 1944.   [33] CSC, *Circular Letter No. 4046,* August 7, 1943.
[34] *Ibid., No. 3863,* October 28, 1942.
[35] *New York Times,* October 24, 29, 31, November 16, 1943.
[36] CSC, *Unnumbered Circular,* September 7, 1944, and *Circular Letter No. 4240,* January 19, 1945.
[37] 88 *Cong. Record* 8416, October 20, 1942.
[38] *Ibid.,* 8353, October 19, 1942, and 8413-23, October 20, 1942.

torial confirmation of War Manpower Commission employees receiving $4,500 per annum salary or more. His appetite whetted by his triumph, Senator McKellar tried much the same tactic in 1943, introducing first *S. 575,* providing that everyone in the executive branch receiving $4,500 or more salary per annum be deemed an officer of the United States appointed by the President with the advice and consent of the Senate. This was reported favorably by the Judiciary Committee and passed the Senate June 7, 1943, by a vote of 43 to 22.[39] The House, however, referred this bill to the Committee on the Civil Service, which clearly doomed it. At that juncture Senator McKellar resorted to his device of the previous year, the attachment of riders to the War Agencies Appropriation Bill and the Labor-Federal Security Appropriation Bill. The House Appropriations Committee furnished stiff opposition to the rider on the former bill and secured a vote of 302 to 29 against it to insist on House disagreement.[40] That threw the rider on the War Agencies Appropriation Bill back into conference in which the House members refused to recede from their disagreement.[41] Twice more the House refused to recede from its opposition and thus killed the rider not only in the War Agencies Appropriation Bill but in the Labor-Federal Security Appropriation Bill as well.[42]

For the most part the Commission retained real control merely over the classification audit and a review of the qualifications of the administrative appointees.[43] Many salaried executives were appointed in much the same manner as the uncompensated executives or dollar-a-year men at first but never with the same confusion characterizing their recruitment. The very freedom which the agencies utilized to such advantage in their search for talent was an invitation to assault from the spoilsmen in the Senate. But as the Civil Service Commission gained in experience during the war period, it was able to render more assistance to the agencies.[44]

[39] 89 *Cong. Record* 5417, June 7, 1943.
[40] *Ibid.,* 7145, July 3, 1943.   [41] *Ibid.,* 7382, July 7, 1943.
[42] *Ibid.,* 7497, July 8, 1943. For a complete account of this issue see Arthur W. Macmahon, "Senatorial Confirmation," *Public Administration Review,* III (1943), 281-96.
[43] Interview with Emmerich, August 28, 1945.
[44] A special rule was adopted for recruitment of regional directors of OPA, WPB, WMC, and OCD by intensive publicity, open competition, and certification of the top three. Later, approval of the central office of the Commission was essential

APPLICATION TO PARTICULAR OCCUPATIONS 77

Its record in that area and its efforts seem to have been creditable.[45]

THE MOBILIZATION OF SCIENTISTS AND PROFESSIONAL PERSONNEL[46]

The search for scientific talent presented more orderly aspects than that for managerial ability primarily because of the registration of scientists which had been developed. When it was realized early in the defense period that scientists and engineers, to say nothing of others professionally trained, would be required in numbers and categories which the Civil Service Commission alone was wholly unprepared to supply, a new approach was deemed essential. Within the National Resources Planning Board the National Roster of Scientific and Specialized Personnel was established on June 28, 1940, as a central clearinghouse of information on the names and qualifications of the nation's scientists.[47] Its physical location, however, was in the Civil Service Commission. Funds were at first secured from the Emergency Fund of the President and later by regular appropriations. The choice of initial location under the National Resources Planning Board was appropriate in the light of the stress given by its predecessor, the National Resources Committee, during the thirties to scientific training as one of the nation's greatest resources. Leonard Carmichael, president of Tufts College, was appointed Director of the Roster. The executive order creating the War Manpower Commission transferred the Roster to that agency where it became a division of the Bureau of Placement but still maintained close liaison with the Civil Service Commission.

The National Roster was a central register of American scientists and technical personnel which coded their qualifications by modern punch card methods for immediate reference. It was

---

for any appointment as regional director of these agencies. CSC, *Circular Letter No. 4046, Revised,* December 9, 1943.

[45] For an account of the recruitment of field service administrators see W. Brooke Graves and James M. Herring, "Recruiting Administrative Personnel in the Field," *Public Administration Review,* II (1942), 302-11.

[46] See Leonard Carmichael, "The Nation's Professional Manpower Resources," in *Civil Service in Wartime,* 97-117, and John McDiarmid, "The Mobilization of Social Scientists," *ibid.,* 73-97. See also Leonard Carmichael, "The National Roster of Scientific and Specialized Personnel," *Public Personnel Review,* II (1941), 120-33.

[47] Carmichael, in *Civil Service in Wartime,* 99.

utilized for referral of names of qualified persons to government agencies, industry, and the armed forces. Through its close relationship with the various professional societies and by means of recurrent circularization of individuals the Roster was enabled to keep its information current on the facts of professional employment and training in various fields. Moreover, several of those organizations had helped to bring pressure for its establishment by reason of their representation on the Technical Advisory Committee of the NRPB, and they co-operated fully with the Roster.[48] From the membership lists of those societies, lists furnished by the colleges and universities, data from occupational questionnaires used by the Selective Service System, and lists furnished by industrial employers a master file of scientific personnel was assembled.[49] Data gleaned from the Roster regarding the supply of scientifically trained personnel in the nation were integrated with other information obtained by the War Manpower Commission for the development of its lists of critical occupations. Likewise, the criteria developed for occupational priorities in recruitment by the War Manpower Commission were utilized by the Roster in recommending persons for transfer from one type of war work to another. In many cases both government appointing officers and private employers turned first to the Roster for assistance in recruiting specialized technicians rather than to the Civil Service Commission or the United States Employment Service, and such procedures were permitted for that type of personnel under WMC regulations. All told, 185,000 persons were certified to various government agencies and the armed forces, which constituted but one phase of the Roster's broad recruitment service for industry and research institutions as well as for the civil service and the Army and Navy.[50]

The unique value of the Roster consisted in listing persons who had never filed civil service applications and would never have evinced an interest in public employment as a career. That a means was developed to seek out such individuals and enlist them on a temporary basis was a notable achievement. Listing on the Roster involved neither a numerical rating nor a determination of eligibility. Rather the record of the individual was there for immediate reference and was evaluated solely in the light of his qualifications to fill a particular position when it opened.[51]

[48] *Ibid.* [49] *Ibid.*, 104. [50] *Ibid.*, 108. [51] *Ibid.*, 109.

APPLICATION TO PARTICULAR OCCUPATIONS 79

The Civil Service Commission continued its activities in recruiting personnel for the lower grades of the professional service and was notably successful in using the junior professional assistant and junior engineer examinations for mobilizing young college graduates in the government service. Thus for the first time in the history of the American civil service thousands could step from the campus into a waiting government position. All college seniors who passed the JPA examinations, which were advertised by faculty and college placement offices as well as by the Commission and were administered annually many months before June commencement and then later on an open continuous basis, were given eligible ratings as of the anticipated date of graduation with immediate provisional appointments to vacancies.[52] This procedure was employed as early as 1941. Appointing officers were repeatedly urged to take cognizance of the shortages and of the competition with industry for this type of youth and seize the opportunity early to use provisional appointments. Senior engineering students were circularized as early as 1941,[53] and during the autumn of 1942 eighteen trips were organized and conducted simultaneously to the nation's engineering schools by direct recruiting specialists with offers in hand of provisional appointments.[54] Interested departments sent their representatives as joint recruiters or placed orders for direct recruitment for such other positions as chemists, physicists, geologists, metallurgists, meteorologists, pharmacists, and architects in the junior grade. By the summer of 1944, when the supply of professional personnel was nearing depletion, the Commission stressed the desirability of recruiting women, men over thirty years of age, IV-F's, or returned veterans, all "draft-proof."[55]

To recruit social scientists in grades above the junior level the Commission appealed to the various professional societies at their meetings, circularized their members, used professional journals, called upon well-known figures in academic circles to reach others, and utilized all the usual publicity devices.[56] The National Roster was likewise of help in this field. Civil Service examiners at

[52] CSC, *Departmental Circular No. 285,* October 30, 1941, and *Circular Letter No. 3545,* January 15, 1942.
[53] CSC, *Circular Letter No. 3243,* May 3, 1941.
[54] CSC, *Departmental Circular No. 371,* September 4, 1942.
[55] CSC, *Circular Letter No. 4182,* July 8, 1944.
[56] McDiarmid, in *Civil Service in Wartime,* 84-85.

times set up recruiting desks at conventions of professional associations. Two recruiting specialists in the field of professional personnel were placed on the staff of each regional director.[57]

Actually through its alliance with the Roster the Commission retained a degree of control over recruitment of scientists which it never possessed over the mobilization of administrators per se. Because there was really but one channel by which to enter the lowest professional grade, namely to take a junior grade examination, the Commission exercised a complete control over the recruitment of young college graduates, and fortunately the Commission saw before the departments the necessity for aggressive and effective action to secure them. Thus the Commission's timely action enabled the government to capitalize as it had never before done upon the educational resources of the nation.

Obtaining Stenographers and Typists

The acute shortage of qualified stenographers and typists which developed during the war years led to some drastic changes in the techniques employed for their mobilization. Indeed, the services of this group of office helpers were well-nigh indispensable, and the "Battle of Washington" fought in quintuplicate was more than a mere quip. Quotas were assigned to the various regional directors for needs in the departmental service when the central office of the Commission was unable to furnish an ample number of eligibles from its registers.[58] Regional directors were authorized to mail or wire eligibles on their lists offers of appointment and request their immediate appearance in Washington at the Commission's Direct Recruiting Office. Transportation was paid for stenographic and typist recruits by some agencies which had Congressional authorization to use funds for that purpose. Lacking eligibles, the regional office placed a job order with USES, just as for laborers, or tried to obtain lists of eligibles from state and local government registers, if they were based on acceptable standards. Or the regional director could always assign specific quotas to recruiting representatives or individual local secretaries who usually turned to business schools and high schools while the regional director turned to the radio and press to publicize openings.[59] Surplus eligibles' papers were never filed away in a re-

[57] *Ibid.*, 86. [58] CSC, *Circular Letter No. 3546,* January 17, 1942.
[59] To leave no stone unturned, retailers and wholesalers who were forced out of

APPLICATION TO PARTICULAR OCCUPATIONS 81

gional office but were sent in to central office registers. Government employees themselves were invited to furnish the names and addresses of qualified persons who might be available for positions in Washington or the field.[60] Colored slides were sent out to the regional offices to assist in departmental service recruitment by depicting life in Washington for the "government girl"—favorably of course.[61]

That the "bottom of the barrel" was being scraped for stenographers in certain parts of the country was evident in 1943 on the West Coast, when the Commission's regional office urged appointing officers to canvass their organizations for persons in messenger, typist, and clerk positions to induce them to take free training in the public schools to meet future needs.[62] The Navy, more fortunate than other departments, used WAVES to offset the deficit in stenographers when the Civil Service Commission certified inability to recruit.[63] The War Department, however, did not use WACS for civilian work.

The Commission in 1944 confessed that it had 6,600 more Washington vacancies for stenographers and typists than it could fill, so difficult had it become to persuade trained women to come to the capital or to keep them there any reasonable length of time.[64] Not one single factor but a matrix of many had created this shortage condition. Joint recruiting programs had to be authorized for the agencies for the recruitment of stenographers and typists, as for laborers. Each June new battalions of dewy-eyed high school seniors, scarcely recovered from the excitement of commencement week, poured into Washington's Union Station to be whisked out to the clamoring agencies by their departmental chaperons. Some of the hardier girls stayed on, but homesickness and disillusionment over the real Washington, so different from the colored slides, soon took their toll, and the recruitment struggle had to be waged once again. The backlog in vacancies for stenographers and typists seemed impossible to overcome.

---

business by consumers' goods shortages or who discharged some of their employees were called on by recruiting representatives to secure lists of their surplus office and clerical employees.

[60] CSC, *Personnel Series No. 4,* December 9, 1943.
[61] CSC, *Circular Letter No. 4177,* June 29, 1944.
[62] *Ibid., No. 3952,* February 3, 1943.
[63] *Ibid., No. 4174,* June 21, 1944.
[64] CSC, *Departmental Circular No. 467,* February 3, 1944.

The Enlistment of Labor[65]

It was in the recruitment of labor for the gigantic Federal industrial expansion that the Civil Service Commission scored its greatest success. That it did seek out and mobilize on schedule the millions needed was no mean achievement. Time pressures were considerable. It was not unusual to produce personnel for War and Navy establishments within seventy-two hours' notice.[66] Recruitment of skilled labor for the Pearl Harbor Navy Yard immediately after December 7, 1941, was, of course, conducted under the greatest stress in our history. Within the space of two weeks recruiting trips had to be planned, undertaken, quotas filled, men examined as to qualifications, physical condition, and loyalty, rated, certified, and started on their way to Hawaii. From December 7, 1941, the pressure never abated for the recruitment of laborers for both War and Navy industrial establishments.

As shortages in skilled labor had become more acute in 1941, the search for those workers intensified. Before the migration of the nation's labor force had become common, local boards had been wont to object to the circularization of their surplus eligibles who had applied for work at a particular Federal establishment. But as competition sharpened, it was clear beyond a doubt that skilled workers would soon be unavailable by reason of private employment inside or outside the area unless their eligibility was promptly transferred to a shortage area for immediate consideration. Therefore, a program of circularization of such individuals as to their willingness to accept employment elsewhere was started.[67] Regional directors were likewise obliged to keep themselves informed of the training programs conducted at that time by the Training Within Industry Branch of the Labor Division of the Office of Production Management, the apprentice training program by the National Youth Administration, vocational courses approved by the Office of Education, and the Civil Aeronautics Administration's aeronautical schools.[68] The Works Projects Administration through the establishment of a Division of Training and Re-employment helped co-ordinate recruitment efforts to notify the registrants of forthcoming examinations and

---

[65] See Flemming in *Civil Service in Wartime*, 118-41.
[66] CSC, *Circular Letter No. 3611*, March 4, 1942.
[67] *Ibid.*, No. 3265, May 16, 1941.   [68] *Ibid.*, No. 3369, August 11, 1941.

openings.[69] The Navy Department instructed its own Naval Recruiting Service early in 1942 to assist in the procurement of skilled workers for Pearl Harbor by referring to Civil Service recruiting representatives the names of those men rejected by the Navy because of age or physical defects.[70]

Inescapably it was the Commission's field staff which bore the brunt of the recruitment load in the laborer category for the simple reason that it was in the field establishments that the labor force was needed. Authority and responsibility to devise methods and plans for recruiting assigned quotas were delegated to the regional directors. Such assignments were as little arbitrary as possible when used for interregional recruitment, for the Commission took into account regional differences in density of population and labor market conditions. Deficits in quotas which could not be filled with expedition in one region were reassigned forthwith to other offices experiencing less difficulty. The USES, of course, rendered invaluable assistance. Certain lower-grade CAF and mechanic-learner registers were transferred from the regional offices to special Commission representatives at local establishments as an aid in delegation to the field.[71] The War Department paralleled that step with its own decentralized procedures in furnishing to the Commission personnel to be trained for the new local board offices.[72] To supplement their recruiting representatives regional directors could utilize labor board personnel from naval shore establishments to meet interregional quotas for all Navy Department establishments; such persons were temporarily placed under the regional director for the period of the assignment and trained by the latter.[73]

Direct recruitment was the unvarying technique in this field, just as the positive recruiting publicity over the radio, through motion picture "shorts," and newspaper articles constituted an almost continuous barrage. All the devices heretofore described, such as liaison with civic groups, veterans' organizations, and labor unions, were utilized to the utmost. The Navy Department even had to go to such lengths in recruitment for Pearl Harbor and the West Coast establishments as to authorize both travel and meal tickets from a recruit's home as his place of recruitment to his

[69] *Ibid., No. 3403,* September 11, 1941. [70] *Ibid., No. 3553,* January 26, 1942.
[71] *Ibid., No. 3376,* August 15, 1941. [72] *Ibid., No. 3431,* September 25, 1941.
[73] *Ibid., No. 4174,* June 21, 1944, and *No. 4189,* July 20, 1944.

duty station, although he may have been out on the West Coast and hundreds of miles from his real home when signed as a recruit.[74] It was a far cry from the days when Representative Wigglesworth, Massachusetts economizer, cried in blank amazement at the idea of positive and direct recruitment of skilled workers, "You do not look for them by travelling around the country, do you?"[75]

TABLE 11

DISTRIBUTION OF EMPLOYEES IN THE WAR AND NAVY DEPARTMENTS, JUNE 30, 1944[a]

War Department:	
Total	1,240,933
By Classification Services:	
Ungraded positions	576,600
Graded CPC service	99,300
Subprofessional service	34,600
By Divisions:	
Departmental Headquarters	37,130
Air Service Command, Air Transport Command, and other AAF field commands and forces	344,327
Commanding general and staff divisions of ASF	16,784
Chemical Warfare Service	24,901
Engineers	79,497
Hospitals, medical depots, etc.	8,063
Arsenals and other Army ordnance plants	170,099
Quartermaster depots, etc.	74,843
Army transportation and signal corps	136,535
Nine Army service commands and Washington Military District	345,965
Miscellaneous field activities	2,789
Navy Department:	
Total	672,169
By Classification Services (only within ungraded):	
Unskilled	1,400
Semiskilled	198,100
Skilled	267,400
Supervisory Mechanical	27,300

[74] *Ibid.,* No. 4170, *Supp.* No. 1, June 30, 1944.
[75] U.S. Congress, House, Hearing on *Independent Offices Appropriation Bill, 1942,* 77th Cong., 1st Sess., December 12, 1940, p. 87.

TABLE 11—*Continued*

By Divisions:	
Departmental Headquarters	19,826
Navy yards	346,943
Naval air stations	75,698
Naval supply depots, fuel depots, net depots, and related procurement and inspection activities	93,218
Naval torpedo stations, ordnance plants, ammunition depots, and magazines	59,920
Naval operating bases	9,895
Naval training centers, schools, and other personnel and recruitment activities	22,753
Naval hospitals	9,245
Marine Corps and Coast Guard field activities	23,521
Miscellaneous naval activities	11,150

[a] Statistics furnished by John W. Mitchell, Chief, Federal Employment Statistics Staff, Office of Administrative Services, U.S. Civil Service Commission, Washington, D. C.

CONCLUSIONS

Although the Civil Service Commission maintained its central and controlling position over the recruitment of labor and the lower grades in the classified service, its inexperience in recruiting higher-grade administrators and professional personnel gave the operating agencies great freedom in developing their own sources of supply where and as they could. The Commission imposed no central controls whatsoever upon the recruitment of dollar-a-year men who were enlisted by widely known business executives, notably in OPM and WPB.

The entire experience with procuring dollar-a-year men who remained on their company rolls while directing vast programs for the government which inevitably affected their companies raised certain questions and problems in connection with the Federal civil service. That this country could not develop within a government service based on an economic system of private enterprise the technical operating skills requisite to direct a war economy seems clear. But it also would seem to serve the public interest more effectively in the long run if a flexible salary scale could be developed for an emergency period to place such technicians on the regular government payroll. That issue Congress never faced although it continually carped about the desirability of paying such men a regular salary at the usual scale. As for the development of general administrators, who were in unprecedented demand during the war, a start may have been made through the establishment of an in-service internship program. Of that more shall be said in the investigation of the subject of training programs in a later chapter. Herbert Emmerich foresaw the necessity for broad training of that kind for the emergency demands at the beginning of the defense period when he wrote: "In fact, members of the permanent service are more needed than ever in emergency times as a focal point of objectivity and loyalty to the main and single objective of defense because they will be surrounded with untrained and undisciplined newcomers who have not the same tradition or the same detachment."[76]

The Commission was never able to cope successfully with the problem of favoritism, personal ties, and institutional nepotism in the recruitment of salaried administrators. Because it did not hold the initiative in the recruitment of administrative personnel at the beginning of the defense crisis, it never caught up with agency recruitment in this field. Moreover, agency administrators resented anything but a postaudit of the qualifications of those persons they had recruited. But the critic of wartime personnel practices cannot gainsay the fact that the agencies were able to attract many able persons into the government service through the use of personal appeals, the old "school tie," and similar devices.

In the recruitment of labor the results the Commission achieved were commendable. With the aid of USES and its own network of recruiting representatives scattered strategically over the land, the entire nation was culled and combed over, appealed to by streetcar, bus, and newspaper advertising, and exhorted by radio announcers to accept a job as a laborer. Thus the Commission fulfilled its solemn commitment made in 1940 to supply personnel promptly in the required numbers.

The ability to recognize the essential "first" things—namely, that an aggressive approach was imperative to recruitment in a

[76] Herbert Emmerich, "Administrative Normalcy Impedes Defense," *Public Administration Review*, I (1940-1941), 324-25.

crisis situation and that willingness to sacrifice the unessential elaborations built up in peace must be demonstrated—enabled the Commission to meet its obligations. It held to mass recruitment for the lower grades wherein it was equipped by long experience and for which it could augment its own staff more expeditiously, and it delegated to those better equipped in the agencies authority to mobilize talent for their own higher posts, subject to standards and review in the case of civil service appointees. By keeping control over the situation there were no patronage "grabs" by the politicians or scandals in recruitment. "A great deal depends upon whether the civil service can shake itself out of old grooves and depart from normalcy long enough to meet new situations in new ways," Herbert Emmerich declared in 1941.[77] The Commission departed from the normal long enough to establish the fact that responsibility for civilian recruitment in war as in peace can be concentrated successfully in the central personnel agency if that agency is willing to pioneer with a bold new approach to its problem.

[77] Ibid., 324.

CHAPTER FIVE

The Deterioration in Standards for Selection

SCARCITY of manpower in the steadily contracting labor market of the war years coupled with the vast expansion in government employment had but one effect upon qualification standards: to reduce them to a faint resemblance to their prewar level. As manpower regulations were promulgated in that complex network of controls described in Chapter II, the primary test for most positions became availability. Government, like industry, had to accept what the labor market offered. The Civil Service Commission, therefore, early delegated authority to its regional directors to gear standards to the labor market. Any available person could easily be termed an eligible. As a matter of fact, the common quip around both public and private production facilities, "If he's still warm, we'll hire him," was not wholly without truth.

To meet the crisis in manning expanding government establishments and bureaus, major adjustments in the selection process were made early in the emergency for a few defense positions and more widely applied as the labor supply dwindled. For example, one was the development of "duration" appointments coupled with noncompetitive selection. The war service regulations in 1942 placed all appointments on a duration basis under emergency procedures. The emphasis on speed in placement led to simplification in examinations, accompanied by some wholly new practices in giving them and rating them as well as by a revolutionary certification procedure. The lowering of qualifications standards made itself felt more drastically in eroding skills and preservice training requirements to the point where subeligibles, even under the deteriorated war standards, were frequently offered to appointing officers. Less significant in their effect upon the quality of work produced were the disappearance of maximum age requirements and changes in physical fitness minima. On the other hand, a more serious change occurred when character requirements, that is, absence of a criminal record, were somewhat attenuated as a *sine qua non* of Federal employment. Fortunately it was not until after the peak of the manpower crisis had been passed that Congress intervened to force the Civil Service Commission back to prewar examination procedures, albeit not standards, through the new veterans' preference legislation of 1944. Thus selection procedures went full cycle from 1939 to 1944 while qualifications steadily deteriorated.

New Types of Appointments for the Emergency

Following hard on the heels of the proclamation of limited national emergency in September, 1939, was the first of a notable series of executive orders which revolutionized the status of the new emergency recruits into government service. This was Executive Order 8257 of September 21, 1939, which empowered the Civil Service Commission to permit immediate appointment of personnel subject only to noncompetitive tests to positions in the defense program. Although such appointees did not acquire a civil service status, the Commission was empowered to exercise its authority only under the "most unusual and compelling circumstances." The latter proviso acted as an unnecessary limitation a year later when Americans looked on aghast as the "Battle of Britain" raged. The "unusual" was fast becoming a tragic commonplace. Therefore, a new kind of appointment was developed to meet the sense of public urgency, namely probational-indefinite appointment.

1. PROBATIONAL-INDEFINITE APPOINTMENTS

A new executive order, No. 8564 of October 8, 1940, established probational-indefinite appointments by mentioning for the first time the duration of the defense program as the maximum tenure for the new appointments made subject to noncompetitive examinations. The order provided that such appointees should not acquire civil service status, but significantly the Commission was no longer limited in the use of such appointments by any factors other than exigency and the public interest. Through this order a streamlined production system to supply the expanding defense agencies sprang up side by side with the slow, intricate "normal" pattern of selection procedures. Eventually the former, modified for competition, swallowed the latter only to have it emerge, like Jonah, untouched by its years of supposed "digestion."

Duration selections under Executive Order 8564 were called probational-indefinite appointments and possessed certain advantages over merely temporary appointments. For one thing, probational-indefinite appointees could be retained for long periods without any lost motion in the form of requests for extension of the appointment; they were eligible for promotion, transfer, or reassignment to other positions, even permanent ones. To them opened the possibility of completion of the probation period, if in a permanent position, and acquisition of regular classified status, a point to which their inclusion under the Retirement Act was related; and they could be utilized most effectively to replace classified Federal employees who left for the armed forces retaining their re-employment rights.[1]

Provisions for temporary appointments were liberalized in 1940 to permit their use under almost the same conditions as probational-indefinite appointments.[2] A relaxation of the rules obviated the necessity in many cases for periodic requests for extension of temporary appointments.[3] Temporary employees in the War or Navy departments who failed competitive examinations for regular appointment could be retained as probational-indefinite employees if their services were deemed necessary by reason of the training they had received during temporary appointment.[4] They had to qualify noncompetitively, however, for retention under Executive Order 8564.[5]

Since the number of employees in defense positions after Pearl Harbor promised to outnumber the regular permanent executive civil service, it was neither feasible nor defensible to retain the old examination procedures or to attempt to fill permanent positions with regular probational appointees who could attain status. From January 1, 1942, the Commission was making from 25,000 to 28,000 placements per week in the War and Navy departments alone.[6] Nor was it desirable to fill all positions noncompetitively. The realistic solution was that adopted: to streamline examination

---

[1] CSC, *Departmental Circular No. 241*, November 16, 1940.
[2] CSC, *Departmental Circular, National Defense Series No. 8,* November 23, 1940.
[3] CSC, *Circular Letter No. 2896,* May 18, 1940.   [4] *Ibid., No. 3246,* May 6, 1941.
[5] *Ibid., No. 3380,* August 18, 1941. In areas already suffering housing shortages local persons not on any registers could be offered temporary positions in the absence of local eligibles even when non-local eligibles were available. *Ibid., No. 3311,* July 9, 1941.
[6] Memorandum of Commissioner Flemming, March 2, 1942.

procedures for competitive selection in so far as possible by reducing standards to the level the labor market allowed and to confer a duration status upon the new recruits. Therefore, Executive Order 9063 was issued on February 16, 1942, conferring on the Civil Service Commission authority to issue its war service regulations.

2. WAR SERVICE APPOINTMENTS

All appointments under the new war service regulations were for a maximum period of the duration of the war and six months thereafter. Aside from maximizing Commission control over recruitment activities of the Federal government, the new rules were designed to attain the greatest speed possible in staffing for the war effort. The following rules were basic:

1. Examinations were competitive for original appointment unless an adequate number of competent persons failed to compete. In that case noncompetitive tests could be utilized. The number of persons admitted to any examination could be limited to that commensurate with the needs of the service.
2. Disqualifications for employment stressed, among other undesirable qualities, reasonable doubt as to a person's loyalty to the government of the United States.
3. No maximum age limits were permitted except where appointing officers established to the satisfaction of the Civil Service Commission that sound administration required them.
4. The Commission could, at its discretion, rate examination papers merely "eligible" or "ineligible" if the demand exceeded the supply.
5. The Commission could utilize direct recruitment on agreement with the departments, in order to fill requisitions for personnel.
6. Requisitions were to be filled without regard to sex.
7. The Commission adopted an unranked register system of certification for most positions. That is, it certified as large a group at the top of a register as would all have appointment opportunities within six months, and selection could be made from the list in any order. The "rule of three" was abandoned in certification inasmuch as the Commission bound itself to supply an adequate number of names from the head of an appropriate list to furnish a "sound discretion" to appointing officers.
8. Apportionment was retained only as nearly as good administration permitted.

9. At first the field service of the Post Office Department, positions in the police and fire departments of the municipal government of the District of Columbia, Schedule A and B appointments, and procedures for appointment to positions under the jurisdiction of the Board of Legal Examiners were all excluded from the operation of the war service regulations.[7]
10. A trial period of one year was established for all war service appointees.[8]

The retention of the competitive principle, even though attenuated by deteriorating qualifications standards, was designed to insure that mobilization of the vast civilian army of Federal employees would be conducted on the basis of merit and fitness. If labor market conditions prevented government from obtaining the most highly skilled and trained workers in the nation, still recruitment was based on the principle that those recruited were among the best who were available. Even in normal times under higher entrance standards the government could not necessarily obtain the best talent in the nation for positions waiting to be filled. It is an obvious fact that any employer can secure only such talent as he can afford to hire in a competitive labor market, other factors than wages being equal. Since other factors are seldom equal and during a war period the emotion of patriotism more frequently is correlated with the public service, the Federal government was able to secure a surprising number of well-qualified professional and administrative employees from business, the professions, and university halls who were not ordinarily available for government work. There is no need to labor this point further in view of the discussion of recruitment in the foregoing chapters. Suffice it to say here that the essence of the merit system was preserved through the war service regulations even though standards were reduced to the level the market would produce.

Because war service appointments were for the duration only,[9]

[7] Executive Order 9378, September 23, 1943, placed the field service of the Post Office Department under the war service regulations.

[8] The war service regulations were first issued as *Departmental Circular No. 323*, February 28, 1942, which underwent many amendments and revisions by the Commission.

[9] Duration of the war was interpreted by the Commission to mean the duration as legally fixed by congressional resolution or presidential proclamation declaring the end of the war. It did not mean the duration of hostilities. CSC, *Departmental Circular No. 511*, December 4, 1944.

the government was subsequently in a position to eliminate from the service the vast majority of wartime recruits who did not meet prewar qualifications standards and to throw those new positions that became permanent open to competition at the old standard of performance. Thus the service was in no way permanently impaired. Furthermore, the youth of the nation, withdrawn from competitive opportunities by long military service, was thereby enabled to compete for the government service with its special preference advantages.

3. TRANSITION PROCEDURES

To make as smooth as possible the change from the two lines of procedure prior to March 16, 1942, the effective date of the war service regulations, certain transition procedures were announced. One was the conversion of the extant probational-indefinite appointments into war service appointments.[10] Another was the completion of regular probational appointments, retaining the opportunity for probationers to secure classified status on completion of their probation. This kind of appointment was, however, conditioned upon the individual's having actually entered on duty before March 16, 1942, from a Commission certification for regular probational appointment or at least upon the report to the Commission of his selection by the agency before March 31, 1942.[11]

Difficulties were encountered in according justice to many employees who had been appointed as excepted or probational-indefinite employees and had eagerly awaited the opportunity for appointment to a regular classified position before March 16, 1942. A probability was allowed at first to become the basis for their classification in this fashion. If their names had been reached for probational appointment on a register from which certification would have been made to fill the position they held on that date when it was reached, or if they had received the usual recommendation for status under the Ramspeck Act from the employing agency, they were considered eligible on the basis of their examination rating.[12] But the Veterans' Preference Act of 1944, if faithfully administered to execute the intent of Congress and the President, necessitated a reconsideration. From December, 1944, no one was to be accorded a civil service status merely because his name had been reached on a regular civil service register unless

[10] *Ibid., No. 323,* February 28, 1942. [11] *Ibid., Revised,* March 30, 1942.
[12] *Ibid., No. 457,* December 3, 1943.

he had actually been selected for appointment from a Commission certification for probational appointment and had entered on duty.[13]

SIMPLIFICATION IN THE EXAMINATION PROCESS

The emphasis on speed in placement gathered momentum from 1940, resulting in a correlative simplification in examinations and the whole selection procedure. Notable developments were a temporarily increased use of selective certification; the enlarged use of unassembled examinations; sweeping changes in assembled examinations such as scheduling them on an open continuous basis; developing shortened forms of the widely used tests and simplifying rating schemes and rules; telescoping recruitment, examination, and certification with appointment by means of direct recruitment; and lastly, modification of the right of appeal of examination ratings. When time was of the essence, the elaborate prewar procedures to ascertain competence had to go, with the result that standards, too, fell when they proved a barrier to speed. The basic essentials and often mere availability alone could be sought in recruits.

1. SELECTIVE CERTIFICATION

During the thirties the Civil Service Commission had developed a useful procedure designed to eliminate the necessity for devising and scheduling special examinations for the many unique positions in the Federal service introduced by social security and farm security legislation, which required unusual combinations of skills or training. Known as selective certification, this procedure permitted certification from the most appropriate relevant registers of persons with the specialized qualifications sought. Names were rerated for certification, and the rerating was often different from or higher than the original rating because of the differing relative importance of the secondary qualifications possessed.[14] This procedure lent itself admirably to the need for accelerated certification of eligibles for the new defense positions, for the establishment of new registers would have caused unconscionable delays and great expense. It was again recommended to the Commis-

[13] CSC, *Departmental Circular No. 515,* January 23, 1945, based on Executive Order 9506.
[14] Interview with Dr. Ernest V. Stocking of the Examining and Personnel Utilization Division, Civil Service Commission, August 12, 1944.

THE DETERIORATION OF STANDARDS 95

sion's regional directors in 1939 and 1940[15] and urged upon them to the fullest extent possible in order to reduce the number of examinations which had to be announced.[16] Ultimately this principle of certification was abandoned with the adoption of unranked registers under the war service regulations, for selective certification involved a numerical rating.

Clearly selective certification needed to be safeguarded against subversion of the merit principle. Therefore, it was permitted only when no suitable register existed for regular certification, a register appropriate for selective certification was actually extant, and the special job requirements were valid and reasonable.[17] When, however, qualified eligibles could be found on registers totally unrelated to the type of vacancy, selective certification was proscribed and a new examination had to be scheduled.[18]

2. ENLARGED USE OF UNASSEMBLED EXAMINATIONS

Well before the launching of the defense program a trend had set in for the wider utilization of unassembled examinations, due in part to the same reasons causing the increased use of selective certification procedure. For example, the number of unassembled examination papers rated in fiscal 1939 had jumped to 156,182 over the 16,110 in fiscal 1938.[19] As the labor market contracted and the number of applicants dwindled, the Commission took the view that too many steps were involved in making up assembled examinations. Speed and the simplification basic to speed were more urgent than intensive testing for quality. Direct recruitment obviously required the adoption of unassembled examination techniques with emphasis on interviewing as the chief means of examination. Indeed, the development of adequate interviewing facilities became imperative as the use of unassembled examinations became increasingly common.

---

[15] CSC, *Circular Letters No. 2829*, September 25, 1939, and *ibid., Revised*, April 8, 1940.
[16] *Ibid., No. 2897*, May 25, 1940.   [17] *Ibid., No. 2829*, September 25, 1939.
[18] The Commission stipulated that appointing officers could not demand an excessive quantity or quality of experience nor too great a diversity of abilities. Further, if the eligibles in the regular order on the register could be adequately fitted for the position in question by brief on-the-job training, the special requirements were deemed unnecessary. The danger to be guarded against was that the special requirements were so peculiar and capricious that they had been devised to "reach" one favored eligible on the register.
[19] U.S. Congress, Senate, Hearing on *Independent Offices Appropriation Bill, 1941*, 76th Cong., 3rd Sess., January 25, 1940, p. 34.

The truly amazing use of unassembled examinations forced upon the Commission by urgency and scarcity is adequately demonstrated not merely by the use of unassembled tests to rate skilled laborers but by their utilization for the selection of stenographers. In some regional offices it was at times not feasible to conduct assembled examinations for typists and stenographers. Applicants were merely rated on the basis of training and experience. One can, therefore, understand how college students employing the time-honored "hunt and peck" method found themselves employed as CAF-3 stenographers for a summer. The familiar Washington aphorism that any girl who could distinguish a typewriter from a sewing machine found employment as a stenographer, therefore, contained an uncomfortable grain of truth. Here, too, the interview became an integral part of the examination.

Ideally, the effective use of unassembled examinations requires the painstaking analysis of experience records by well-trained examiners familiar enough with the field of the examination to exercise a nice sense of discrimination and judgment. Practically this has never been attained by the Civil Service Commission as it has never had the funds at its disposal to employ personnel for this type of rating at the proper classification level to achieve those results. Indeed, during the war years when the caliber of clerical employees fell so markedly, the situation worsened. The only recourse was to devise a mechanical rating scale so simplified that any real discrimination was nullified in any event. The instructions accompanying the rating scale below were that the applicant's experience as a whole determined the quality or grade rating.[20] Only three quality groups were used: barely qualifying, good, and excellent experience. Thus the advantage lay with the individual who may have had long experience of an indifferent quality as against the person who possessed good experience or advanced training at the bare minimum demanded in the examination announcement. The second type of person was saved from unfairness in rating because no rating except as to eligibility was required under the war service regulations when the demand exceeded the supply, as it virtually always did for the more important positions. This technique of rating unassembled examinations, however, left the problems of validity and fairness to be solved in postwar years.

[20] CSC, *Circular Letter No. 3634,* March 26, 1942.

Rating Scale for Unassembled Examinations[21]

Years of experience beyond prerequisite	0	1	2	3	4	5	6
Barely qualifying experience	70	73	73	75	75	78	78
Good experience	75	78	83	85	88	88	90
Excellent experience	80	85	90	93	95	95	98

Fortunately the Commission itself recognized the shortcomings of the foregoing rating system and instituted personal investigations through its Investigations Division to assess the qualifications of those considered for higher-grade administrative posts. No examination, of course, is valuable unless it is valid and reliable. Investigation of experience records represented an attempt to achieve validity, but the value of the investigation depended largely upon the skill of the investigators. The Commission first employed personal investigations in 1943 to fill the positions of WMC regional, state, or area directors and top budget and personnel officer positions.[22] In 1945 these investigations were extended on a more ambitious scale to cover all executive and administrative positions at CAF-13 and above.[23] Through adoption of the personal investigation procedure the Commission came to the advocacy of the examination technique which had constituted one of the special contributions of TVA personnel administration, that is, an intensive check into experience records and recommendations of applicants.

In those cases where applicants appeared in person, interviewing facilities were valuable in offsetting the mechanical nature of experience rating. Central interviewing offices were established in Washington and in the field, but at the Washington office the primary purpose was to supply information about openings within the service and explain to applicants the best use of their qualifications.[24] Agency employees acting as accredited interviewers of the Commission were stationed in a number of employing agencies. They conducted orthodox placement interviews and sent reports of the interviews to the Applicant Supply Section of the Examining and Personnel Utilization Division of the Commission for analysis and rating. Agencies still continued to do

---

[21] Experience beyond six years not credited.
[22] CSC, *Circular Letter No. 4268*, April 12, 1945.
[23] U.S. Congress, House, Hearing on *Independent Offices Appropriation Bill, 1946*, 79th Cong., 1st Sess., January 17, 1945, p. 1167.
[24] CSC, *Manual of Instructions, Policies, and Procedures*, E6.01.02, May 10, 1943.

their own independent interviewing on an extensive scale, however, despite Commission instructions to refer persons seeking employment to the central interviewing offices to avoid duplication of effort and render applicants eligible to more agencies.

Placement interviews were also conducted by direct recruiting representatives wherever eligibles were found and at agency request for filling higher grade administrative and professional positions.[25] These were in addition to the personal investigations described above, and applicants were called to some central point if possible. Telegraph or radio reports were made of such interviews for immediate service.

3. CHANGES IN ASSEMBLED EXAMINATIONS

Clearly it was in the administration of assembled examinations that shortened procedures were most urgently needed. Even the process of application for employment required simplification in 1942. Thus almost contemporaneously with the issuance of the war service regulations two much-needed revisions of standard application forms made their bow. For all except laborer positions Form 57 was worked out between the Council of Personnel Administration and the Civil Service Commission.[26] Form 57 was shorter than the outmoded form, more compactly arranged, and was designed to serve as a personal history of Federal employment for agency files. For laborer positions requiring an even simpler record of qualifications another new form, No. 60, was introduced.

Under the war service regulations, in fact, competitive examinations were announced only when the establishment of the resultant formal eligible lists would expedite the recruitment and placement of the best qualified persons for the war program.[27] When formal announcements were not issued, the Commission did, however, require a definite understanding in writing with appointing officers regarding the minimum qualifications for specific positions, which had the same force and effect as the qualications paragraph in a public announcement. For the field service the regional directors of the Commission enjoyed discretion in deciding the scope and intensity of publicity and whether the examination would be of the open continuous type. The Commission's

[25] *Ibid.*, E6.01.04, May 10, 1943.
[26] CSC, *Departmental Circular No. 332*, April 20, 1942.
[27] CSC, *Circular Letter No. 3608*, February 28, 1942, and *Departmental Circular No. 323*, February 28, 1942.

responsibility for carrying on a recruiting program was the same whether or not an examination announcement was issued.

a. *Open continuous examinations.*—Although the use of open continuous examinations became a commonplace under the war service regulations, it was really authorized much earlier. Open continuous examinations have no closing date for applications, the examinations, if assembled, are held at frequent intervals, and names are continuously added to the register. The Commission limited the use of open continuous examinations in 1940 to positions it designated as defense or in defense agencies.[28] This restriction was part of the general policy to give examination priorities to needs connected with national defense while the Commission was also struggling to replace old and obsolete registers as extensively and rapidly as possible.[29]

By 1941 the demand for typists and stenographers had reached proportions which called for open continuous examinations in that occupational group. Because the examinations were scheduled irregularly and sometimes at extended intervals, with the result that examination quarters were frequently overcrowded, the Commission specifically directed its regional offices to schedule these examinations for local registers twice monthly.[30] The number of places for holding examinations was also soon doubled. Even more clearly calculated to accelerate service to the agencies was the provision for immediate service daily in administering examinations to all who appeared at the central Commission offices before 3:30 P.M. with requests from the agencies for immediate certification and appointment if the examinations were passed.[31] This procedure enabled the Commission to rate examinations and certify eligibles with such celerity that their appointment could be consummated within a possible two hours. By September, 1942, junior stenographer and typist examinations were held at least weekly and sometimes daily in the regional offices and could even be scheduled on Sunday and during the evening hours if essential to meet the quotas for direct recruitment.[32]

b. *Abbreviated examinations.*—The necessity both for lowering standards and rapidity in rating led to materially abbreviated

[28] CSC, *Departmental Circular, National Defense Series No. 1,* September 3, 1940.
[29] CSC, *Circular Letter No. 2868,* March 8, 1940.
[30] *Ibid., No. 3475,* November 15, 1941.
[31] CSC, *Departmental Circular No. 331,* April 11, 1942.
[32] CSC, *Circular Letter No. 3814,* September 14, 1942.

examinations. Often quality had to be sacrificed for speed, since war placed priority on speed. Two excellent illustrations of what happened to examinations are to be found in the changes in the junior typist and junior stenographer tests as well as those for junior professional assistant. In the case of the former, two subjects were early eliminated entirely from the examination, namely, a general test and a test in copying from rough draft, in order to simplify machine scoring.[33] Departmental appointing officers were warned that additional training was, therefore, required after appointment of eligibles, not merely in typing and stenography skills but in a review of English usage, punctuation, spelling, and paragraphing. The Commission attributed the abbreviation of its examinations directly to the difficulty of furnishing an adequate supply of eligibles at the higher standards. The junior professional assistant examination, designed for college seniors, was reduced from a long examination of two parts, one an intelligence test and the other a broad test in the options,[34] into an intelligence test alone which consumed only about one-third the time for actual administration. Academic specialization of the eligibles was coded and recorded for certification purposes. The Commission, in addition, eliminated the requirement that JPA eligibles furnish transcripts or proof of completion of their courses.[35]

c. *New rules for rating examinations.*—Again in connection with rating, the war service regulation that papers could be rated simply eligible or ineligible where demand exceeded supply was preceded by a rule earlier in 1942 to much the same purpose.[36] Examinations which had required both written tests and experience elements were ordered to be kept at a minimum and the averaging of one rating with the other was discontinued.[37] Only one test of the combined examination type was rated and the other simply used to determine eligibility.

In the event the Commission anticipated the number of eligibles

---

[33] CSC, *Departmental Circular No. 287,* November 10, 1941.

[34] The options were the fields of specialization or college majors, *e.g.,* economics, sociology, statistics, etc.

[35] CSC, *Departmental Circular No. 351,* June 30, 1942.

[36] Rating an application form eligible or ineligible without a percentage grade was permitted for specific kinds of positions in particular areas or all areas if a shortage of eligibles existed there and open continuous examinations were used. CSC, *Circular Letter No. 3552,* January 20, 1942.

[37] CSC, *Circular Letter No. 3608,* February 28, 1942.

THE DETERIORATION OF STANDARDS 101

would exceed the demand over a considerable period, eligibles were classified into two groups.[38] Only enough papers were rated to supply personnel requisitions for six months. The "A" group included those from the top down, rated numerically, who were necessary to meet the demands for certification within the ensuing six months. If that number proved inadequate, more names were lifted into the "A" group. The volume of requisitions soon forced a redefinition of the "A" group into those estimated as necessary for the next two months.[39]

Beginning in 1940 subeligible ratings could be assigned when the number of eligibles fell short of the demand.[40] They were then utilized in the case of temporary appointees who could be retained even though not within reach for certification, for the reason that all eligibles could become appointees. Simultaneously, rejected applicants were already regarded as potential eligibles for notification of future examinations, especially if events forced a lowering of examination requirements.[41]

Simplification of rating had important repercussions upon the appeal of examination ratings, in that it largely obviated the necessity for appeal. Even before the war service regulations were adopted, the Commission determined that the central office Board of Appeals and Review could not entertain appeals for a higher grade when the original action had already resulted in eligibility.[42] Complaints and appeals from oral examinations as to ratings were made a part of the review procedure handled by the Examining Division.

The wartime emphasis on loyalty with its resultant appeals work, coupled with the simplified rating system under the war service regulations, led the Commission to decide that for the duration the Board of Appeals and Review would concentrate on suitability cases, presidential and fourth-class postmaster examinations, retirement appeals, and appeals relating to residence.[43] Regional boards of appeals continued to handle appeals only of suitability and residence. All other matters were considered "requests for review" and not appeals; consequently they were routed to appropriate divisions of the Commission instead of to

[38] *Ibid.* [39] *Ibid., No. 3645,* April 3, 1942.
[40] *Ibid., No. 2896, Supp. No. 8,* September 28, 1940.
[41] *Ibid., No. 2897,* May 25, 1940.   [42] CSC, *Minute No. 2,* February 17, 1942.
[43] CSC, *Circular Letter No. 3721,* June 26, 1942.

the Board of Appeals and Review. The Examining Division was ordered to refrain from reviewing ratings in an assembled or unassembled examination unless there was an obvious error.[44]

THE CYCLE IN CERTIFICATION

Possibly the revolution in wartime procedures was best illustrated by the radical departure in certification from the hallowed "rule of three" to the unranked register and resultant certification of a large group of names for consideration. At any rate that particular wartime departure was the first restored to its pristine strength by reason of deep congressional devotion to the "rule of three." Over a year before V-J Day the Civil Service Commission found itself committed for all time by statutory mandate to its traditional practice in certification. The wartime urgency of placement was superseded in the congressional mind by a new exigency: the necessity of enlarging veteran's reference in the civil service, probably impossible without a rigidly prescribed certification system based on a numerically ranked register.

1. EARLY DEFENSE PRACTICE

The first relaxation in certification procedure was the provision in 1940 for transfer of eligibility between civil service regions and between the central office and the several regions for registers used in the defense program.[45] This procedure was accompanied by orders to circularize all such registers to check the availability of eligibles.[46] The Commission in 1941 permitted defense agencies to select proposed eligibles not within immediate reach for certification when there were opportunities for appointment numerous enough to use all eligibles. The Commission deemed it unjustifiable to insist on selection of higher eligibles if that meant delay in filling a defense position.[47]

The problem arose of how to handle the eligibility for certification of those called into the armed forces. Suspension of eligibility in 1940 of those on active duty in the armed forces seemed logical for but a very short time. It had to fall with the inception

[44] *Ibid., No. 3738,* July 14, 1942.   [45] *Ibid., No. 2897,* May 25, 1940.
[46] Field appointing officers could appeal to the Commission's central office for certifications; in those cases names were radioed or telegraphed to the officers and the actual certificate sent by mail. CSC, *Departmental Circular, National Defense Series, No. 5,* September 4, 1940.
[47] CSC, *Circular Letter No. 3366,* August 8, 1941.

THE DETERIORATION OF STANDARDS 103

of compulsory military service under the Selective Training and Service Act of 1940 in order to preserve civilian opportunities for the men inducted through no fault of their own. This was recognized in Executive Order 8602 of November 25, 1940, which extended the eligibility of inductees and National Guardsmen to cover the period of active military service. The only limitation in this order was that the inductee had to apply for restoration within forty days of his discharge; later this was extended to ninety days after discharge or hospitalization.[48] Implementing this order, the Commission ruled that those who had applied for restoration to a register after military service were entitled to certification ahead of all other eligibles until they had received as many certifications as they had lost.[49] Then they fell to the place on the register to which their examination rating entitled them as augmented properly by their preference points. Executive Order 8937 of November 7, 1941, applied the extension of eligibility to all those who had entered the armed forces after May 1, 1940.

2. CERTIFICATION UNDER THE WAR SERVICE REGULATIONS

Inasmuch as the war service regulations had eliminated the need for numerical rating whenever demand exceeded supply, the entire list of available names rated eligible could be sent to an appointing officer.[50] Because everyone on the register had the opportunity for appointment there was little need to hold back any names or discriminate between the top three and anyone else. Even when numerical ratings were assigned, the war service regulations required a sufficient number of names to give appointing officers a "reasonable opportunity for exercising a sound discretion." Naturally appointing officers were supposed to adhere to the certificate in making selections unless the Commission could furnish the names of other eligibles from other lists or by going outside the registers entirely.[51]

Since apportionment was not allowed to impede the needs of

[48] Executive Order 9579, June 30, 1945.
[49] CSC, *Departmental Circular No. 255*, April 16, 1941.
[50] CSC, *Circular Letter No. 3608*, February 28, 1942.
[51] When large numbers of vacancies were to be filled, the Commission furnished a sufficient number of names for consideration for ten vacancies if the positions were at salaries of $2,000 per annum or more or enough names for fifty vacancies if the salary was below the $2,000 level. Subsequent lists followed of similar length in the next two or three days to fill remaining vacancies. CSC, *Departmental Circular No. 352*, July 1, 1942.

the service under the war service regulations, it was a factor which was largely in abeyance in certifying for war service appointments in the departmental service.[52] Technically it was held at first to apply, however, to departmental service positions moved out of Washington by the wartime decentralization of some agencies to other cities. Here, since it was necessary to certify only eligibles actually willing to accept appointment at the new location, apportionment was soon found to be impossible to apply.[53]

The Civil Service Commission could omit names proposed by the agencies if, in the opinion of the Commission, the nominees were not among the best qualified persons known to the Commission.[54] Indeed, the Commission held that it would not normally certify agency-proposed names until it had had a minimum of two weeks in which to certify qualified applicants unless the requisition of personnel was to meet emergency conditions. If the person proposed was disapproved, no other names were certified unless requested.[55]

The unique survival of the "rule of three" in undiluted form was in connection with the staffing of the major field administrative posts in OPA, WPB, OCD, WMC, and the Commission itself. Examinations were widely publicized for a limited period, rated numerically, and certification always followed the "rule of three."[56] No temporary appointments were permitted to those positions, and the rule was never attenuated.

The Commission made it more difficult for appointing officers to reject eligibles also. Objections to eligibles in order to be maintained had to be based upon sufficient evidence to convince the Civil Service Commission that had it been in possession of those facts before certification was made, the objectionable in-

---

[52] CSC, *Circular Letter No. 3796,* August 26, 1942. It was applied insofar as possible to filling positions for which the supply exceeded the demand for eligibles. *Departmental Circular No. 386,* October 27, 1942.

[53] The rule limiting the number of members of a family in the civil service to two was suspended with respect to those employees who entered active military service. During their absence third members of the family could be certified, and in any event temporary employees, probational-indefinites, and later war service appointees could be certified without regard to the rule. CSC, *Departmental Circular No. 310,* January 16, 1942.

[54] CSC, *Departmental Circular No. 323, Revised, Supp. No. 12,* February 2, 1943.

[55] *Ibid., No. 346,* June 10, 1942.

[56] CSC, *Circular Letters No. 4046,* August 7, 1943, and *ibid., Revised,* December 9, 1943.

dividual would have been rated ineligible or would not have been within reach for certification.[57] Objections generally not sustained were those based on unproved charges of disloyalty, foreign birth, unsuitable personality, lack of education, age, physical condition, management or union affiliation, and lack of local residence. Acceptable objections covered I-A draft status of males, lack of WMC clearance, and lack of sympathy with the objectives of a program when that objection could be acceptably documented and presented in writing.[58] Inability of an appointing officer to interview an eligible was never a valid objection regardless of the duties or the grade of the position.[59]

The probation period under the war service regulations was increased in length from six months to one year as a deliberate policy of the Commission to enable appointing officers to rid themselves of incompetents after an adequate trial.[60] The successful completion of this period was always regarded as part of the entrance examination, but labor shortages probably prevented any more effective use of it as a trial period than in the prewar period. At least there is no proof to the contrary. Therefore, it is not surprising to find that the probationary period went back to six months in 1944.[61] Oddly enough, the Civil Service Commission was under the impression that labor turnover might be reduced under the war service regulations by the reverse kind of

[57] *Ibid., No. 4193,* August 2, 1944.

[58] Charges of disloyalty or foreign birth were not sufficient to suspend eligibility except for positions of a confidential nature or in war production work which offered opportunity for sabotage. Charges of unsuitable personality were sustained only when minimum qualifications statements clearly contained a description of required personality traits or such traits were recognized by the Commission as essential to the position. Lack of education was sustained only when the Commission had established minimum educational requirements for a specific position. Clearance with WMC had to be secured within two weeks to escape sustainable objection. Age objections were accepted only when the eligible's age was above established maximum or below minimum limits. Objection as to physical condition was referred to the Commission's Medical Division for its final decision.

[59] Departments were reminded frequently to return certificates, which they often held indefinitely without action unless prodded. Although the Commission at one time tried to secure reports within seven days on certificates not in plentiful supply, it was compelled later to make the period one or two weeks. After the war service regulations were issued, it allowed but one week and threatened to resubmit the certificate to other agencies if not returned within that time.

[60] CSC, *Departmental Circular No. 345,* June 8, 1942. See Commissioner Flemming's statement in *Investigation of Civilian Employment,* Part I, 57.

[61] 9 *FR* 4127, April 19, 1944.

rule: a categorical statement to each new appointee that he was expected to serve a minimum period of six months and that resignation during that period would be accepted with prejudice.[62] Revocation of this rule followed shortly with the significant postscript to the departments to record and report exit interviews and turnover data.[63]

3. EFFECT OF THE STARNES ACT

Congress reinstated the "rule of three" through the Veterans' Preference Act of 1944. By that year increased veterans' preference was politically inescapable. Since the Commission had never explained to Congress how to enforce veterans' preference effectively without a ranked register but had urged the "rule of three," Congress provided in the Veterans' Preference Act, or Starnes Act:

> The nominating or appointing officer shall make selection for each vacancy from not more than the highest three names available for appointment on such certification, unless objection shall be made, and sustained by the Commission, to one or more of the persons certified, for any proper and adequate reason, as may be prescribed in the rules promulgated by the Civil Service Commission.[64]

The continuing manpower shortage, however, modified the application of this provision in that so long as demand exceeded supply for any position it was possible to adhere to the war service regulation to rate merely as eligible and ineligible. Nevertheless care had to be exercised to insure ten-point preference veterans (disabled) first place on every certificate,[65] except those for professional and scientific positions where the entrance salary was over $3,000 per year. The establishment by law of absolute preference for veterans in certain positions for five years led to an outpouring of complex certification rules as, for example, rules on zones of certification in the field service,[66] areas of competition, and merger of registers.[67] Fortunately these intricate regulations

---

[62] CSC, *Departmental Circular No. 323, Revised, Supp. No. 2,* June 9, 1942.
[63] *Ibid., Supp. No. 11,* October 27, 1942.   [64] 58 *U.S. Statutes* 387 (1944).
[65] CSC, *Circular Letter No. 4254,* February 17, 1945.
[66] Zones of certification were established governing residence in local areas for field service vacancies. Only residents within the prescribed areas wherein vacancies occurred could compete as a rule unless an insufficient number of eligibles applied.
[67] CSC, *Circular Letter No. 4222,* November 14, 1944. Time limits for reporting on certificates were necessarily extended to twenty-one days (CSC, *Departmental Circular No. 512,* December 13, 1944), because of the technicalities involved in objecting to veterans. For rules on zones of certification see *Circular Letter No. 4222,*

were not allowed to impede staffing during the remainder of the war, particularly in shortage categories, such as for guard and custodian positions. They were designed to set the stage for the postwar influx of veterans.

The entire certification process was retarded by the Starnes Act. Reasons for passing over veterans and tentatively selecting nonveterans had to be submitted to the Commission. Further the nonveteran was not permitted to enter on duty until after the appointing officer had received and considered the Commission's findings as to the sufficiency of the objections.[68] Any authority previously granted by the Commission to the employing agencies to determine that eligibles certified were not qualified physically was withdrawn. Additional names beyond the three certified were submitted to consider in the event of declinations or unavailability of the first three, but this, of course, was a mere wartime convenience to prevent staffing from becoming hopelessly bogged down. Always, however, the names had to be considered in groups of threes. And not to be overlooked, the "rule of three" was extended to the unclassified service, a revolutionary new application.[69] Agencies were expected to follow definite and fixed procedures based on selection of one of the highest three names in order to insure that preference applicants would have fair opportunity to apply for the unclassified service and receive the consideration to which the Starnes Act entitled them. This meant, among other things, that standards had to be established for unclassified positions, a system of rating devised for evaluation of qualifications under the standards, and employment lists established of applicants entered in the proper order of their rating from which certification could be made. The only Federal positions which remained outside the scope of these requirements for veterans' preference respecting certification were those posts which required senatorial confirmation.

It is apparent, therefore, that it is really understatement to aver that the Commission went through a full cycle in certification procedures. In truth, it came through at the end of the war with a much more rigid system of certification than it possessed

---

Supp. No. 1, December 13, 1944, *Supp. No. 3,* March 1, 1945, and *Supp. No. 5,* May 9, 1945.

[68] CSC, *Departmental Circular No. 493,* July 3, 1944.

[69] *Ibid., No. 519,* March 20, 1945.

in 1939. Due to the efforts of Congress and its own willingness to restore the "rule of three," it found itself enmeshed in intricate new coils of red tape superimposed upon the prewar network. Despite Commission experience with the more flexible certification procedures during the war, Commissioner Flemming testified that the "rule of three" provided sufficient discretion to appointing officers and maintained proper standards.[70] Willingness to accept rigid certification procedures Floyd W. Reeves has characterized as a "major disaster" in personnel administration.[71]

Lowering of Qualifications to Adjust to Labor Shortages

1. AGE AND PHYSICAL STANDARDS

The relaxation of standards respecting age and physical condition was a gradual process aided and abetted wholly by labor market conditions and not at all by congressional concern over the existence of maximum age requirements.[72] One of the first changes in age requirements was that permitting maximum age limits to be raised under emergency conditions to a point ten years below retirement age, instead of the usual fifteen or seventeen, by joint agreement between the Commission and the employing agency.[73] By the spring of 1941 the maximum recruitment age was sixty-five for ordnance positions,[74] and the minimum age was eighteen for welders in the Navy yards.[75] Almost simultaneously the minimum age for stenographers and typists could be reduced

---

[70] U.S. Congress, Senate, Committee on Civil Service, Hearings on *Bills to Give Honorably Discharged Veterans, Their Widows and Wives of Disabled Veterans Who Themselves Are Not Qualified, Preference in Employment Where Federal Funds Are Disbursed*, 78th Cong., 2nd Sess., May 19 and 23, 1944, p. 26. See also Commissioner Flemming's replies to Representative Starnes' questions at an appropriations committee hearing, U.S. Congress, House, Hearing on *Independent Offices Appropriation Bill, 1945*, 78th Cong., 2nd Sess., December 9, 1943, pp. 1051-1052.

[71] Floyd W. Reeves, "Civil Service As Usual," *Public Administration Review*, IV (1944), 334.

[72] U.S. Congress, Senate, *Relating to Age Requirements for Civil Service Examinations*, Sen. Report 341, 76th Cong., 1st Sess., 2.

[73] CSC, *Minute No. 1*, January 17, 1940.

[74] CSC, *Circular Letter No. 3236*, April 25, 1941.

[75] *Ibid., No. 3250*, May 9, 1941. The maximum age limit at the beginning of the defense program was sixty-two years or the retirement age for any trades or skilled occupations in the Navy Department suffering shortages. *Ibid., No. 2938*, June 28, 1940, *Supp. No. 1*, July 12, 1940, *Supp. No. 2*, July 24, 1940, and *Supp. No. 5*, September 3, 1940.

THE DETERIORATION OF STANDARDS   109

to sixteen by regional directors if necessary to obtain a sufficient number of eligibles.[76] The war service regulations abolished maximum age limits for the duration except where appointing officers could establish to the satisfaction of the Commission that they were essential for a particular position.[77] The setting of maximum age limits or reduction of minima below sixteen years of age was forbidden to regional directors.[78]

The reduction of physical standards followed a pattern similar to that for age requirements, first applying to War and Navy Department positions, then to all other defense positions, and finally generally.[79] The guiding principle adopted by the Commission for its program of liberalization was that physical standards should be so adjusted as to secure persons capable of performing assigned tasks without danger to their fellow workers. During the emergency, standards were only secondarily related to retirement provisions. Attention has already been called to the policy sponsored by the Commission of attempting to secure a re-examination and change of physical requirements by agencies in order to promote the employment of the physically handicapped.[80] Defense agencies were granted power to offer temporary appointments to those who had been reached for probational appointment but did not meet the physical standards therefor.[81] Almost the only disease considered absolutely disqualifying was active tuberculosis. Venereal diseases, if brought under control by treatment, were not disqualifying, and epilepsy as well as mental disease were considered serious enough to require consultation with the Commission's Medical Division before appointment was offered.[82] The following quotation throws some light, not without humor, on physical standards during the war:

> In view of the critical shortage of manpower, every effort should be made to place applicants with a history of mental

[76] *Ibid., No. 3295*, June 21, 1941.

[77] CSC, *Departmental Circular No. 325*, March 18, 1942.

[78] *Ibid., No. 3785*, August 21, 1942. Certification of those under eighteen was forbidden for hazardous work. *Ibid., No. 3797*, August 27, 1942. See Chapter III for discussion of age minima.

[79] *Ibid., No. 2906*, June 5, 1940, *Supp. No. 1*, June 24, 1940, *Supp. No. 2*, July 12, 1940, *Supp. No. 6*, December 17, 1940.

[80] See Chapter III, pp. 58-59.

[81] CSC, *Departmental Circular No. 283*, October 21, 1941.

[82] CSC, *Departmental Circular Regarding Physical Defects Found on Medical Certificates* (to accompany war service regulations).

disease if, after a careful study of the entire case, it is apparent they will be able to perform satisfactorily, without hazard to themselves or others, the duties of the position involved.

Applicants who have a history of mental instability are not to be instructed to report to Washington, D. C., for employment, inasmuch as they might have more difficulty in adjusting to conditions in Washington during wartime than would an individual with a perfectly stable nervous system.[83]

Departments were warned against requesting employees to furnish statements from the Selective Service System regarding the reason for their classification as IV-F, for the Commission looked upon such requests as an unjustifiable invasion of confidential information.[84] Departmental officers were reminded that Selective Service classification was solely for fitness for active military duty and not necessarily relevant to civilian employment.

2. RELAXATION OF CHARACTER REQUIREMENTS

The manpower shortage liquidated a Federal rule prohibiting the certification of convicted felons until a lapse of at least two years after their discharge from prison. Soon after the war service regulations were adopted, provision was made to accept applications from discharged and paroled Federal felons or those on probation from Federal district courts regardless of the length of time elapsed since their release, pending a complete report on the individual from the prison warden or probation officer.[85] This liberalization was later extended to persons convicted of felonies in the state courts.[86] The Commission took the warden's report as well as the nature of the offense into consideration and attached great weight to the warden's opinion of the individual's suitability for Federal employment.[87] Naturally, former felons were not acceptable for law enforcement positions.

3. THE DISAPPEARANCE OF SKILLS REQUIREMENTS

The wide application of direct recruiting during the war, coupled with the unassembled examination procedure, swept away many skills requirements for types of positions that had formerly been characterized by fairly high standards of competence. Although there was some reluctance to admit the fact that

---

[83] CSC, *Manual of Instructions*, E5.03.08, March 28, 1944.
[84] CSC, *Departmental Circular No. 513*, December 16, 1944.
[85] CSC, *Circular Letter No. 3711*, June 8, 1942.
[86] *Ibid., Supp. No. 1*, February 26, 1943.
[87] CSC, *Departmental Circular No. 426*, May 25, 1943.

THE DETERIORATION OF STANDARDS 111

standards in many areas had collapsed, the very fact that selection was so largely based on unassembled examination techniques, that is, by the rating of experience and training statements and by interviews, rather than through specific performance tests to demonstrate skills, indicated a real abandonment of standards. Selecting a welder or a typist by interview or paper record of training is a tenuous procedure at best.

At first the pressure for lower standards came from the employing departments as sporadic shortages developed, but once the responsibility for producing the quotas of eligibles requested was placed squarely on the Commission, the pressure for deterioration of standards to meet those quotas shifted to the Commission itself. As previously pointed out, shipyards experienced the first labor shortages in the defense period. Consequently it was there that the Navy Department first requested a relaxation, cutting experience requirements in half for helper shipfitters.[88] Commission regional directors were authorized to make similar cuts for other trade helper positions suffering from labor shortages. Direct recruiting of laborers for Pearl Harbor and testing by experience ratings early disclosed the weakness of that technique unless checked by investigations of experience claims for exaggeration of quality and quantity.[89] In fact, 14 per cent of those who applied for Pearl Harbor work during the autumn of 1940 were revealed by "spot" investigations to be unqualified.[90] The pressures of time and volume prevented an effective investigation of claims as time passed. By the summer of 1941 the Commission ordered its regional directors to institute aggressive steps to lower examination requirements below those insisted upon by appointing officers whenever necessary to produce eligibles for critical and semicritical positions.[91] For example, in simplifying the assembled examinations for typists and stenographers, not only was the content abbreviated, but the rating standards were relaxed for what was left.[92] When assembled examinations continued to be held for typists, as they were in some regions, the required speed in number of words per minute fell drastically below the prewar level

---

[88] CSC, *Circular Letter No. 2805, Supp. No. 2*, January 23, 1940.
[89] *Ibid., No. 3079*, October 29, 1940.
[90] U.S. Congress, House, Hearing on *Independent Offices Appropriation Bill, 1942*, 77th Cong., 1st Sess., December 12, 1940, p. 529.
[91] CSC, *Circular Letter No. 3347*, July 23, 1941.
[92] CSC, *Departmental Circular No. 287*, November 10, 1941.

and fluctuated with labor market conditions. Commissioner Flemming admitted to the House Appropriations Committee that standards for some clerical positions had been too low and had to be raised.[93] Hence, no unassembled examinations were allowed for those positions from 1943 on. Difficulties experienced in recruiting enough higher level administrative technicians, business analysts, and economists, even as early as December, 1941, induced the Commission to advise the departments to accept college seniors through provisional appointment and by arranging proper in-service training programs to advance them rapidly.[94] Likewise enrollees in trade schools were offered provisional appointments if they were within two months of completion of their courses, appointments which were consummated upon proper evidence of completion.[95]

The basic policy of the Commission on the fluctuation of standards with labor market conditions is best expressed by advice given in 1944 to regional directors:

> In many cases it has been necessary to lower requirements because of labor shortages. It is desired to emphasize to regional directors that they have the authority to raise specifications. This authority should be exercised as labor market conditions improve so that standards can be brought back to the normal level as soon as possible. Where there is evidence of labor market improvement, outstanding announcements should be reviewed to determine where requirements may and should be revised.[96]

a. *Use of subeligibles.*—Another illustration of how standards were reduced in actual practice was found in the certification both of subeligibles and of those who had failed their examinations to attain civil service status under the Ramspeck Act. As early as 1940 those rated ineligible in junior engineer and JPA examinations with engineering options could be considered immediately for other examinations for which their applications could be utilized, with a waiver of the six months' wait previously required for such reconsideration.[97] Identical relaxation was extended in

---

[93] U.S. Congress, House, Hearing on *Independent Offices Appropriation Bill, 1944,* 78th Cong., 1st Sess., January 14, 1943, p. 850.
[94] CSC, *Departmental Circular No. 297,* December 10, 1941.
[95] CSC, *Circular Letter No. 3507,* December 20, 1941.
[96] *Ibid.,* No. 4227, December 12, 1944.
[97] CSC, *Minute No. 5,* September 4, 1940.

THE DETERIORATION OF STANDARDS 113

1941 to all national defense examinations for which there was a scarcity of eligibles and insufficient competition.[98] Those who failed in one field service examination might have their names transferred to another examination for a different position for which they could be reconsidered and gain eligibility.[99] Under the Ramspeck Act those who failed their examinations for status had to be separated immediately from positions classified into the permanent civil service, but they could be retained as war service appointees in the same positions without any break in service.[100] Subeligibles, on the other hand, were actually not certified as qualified but offered as persons who might develop into qualified workers in the absence of eligibles and proposed only at the request of appointing officers.[101] But it is hard to see that there was anything more than a technical distinction without a difference in "offering" subeligibles in lieu of certifying them. No numerical rating was shown for subeligibles, as indeed it often was not for eligibles. Inasmuch as subeligibles were not certified eligibles, veterans could be passed over without stating reasons therefor.

In raising qualifications for reappointment and re-entry into the Federal service in 1944, the Commission admitted that many persons appointed under the relaxed examination standards were unable to fulfil satisfactorily the duties assigned to them.[102] In other words, when the government was able to rid itself of incompetents, it proposed to keep them out thenceforth by compelling them to meet the standards established for open competition. If the standards were higher than when such persons had formerly attained eligibility, they were, of course, re-examined. They were certified, if not actually requested for reappointment by any employing agency, only if they were among the best qualified and available eligibles. But this safeguard necessarily came late in the war, when it seemed that the labor market would ease in the near future.

b. *Stress on experience versus education.*—The general philosophy of the Commission and of Congress regarding the American public service has always been to stress experience as against edu-

[98] CSC, *Minute No. 2,* January 3, 1941.
[99] CSC, *Circular Letter No. 3015,* September 6, 1940.
[100] CSC, *Departmental Circular No. 291, Supp. No. 12,* December 26, 1942, and *Supp. No. 12, Revised,* July 8, 1943.
[101] CSC, *Circular Letter No. 4190, Supp. No. 10,* February 21, 1945.
[102] *Ibid.,* No. 4116, February 15, 1944.

cation.¹⁰³ But during the war Congress almost outdid itself in finding every means at hand to maximize this emphasis. The *coup de grâce* to any remote hope of establishing a trend toward a reverse emphasis on educational requirements was administered by the Starnes Act despite the fact that opportunities for higher education had been broadened as never before under the G. I. Bill of Rights. The Starnes Act forbade any minimum educational requirements in any civil service examinations except for scientific, technical, or professional positions for which the Commission determined that they were essential. The Commission's reasons for such decisions had to be made a part of its public record.

OPA became the unhappy target of Congress in the controversy over practical experience because of the large number of academic economists it employed. Not only were there countless denunciations of the economists on the floor of Congress,¹⁰⁴ but the Ramspeck Committee in its first report said:

> It also appears that in some agencies too much stress has been placed upon educational background [college degrees] and not enough attention paid to securing persons having practical experience. Too many people have been employed without actual experience in dealing with the public. Many experienced business men have failed of employment while college professors, economists, and young lawyers have been engaged. That is particularly true of the Office of Price Administration.¹⁰⁵

Congress had rationalized senatorial confirmation of War Manpower Commission employees on the loftier grounds that only in that way could employees with practical experience be secured.¹⁰⁶ But Congress made clear its intent to insist upon practical experience to the exclusion of academic training in the rider attached to the National War Agencies Appropriation Bill for 1944 that no part of the appropriation was to be used to pay the salary or

---

103 CSC, *Manual of Instructions*, E4.02.03, May 3, 1944.

104 See attacks by Representative Taber, 89 *Cong. Record* 617, February 4, 1943; Representative Harness, *ibid.*, 135, January 12, 1943; and Representative Jones of Ohio, *ibid.*, 3073, April 7, 1943, as typical outbursts.

105 U.S. Congress, House, Committee on Civil Service, *Investigation of Civilian Employment*, House Report 2747, 77th Cong., 2nd Sess., 2.

106 See above, p. 75. This requirement of confirmation of WMC employees receiving $4,500 a year or more expired with the deficiency appropriation of 1942, on July 1, 1943.

THE DETERIORATION OF STANDARDS 115

expenses of anyone who directed the "formulation of any price policy, maximum price, or price ceiling with respect to any article or commodity unless, in the judgment of the Administrator, such person shall be qualified by experience in business, industry, or commerce."[107] This was reflected in the Commission mandate for the recruitment of top administrators of OPA, WPB, OCD, WMC, and the Commission that there must be no positive education requirement.[108] As usual, the Commission seemed to go farther than was necessary.

The Starnes Act, however, soon finished what the Commission had started in ruling out educational requirements for administrators by stipulating that no minimum educational requirement could be prescribed except for professional, scientific, or technical positions. Even for those positions the Commission had to make public its reasons for determining that the duties involved could not be performed by anyone lacking the required education.[109] The Commission, therefore, stated that both the labor market and the Starnes Act made it imperative in 1945 to substitute more practical tests for some of the customary prerequisites of education *or experience* in order to make the fullest possible use of persons who had needed skills but had been denied normal opportunities to demonstrate them in formal education or experience.[110] Again the Commission went beyond the statutory requirements. One purpose of this pronouncement, on the other hand, was to effect a closer correlation between selection standards and actual success on the job. The employing agencies were accordingly requested to re-examine all qualifications specifications in the light of the new policy. What this step seemed to portend was a movement back to wider application of assembled tests, both written and demonstration, to discover basic intelligence and aptitudes of applicants.

CONCLUSIONS

Qualifications for Federal positions were perforce geared to the labor market. Not only were they changed by directives from the Commission in Washington as conditions changed, but authority

---

[107] 57 *U.S. Statutes* 522 (1943). [108] CSC, *Circular Letter No. 4046,* August 7, 1943.
[109] 58 *U.S. Statutes* 387 (1944).
[110] CSC, *Departmental Circular No. 524,* May 11, 1945.

was given to regional directors with respect to many occupations to adjust standards to the local labor market conditions prevalent in their jurisdictions. The result was that many standards were eroded by the diminution of the labor supply and the flood of requisitions to staff the nation's vast wartime organization.

Only a doctrinaire would have tried to avert what happened to the quality of Federal personnel, so great was the urgency the personnel system faced. Crises seldom leave a choice of means or instruments; often any tool at hand which may bear but a slight resemblance to that desired must be employed to achieve an objective. Sometimes when an inferior instrument is used, more must be utilized than would otherwise be the case. But rarely can the inferior article be scorned.

Although simplification is often correctly praised, wartime simplification meant for the most part a deterioration in quality in order to produce the required quantity. What both Congress and the Commission failed to realize is that simplification and flexibility need not be linked with relaxed qualifications standards in a normal period.

But new types of "duration" tenure mitigated the effects of lower standards. The war service regulations took cognizance of the undesirability of conferring regular civil service status upon employees who could not meet the former higher competitive requirements. Thus there were no legal entanglements to a service-wide dismissal of war service employees. Little thought was, however, devoted to any means for retaining the best of the new recruits permanently, for the war service regulations were designed for the immediacy of the moment, not for the distant future of the service.

CHAPTER SIX

The New Emphasis on Loyalty

As EDUCATION and experience standards were discarded under the pressure of wartime exigencies, another type of qualification standard, that of loyalty, became by congressional mandate indispensable. For the first time probing of the attitudes of many Federal employees toward their government became an integral part of the examining process. The size of the service, of course, precluded the possibility of examining all recruits on this score, but for important defense and war positions, or for those in which sabotage was possible, the necessity of a loyalty investigation was established.

Congress first conceived the idea of instituting a loyalty requirement in 1939, but never at any time did it clearly define what it meant either by loyalty or by the "subversive activities" it forbade. Instead, it delegated to the Civil Service Commission the responsibility for preventing the entrance into the service of disloyal persons. Upon the Commission, therefore, fell the task of deciding for its own purposes what subversive activities were and what procedures for investigation and appeals would be fair. Over employees already in the service their employing agencies had full jurisdiction. However, when the Commission and the employing agencies failed to take the summary action Congress favored in dealing with those suspected of subversive activities, Congress intervened in 1943 to create one of the *causes célèbres* of recent years, the "bill of attainder" case of that year. Congressional concern over loyalty continued unabated into the postwar period.

STATUTORY REQUIREMENTS

The outbreak of war in Europe in 1939 had brought to the forefront the idea of excluding and dismissing from the service those who had espoused disloyal ideas or had engaged in that nebulous kind of operation known as "subversive activities." The first Hatch Act of 1939 contained the following prohibition:

> Sec. 9A (1) It shall be unlawful for any person employed in any capacity by any agency of the Federal Government, whose compensation or any part thereof, is paid from funds authorized or appropriated by any Act of Congress, to have membership in any political party or organization which advocates the overthrow of our constitutional form of government in the United States.
>
> (2) Any person violating the provisions of this section shall be immediately removed from the position or office held by him, and thereafter no part of the funds appropriated by any Act of Congress for such position or office shall be used to pay the compensation of such person.[1]

Removal from office was mandatory under the Hatch Act for membership in a subversive organization, and for many positions certification was not completed until the individual had been cleared as to loyalty by the Commission's Investigations Division. Prior to the passage of the Hatch Act investigations of new employees had been conducted only for law enforcement and postmaster positions.

The Emergency Relief Appropriation Act for fiscal 1941 was the first of a long series of appropriations acts to require an affidavit of citizenship and loyalty of Federal employees. It stated:

> Sec. 15 (f) No alien, no Communist, and no member of any Nazi Bund Organization shall be given employment or continued in employment on any work project prosecuted under the appropriations contained in this joint resolution and no part of the money appropriated in this joint resolution shall be available to pay any person who has not made or who does not make affidavit as to United States citizenship and to the effect that he is not a Communist and not a member of any Nazi Bund Organization, such affidavit to be considered prima facie evidence of such citizenship, and that he is not a Communist, and not a member of any Nazi Bund Organization. . . .
>
> Sec. 17 (b) No portion of the appropriation made under this joint resolution shall be used to pay any compensation to any person who advocates, or is a member of an organization that advocates, the overthrow of the Government of the United States.[2]

On the one hand, the Commission enforced the loyalty provisions with respect to new employees by making their certification

---

[1] 53 *U.S. Statutes* 1147 (1939).   [2] 54 *U.S. Statutes* 611 (1940).

subject to investigation, but, on the other, the responsibility fell to the employing agencies to investigate and take final action in the case of those employed by the Federal government at the time the above laws were passed. The Commission had no statutory power to review removal of employees unless the procedure of the Lloyd-LaFollette Act of 1912 was not followed or a removal had been made for political or religious reasons.[3]

Administrative Procedures in Loyalty Cases

1. Civil Service Commission Investigations

The policy of the Commission with respect to the recruitment of new employees was that responsibility centered in it to insure that everyone recruited was of unquestioned loyalty and that all doubts were to be resolved in favor of the government.[4] Therefore, its staff of investigators underwent a sharp increase after May, 1940, and eventually a Loyalty Board was established to review findings adverse to employees investigated. Five times as many investigations were required in fiscal 1941 as fiscal 1940,[5] and the number of investigators climbed during the war years from 80 to 755. Not all positions required special investigation, and the Commission did not have to investigate for all agencies inasmuch as War, Navy, the Treasury, and the Federal Works Agency conducted their own investigations. The Federal Works Agency, in addition, investigated dollar-a-year men for WPB. Enemy aliens and stateless persons formerly subjects of Germany, Italy, or Japan were subject to a thoroughgoing investigation before certification to any position and upon either inter- or intra-agency transfer if not previously investigated.[6]

The problem of recruiting competent investigators and training them in a field new to the Commission was one in itself of some considerable proportions. Applicants for these posts were given oral examinations and investigated. The fact that 60 per cent of the applicants for investigator positions failed the orals and an additional 15 to 20 per cent were rated ineligible after investigation during the years 1940 to 1943 is indicative of the staffing

[3] The Commission had no authority over suitability of overseas personnel of OWI, OSS, or FEA. U.S. Congress, House, Hearing on *Independent Offices Appropriation Bill, 1945*, 78th Cong., 2nd Sess., December 9, 1943, p. 1066.
[4] CSC, *Fifty-Seventh Annual Report*, viii.
[5] *Ibid.*, 2.   [6] CSC, *Circular Letter No. 4148*, April 21, 1944.

problem.[7] In December, 1940, Commissioner Flemming asserted to the House Appropriations Subcommittee his conviction that the Commission had not only assembled competent investigators but that an excellent program for training the new investigators had been created.[8]

The new staff carried a heavy load. Of the 273,429 cases closed out by the Investigations Division from July, 1940, to December 31, 1944, 34,576 were rated ineligible for all causes. But only 1,180 persons were rated ineligible solely on loyalty grounds.[9] Up to the end of fiscal 1943, 313 of the latter number had been found to be pro-Axis and 461 pro-Communist or adherents to the Moscow "party line."[10]

The training of the Civil Service Commission investigators in the early years proved to be far less adequate than Commissioner Flemming had believed. In fact, the Commission had to take corrective steps in 1943 after complaints from the public, adverse publicity,[11] and protests from the United Federal Workers of America, the CIO employees' union, respecting investigators' attitudes had brought the Commission into unfavorable notice. The common complaints centered about the ineptitude of the investigators and their bias against liberal affiliations on the part of those being investigated. They followed the "guilt by association" standard established by the Dies Committee. Leonard D. White, professor of public administration of the University of Chicago and former U. S. Civil Service Commissioner, said of them:

> Earlier leadership in the Investigations Division of the Civil Service Commission had been relatively uninspired. The investigating staff was characterized by integrity but not by exceptional competence. The heavy demands of 1940-45 came at a time when competent investigators were difficult to secure. The Commission did what it could and trusted to close supervision and some elementary training to produce satisfactory results.

[7] CSC, *Sixtieth Annual Report*, 11.
[8] U.S. Congress, House, Hearing on *Independent Offices Appropriation Bill, 1942*, 77th Cong., 1st Sess., December 12, 1940, p. 530.
[9] U.S. Congress, House, Hearing on *Independent Offices Appropriation Bill, 1946*, 79th Cong., 1st Sess., January 17, 1945, pp. 1283, 1237-38.
[10] CSC, *Sixtieth Annual Report*, 12.
[11] "Washington Gestapo," *Nation*, CLVII (July 15, 1943), 64-66 and (July 24, 1943), 92-99.

> During the years 1941-44 a considerable number of these investigators called at my office for information about former students. . . . The Civil Service Commission investigators were on the whole competent to ascertain factual information. Some of them gave offense in their attitudes with respect to allegedly radical tendencies of persons about whom they made inquiries. Membership in innocuous student societies was pursued with avidity and at times apparently with relish. The orientation of these investigators as a group was distinctly conservative. . . .
>
> The proper orientation and training of investigators was a constant subject of solicitude on the part of the Civil Service Commission. The Commission recognized that its staff was in some respects inadequate and took progressive steps to improve the quality of this part of its work.[12]

Floyd W. Reeves, professor of administration of the University of Chicago and first personnel director of TVA, described their attitudes in these terms:

> During the period from June 1940 until June 1943, I was interviewed many times by investigators of the United States Civil Service Commission concerning the character and loyalty of men and women who had formerly been employed in agencies under my direction. My general impression of the investigators was highly unfavorable. The major interest of almost all of them seemed to be that of finding out whether or not the person being investigated might be sympathetic toward Communism, toward our ally, Russia, or toward the Spanish Loyalists. The questions asked relating to matters such as membership in national or local associations, books and literature read, and associations with other persons, seemed to imply that one who had read books about Russia, visited Russia, was a friend of someone who had visited Russia, or had been sympathetic with the Spanish Loyalists was a dangerous person to employ in a government agency. I cannot recall ever having been asked a question that implied that the person under investigation might be or have been sympathetic toward Germany or Japan. When the position for which the man or woman was being considered was an important administrative position, questions might be asked about his or her administrative ability. Such questions, however, were rarely asked, and when they were, I received the impression that the investigator was not particularly interested in the answers given.[13]

[12] Interview, April 11, 1946.   [13] Letter to the writer, April 12, 1946.

122   IMPACT OF WAR ON FEDERAL PERSONNEL

William C. Rogers, secretary of the Personnel Exchange, Public Administration Clearing House, said of the investigators:

> Civil Service Commission investigators were uniformly poor. They were a very low grade of personnel who were almost 100 per cent interested in whether a man was a Communist rather than whether he was sympathetic with the countries we were fighting against. The worst thing about them was their terrible persistence. Civil Service Commission investigators were inferior in ability to the other Federal investigators from the War and Navy Departments and the F.B.I. They also showed a lack of training. It was ridiculous that such investigators should ask about an individual's qualifications for a high administrative position. What could such poor personnel bring back?[14]

W. H. Spencer, Hobart Williams Distinguished Service Professor of government and business, University of Chicago, and from 1942 to 1946 Regional War Manpower Director of the Sixth Regional WMC Office in Chicago, declared:

> Very superficial investigations were conducted by the Civil Service Commission. The investigators' questions were not searching—not nearly so searching as those of the F.B.I. and Department of Justice investigators. The F.B.I. would have some specific object in mind as to whether a person could be trusted on a particular project. I always felt that the Civil Service Commission investigators were immature as contrasted with the others and not quite as competent, not quite as well-trained, not quite as resourceful in digging out information. I felt definitely that if I had been the type of person who would have wanted to "put something over," I could have done so easily.[15]

One of the difficulties with Commission policy respecting loyalty investigations was that the Commission had no clear standard from Congress as to what it was searching for in connection with subversive activities. In lieu of a directive, it substituted some vague notions of its own, reflected in the statement of Commissioner Flemming at a House Appropriations Subcommittee hearing in 1940:

> In connection with all of our investigations, we are keeping this policy in mind; if we find anybody has had any association with Communists or the German Bund, or any foreign or-

[14] Interview, April 10, 1946.   [15] Interview, April 15, 1946.

ganization of that kind, that person is disqualified immediately. All doubts are being resolved in favor of the Government.

In addition, we believe it is just as important to make sure that persons obviously of weak character are not put in navy yards and arsenals and other key defense positions at the present time. They may have had no association, up to the present time, with Communists, bunds, and so on; but, if they have a weak character, they are good prey for those who want a representative on the inside of our defense establishments. Consequently, we are eliminating that type of person—again resolving all doubts in favor of the Government. . . .

It seems to me, however, that it is equally as important to do everything we can to prevent undesirable persons from getting into the service and creating difficult situations. That is our function and that is our responsibility, and we are trying to discharge it in the very best way we can.[16]

"Weak character" or "undesirable persons" are terms as nebulous as "subversive activities" and quite as open to abuse and misinterpretation by overzealous investigators. That fact the Commission learned in the years after 1940. To correct the bias manifested by some investigators against so-called liberal activities the Commission issued instructions in August, 1942, and reaffirmed them on November 3, 1943, detailing the types of questions which should not be asked by investigators. The nature of these instructions reveals indirectly some of the line of questioning previously pursued which had caused protest from UFWA and others. The instructions of November 3, 1943, were:

1. Under no circumstances should any question be asked of an applicant or a witness involving union membership, union associations, or union activities. . . .

2. If in the course of the investigation witnesses say that a certain person is a Communist because he has associated with certain persons in a union known or said to be Communists, the investigator should not ask the applicant about his associations with these particular individuals, since the asking of such questions would expose the Commission to the charge that this is an indirect way of connecting the applicant with union activities. In other words, the question of unionism should not be brought up in any way in an investigation, either directly or indirectly.

---

[16] U.S. Congress, House, Hearing on *Independent Offices Appropriation Bill, 1942*, 77th Cong., 1st Sess., December 12, 1940, pp. 529-30.

3. Do not ask any question whatever involving the applicant's sympathy with Loyalists in Spain. This means that the investigator should avoid not only asking about the applicant's sympathy in the Spanish war, but no reference should be made to any such organizations as the Abraham Lincoln Brigade or any other of the many Spanish relief groups. The whole matter of the war in Spain should be scrupulously avoided by the investigator as having any bearing on pro-communism. . . .

5. In asking an applicant whether he knows a certain individual, that individual should not be characterized in any way so as to show the individual's views or leanings. . . .

8. In speaking to the applicant or to a witness do not characterize an organization as communistic or Fascist. Do not characterize it at all. . . .

10. Under no circumstances ask any question or make any statement to the applicant or to a witness relating directly or indirectly to the color, race, creed, or religion of an applicant or witness.

11. Obtain all available information from witnesses which will help establish whether the applicant was a Communist Party line conformist. Do not discuss the party line with the applicant or with witnesses. Familiarize yourself thoroughly with the party line test and ask questions which will specifically bring out whether the applicant changed his views at certain periods but do not mention party line unless the witness offers the information that the applicant did follow the Communist Party line. In that event ask the witness specifically what statement or actions on the part of the applicant he has in mind or knows about which leads him to the conclusion that the applicant was a party line follower. Again, have in mind it is not your function to argue or give information but merely to elicit information.

12. Do not ask any question regarding the type of reading matter read by the applicant. This includes especially the Daily Worker and all radical and liberal publications. Remember that the mere fact that a person reads a certain publication is no indication that he believes in the principles advocated by such publication. Citizens are free to read anything they like.

13. Do not ask any questions as to so-called mixed parties, that is to say, whether the applicant associates with Negroes or has had Negroes in his home.

14. Do not ask regarding membership or interest in the Lawyers Guild, the American Civil Liberties Union, the Socialist Party, the League of Women Shoppers, or the Harry Bridges Defense Committee. This is not a complete list of organizations about which no questions should be asked, but

THE NEW EMPHASIS ON LOYALTY

investigators should avoid asking any questions regarding any organization unless it has been authoritatively designed [sic] as subversive. If the investigator is in doubt the best policy is not to ask the question. . . .

15. Do not ask general questions regarding the political philosophy of the applicant, such as whether he believes in capitalism or what his opinion is regarding certain events of a current or historical nature. . . .

17. Exercise intelligence. Keep in mind what you are looking for. Remember that you are investigating the loyalty of the applicant to the United States. You are not investigating whether his views are unorthodox or do not conform with those of the majority of the people. What you are looking for is to determine whether there is evidence that the applicant's interest in the welfare of another country transcends his interest in the welfare of the United States. Remember that a question of an improper nature will result in criticism of, and embarrassment to, the Commission. Do not ask any question which is immaterial and has no bearing on the ultimate issue involved.[17]

Some members of Congress did not, of course, agree with the Commission's instructions of 1942 and 1943. The following questions asked in the House Appropriations Subcommittee hearing in December, 1943, indicate the hostility felt toward Commission policy by Dies Committee adherents:

Mr. Starnes. In stopping its agents and investigators from really going into the background of a governmental employee or a man wanting to be employed by the Government, and estopping those people from getting some real and vital information about his connections with subversive organizations and groups, and that is a matter in which the Congress and the whole country should be deeply interested [sic]. Nothing you say about it—I do not want to go into this, because I think it is a subject that is going to have to be threshed out by a special committee and gone into very thoroughly, but there will be quite a bit of information that will be quite enlightening to the gentlemen who head the Commission, who are willing to take responsibility for it [sic].

Mr. Wigglesworth. Do you think, Mr. Flemming, that these instructions are conducive to carrying out the congressional intent?

Mr. Flemming. We certainly do, and the basic reason—

[17] U.S. Congress, House, Hearing on *Independent Offices Appropriation Bill, 1945*, 78th Cong., 2nd Sess., December 9, 1943, pp. 1078-79.

Mr. Wigglesworth. Do you think they are conducive to maintaining the morale of your investigating force?

Mr. Flemming. We do.

Mr. Wigglesworth. Do you endorse the policy reflected in these instructions?

Mr. Flemming. I certainly do.[18]

Mr. Wigglesworth. . . . I just want to observe for the record that, personally, I should hate to be an investigator for the Civil Service Commission and try to obtain the results that I believe everyone around the table feels absolutely vital to this country, under any such prohibitions as are contained in the instructions embodied in the letter of November 3, 1943.[19]

The procedure for determining loyalty was to have the investigators, all of whom worked from the regional offices, look into the case assigned for investigation and close it out unless derogatory information was disclosed; only in the latter event were further proceedings necessary. If the latter happened, a special hearing might be called by the regional office to give the appointee an opportunity to present his side orally or in writing. If the recommendations were adverse to the individual, the case was turned over to a rating unit in the central office composed of persons who had had no previous connection with the investigation and was summarized by them with recommendations for the chief of the Investigations Division. If still adverse, it was next sent to the Office of the Executive Director of the Commission, where it was reviewed by the Loyalty Board, especially created to review loyalty cases.[20] To their recommendations the Executive Director might add his own when the file returned to him before it went to the Commissioners for decision. If they decided to rate the individual unsuitable and either he or his employing agency decided to appeal, the matter was referred to the Board of Appeals and Review, which reviewed the entire case and made recommendations to the Commissioners. The appellant had an opportunity to request a hearing before the Commissioners before they made their final decision.[21]

[18] *Ibid.*, 1081.   [19] *Ibid.*, 1088-89.

[20] U.S. Congress, House, Hearing on *Independent Offices Appropriation Bill, 1946*, 79th Cong., 1st Sess., January 17, 1945, p. 1200. The Loyalty Board was established in 1941.

[21] CSC, *Sixtieth Annual Report*, 13-14.

2. THE INTERDEPARTMENTAL COMMITTEES

The investigation of employees already in the service before 1940 was left to each department. To co-ordinate this work the Attorney General established an Interdepartmental Committee in 1942 within the Department of Justice, which was succeeded in 1943 by a new Interdepartmental Committee created by President Roosevelt.[22] All complaints made to the employing departments were to be referred to the F.B.I. for investigation, for the work of the Interdepartmental Committee was to recommend policies, receive reports from the F.B.I. on complaints received, and advise the departments on fair procedure for determining action. The departments reported back with respect to the procedures followed and action taken. On request of an agency or on its own motion the committee might review the case and give an advisory opinion. The establishment of the two committees was regarded as an important step for attaining fairness in establishing just procedures and standards for removal, but in no way was it to limit departmental action. Congress had nowhere defined the term "subversive" for the executive branch, and the establishment of the committees was deemed a means of assisting the departments to act fairly in an ill-defined area.

But the Attorney General's Committee had questioned the value of the loyalty investigations as a personnel policy in that they were time-consuming and produced little in the way of substantial results. Dismissals had been ordered by the departments in only three cases out of 1,121 complaints from the Dies Committee and 3,500 from other sources.[23]

Its successor committee made a significant contribution to administrative procedure in outlining and recommending eight standards for fair hearing procedure: (1) formal charges in writing against the employee; (2) formal hearing with an adequate opportunity for the employee to prepare for it; (3) notice to the employee that charges, if sustained, would necessitate his dismissal; (4) the right of representation by counsel; (5) the right of the employee to produce witnesses in his own defense and the recognition of the obligation on his part to answer all questions

---

[22] Executive Order 9300, February 5, 1943. See Robert E. Cushman, "The Purge of Federal Employees Accused of Disloyalty," *Public Administration Review*, III (1943), 297-316.

[23] Cushman, "The Purge of Federal Employees," *loc. cit.*, 309.

128   IMPACT OF WAR ON FEDERAL PERSONNEL

put to him; (6) freedom from rigid rules of evidence in the hearing; (7) the keeping of a record of hearing proceedings with copies furnished the employee; (8) findings of fact and a decision in writing with the privilege to the employing agency, not to the employee, to appeal to the Interdepartmental Committee for a review and an advisory opinion. There is little doubt that the Interdepartmental Committee felt that a stronger case was required to dismiss an employee in the service than did the Civil Service Commission to deny eligibility. This is understandable in that the individual in the former case had a materially different status as an employee from that of one who was merely an eligible.

Congressional Purges

The loose accusations and "witch hunt" atmosphere provoked in the House of Representatives by the Dies Committee, the special House committee to investigate un-American activities, were calculated to provide victims for the frenetic zeal of Congress. The first hapless individual upon whom congressional wrath lighted and who provided the "trial run" for the real effort in following years was one David Lasser, onetime head of the Workers' Alliance, a union of WPA employees, and employed in 1941 by the Works Projects Administration. The technique resolved upon was to attach a rider to the Emergency Relief Appropriation Act for 1942 barring the payment of salary to Lasser.[24] When even the Dies Committee could not make a substantial case against him, the principal charge left seemed to be that he "runs with the wrong crowd."[25] No sooner was the act passed than a resolution for its repeal forced the Appropriations Committee to hold hearings later in the year at which Lasser categorically denied ever having been or being a Communist. The committee had this to say of the rider, in recommending reconsideration by the House:

> Personal legislation of the character enacted in Mr. Lasser's case is rare. It was taken, the committee feels, without suffi-

[24] 55 *U.S. Statutes* 396 (1941).
[25] 87 *Cong. Record* 5110, June 12, 1941. The rider was proposed by Representative Dirksen, Republican, of Illinois. The vote on the amendment was 131 for it, 88 against it in the committee of the whole (p. 5113), and 214 ayes to 114 noes on the final vote, June 13, 1941 (p. 5151). Senator Murray moved to strike out the rider in the Senate, but his motion was rejected without a recorded vote, June 20, 941, pp. 5384-85..

cient previous consideration and in recommending the repeal of the limitation opportunity is provided for reconsideration of what many feel has been an injustice to Mr. Lasser. . . . Congress has by law established a damaging reflection upon Mr. Lasser.[26]

The appropriation act did not contain a repeal of the bar against David Lasser because of a point of order raised against the clause for repeal by Representative Taber. He objected to the repeal on the ground that it represented legislation in an appropriation bill, although no such objection was sustained against the original bar.[27] But the whole question soon became academic with the expiration of fiscal 1942, for the bar expired with the Emergency Relief Appropriation Act of that year. Lasser was subsequently employed by WPB.

The year 1942, however, saw the preliminary skirmish in a real *cause célèbre,* the case of Goodwin B. Watson, foreign broadcast analyst in the Federal Communications Commission. The full Appropriations Committee of the House had voted to deny funds to pay any salary to Watson. Representative Plumley added, "We should send him to a concentration camp for the duration and watch him if we were not so complacent and so dumb as not to know enough to protect our own interests."[28] Senator Barkley, majority leader in the Senate, however, viewed this procedure as both a cowardly method and a bill of attainder and moved to strike it from the bill.[29] Senate opposition thus killed the House-approved rider for the time being.

Not visibly discouraged, the Dies Committee and its adherents simply renewed the fight on a grander scale against a whole coterie of Federal employees, among them William Pickens and Mary McLeod Bethune, both Negroes, Frederick L. Schuman, Goodwin B. Watson, William E. Dodd, Jr., Paul R. Porter, David Lasser, Robert Morss Lovett, Walter Gellhorn, David J. Saposs, and twenty-nine others.[30] Representative Hendricks of Florida offered an amendment to the Treasury and Post Office Appropriation bill for 1944 to bar salaries to them, but when it developed

---

[26] U.S. Congress, House, Committee on Appropriations, *Third Supplemental National Defense Appropriation Bill, 1942,* House Report 1470, 77th Cong., 1st Sess., 39.
[27] 87 *Cong. Record* 9494, December 5, 1941.
[28] 88 *Cong. Record* 568, January 22, 1942.   [29] *Ibid.,* 3997-98, May 6, 1942.
[30] 89 *Cong. Record* 645, February 5, 1943.

that Pickens alone was employed in the Treasury Department, the motion was rejected by a slight margin and another offered by Hendricks to bar Pickens alone.[31] This was carried, but many faces soon turned crimson when it was discovered Pickens' color was black, and Representative Cannon proposed vacating the amendment against Pickens in favor of a motion for hearings for all thirty-nine accused employees before a special subcommittee of five members of the Appropriations Committee.[32] Amid many approving remarks that now everyone would have "his day in court," Cannon's motion was duly passed.

The hearings held by the subcommittee consisting of John H. Kerr of North Carolina, chairman, Albert Gore of Tennessee, Clinton P. Anderson of New Mexico (Democrats), D. Lane Powers of New Jersey, and Frank B. Keefe of Wisconsin (Republicans) were characterized by such highhanded procedure as would have vitiated any administrative hearing in the United States. There was no notice in the sense of a summary of charges against the victims to give them foreknowledge of the nature of the accusations. No time was allowed to prepare a defense since all were given one day's notice of the hearing. No representation by counsel was permitted, and not even employing agencies could appear on behalf of their employees or have observers present. No opportunity was allowed to bring in witnesses, and no witnesses were presented by the committee to confront the accused for cross-examination.[33] The attitude of the committee was wholly that of a prosecuting attorney.[34]

The evidence adduced at the hearings showed that Lovett had been an inveterate joiner of many organizations labeled "fellow traveling" by the Dies Committee, Watson had expressed in writing criticism of the profit system, and Dodd had entertained Harry Bridges, whose deportation case was then still pending before the courts, at a cocktail party in his apartment. Or to be more ac-

[31] *Ibid.*, 655-56.

[32] *Ibid.*, 709, February 8, 1943, and 734, 742, 754-57, February 9, 1943.

[33] See Frederick L. Schuman, " 'Bill of Attainder' in the Seventy-Eighth Congress," *American Political Science Review*, XXXVII (1943), 819-29, especially 821 on procedure.

[34] See U.S. Congress, House, Hearings before the Special Subcommittee of the Committee on Appropriations, *Fitness for Continuance in Federal Employment of Goodwin B. Watson, and William E. Dodd, Jr., etc., and Robert Morss Lovett, etc.*, 78th Cong., 1st Sess., April 9, 12, 13, and 15, 1943.

curate, Dodd had allowed his apartment to be used for that purpose and had been present. This evidence and the failure of all the accused persons to withdraw from the questionable organizations after the Russo-German treaty of 1939 led the committee to hold them unfit for government employment. The committee, for the guidance of Congress, had formulated a definition of subversive activities which did little to clarify what they might be.[35]

The committee recommended a rider to be attached to the Urgent Deficiency Appropriation Bill for 1943 to bar the payment of salaries to the three individuals.[36] That recommendation was accepted by the House as though from a trial jury after a full and fair hearing. Secretary Ickes, appearing before the Senate Appropriations Committee in defense of Lovett, in his blunt way declared: "This is a pretty weak pail of garbage with which to find a man guilty of being disloyal to his Government."[37]

A sharp, stubborn battle ensued between the two houses of Congress. Since only a small contingent fought the rider in the House of Representatives, it was overwhelmingly adopted by a vote of 318 to 62.[38] But the Senate, to which the Kerr Committee report was not at first accessible, raised serious doubts about the constitutionality of the proposed procedure to remove named Federal employees by cutting off salaries. Even the Senate Appropriations Committee led by the redoubtable Senator McKellar opposed the rider.[39] The House, however, adamantly refused Senate deletion of the rider,[40] while the Senators continued to "shrink at the contemplation of a proceeding which amounts to a bill of attainder," in the words of Senator Bone.[41] By unanimous vote the Senate rejected it a second time. Thinking to

---

[35] "Subversive activity in this country derives from conduct intentionally destructive of or inimical to the government of the United States—that which seeks to undermine its institutions, or to distort its functions, or to impede its projects, or to lessen its efforts, the ultimate end being to overturn it all. Such activity may be open and direct as by effort to overthrow, or subtle and indirect as by sabotage." *Ibid.*, 331.

[36] U.S. Congress, House, *Fitness for Continuance in Federal Employment of Goodwin B. Watson and William E. Dodd, Jr., etc., and Robert Morss Lovett, Arthur E. Goldschmidt and Jack Bradley Fahy, etc.*, House Report 448, 78th Cong., 1st Sess.

[37] U.S. Congress, Senate, Hearing on *Urgent Deficiency Appropriation Bill, 1943*, 78th Cong., 1st Sess., May 20, 1943, p. 8.

[38] 89 *Cong. Record* 4605, May 17, 1943.   [39] *Ibid.*, 5023-24, May 28, 1943.
[40] *Ibid.*, 5517, June 8, 1943.   [41] *Ibid.*, 5605, June 10, 1943.

teach the recalcitrant Senators a lesson in tactics, Representative Taber, ranking Republican member of the Appropriations Committee, held up House consideration of Senate rejection for a number of days, sensing the fact that the nearer the conference was held to the end of the fiscal year the greater the likelihood of Senate surrender. His surmise was correct in that the Senate conferees receded, an action defended by Senator McKellar on the ground that it was unfair to delay salaries for others and that the three employees could test the question in the courts anyway.[42] Nevertheless, the vote in the Senate was 52 to 17 against agreeing to the conference report.[43] Still the conference managers again agreed to reinsert the rider, but it was June 29 and the Senate was wavering. It rejected the rider a fourth time by a vote of 53 to 32.[44] Time was, as Taber expected, with the House, for the next conference report to accept the rider passed the Senate on July 2 by a vote of 48 to 32.[45]

The challenge to executive control over the removal of employees in its own branch was a precedent so dangerous to presidential authority that it could not be ignored. Not only did President Roosevelt denounce the action, but Secretary Ickes defied congressional abolition of Lovett's position as Secretary of the Virgin Islands by appointing him without delay to a position he created, Executive Secretary to the Governor of the Islands. The lines were drawn for a long legal battle. When salary suits were filed by the three proscribed employees, Attorney General Biddle informed Congress of his regret that he found "it impossible to advocate with conviction the view of Congress,"[46] thus forcing that branch to hire a private attorney to represent it. The three plaintiffs received an offer of representation from one of the leading law firms of Washington and won the opening round in the courts before the Court of Claims on November 5, 1945.[47]

The Supreme Court in June, 1946, speaking through Justice Black, declared the action of Congress constituted a bill of attainder, falling "precisely within the category of congressional actions which the Constitution barred."[48] The rider, Justice Black held, "clearly accomplishes the punishment of named in-

[42] *Ibid.*, 6407-6408, June 24, 1943.
[43] *Ibid.*, 6415.
[44] *Ibid.*, 6737-38, June 29, 1943.
[45] *Ibid.*, 7014, July 2, 1943.
[46] *Ibid.*, 10401, December 8, 1943.
[47] *New York Times,* November 6, 1945.
[48] *U.S.* v. *Lovett,* 328 *U.S.* 303 (1945).

dividuals without a judicial trial. The fact that the punishment is inflicted through the instrumentality of an Act specifically cutting off the pay of certain named individuals found guilty of disloyalty makes it no less galling than if it had been done by an Act which designated the conduct as criminal." Justices Frankfurter and Reed concurred in upholding the claim to back salaries awarded to the litigants but found no unconstitutionality in the rider.

Conclusions

The emphasis on loyalty as a major qualification for eligibility and, indeed, for the right to continue in a Federal position had created troublesome new procedures and problems not merely for the Commission but also for the employing agencies. The Congressional mandates requiring loyalty of Federal employees created a wholly new basis for examining into the suitability of eligibles and placed an unsolicited responsibility on both the Commission and the departments for executing the will of Congress justly. For the former body the task was more difficult in that it could not ignore the grave duty of certifying only loyal recruits for the war program.

Even more significant the loyalty mandate had given rise to a disturbing precedent for congressional interference with the executive power of removal of employees. The furore created by the Dies Committee over an infusion of "reds" into the Federal government was not sustained by the facts. When it is recalled that scarcely more than 1,000 persons or .014 per cent were barred from Federal employment out of more than 7,500,000 recruited during the years of defense and war, the loyalty of Federal employees appears to have been steadfast. But a dangerous pattern had been set nevertheless for the postwar years.

Administrative procedures were, on the whole, quite fair in handling this vexing question. The Commission did what it could to correct allegations of bias and stupidity in investigative work at the same time that the Interdepartmental Committee took pains to advise equity in the departmental proceedings and decisions. Congressional procedure, in contrast, seemed a subversion of the very Americanism the congressional "purgers" were shouting so vociferously to protect.

But the legislative body felt no restraints on an excess of zeal as did an administrative agency. Carried away by the Dies Committee, it challenged the power of the executive over removal of employees as it had not been challenged since the days of Andrew Johnson. Further, it seriously challenged the civil rights of American citizens in attempting a bill of attainder. The loyalty issue stands forth all the more starkly when one reflects on what happened to the other qualifications for Federal employment at the time it was magnified out of all proportion to its due importance.

CHAPTER SEVEN

Development of Training Policies and Organization

MANIFESTLY the decline and fall of qualifications standards could well have had catastrophic results on production activities within the Federal government had not steps been taken to institute training programs at all organizational levels and for a great variety of skills. Indeed, the universality of interest in training activities among both personnel technicians and operating officers was phenomenal in comparison with the "spotty" prewar training situation. Supervisory and administrative training had formerly been largely neglected, little orientation or indoctrination had been given to new employees, and the teaching of basic skills was, of course, superfluous when highly trained employees could be recruited with ease. There were a few notable exceptions to be found, such as in the Forestry Service, Federal Bureau of Investigation, Social Security Board, and Farm Credit Administration. But wartime deterioration in the quality of recruits, coupled with their enormous quantitative expansion, created an imperative need for a wholly new approach to the training problem. Urgency for production, too, forced agencies to face this problem.

Training alone could not have met production demands. Reinforced by job dilution, that is, the breakdown of skilled, complex tasks into their simpler component parts, it could go a long way to compensate for deficiencies in preservice schooling and experience. Indeed, job dilution is the technique that has been long employed by American industry to make possible assembly-line methods for mass production. That it was not earlier adapted to government establishments may be attributed to two reasons; one, normally the direct mechanical production to which job dilution best lends itself is but a small part of total Federal activities, and two, job dilution is not used so successfully where a high degree of skill and a low degree of standardization are found and must exist. When few ships are built and each is custom-built to an individual design, it may be deemed best procedure to employ none but skilled mechanics in their construction. But when dozens of ships are constructed, all of a standard design and turned out in the least possible time, job dilution can and must be applied. A machinist's work must be divided into a dozen or more small operations, such as having one man do nothing but fit one part of an engine into another all day, another follow with the tightening of bolts as the engine moves along the line, and a third turn a set of screws. Thereby the totally inexperienced can be employed and training simplified. On the whole, job dilution is not too adaptable to office routine or professional work. It is possible to streamline paper procedures, but a typist must still be a typist and a junior engineer still be a graduate of an engineering college if the work is to be turned out.

That training programs were installed was due to sheer necessity and not to well-planned preparation in the executive branch or clear delegation of authority from Congress. As a matter of fact, the war began and ended with no clarification from Congress of the role of the Civil Service Commission with respect to training. For a time the Commission struggled to serve the departments in a consultative capacity, but the War and Navy departments, the great employers of new appointees, early found their needs so pressing that they went their own way on training and brought in educators and industrialists to provide the expert knowledge for thoroughgoing programs. The two fields in which the Civil Service Commission took the lead were in promoting supervisory training throughout the service and in working with the Council of Personnel Administration in 1944 to establish an in-service internship program for administrative training.

In order to effectuate the smooth functioning of training activities it was essential to define the relationship of the training staff to the operating officers in each agency. Likewise it was necessary that the top command define the training policy of the department in so far as training obligations and areas for activities could be defined. Invariably the relationship of the training branch to the line activities was a consultative or staff relationship. This was logical in view of the fact that the line officers had full responsibility for work production and could not allow training for training's sake to be foisted upon them by zealots in a service office.

Confusion in the Responsibility for Training

Unlike the field of recruitment, training possessed no statutory guideposts to clarify responsibility for the institution, guidance, or control of training programs in the Federal service. For example, the authority and responsibility of the Civil Service Commission had never been made explicit. The only indication of the Commission's responsibility was that given in Executive Order 7916 of June 24, 1938, which in Section 8 declared, "The Civil Service Commission shall, in cooperation with operating departments and establishments, the Office of Education, and public and private institutions of learning establish practical training courses for employees in the departmental and field services of the classified civil service." But under Section 6 of the same order the departmental personnel director's functions included supervision of training and the initiation of such programs as were approved by the department head after consultation with the Civil Service Commission. Thus it was not made clear whether the Commission possessed specific control or merely consultive power.

Under the impetus of Executive Order 7916, however, the Commission in 1939 requested funds from Congress to establish a Division of Training in fiscal 1941.[1] Thereby it hoped to furnish consultative services to the departments in the critical period it foresaw and justified the request by pointing out that during any emergency period the primary emphasis would be on training employees suddenly called upon to assume supervisory responsibilities. With this modest beginning it might have been able to forge ahead had there been a determination to impress upon the Appropriations Committees the significance of the training function and the Commission's connection therewith. But the request for funds was denied by the committee. The emphasis in subsequent committee hearings was centered upon the recruitment responsibility of the central personnel agency with scant attention to other personnel functions. This may have been due to a lack of agreement within the Commission that it was anything more than the central recruitment agency or to a fear of

---

[1] U.S. Congress, House, Hearing on *Independent Offices Appropriation Bill, 1941*, 76th Cong., 3d Sess., December 12, 1939, p. 654. The request was for a modest sum: $82,040.

congressional disfavor induced by a lack of sympathy with a broad and inclusive program.

Not until early in 1942 did the Commission establish a Training Division, which acted purely on a consultative basis with the agencies. There is little evidence that those agencies faced with acute training needs looked to the Commission for guidance. Instead, they brought in their own consultants and experts and worked out independent programs for training. Often the Commission remained uninformed of training under way in the departments, so poor was liaison between the Training Division and the agencies. At any rate, the Training Division disappeared in a Commission reorganization in March, 1943, when training activities were integrated into a larger program of personnel utilization laid upon the Commission by Congress.

A new name and a new approach were tried in 1943. Within the enlarged Examining and Personnel Utilization Division of the Civil Service Commission was located the Federal Work Improvement Program. Three roles were assigned to the latter: as a stimulator of training programs, it was to urge their value upon the departments for the more effective utilization of their personnel and for reduction of the recruitment load; as an information agency, it was to keep the agencies informed of training methods employed successfully elsewhere in the government; as a consultant, it was to serve as a two-way channel for the expression of government needs to the War Manpower Commission and to the departments for advice on WMC training resources available to them.[2] Actually in order to bring WMC training facilities to the agencies, the Commission trained the departmental instructors for the "J" courses for the improvement of supervision. The instructors trained by the Commission at agency request were then used by the departments to spread supervisory training throughout the Federal service.[3]

The House Appropriations Committee, however, viewed the whole Federal Work Improvement Program darkly, especially the "J" institutes conducted by the Commission. Because the Appropriations Committee did not appreciate the manpower short-

[2] CSC, *Manual of Instructions*, A7.03.04, July 13, 1943. The Commission stated in its *Fifty-Ninth Annual Report*, 5, that its function was to encourage the departments to establish training facilities for their own employees, not to give training directly.
[3] See Chapter VIII for a description of the "J" courses.

age existent in 1945, it failed to attach due importance to the need for training in Federal personnel activities. Congressman Wigglesworth epitomized the feeling of the majority by his comment: "Is not the real way to get at the root of the trouble to appoint competent people in the first place? . . . Why should we set up another brand new agency to teach the Civil Service Commission how to teach the teachers at the various agencies how to teach the employees? You can carry that idea on almost indefinitely."[4]

It occasioned no surprise, therefore, when the committee struck out $106,678 from the Federal Work Improvement Program in the Commission appropriation for fiscal 1946.[5] Thus the program was virtually forced into limbo. But the end of the war nearly coincided with the action of Congress, easing off somewhat the pressure for training.

The war began and ended with no clear directive from Congress or the executive branch and no firm determination within the Commission to recognize the obligation of the Federal government to provide in-service training or to fix the responsibility for it. Since the need for extensive in-service training ranked next in urgency to that for recruitment, the employing agencies eventually "took the ball and ran with it" as far and as fast as funds and initiative allowed. Urgency was greatest, of course, in the War and Navy departments, and Congress allotted them appropriations most freely. As a consequence, their leadership in the field of training activities in variety, scope, and intensity was natural. By their bold efforts they validated conclusively the idea that there is an obligation resting on the Federal government to undertake training activities to improve the caliber of recruits in order to attain program and production goals. The responsibility for leadership in assuming that obligation seemed to rest with the appointing power, namely the departments.

AGENCY ORGANIZATION FOR TRAINING

While each agency was free to develop what organization and approach it would for the conduct of training programs, this brief comparative survey will be limited to four agencies. They are

[4] U.S. Congress, House, Hearing on *Independent Offices Appropriation Bill, 1946*, 79th Cong., 1st Sess., January 17, 1945, pp. 1230-31.

[5] U.S. Congress, House, *Independent Offices Appropriation Bill, 1946*, House Report 54, 79th Cong., 1st Sess., 5.

the War and Navy departments, the Office of Price Administration, and the Department of Agriculture, chosen for study because they furnished a cross section of wartime Federal establishments as well as an illustration of very different ways of viewing the training problem. The size and complexity of operations and working force in the military departments aggravated their problems and evoked programs unrivaled in the government, if not in industry. As the Army Service Forces boasted, it was the "largest employer of free civilian labor in world history."[6] Agriculture, as one of the "old-line" agencies, had engaged in some specialized types of training before the war. With the accretion of new wartime functions in every bureau and the same personnel problems other agencies faced, it was forced to broaden its program and adapt its offerings. OPA, as a wholly new war agency plunged into three intricate regulatory fields unexplored by the Federal government before the war—price control, rationing, and rent control—with an entirely new staff and many organizational and political problems, was in a position radically different from both the military and "old-line" agencies. It was logical, therefore, that its training program should have been adapted to its own peculiar needs.

1. WAR DEPARTMENT

Unlike Agriculture and some of the other "old-line" agencies and in sharp contrast to the emphasis it placed upon training in military life, the War Department had no top organization for civilian training activities before 1941. Indeed, it had no civilian personnel director even after Executive Order 7916 until President Roosevelt issued a peremptory command for compliance in 1940.[7] Civilian training was at best haphazard, conducted locally without plan or support from the highest echelons and only as local crises dictated.[8] During 1940 reliance was placed upon preservice training offered as a part of the defense training program of NYA, WPA, and the Office of Education. In addition, at that time there was an in-service apprenticeship for skilled workers in aircraft maintenance.

---

[6] ASF Manual, *Civilian Personnel Officers' Handbook M212* (Washington: ASF, April, 1945), 21. One wonders what the U.S.S.R. might say of this boast.

[7] *Investigation of Civilian Employment*, Part III, Hearing on June 10, 1943, p. 510.

[8] Interview with Lee P. Brown, Office of the Secretary of War, Director of Civilian Training, War Department, June 23, 1945.

TRAINING POLICIES AND ORGANIZATION   141

A policy and a program began to take shape after Secretary of War Stimson called in Lawrence A. Appley as a consultant early in 1941. Appley, as vice-president of the Vicks Company, offered a wealth of industrial experience upon which the War Department could draw. Appley found imbedded in department thinking not merely a misunderstanding of labor conditions and therefore a misconception that the Civil Service Commission owed it the duty of supplying fully qualified workers, but worse, dismissal of responsibility for any civilian employee training.[9] Not only did the department lack top organization for training, but facilities, equipment, and money were wanting. Those facilities actually used at various commands for civilian training were usually diverted from military training by subterfuge.[10] The direct result of Appley's survey was the first statement of policy from the Secretary of War on July 10, 1941, which attached to civilian employee training equal importance with military training. Training was thereby made a function of management and line operations at each level in the hierarchy. At each echelon of authority in the field and departmental service a competent training staff was established through a supplementary policy statement of October 20, 1941. The supplementary statement also provided for a close liaison between the Director of Training in the Office of the Secretary of War and the civilian training officers throughout the echelons or levels of authority, on the one hand, and, on the other, the line administrators of the various divisions or services of the War Department. Training officers were always in a staff relationship to commanding officers. The two statements of 1941 were combined in a new comprehensive summary of policy issued by the Secretary of War on June 30, 1944. From the 1941 statements burgeoned the program which trained approximately 3,000,000 persons, at the rate of about 100,000 each month, in activities varying from a few hours a day to as long as six to nine months of comprehensive instruction.[11]

---

[9] At Frankford Arsenal otherwise qualified machinists were being turned away in 1940 because they could not read drawings and handle precision instruments. Commissioner Flemming visited the arsenal and induced the authorities there to accept recruits and train them at a trade school at the arsenal. CSC, *Circular Letter No. 3083*, November 2, 1940.

[10] Interview with Brown, June 23, 1945.

[11] As reported by Brown, the monthly total was down to a figure between 50,000 and 60,000 by the summer of 1945.

William H. Kushnick,[12] who held the position of Director of Civilian Personnel and Training in the War Department during most of the war period, was brought in to head training activities in particular. He found certain tasks immediately pressing in 1941. It was his responsibility to provide the personal leadership to launch the program successfully. The tasks to be accomplished were to provide consultative service to the forces, services, and commands in the development of their own training programs, to assist in the organization of competent training staffs for the various echelons, and to co-ordinate training activities. Within each force, service, and command the training staff reported to the commanding general and not to the training office in the echelon immediately above it. The problem of training was already acute at that time inasmuch as employees were entering the War Department at the rate of 5,000 per week, a rate stepped up to 15,000 in 1942.[13]

Securing centers for large-scale training activities and a competent staff posed knotty problems. Economy and the need for quality and quantity control dictated the use of large centers in so far as possible or alternatively at large establishments the use of limited facilities around the clock. Vocational schools, factory schools, public institutions, and even private airports were in some instances obtained not only for mechanical facilities but for recruiting teaching personnel. As time passed, training at the installation was more favored, for it could be given more specific direction toward a definite job or assignment. The War Department found in securing instructors and staff members for training that educators, industrial psychologists, and personnel technicians might be taught the work of an installation or that employees who knew the latter might be trained briefly in the techniques of instruction. But the former proved preferable for the administration of training programs. Some of the civilians recruited for the administration of training were commissioned; others remained civilian employees working side by side with the officers.

The training of 3,000,000 employees obviously cost money such as nonmilitary departments would have blanched at requesting and Congress would have boggled at appropriating. But Congress

[12] For fifteen years prior to his War Department work, Kushnick was a plant manager for Anchor-Hocking Glass Co.
[13] As reported by Brown.

thoughfully relieved itself of any anxiety that might have been caused by the knowledge of large amounts going for such unprecedented activities. Surrendering the itemization of training along with that for most War Department programs, it authorized the War Department to finance training from the general departmental appropriation in fiscal 1944, the first blanket authority so granted. This was repeated the following year. This authorization, incidentally, covered the payment of tuition for War Department employees when departmental or public facilities were inadequate. This was known as "contract training," and for internal purposes at first required both a justification from the officer who ordered it and approval of the Director of Personnel. In 1944 authority to approve contract training was delegated to the commanding generals of Air, Ground, and Service Forces with a post-audit by the Director of Personnel.

War Department personnel organization in general, including that for training, differed from that in other departments in the institution of at least three policy levels in Washington. Other departments had but one policy level in Washington. Because the organization of the War Department was so vast and its industrial activities were so various, considerable latitude with respect to programs had to be permitted to the two large forces, ASF and AAF, and less by the forces to the ASF branches, such as Quartermaster General, Adjutant General, Ordnance, etc. The interposition of the middle policy level in the two forces served to bring about an element of uniformity among related types of work and was an advancement over the heterogenous prewar organization of the department.

Military administration on a vast scale like that after Pearl Harbor raised inevitably the necessity for controls to insure compliance with policy directives. The inspection function was located in the Office of the Secretary of War after a preliminary trial in 1942 of a field training consultant and specialist who visited installations to advise the officers in charge and report on their progress. Following up his success, the Office of the Secretary of War furnished a check-list for other training specialists assigned to the field. Eventually a questionnaire was developed in July, 1943, as a yardstick for evaluation of particular phases of a local training program. Expansion of the questionnaire into an inspectional outline to serve the auditing and investigative functions of the field representatives and training specialists completed the development of control instruments by 1944.

Inasmuch as the inspection function was vested in the Washington personnel headquarters, together with the "training of trainers" initially through institutes and the dissemination of much literature on training, the existence of three staff levels is both comprehensible and justifiable. The three levels of personnel offices in Washington were, in fact, much more than mere consultative and policy-making units, for they were an important informational arm for the execution of policy. In that respect they approached the traditional concept held by many students of public administration, that the staff function includes inspection authority, with actual control and enforcement on the basis of staff reports remaining in the hands of the commanding line officers.

Within the operational echelons in the field installations the civilian personnel officer was responsible for the development of all training activities. On behalf of the commanding officer he determined the individuals and groups in need of training, the kinds of training required, the development of facilities for it, the programming of all training activities, and the follow-up to measure the efficacy of training. In large installations the civilian personnel director's staff included a director of training with his own staff. In the event that line supervisors refused to co-operate with either the training director or his chief, the personnel director, the latter appealed to the commanding officer under whom he served directly.[14] The civilian personnel officers possessed no command authority in themselves but could direct only in the name of the highest line officer at the installation.

That there were problems inherent in the dichotomy between military officers in command and civilian personnel as training directors is not to be denied. In many instances commanding officers sought to alleviate the strain by making commissioned officers personnel officers and training officers. In some instances uniformed personnel officers had been in industrial or government personnel management in civilian life; in others they were wholly inexperienced in that field. There was no recourse to correct a bad situation created by poor appointments except the regu-

[14] *Investigation of Civilian Employment*, Part III, Hearing on June 10, 1943, p. 508.

lar command channels. Anyone who spent much time in the Washington War Department civilian personnel offices was inclined to adopt the "horseback" opinion that civilian and military officers were in many cases duplicating each other's work. This opinion was inescapable because some military officers seemed to rely unduly on their civilian assistants who appeared to have the necessary expert knowledge to keep the office running. The military officers seemed to have been placed in charge or superimposed in some cases to satisfy the necessity of securing the co-operation of other military officers in the line of command. Chairman Ramspeck brought this situation into the open in the House investigation of civilian employment through the following colloquy with Kushnick in 1943:

> *The Chairman.* I have wondered . . . why it is necessary, in a purely clerical function, where the work being done is being done by clerks and stenographers and statisticians and those sorts of people, why it is necessary to have all this military set-up on top of it. Have you any ideas about that?
>
> *Mr. Kushnick.* I would say that perhaps the Under Secretary the other day probably gave you as frank an answer as I can give you, and that is, to the extent that in many instances it has been necessary to recruit competent supervision through the inducement of a commission. . . .
> I would say, too, that there are many activities which we may call clerical . . . which are traditional activities of the War Department during peacetimes, and that during peacetimes those jobs are normally the activities of the Army, and that therefore military men perform those in wartimes also.
>
> *The Chairman.* . . . Well, now, frankly, unless some good reason can be given to me, I think it is a lot of bunk. . . . It looks to me like the War Department set up an organization where they have all of the civilian set-up that any other agency would have, and then they superimpose on top of that a lot of commissioned officers. . . .
>
> *Mr. Kushnick.* . . . I would say that essentially that is not correct.
>
> *The Chairman.* Why?
>
> *Mr. Kushnick.* Because I must say this: That I feel the military personnel are performing a job. Whether it should be military or civilian I am not in a position to say here, because I have no discretion as to whether a supervisor, as an example, shall be an officer or civilian, but at least my feeling is that

every one of those officers is doing a job that is necessary in that organization, and therefore I cannot go along by saying that if you remove all of that top structure of military, the rest of the organization could produce without any increase of personnel.

The Chairman. You are a personnel expert. You have had many years' experience in handling personnel. Don't you know that it is not necessary to have 5 high-ranking officers in charge of 326 civilians when you have got at the top an administrative officer CAF-11 and a junior administrative officer CAF-10, with all the complement of supervisors below that? [Description of routine clerical operations in the Office of the Chief of Finance.]

Mr. Kushnick. With the facts as you present them, I would say that it looks as if probably it was not necessary, but to be honest with you I would rather study the facts and bring the story back to you.[15]

Personnel management, and certainly training activities, could not follow the identical organizational pattern to which Chairman Ramspeck alluded in describing the routine clerical operations of the Office of the Chief of Finance. Training activities required more technical specialists in higher classification brackets and fewer lower clerks, but the point at issue before the Ramspeck Committee struck anyone who visited Pentagon personnel offices. To discover whether there was overlapping and duplication as between military and civilian officers would require an intensive personnel investigation such as even the Ramspeck Committee did not make. If such duplication did exist, its justification could not be sought in the exigencies of military organization per se, as will be pointed out later in the discussion of Navy Department personnel organization. It must be sought on other grounds still obscure to the lay investigator.

2. NAVY DEPARTMENT

Although the Navy Department possessed one of the oldest Federal in-service civilian employee training programs in its well-established apprentice system, the administration of training was completely decentralized until the war years. The first move to provide more guidance from headquarters came as result of Executive Order 7916, namely, the establishment of a Training Di-

[15] *Ibid.*, 510-12.

vision in the Division of Personnel Supervision and Management in November, 1939.[16] During 1940 the energies of the Training Division were devoted to the establishment and co-ordination of field training for the mechanical employees, especially in the Navy yards already suffering from shortages of skilled workers. The first policy statement on training was a circular letter on June 24, 1941, leaving responsibility for the establishment and conduct of training programs with each shore activity and placing responsibility for co-ordination of all such programs in the Training Division. Until February, 1945, there was no single departmental policy on training. Instructions were issued from time to time by the Secretary of the Navy on the desirability of training workers for various occupational fields. For example, in-service training was extended from the Navy yards to ordnance and aviation stations in April, 1940. The usual practice at shore establishments was to appoint as training officers members of the Naval Reserve who had acquired years of experience in vocational training.[17]

A complete reorganization of all civilian personnel activities was effected in the spring of 1944. The administration of all civilian personnel of the shore establishments was consolidated into a Division of Shore Establishments and Civilian Personnel, called SECP, under a director responsible to the Secretary of the Navy.[18] Under SECP was the Training Branch. The District Commandants were asked to establish an office similar to SECP in each Naval District. The District Civilian Personnel Director who reported directly to the District Commandant had under him divisions for employment, training, wage and classification, and employee relations. Viewed as a staff adviser at both the district level and the departmental level, the training officers possessed no direct supervision over line officers executing training plans. Nor did the Training Branch in Washington have any supervisory jurisdiction over training officers in the field.

A standardized training policy and program came late in the

[16] From an unpublished report on in-service training prepared in the Training Branch, Shore Establishments and Civilian Personnel, Executive Office of the Secretary, and from an interview with Commander S. L. Owen, Chief of the Training Branch, SECP, on July 6, 1945.

[17] Navy Department, *Navy's Training Program for Civilian Employees* (Washington, 1943), 3.

[18] Navy Department, *Circular Letter, SECP-110: MLM,* District Civilian Personnel Offices, Establishment of, April 6, 1944.

war in the Navy Department. Possibly this failure to standardize early in the crisis was due to the well-established tradition for mechanical training and also the ability of some commandants to carry on satisfactorily alone. Each training officer had been encouraged to use his own ingenuity and initiative to develop a program that would meet local needs.[19] The Training Division had acted in a very limited advisory capacity. Each local program had been shaped not merely by needs but also by facilities and instructional materials available, production pressures, rate of expansion, and the support granted by top management and civilian supervisors. The Training Branch said of these local programs: "Despite the fact that all of the programs were developed amidst wartime confusion and with emphasis on speed, many have proved outstanding but a number have proved only fair."[20]

The first general policy statement on civilian training ever made by Navy, that of February, 1945, was a declaration announcing a standardized program to be launched later in 1945 known as the Navy Work Improvement Program. This was to serve both as a pattern and as a yardstick in evaluating individual programs. Not alone a wartime measure, it was regarded as a permanent plan for on-the-job training, related technical instruction, after-work assignments, and supervisory improvement, and covered the major categories of civilian employees. It was completed for all groups by August 1, 1945.

Navy organization for civilian personnel administration was in striking contrast to that of the War Department. For one thing, there was a single policy level in Navy, that in SECP. Training policies enunciated late in the war were developed in the Training Branch of SECP. Reports from the field came to the Training Branch, and inspections were made by it; the results of both were passed up the line to the Secretary of the Navy. The training staff in Washington was probably not one-tenth the size of that in the War Department although it was engaged in planning for half as many civilian employees, many of whom were engaged in work requiring a higher degree of mechanical skill than that needed in War Department establishments. The size of staff may, however, be attributed to the stress on decentralization and to the

---

[19] Navy Department, *Navy Work Improvement Program*, prepared by the Training Branch, SECP.
[20] *Ibid.*

prolonged lack of standardization of program. In sharp contrast to the staffing of the War Department personnel offices with military officers and civilians working side by side on identical assignments, the Navy practice favored the use of commissioned officers whose civilian experience prior to the war was in industrial and vocational training. The number of civilian training branch employees above the clerical level was comparatively small, and all were assigned to technical phases of the program. Thus military necessity can scarcely have imposed upon it the pattern used by the War Department.

The Navy Department managed to meet its production goals in quite as astonishing a manner as did the War Department despite its long decentralization of training responsibility and its vast expansion of civilian personnel. A factor contributing to its success may well have been the respected tradition recognizing the importance of civilian employee training in the naval program. The War Department, with no roots in the past in that particular area and faced by more acute growing pains, was forced to turn to centralization and standardization when it recognized the problem. In order to get results in the field, therefore, policy had to be enunciated from the highest echelons in the Army in unmistakable terms.

3. THE DEPARTMENT OF AGRICULTURE

Even less than the Navy did the Department of Agriculture change the organization of its training program during the war years. Before the war started, it had a training officer on the Personnel Director's staff, a training council composed of one representative from each bureau which met with the training staff, and a policy.[21] In December, 1944, that policy was redefined in terms of six objectives: (1) the orientation of each employee to the purpose and place of his job in the work of the department and his responsibility in it; (2) instruction of each employee in his job with respect both to what it is and how to do it; (3) provision of an opportunity for each employee to fit himself for the job ahead as well as to develop an understudy to take his place; (4) development of supervisory skills in each supervisor; (5) encouragement in management of a knowledge of the principles and practices of

[21] Interview with Dr. H. E. Eisele, Training Division, Personnel Office, Department of Agriculture, July 11, 1945.

administration; and (6) professional development by providing management with the methods of exercising and developing scientific leadership. Training problems received recognition at regional personnel officers' meetings of the Department of Agriculture.[22]

From the time the department took public cognizance of training needs in 1939, it pursued the policy of locating responsibility for the conduct of on-the-job training in the bureaus, each of which had bureau personnel officers, including usually a bureau training officer. They worked with supervisory officers in an advisory relationship, stimulating their interest in training, setting up standards to evaluate it, and offering concrete suggestions and facilities. The Training Division of the department acted in a staff capacity, standing by to offer consultative services. When the quality of wartime recruits created the need for certain department-wide programs, as in office skills and supervisory training, the Training Division took the initiative in organizing these programs which were actually carried on by the bureaus. For supervisory training the "packaged" program of the "J" courses was adopted and is the one example of a standardized training program in the department. (See Chapter VIII.)

4. OFFICE OF PRICE ADMINISTRATION

If Agriculture stood midway between the military departments at one extreme of standardization of programs, OPA stood at the other end of the scale of complete lack of standardization. Training in OPA was built around the supervisor, and programs were adapted to individual needs in so far as possible in both the field and Washington. OPA declared training and supervision to be identical.[23] The training staff in the departmental personnel office was advisory and followed what it described as a "sophisticated approach" to the problem of employee training.[24] By that OPA meant that training needs had to be postulated upon organizational needs and problems, and training responsibility had to rest in the supervisor. Because supervisors' needs varied with the organizational problems, standardized programs were not con-

---

[22] See *Personnel Officers' Meeting*, St. Louis, November 30-December 4, 1943 (Washington, 1943, mimeographed).

[23] Office of Price Administration, *OPA Manual*, Sec. 8-2202-01.

[24] Interview with William Wolfrey, Training Staff, Personnel Office, OPA, July 17, 1945.

sidered effectual. Whenever a problem presented itself which seemed to indicate the necessity of training, established policy outlined eight steps which had to be followed in the development of a program by the supervisor in consultation with the training staff. They were: (1) to determine the location of need, (2) to select personnel to be trained, (3) to analyze the job requirements, (4) to determine the information and skills needed, (5) to discover and locate sources of needed information and skills, (6) to test the training plan against the organizational environment, (7) to determine the training method, and (8) to appraise the results.

Since the training staff in Washington was very small and flexible, it was assisted by the major line divisions which set up training offices. In the field the regional offices each had a training officer on the staff of the regional personnel director and an enforcement training specialist. In the district offices an OPA enforcement officer (that is, a line officer responsible for the enforcement aspects of OPA rationing, price, or rent control work) served as a training officer. In addition, advisory training committees of operating personnel, with a training officer as executive secretary, were utilized in both the divisions and regional offices. The task of the regional training officers was that of influence, not operations, in persuading the regional executives to fix training responsibility upon their subordinate supervisors. The training officer's role was described as anonymous.[25] "The more fully he succeeds in making supervisors sensitive to training needs and equipped to carry out their responsibilities for training—the more *they* do the less *he* does—the better the training officer."[26] The special responsibility of the training officer was induction of new employees and the office skills training program, because they could be administered centrally in a more efficient manner.

The changing nature of OPA programs required considerable retraining in addition to the training of new employees. One member of the Washington training staff was assigned to review all regulations and directives put out by the agency in order to analyze and isolate resultant training needs. By conferences with regional executives, problems in training were brought out into the open and past efforts criticized and evaluated. Some written

[25] *OPA Manual,* 8-2202.03.   [26] *Ibid.*

materials were developed by the central office training staff, especially memoranda for management training. A regular fortnightly bulletin was also issued to aid in the training of volunteer workers, so vital to OPA administration. The latter was written by individuals in the appropriate operating division although issued by the Personnel Division.

OPA training was postulated upon the assumption that effective training was geared to particular jobs and was not a broadside attack. The novelty, complexity, and sudden mutations of its own tasks reinforced that assumption. Likewise, for work involving a high degree of administrative skill and professional training, as for example in law, economics, or statistics, this assumption seems valid. On the other hand, for direct mechanical production by shifting armies of low-grade inexperienced employees, broadside attacks developed to a high degree of standardization have an obvious value. Whether or not the OPA training program was "sophisticated," the training staff appeared to have possessed considerable sophistication and acumen in differentiating its training problem from that of the other agencies and in pioneering an individualistic approach to it. However, there seemed to be a latent danger in that approach. Because all supervisors did not have a common frame of reference with respect to training and the training staff had to spread itself very thinly to render individual assistance, it was difficult to avoid superficiality. Standardized programs for training may offer much less than a fundamental answer to the training problem, but they can at least provide a uniform frame of reference.

Conclusions

Into the vacuum in 1941 and 1942 rushed those agencies ground between the pressures for high production based on reasonably good performance and the continuously deteriorating quality of recruits. One of these, the War Department, had neither organization nor tradition for civilian training activities, and another, OPA, just born in 1942, faced tasks so new that whatever it established for training purposes had to be done empirically. Two others, Navy and Agriculture, had recognized traditions for the conduct of training programs. The latter even had an organization with principal responsibility for programs delegated to the bureaus of the department which were to act within a departmental policy statement. OPA built both the organization and the policy in the beginning which it carried through the war. The Navy Department, which had long been satisfied with complete decentralization of operation and lack of standardization in training programs, finally ended the war with an organization for control purposes and with a completely standardized program. The War Department, at first blind to the civilian employee training demands, marshalled the best talents it could find in industry and education in the training field and mobilized them to help it set up a complex organization, once it recognized the problem. Elaborate standardized programs encompassing all types of training activities were formulated by the two chief services, ASF and AAF, and financed out of the general funds appropriated to the department.

On the whole, War and Navy Department experience points out that training activities in a large organization embracing many varieties of occupational skills, many of them manual in type, required clear policy statements and a well-defined organization. Policy had to come from the highest echelons through an organization at the center to advise and assist local establishments. Their experience also pointed to the value of standardized training programs enforced by such controls as adequate reporting media and regular inspections. But a large professional staff engaged principally in professional and technical research activity resented interference and too definite a training policy coming from the center of the organization as much as it resisted uniformity and the controls to enforce it. Therefore, the Department of Agriculture and, to a much greater extent, OPA had to allow their principal organizational units considerable autonomy in training activities. The more unique and technical the activity, the more individualistic the approach and decentralized the responsibility appeared to be the rule in the training field. Clearly there was no one answer to the kind of departmental organization and policy for employee training that was needed in the Federal government.

CHAPTER EIGHT

Development of Training Programs

DIVERSE AS were training policies and the organization to effect them, training programs fell into seven principal categories: (1) preservice, (2) orientation or induction, (3) apprenticeship, (4) instruction in basic mechanical skills and for upgrading, (5) instruction in office skills, (6) supervisory training, and (7) administrative internship. One of these types, preservice, was uncommon outside the War and Navy departments. Another, supervisory training, was frequently given in a "packaged" program—that is, by neat formulae prepared materials were presented uniformly in a concentrated dosage throughout an agency. But almost all were distinguished by specific adaptations to the peculiar needs of each agency, even in the case of "packaged" programs. At least two types of training attacked areas of weakness in Federal administration, the lack of systematic supervisory and administrative training. For that reason, if for no other, they carried potentialities of great usefulness for the future of public personnel administration and established important precedents for permanent postwar advances.

Zealots for training may be inclined to urge training for the sake of training because they believe so firmly in the value of their wares. The urgency of war and lack of vitally needed skills among those recruited in the wartime labor market combined to rule out nonessential training activities, however earnestly advocated. Since there were specific positions to be filled in the government service, training had to be particularized to supply the exact skills and abilities required within a minimum time. The tendency was, therefore, for wartime training programs to become intensely practical. Industry had long justified training activities on the basis of their contribution to profits. Government in war justified them on the basis of their contribution to productivity. Training which did not serve that purpose could not be rationalized. That is not to say, however, that all training was designed for discrete positions, for much was general in applicability.

Preservice and Contract Training

Leaving out of consideration the defense training courses sponsored by the Office of Education, NYA, and WPA because they were designed to prepare participants for industrial as well as for governmental work, preservice training was largely confined to the War and Navy departments. The reason for this limitation was simple: Congress generally disapproved payment for the training of recruits by private agencies. Only sheer desperation and their own lack of specialized facilities led the War and Navy departments to utilize this type of training, and it was carefully controlled by the requirement of justifications and by audits.[1]

Preservice training was commonly referred to as contract training because the employing agency entered into a contract for the payment of tuition for a fixed period per recruit assigned to a private school or factory for specialized instruction. During the training period the recruit received the salary of the trainee grade or wages at the hourly rate of the mechanic-learner. Upon satisfactory completion of the course of instruction he was upgraded to the full entrance salary for the regular grade for which he had been recruited. Of course, not all contract training was preservice. Sometimes selected employees already in the service were sent to schools for special instruction.

Forest Products Laboratory at Madison, Wisconsin, was one of the institutions most generally utilized by the War and Navy departments for contract training. The Navy[2] and Army Service Forces,[3] Ordnance,[4] and the Quartermaster General's Office[5] were among the chief clients of this service to train their own supervisors as trainers in palletizing[6] and packaging all the material of war for storage and overseas shipment. Many trade schools en-

---

[1] See Chapter VII.
[2] Interview with Lt. Roy Fornwalt, SECP, Training Branch, Navy Department, July 7, 1945.
[3] Interview with Lt. Col. Everett Conover, ASF, Civilian Personnel Division, Training Branch, July 5, 1945.
[4] Interview with W. C. Williams, Civilian Personnel Division, Training Branch, Ordnance, ASF, War Department, July 3, 1945.
[5] Interview with M. Yetter Schoch, Training Branch, Office of the Quartermaster General, ASF, July 4, 1945.
[6] Palletizing means packing a number of boxes or crates into one unit on a wooden pallet which is stored, moved by rail or freighter, and taken out of the ship's hold for unloading at an overseas depot exactly as put together.

gaging in the instruction of airplane mechanics and repairmen, and even plane manufacturers, were employed on a contract basis by the Army Air Forces, especially in 1942 and 1943 when the pressures for plane servicing were running high and the supply of trained mechanics had been exhausted.[7] For example, AAF employees were sent to Boeing Aircraft to learn the repair and servicing of B-29's to prepare for the widespread use of that plane.[8] General Motors Institute was utilized by many branches of ASF for maintenance instruction for trucks and other kinds of motorized equipment.[9] The Navy took advantage of all emergency programs for contract instruction, especially for the training of welders and machinists.[10] Radio and radar technicians and repairmen were trained by the Bell Laboratories to become government instructors.

Impatience with the number and caliber of stenographer and typist recruits enlisted by the Civil Service Commission led AAF to employ preservice contract training in that field from 1943 to the end of the war.[11] The Commission still supplied the recruits who were appointed as trainees and assigned to business schools for the completion of abbreviated streamlined courses of eight to twelve weeks. In no other agency was this type of training employed for stenographers and typists.

Because it was too difficult to control, contract training did not meet with general acclaim in the War Department.[12] For all but marginal areas or highly technical work it was not recommended by the Quartermaster General's Office and was used but sparingly. This attitude prevailed in that branch despite the great variety of resources available for training purposes under contract training. Generally in-service training was deemed much more satisfactory on all sides even if outside specialists had to be hired as instructors for brief periods.

---

[7] Interview with Lt. Col. F. L. Miller, AAF, Civilian Personnel Division, Training Branch, July 2, 1945.

[8] Interview with Lee P. Brown, OSW, Civilian Personnel Division, Training Branch, June 23, 1945.

[9] Interview with Miss Arlein Brown, ASF, Civilian Personnel Division, Training Branch, July 5, 1945.

[10] Interview with Lt. Fornwalt, July 7, 1945.

[11] Interview with Lt. Col. Miller, July 2, 1945.

[12] Interview with Dr. John C. Duff, Office of the Quartermaster General, Training Branch, July 4, 1945.

Orientation of New Employees

The wartime influx of new Federal employees, many of whom had never before been subjected to the discipline of daily work in a compensated position, required a planned introduction to their new status as Federal employees. In normal prewar years new employees filtered into the organization gradually, and departments felt less constrained to design a uniform introduction to the agency and its work. The burden could be and usually was left to individual supervisors, some of whom performed this task acceptably. But during the long war period supervisors were themselves often new and inexperienced in government employment. Leaving induction to them would have meant leaving it to chance. Further, it was more economical to standardize it where large numbers were involved.

Induction of new employees during wartime also required their indoctrination in the significance of their own tasks with reference to the work of the entire employing agency and the total war effort. Orientation was also of substantive concern to the employee relations staff as well as to the training staff inasmuch as most new employees required information respecting housing, transportation, food, and recreational facilities in the community.[13] When turnover was an acute problem, recruits needed practical solutions to pressing extraemployment problems at the outset of their employment. The new worker had to fit himself into the scheme of things with his fellow workers, his community, and his nation.

The Civil Service Commission through the Federal Work Improvement Program developed orientation suggestions for both agency personnel offices and for supervisors. Among the steps they recommended that the personnel office should take were induction interviews on the day of entry into the service; group meetings the first week, featuring both an official welcome to the agency from a top executive and talks explaining the organization, functions, and responsibilities of the agency and its relationships with other parts of the Federal government; and explanations of the personnel office and its services, the privileges, rights, and responsibilities of employees, and community facilities in the fields of education, recreation, religion, finance, commerce, culture,

---

[13] CSC, *Guide for Orienting New Employees,* Part I, January 3, 1945.

athletics, and the like. In addition, the Commission stressed the desirability of follow-up activities on the part of the training officers, counselor, and placement officer at regular intervals during the first few months of service.

Other aspects of orientation the Commission proposed as part of the supervisor's responsibility, as, for example, getting ready for the new employee, making him welcome and introducing him, and describing the work of the unit and its organization, its special rules, and his own work assignment.[14] Supervisors were likewise advised to "follow through" by means of additional instruction, coaching, appraisal and explanation of the standards of performance, culminating in the review of the first efficiency rating with the employee.

The War and Navy departments, as well as the Department of Agriculture, used film material extensively to explain the respective operations in their departments. From November, 1941, all new Navy civilian employees in the departmental service were required to attend six one-hour sessions for indoctrination in the history, work, and organization of the Navy Department, its role in the world, the uniform insignia, and even in the building of naval vessels. Each new employee was also welcomed by a letter from the Secretary of the Navy. On all sides employee handbooks were recognized as a useful collateral orientation instrument, summarizing such information as civil service rules, agency employee relations and grievance policy, and agency organization by means of charts. Each Navy yard and shore establishment not only produced its own employee handbook but designed its own orientation program using the film materials it desired from the list recommended by the Training Branch.

An individualistic reversal of the usual procedure was demonstrated by the Quartermaster General's Office in scheduling an orientation course of six hours divided into three sessions sometime after the employee had been inducted into the establishment.[15] Supervisors assumed the responsibility for the immediate phases of orientation by appointing a sponsor, an older employee to act as host for each new recruit. Orientation into the actual working assignment was the immediate supervisor's own responsibility, that into the division's body of knowledge and

---

[14] *Ibid.*, Part II, January 3, 1945.   [15] Interview with Schoch, July 4, 1945.

rules the task of the division's administrative assistant for training, and that into the installation by the regular course of group meetings at the end of the first few weeks the responsibility of the training staff assisted by all branches of the personnel office.

Employment of women at manual labor in the Navy yards raised new orientation problems inasmuch as few of the new female employees had any prior experience in heavy industry. Since many were not possessed of confidence in themselves in this strange setting, importance was attached to discovering their I.Q.'s and aptitudes immediately in order to train them properly at the outset and provide suitable placement. Safety regulations had to be especially stressed through both lectures and films, suitable dress for manual labor was explained, and selected women employees of demonstrated success in the yard were pointed out to inspire confidence in the tyros.[16] After three days of tests and lectures the personnel office was ready to make a placement in a vestibule shop to accustom the women to the noise, atmosphere, and hazards before they were sent out as helper-trainees to the main shops.

Apprentice Training

Apprentice training is still the only accepted method of learning the skilled trades. Although ordinarily referred to in connection with the training sponsored by labor unions, it was utilized in the training of skilled mechanics by both the Navy and the Army Air Forces. By apprenticeship is meant a long period, that is, three to four years, of tutelage in all the component skills which make up such trades as machinist, electrician, or shipfitter. For generations the Navy yards of this country have provided apprentice training, but the modern apprentice schools providing both classroom instruction and practical shop experience date from 1912.

War shortened and diluted the quality of Navy apprenticeship training just as the caliber of apprentices deteriorated,[17] but the basic program was retained. This was due to two factors: one, that Navy yard work is, in part, based upon skills that defy job

[16] Interview with Comdr. S. L. Owen, SECP, Training Branch, July 6, 1945.
[17] Before the war at one yard, out of 12,000 to 15,000 applicants for apprentice training, 10,000 made the eligible list, but only 500 were actually selected. During the war 100 per cent who applied made the eligible list and 100 per cent were selected. Interview with Lieut. Fornwalt, July 7, 1945.

dilution for conversion to assembly-line production methods, and the other, that those in charge of training at the various yards were deeply convinced of the value of apprentice training in a well-balanced Navy program.[18] Selected by competitive civil service examinations administered semiannually, apprentices had to be within the age range of sixteen to twenty-two years, for their school work was in part a continuation of high school work. Before the war they were paid during the four-year training period at the rate of $3.20 per day the first year up to $6.08 during the last year. One week out of every four was spent in the classroom studying such subjects as English, civics, mathematics, physics, and mechanical drawing. Formal school totaled 1,100 hours, and the remainder of the training time on a five-day week basis was devoted to shop training. Originally up to 1938 the number of apprentices in each trade was limited to 20 per cent of the journeyman mechanics in that trade, but this percentage was never attained.[19] Early in 1941 the four years of training was translated into 8,000 hours or the equivalent of the number formerly spent learning the skills of the trade because most apprentices were scheduled for a six-day work week by that time. The next step, taken on December 11, 1942, was the reduction of time for apprenticeship to a straight three years with a correlative reduction in the number of hours in shop instruction. The new program was called War Time Apprentice Training Program. Apprentices thereafter spent every fourth day in the classroom and the remainder of their time under the immediate supervision of a carefully selected skilled journeyman working on production jobs in the proper learning sequence. Working a forty-eight hour week and paid regular overtime, they started at $4.64 per day, which was increased by $0.96 per day on the completion of each quarter of training. The total wartime program covered 5,448 hours, with 1,362 in school attendance. Thus it was evident that the time spent in acquiring mastery of manual skills suffered. Only boys were accepted as apprentices, and those away from home were housed in separate government dormitories away from older employees at some Navy yards. Twenty shipyard trades were taught in most Navy apprentice schools.

Under the Navy Work Improvement Program adopted in 1945

[18] Interview with Comdr. Owen, July 6, 1945. [19] *Ibid.*

the age range established was sixteen to nineteen years except for veterans for whom the age limits were waived.[20] Convinced of the value of the prewar four-year course, the Navy waited impatiently to return to it. Commander S. L. Owen, director of the Training Branch in SECP and formerly in charge of training at the Mare Island Navy Yard, declared that war had proved the value of apprenticeship training in that the men so trained, only 5,000 all told, rapidly upgraded to supervisory and instructor positions in the yards, were the nucleus for the wartime training program. On the other hand, those trained in the three-year course were often substandard in caliber and had not received sufficient time for practice or assimilation of the information taught. The near wrecking of the apprenticeship program was attributed by naval officers to the "infantry complex" of the Selective Service System which never appreciated Navy's construction requirements.

In contrast to the Navy Department's program, Army Air Forces' apprenticeship program, which had provided a small number of workers in its shorter life span, was an early wartime casualty. Job dilution was the only recourse for AAF to complete the production work required of it. That type of work lent itself to job breakdown and simplification. Before the end of the war AAF laid plans for an early return to a three- or four-year apprenticeship for maintenance mechanics with less classroom work than was provided by the Navy. Plans for rebuilding the apprenticeship program were predicated upon the expectation that AAF civilian tasks would be primarily those of maintenance. The AAF was firmly convinced of the long-term values of apprenticeship training to the force.[21]

Training in Mechanical Skills and for Upgrading

Effective training of several millions of labor force employees would have been well-nigh impossible without job dilution in order to shorten the training period and get workers into production. There were certain analytical steps in the training process which had to precede dilution of any set of operations. First of all, the capacity—that is, the knowledge, skill, background, aptitudes, and attitudes of the trainee group—had to be estimated.

---

[20] CSC, *Circular Letter No. 4282*, May 24, 1945.
[21] Interview with Lt. Col. Miller, July 2, 1945.

162   IMPACT OF WAR ON FEDERAL PERSONNEL

Then the maximum period of time allowable for training was computed on the basis of the operating schedule. Training deadlines had to be met to satisfy production deadlines. That done, the average degree of skill feasible for trainees to acquire during the training period was computed as well as the level of work the trainees could be expected to produce with the allowable degree of training. Only then could the work itself be adapted to the workers' capacity. In other words, both time elements and worker capacity had to be the known elements precedent to job dilution.[22] By careful preliminary studies for simplification it was possible to adapt tasks, and more specifically their tools, to the capacities of both the physically handicapped and women workers, when necessary, and then to plan training intelligently. Exactly the same techniques were employed to train Arabs, Iranians, and other overseas civilian employees engaged in maintenance work for the Army abroad.

The Civil Service Commission had recommended job dilution for the consideration of personnel officers in mechanical production establishments as early as September, 1940.[23] Repeatedly it called the attention of employing agencies to the steady deterioration in examination requirements and the fact that the work of their organizations would suffer unless in-service training were instituted to overcome deficient qualifications.[24] Paralleling these efforts to stimulate interest in training were exhortations to explore the possibilities of employing women and to prepare the concomitant training programs necessary to make them effective employees.[25]

More than 3,000,000 civilian employees were trained by the War Department from 1940 to 1944, almost all of whom were totally inexperienced and required training in the entire task to which they were assigned. At least 75,000 employees received initial training every month during 1943 and an additional 25,000 to 40,000 training for upgrading. The War Department

[22] Interview with Lee P. Brown, June 23, 1945.
[23] CSC, *Circular Letter No. 3024*, September 14, 1940.
[24] CSC, *Departmental Circular No. 262*, June 3, 1941; *Circular Letters No. 3415*, September 16, 1941, and *No. 3550*, January 21, 1942; and *Memorandum to Heads of All Departments from the Three Commissioners as to Federal Recruiting Policies*, February 8, 1943.
[25] CSC, *Departmental Circular No. 266*, June 16, 1941, and *Circular Letter No. 3377*, August 16, 1941.

DEVELOPMENT OF TRAINING PROGRAMS 163

preferred training at the installation and on the job when that was possible without prohibitive expense from spoilage of materials.

Training had to be a continuous process in order to meet a major personnel problem, that of turnover. But, in addition, ASF emphasized that training officers must search incessantly in present and anticipated operating problems for training needs.[26] That is, they had to look to production quotas, changes in emphasis in production, and to the quality of work to determine training programs. Such programs, therefore, required a follow-up to see that instruction was utilized and supplemented where necessary as well as to discover where it was defective. ASF held it to be basically maladroit to look negatively at poor production records, absenteeism, and high turnover.[27] Better regarded was the positive effort to assess in advance the specific skills employees needed to develop for adequate performance and to work through the supervisors to ascertain how much training they could give at the work location and how much had to be given in some other place by regular specialist instructors in formal courses. In this way training activity in 1945 had to be geared to 1945 changes in jobs and personnel, not to a 1942 or 1943 situation. Once present and future needs were analyzed, training activity could be programmed exactly and a timetable made to insure a steady flow of trainees.[28] Successful skills training was custom built, it was discovered, not fixed for all time or designed a priori.

Ordnance in the War Department stressed not merely the aforementioned approach but the need for original placement on a job a recruit could perform with simple on-the-job training. Supervisors were to follow initial training with continuous testing and training for upgrading.[29] Job breakdowns were required of supervisors for instructional purposes, as well as training timetables and job assignment timetables. The objectives of training were not merely to bring all employees up to standard performance but to impart a versatility of skills to take care of variable factors, such as illness, leave, and separations as well as sudden rush orders. Toward versatility office workers were given general

[26] ASF Manual, Civilian Training, *Guide for Commanding Officers, M205,* June 6, 1944, p. 2.
[27] ASF, *Civilian Personnel Officers Handbook, M212,* April, 1945, p. 22.
[28] *Ibid.,* 24. [29] Interview with Williams, July 3, 1945.

training in manual operations so that they might be employed in such emergencies as required immediate loading of boxcars and similar tasks. Some ordnance training which should have been given over a four-year period, such as optical and firearms manufacture, maintenance and repair of telescopic gun sights, and ammunition inspection, were stripped to the bare essentials and telescoped by means of institutes into intensive twelve-week, fourteen-hour per day courses. Significantly, safety training was not administered separately but was intrinsic in all ordnance training on the theory that the right way is the safe way. Bad habits were caught by the supervisor and corrected in his follow-up.[30] The employment of women did not allegedly cause any difference in training procedures inasmuch as proper placement took care of sex differences in aptitudes. At many ordance tasks women were found easier to train because they had more manual dexterity, were quicker, and sat at repetitive tasks with less irritation. Strong, muscular women could be as easily trained as men to run heavy equipment like fork-lift trucks.

No less spectacular results were obtained by AAF through the application of job dilution to its production work and maintenance. Some prewar training that had been given by outside agencies, public and private schools, and had taken two years was transferred to air bases, installations, and depots, broken down, simplified, resimplified, and progressively reduced in time first to six months, then twelve weeks, and by 1944 and 1945 to a few days or even in some cases a few hours.[31]

Essentially the same thing happened in the Navy yards and other shore establishments. For example, the basic elements of welding were streamlined into a course covering a few weeks taught to both men and women through lectures and actual practice under supervisors.[32] A course in experimental welding for upgrading, that is testing, analysis, and specialty welding, followed a similar pattern for those with special aptitudes. Cable sealing was taught in six days through streamlined methods of instruction. Instructors were secured by the Navy yards from all relevant

---

[30] Ordnance maintained that it was safer to work in an ammunition plant than at street repair work as 88 per cent of all accidents could be controlled by proper training in the correct work procedure which they attempted to give.

[31] Interview with Lt. Col. Miller, July 2, 1945.

[32] Interview with Comdr. Owen, July 6, 1945.

DEVELOPMENT OF TRAINING PROGRAMS

trades, trained as teachers, employed in the trainee schools for upgrading, and paid six cents per hour additional for teaching over and above the comparable rates paid those working in the shops in the same tasks. Supervisors selected recruits rated as first-class mechanics or "snappers" for training as job instructors. The trades trainee schools included five days each week of shop work and one day of classroom work. Those who completed the courses for upgrading were soon rerated to mechanics third-class. By the spring of 1944 there were no age limits or educational requirements for admittance to the schools, and women trainees were in the majority at many shore establishments.[33] As was true of Ordnance in the War Department, the Navy integrated safety training with job instruction except for women employees who required special preliminary instructions on suitable work costume, coiffure, and behavior, usually given during orientation. Supervisors had to devote special attention to safety instruction for expectant mothers, who were encouraged to retain their jobs as long as possible.

Training in Office Skills

The collapse of standards for stenographers and typists compelled even such conservative agencies as the State Department to establish training courses for the development of basic office skills. Often such courses were euphemistically labeled "refresher" classes although many employees entered them innocent of previous training.[34] The Commission in 1942 suggested not only the need for the establishment of these courses in all agencies but the desirability of agency retention of experienced teachers of stenography and typing already in the Federal service for summer vacation employment. In specialized fields, particularly as of tabulating equipment and teletype operation, the Commission secured the co-operation of International Business Machines Corporation and of American Telephone and Telegraph Company to instruct trainees properly in the use of their respective equip-

---

[33] Trades taught and time to complete training were: machinist 35 weeks, shipfitter 43 weeks, electrician 43 weeks, sheet-metal worker 32 weeks, and pipefitter 30 weeks.

[34] This euphemism was doubtless adopted to allay Congressional antipathy against providing training which Congress felt recruits should have acquired prior to employment.

ment. It was left to the departments to act upon their proposals.[35]

Classroom instruction usually for an hour daily during working hours was the training arrangement commonly utilized in the subjects of typing and stenography for those persons recommended by their supervisors as standing in need of skills improvement. Even as late as 1942, however, the Navy Department provided classroom teaching after working hours as departmental rules then forbade training on-the-job. It was, nevertheless, soon forced to change the rule and move the classes into the scheduled hours of employment.[36] Most classroom instruction was predicated on the traditional approach of the business schools that a standard speed must be attained by trainees regardless of the type of work performed.

Two agencies evolved a different approach to the determination of the intensity of instruction. One was the Navy Department, which in its Work Improvement Program advocated classroom work merely for basic information, drill, and practice, followed up by further training under the supervisors through production pools and "at the desk" training in specific information, job skills improvement, procedures and methods, and for upgrading. In addition, the new Navy program organized developmental office training on an internship pattern with rotation of assignments to provide a career basis in secretarial work.

The other agency which departed from the traditional pattern for classroom instruction was the Adjutant General's Office in the War Department, which, although using that medium, requested an indication on a check list from the supervisors of the specific skills in which the employee was deficient and the purpose for which they were required. For one and one-half hours daily the instructors concentrated attention in class on improving the skills to the point which represented required performance in that particular item of work rather than in building speed up to an arbitrary level which might have no reference to adequacy in performance.[37]

Although not much was done with strictly clerical training, the

[35] CSC, *Departmental Circulars No. 353*, July 9, 1942, and *No. 316*, February 10, 1942.
[36] Interview with Lt. Earl P. Strong, Navy Department, SECP, Training Branch, Field Service Section, July 7, 1945.
[37] Interview with Dr. Charles Bish, ASF, Adjutant General's Office, Civilian Personnel Division, Training Branch, July 5, 1945.

Department of Agriculture Graduate School was compelled by wartime demands made by a different category of employee from their prewar professional clientele to offer courses in administrative procedures of a semiclerical nature.[38] Many war service employees sought courses which would provide them with vocational techniques for upgrading rather than with the principles of administration. For example, during the spring of 1942 and 1943 the Graduate School offered special war training courses in procedures in government accounting, audit clerk, personnel procedures, and multilith operation. The effect upon its regular offerings was to force the school to establish two levels for the study of administrative procedures, especially in the personnel and budgetary fields.

Supervisory Training

Long neglected by any formal attention, supervisory training was forced to the forefront in all Federal employee training programs. The fact, if not ignored, was usually glossed over that the first-line supervisor is the linchpin of both production and sound personnel administration. Normally, however, because promotion was slow in most government establishments, supervisors knew thoroughly the work being supervised and had so few new employees coming into their units at any one time that the tasks of supervision somehow were performed in a manner that enabled departments to carry on their business. When the pressures of crisis administration accumulated in 1941 and 1942 and hordes of recently inexperienced employees bolted upward into supervisory ranks simply because they had learned to do a simple task, training officers everywhere were forced to face the fact that the supervisor held the key to job performance as the most important trainer in any organization. He had to be equipped to do his job or the whole structure was in danger of breakdown.

The weakness of the supervisor in performing the tasks of training and handling employee relations was pointed out by a special investigating committee under Senator Allen J. Ellender in 1939 and 1940.[39] The Ellender Committee heard a staggering

[38] Interview with Dr. Eldon Johnson, Director of the Department of Agriculture Graduate School, July 24, 1945.

[39] U.S. Congress, Senate, Hearings on *Investigation of the Administration and Operation of Civil Service Laws,* 76th Cong., 1st Sess. and 3d Sess., Part I, 1939, and Part II, 1940.

number of grievances from many employees who from the evidence appeared to be neurotic, if not borderline mental cases. The hearings did serve to emphasize the supervisory problem, however, if nothing else. Again and again the hearings made clear that supervisors were usually promoted to that position because they were excellent producers of work but were unable to teach others their "know how." In some final meetings the committee held in 1940 with a number of Federal personnel directors to summarize the evidence and point out remedies, this exchange came to the heart of the problem:

> *Mr. Piozet* [Navy Department Civilian Personnel Director]. I just want a minute to say that the average production supervisor is not a trained personnel technician. That is the whole trouble with the Government service. They are hired primarily to get the work out. Apparently there is room for a tremendous training program of Government supervisors. However, the Appropriations Committee has not been sold on it yet. That means extra personnel and added expenses to the government. . . .[40]
>
> *Mr. Short* [Commerce Department]. . . . And you spoke of a magic formula a few minutes ago. The only magic formula is to train this first line supervisor to deal with his subordinates and handle the human cases right there, and do not make any necessity for them to go beyond that point. And the things that he must have, he does not have now, but they are things that can be taught him. . . .
>
> *The Chairman.* In your experience, have you found many instances in which the fault lay with the supervisor and not with the subordinate?
>
> *Mr. Short.* I suspect in most instances it is fundamentally with the supervisor rather than with the worker.
>
> *The Chairman.* I have found that to be true.
>
> *Mr. Short.* Pardon me. I do not want to leave the impression that they are at fault. They just do not know.[41]

Chairman Ramspeck of the House Civil Service Committee[42]

---

[40] *Ibid.*, Part II, Hearing on May 9, 1940, p. 772.
[41] *Ibid.*, Part II, Hearing on May 10, 1940, pp. 870-71.
[42] U.S. Congress, House, Hearings on *A Bill to Amend Section 13 of the Classification Act of 1923, as Amended*, 77th Cong., 1st Sess., December 16, 17, and 18, 1941, p. 55.

and Commissioner Flemming[43] agreed that the signal weakness in the Federal government was the lack of competent supervision. But there was no organized attack upon the source of that weakness, namely, lack of systematic training of supervisors, until the War Manpower Commission blazed the trail for industry through the "J" courses sponsored by the Training Within Industry Branch.[44] As a matter of fact, the principles in the "J" courses had been employed for many years in those industries distinguished by systematic training policies, but they were "packaged" by the Training Within Industry Branch and promoted intensively throughout the nation.

Three in number, the "J" courses were so called because of their titles: Job Instruction Training or JIT, Job Methods Training or JMT, and Job Relations Training or JRT. The first was designed to teach supervisors how to instruct workers, the second, how to improve work methods of procedures, and the third, how to work with employees. Instruction manuals were published for the three courses by the Civil Service Commission together with illustrative materials, such as sample job breakdown sheets and training timetables. When the courses were actually given to first-line supervisors, the essential information was condensed on small cards easily carried in pockets or billfolds and readily accessible. Based on the long-known four-step teaching method advocated by Frank Cushman and Charles R. Allen, JIT demonstrated instruction by teaching a very simple mechanical operation. Supervisors were thus instructed how to prepare the employee, to present the job by telling and showing one step at a time, to have the employee try out the operation and explain the what, why, and how of it, and to follow up by checking and encouraging the employee after he had been placed on his own. These procedures constituted the four steps. JMT, centered about a simple mechanical operation, showed how to break down a job in its existing methods, step by step, to question every detail, to develop a new work method by eliminating, combining, rearranging, and simplifying, and how to apply the new method after it had been "sold" to the next higher supervisor and to the employees. The basic

---

[43] U.S. Congress, House, Hearing on *Independent Offices Appropriation Bill, 1945*, 78th Cong., 2nd Sess., December 9, 1943, p. 1033.

[44] Transferred from Federal Security Agency to War Manpower Commission by Executive Order 9247, September 17, 1942.

principles of JRT, designed to handle individual cases or problems in human relations, were also arranged in a four-step plan: get the facts, weigh and decide the justice of the matter, take action, and check results. JRT principles to promote good employee relations were to tell the employees how they were getting along, to give credit where it was due, to make the most of each person's ability, and to inform employees of changes that affected them.[45]

Through institutes or sessions to "train the trainers" the Civil Service Commission spread the supervision improvement program as far as it could throughout the Federal government. The matter of co-operation by the departments was voluntary, but the Commission offered its facilities to assist agencies which desired help.[46] If the latter indicated a desire to learn the elements of the "J" courses, a Commission representative presented a condensed version of the courses at a meeting with the departmental head and his staff. Upon a request to secure the program, the Commission conducted ten-hour institutes in Washington for the development of agency trainers in the departmental service and in the field for field office trainers. Once a corps of agency trainers was schooled by a Commission institute, it carried the "J" program down through the department, "training the trainers" in all branches until the principles were conveyed to the first-line supervisors. Responsibility for maintaining quality control was the problem of the co-operating department. The program did not really spread to the field offices of the Commission in full strength until late in 1944, although it was started in the fall of 1943.

By the end of 1944 thousands of Federal supervisors had been reached by these courses. Commissioner Flemming testified to the House Appropriations Committee that 26 JIT institutes had been conducted in 1944 for approximately 260 agency representatives, who then trained 13,000 supervisory officers.[47] In JMT 290 agency representatives had been trained and had passed the training along to 14,500 supervisors. JRT had been given to 130 agency representatives by whom 6,500 supervisors had been

---

[45] CSC, *A Program for Supervisors in the Federal Service*, Federal Work Improvement Program, Examining and Personnel Utilization Division.

[46] CSC, *Departmental Circular No. 430*, August 2, 1943.

[47] U.S. Congress, House, Hearing on *Independent Offices Appropriation Bill, 1946*, 79th Cong., 1st Sess., January 17, 1945, p. 1193.

DEVELOPMENT OF TRAINING PROGRAMS 171

trained. These figures do not tell the whole story, for JIT had been well started in 1943 and JRT was just getting into full stride by the end of 1944.

Army Service Forces was probably the most extensive user of the "J" courses, receiving them directly from TWI. Top management in ASF was not at first convinced of the value of the "J" program but had to be persuaded of its worth by the training staff. Once adopted, the program was elaborated by seven films developed by ASF to be used in teaching the courses and by its own JRT manual.[48] Reversing the usual order, ASF started with JRT as the first course on the theory that man-to-man relations were of major importance. Two weeks after JRT had been given, JIT followed, with JMT a month after JIT.[49]

One lesson soon learned in the vast organization of ASF was that a follow-up on the "J" courses, especially JIT, had to be undertaken by the training staff. A follow-up was needed to discover how much and what part of the instruction every employee needed fell within the reasonable capacity of the supervisor to give.[50] Equally it was necessary to see that supervisors actually made job breakdowns, used the four-step method in teaching and the other tools of supervision with which they had been provided.[51] Follow-up procedure through conferences had to be continuous and a part of the courses themselves; if neglected, supervisors tended to forget by disuse the principles learned. Ordnance required that supervisors who had not learned to apply the principles taught must retake the course, costly as that requirement was.[52]

During the latter part of the war ASF attempted to control the quality of instruction in "J" courses by requiring certification of trainers to qualify them to run institutes. A fourth course for trainers alone in conference leadership was added to the repertory.[53] "Conference" took on a somewhat different meaning from that ordinarily used, and in Army circles connoted teaching by the Socratic or discussion method.

[48] Interview with Carl Hawk, ASF, Personnel Division, Training Branch, July 5, 1945.
[49] ASF Manual, Civilian Training, *Guide for Commanding Officers*, M205, p. 7.
[50] ASF Manual, *Civilian Personnel Officers Handbook*, M212, p. 22.
[51] *Ibid.*, 26.   [52] Interview with Williams, July 3, 1945.
[53] Interview with Hawk, July 5, 1945.

172   IMPACT OF WAR ON FEDERAL PERSONNEL

Army Air Forces, on the other hand, took the principles of the "J" courses, which really covered fifteen two-hour sessions with supervisors, and converted them into twenty-six two-hour sessions. Theirs was a more elaborate "package," fancifully illustrated and underlined by more films than ASF developed. Also added were lessons on conference leadership, the technique of administering a reprimand, the functions of management, developing morale, managing time, and developing an understudy. AAF trained its instructors in three-week institutes, and they in turn presented the lessons once a week over the twenty-six weeks. Separate manuals for trainers were designed for guidance in teaching and conference leadership.[54] The AAF course was first presented in February, 1943, optionally side by side with the regular "J" courses, but it superseded the latter and became the standard single offering in June, 1944.[55] By midsummer, 1945, AAF estimated that at least 40,000 supervisors had completed their training in AAF. Continuing conferences were used as a follow-up on basic courses, as in ASF,[56] to help supervisors put their principles into practice. Since AAF had more training funds at its disposal than any other branch of government, it is not surprising that it possessed the most numerous and lavish charts, graphs, and films for use in supervisory training. Their program was strikingly dressed to impress but of no better quality basically.

Specialized supervisory training for particular problems was designed by Ordnance to add to the "J" courses. For example, that branch installed a work simplification program along the line designed by the Bureau of the Budget and had completed administering it by late summer, 1945.[57] Work simplification was really an advanced version of JMT and taught procedures analysis, office arrangement, and proper distribution of tasks. Other special instruction was given in work measurement, placement, employee relations, wages and classification, reduction-in-force, and rehabilitation of veterans.

The Quartermaster General's Office was compelled by the nature of the logistics problem to devote special attention to one

[54] AAF, *How to Instruct, Instructor's Guide, T. O. No. 30-1-3,* November 15, 1943.
[55] Interview with D. W. Clausen, AAF, Civilian Personnel Division, Training Branch, July 2, 1945.
[56] AAF Regulation No. 40-11, *Personnel, Civilian, Supervisor Training Programs,* August 2, 1944.
[57] Interview with Williams, July 3, 1945.

phase of its work—the storage and handling of goods for shipment. It added substantively to the "J" courses by providing institutes to train supervisors in warehouse handling and storage activities.[58] Experience in using the depot training staff to learn the principles of storage handling to teach the operators did not achieve the desired results because of the time element involved. It was simpler to teach the operating chiefs directly and rely on them to teach their subordinates, the method pursued after May, 1944. This substantive training was given at Jersey City in six sessions. Those in charge of storage operations were sent to a separate school at Ogden, Utah, for six-week courses involving lectures, films, demonstrations, class problems, reports based upon on-the-job observations, and a seven-hour comprehensive essay examination. The Storage Division learned by February, 1944, that the procedures staff had to work very closely with the training staff at each depot on joint problems to make storage training effective.

Another variant to the supervisory training program in the War Department was added by the Adjutant General's Office in February, 1945, in the form of its in-service placement program for the development of the personal interview as a tool of management.[59] Each branch chief of AGO appointed a personnel representative from his staff to interview all supervisors four times a year to discover how the tasks of supervision had been handled and what training needs had not been met. Interviews with first-line supervisors were checked against those with second-line su-upervisors. In this manner AGO hoped to isolate the training needs for emphasis in the follow-up on the "J" courses.

The Navy Department did not use the "J" courses as such but employed the same principles in a longer instructional program for supervisors. Commander Frank Cushman, who was in charge of civilian employee training during the war years until November, 1944, had years before when he was in the Office of Education, along with Charles R. Allen,[60] developed the basic principles of the four-step teaching method. He naturally felt that the Training Within Industry Branch of WMC in designing the "J" courses without bows in his direction had "stolen his thunder." In addition, by 1942 Commander Cushman was convinced that the "J" courses were but a slender foundation for effective training and

[58] Interview with Schoch, July 4, 1945. [59] Interview with Dr. Bish, July 5, 1945
[60] Author of *The Instructor, the Man and the Job* (Philadelphia, 1919).

that the Navy needed something more fundamental.[61] A sidelight on training methods was illustrated by Navy's avoidance of the use of the term "conference" methods. The Training Branch was convinced that conferences could be held satisfactorily only among those who brought equivalent background and knowledge for an exchange of views. Therefore, it employed the term "discussion method" of teaching.

The Navy Department, consequently, developed its own manuals and films which it employed in courses for supervisors at weekly sessions of one and one-half hours each for thirty-two weeks.[62] The topics in the supervisors' course covered a wide range: leadership, development of interest in work and satisfaction in work, promotion of co-operation, handling of negligence, disciplinary problems, elimination of wasted time, safety and accident prevention, placement, planning for efficient production, procedures improvement, care of materials and equipment, wages and hours, analysis of teaching steps (the four-step method), orientation of the new workers, self-rating, industrial organization in the Navy yard, personnel problems of the labor board, medical services, and purchasing and accounting procedures. Job instructors for trade training were schooled one and one-half hours twice a week for twenty-five weeks in instructional techniques, job analysis, and human relations. They were usually "snappers" or first-class mechanics selected for this training by shop masters. Eventually a selected group of job instructors was advanced to the supervisory classes. Shore establishments were autonomous in training programs; therefore, the foregoing program varied up to 1945 from one establishment to another. From July, 1940, to July, 1945, 82,000 persons were given the Navy supervisory training.

In the field of clerical and office supervisory training, known as IVb positions in the Navy, the Training Branch of SECP conducted twenty-hour institutes at shore establishments.[63] This program stressed principles of handling human relations in an office and improvement of work production. The latter phase was a marked departure from the "J" courses in providing a five-step method of attack by the supervisor: (1) analysis of duties, (2) set-

[61] Interview with Lt. Strong, July 7, 1945.
[62] Interview with Comdr. Owen, July 6, 1945.
[63] Interview with Lt. Strong, July 7, 1945.

ting of standards of performance, (3) improvement of job skills, (4) use of effective training methods, and (5) evaluation and follow-up of employees. The difference was, of course, in the stress laid upon improvement of skills. Instructors in the IVb institutes made up their own manuals in the course. The goal set by the Training Branch was that each office or unit produce its own operations manual. Uniformity under this program was achieved by follow-up field visits and conferences with the Washington staff. The IVb supervisory training program actually started April 1, 1944, and formed the principal part of the new standardized Navy Work Improvement Program for IVb's inaugurated August 1, 1945.

For the training of supervisors in shore establishments the Navy Work Improvement Program provided preliminary instruction on a voluntary basis for artisans, leadingmen, quartermen, and masters and foremen.[64] The method of presentation was through reading, study assignments, lectures, and tests. Manuals were sent out by the Training Branch to shore establishments to provide a uniform basis for this training. Where standardized materials were not deemed effective, local establishments had the responsibility of developing detailed material of their own. As vacancies occurred or would occur, those who had successfully completed the training for the next higher grade had an opportunity to take the competitive examinations for it if they had completed their training within the three years preceding the examination.[65] The time limits and examination requirements were established to insure that supervisors promoted under wartime conditions received an opportunity to develop their skills adequately through training. Indeed, to continue in their grades, they were required to participate in the relevant training program.

The Department of Agriculture found the "J" courses helpful after some modification. The JMT course was not so useful as usually presented, based on a mechanical assembly problem, and Agriculture adopted the modified JMT designed by Social Security Board for its employees.[66] Another innovation was the prac-

---

[64] Labor force grades from lowest to highest among skilled laborers.

[65] Navy Department, *Work Improvement Program for Groups II, III and IVa Employees*, NAVEXOS-P-118.

[66] Interview with Dr. H. E. Eisele, Department of Agriculture, Personnel Office, Training Division, July 11, 1945.

tice in Agriculture of giving JMT to all employees, not merely to supervisors. Taking advantage of Civil Service Commission institutes from the first, Agriculture eventually trained 405 persons as instructors who in turn trained 9,000 supervisors in JIT, 7,108 employees in JMT, and 3,160 in JRT. The Work Simplification Program sponsored by the Bureau of the Budget was introduced by Agriculture early in 1945 as an advanced part of supervisory training. Five or six employees in the departmental service were trained to assume leadership as a kind of "task force" to instruct others in work simplification.

OPA tried to discourage the use of the "J" courses because of its dislike of stereotyped training. Some regional offices did, nevertheless, utilize them for supervisory training.[67] One standardized approach, the Work Simplification Program, was modified by OPA and was used to improve local board operations. The Training Section trained and organized a team in this program, consisting of one person from Training, one from Board Management, and another from the Rationing Division to train local board personnel. The Rent Division, upon developing interest in work simplification, trained a Rent Control employee in each regional office to pass the program along to the local offices.

Through influence, not directives or standardized programs, the Training Section sought to attract the attention of operating officers in OPA to management training. The distinctive approach OPA developed toward supervisory training was the preparation of memoranda to supervisors on specific principles of administration and the sending of checklists to the same persons for their evaluation. Regional conferences of employees engaged in a special program were helpful to secure co-operation between the training staff and the operating officers by indicating the training needs of the latter. The desideratum was the recognition of training needs by individual supervisors and the building of their confidence in the training staff to help them meet those needs.

The wartime promotion of thousands of inexperienced persons to supervisory responsibilities forced upon the attention of both the central personnel agency and the employing agencies the critical need for supervisory training. Sooner or later this area of training was characterized in most agencies by standardized pro-

[67] Interview with William Wolfrey, OPA, Personnel Division, Training Section, July 17, 1945.

grams based in principle, if not in detail, upon the "J" courses. A fair conclusion seems to be that the "J" courses probably oversimplified the aspects of supervision by the necessity for "packaging" them for mass distribution. Just as job dilution itself requires uniformity, as exemplified by the production of interchangeable parts by an assembly-line system, so mass training to be given quickly and widely requires simplification and standardization. To reach all supervisors required an approach so simple any normal person in an administrative or supervisory position could give it as training to others or receive it. The "packaged" programs, for the most part, simply scratched the surface of needs in the Federal service for training in teaching tasks to others, in analysis and correction of work methods, and in establishing sound relationships with those supervised. But that the surface was at last touched was of vast importance in personnel administration. Never again could personnel officers overlook this critical area without hazarding accusations of wanton negligence.

Administrative Training

Training for administration as for supervision was neglected by the Federal government before the war. That this condition prevailed was due, no doubt, to a number of factors, such as the late recognition of responsibility for in-service training by employing agencies, the tacit assumption that administrative experience should be presented as a qualification by competitors for such positions, and the belief that those promoted from the ranks because of specific job skills or professional competence would pick up in their own way the "know how" of administration. Of course, there have always been those who have questioned that there is any way to teach administration, maintaining that administration is learned by administering. Systematic preservice training was provided by one private organization, the National Institute of Public Affairs, through its unique internship program based on rotating assignments arranged with individual co-operating government agencies. Before the war, however, there was no means of insuring that interns would actually obtain government positions upon completing their internship. Some did not, and others had to accept mediocre positions at the CAF-3 grade to enter the government service at all. In both such cases their training was not used, at least for some time. By 1941 interns were eagerly sought for vacancies by the agencies in which their internship had been conducted.

The Committee on Administrative Personnel, appointed by the Civil Service Commission in December, 1941,[68] had pointed to the current need for training administrative personnel at one of its earliest meetings, namely, in January, 1942.[69] Their first proposal was that the Commission recruit about one hundred junior professional assistants for an organized training program of regular rotating work assignments on an experimental basis. In addition, the committee pointed to the need for training those in the middle management group for additional administrative responsibilities. The committee proposal, however, did not receive Commission support, for the Commission stated its training policy in terms of conducting training programs for its own personnel only and acting merely in an advisory capacity to other Federal agencies.[70] The Commission training policy likewise caused rejection of another committee proposal of a training program in the field of personnel administration. The latter program the committee had suggested should be conducted by the Commission with participants selected and appointed by the agencies, and the course should run for forty hours, conducted by the conference method by competent persons from the various agency personnel offices. The Council of Personnel Administration through its committee on training prepared a memorandum of May 14, 1942, to the White House requesting Commission authority to undertake the personnel training program.

In the meantime the Committee on Administrative Personnel had spent considerable time in 1942 exploring the possibility of training Federal administrative personnel through a program directed by the Office of Education, with the Civil Service Commission acting in an advisory capacity. Plans were laid to draft the necessary statutory clauses and request appropriations for the program. But because of Commission preference for responsibility for this type of training, the plan was scrapped in the autumn of 1942.[71] The only concrete results achieved by the committee

[68] See Chapter IV.
[69] Summary of meeting of Committee on Administrative Personnel, January 3, 1942.
[70] Summary of meeting of Committee on Administrative Personnel, May 16, 1942.
[71] Summary of meeting of Committee on Administrative Personnel, October 24, 1942.

DEVELOPMENT OF TRAINING PROGRAMS 179

in the field of administrative training were in the establishment of a personnel exchange program for training Commission employees alone.[72] By exchange of personnel between the Commission's Washington and field offices for details of individual employees for a maximum of four weeks promising individuals profited by assignments in work complementary or supplementary to their usual assignments.

The first pioneering step in administrative training was taken by the National Institute of Public Affairs to show what could be done in the expectation that the Council of Personnel Administration or the Civil Service Commission would continue the plan permanently if it were deemed successful. An in-service internship program for selected employees in the departmental service was, therefore, proposed by NIPA in 1943 and accepted on October 7, 1943, by the Council of Personnel Administration.[73] The training and selection of in-service interns was similar in many ways to the methods used for the preservice interns. Twenty-two agencies which agreed to co-operate appointed representatives to plan the program with NIPA and act as a committee on appointments; others from the Bureau of the Budget, the Civil Service Commission, and the Council of Personnel Administration served as advisers. Applications were received from interested employees of co-operating agencies in December, 1943, and sifted by the employing agency which made the nominations. Seventy-one persons were nominated by twenty-one agencies. The nominees had to be under thirty years of age and have had a record of successful work achievement in which they had demonstrated a capacity for leadership. They were tested and interviewed by the committee on appointments through a panel of the latter acting with NIPA. Thirty-two persons were finally selected as interns from eighteen agencies.[74] Half were not college graduates.[75] The period of internship ran eight months, from January 31, 1944, to September 30, 1944. All but six completed the course.[76] Their training comprised, in addition to rotating work assignments and agency super-

---

[72] CSC, *Circular Letter, Personnel Series No. 18,* February 10, 1944.

[73] Henry Reining, Jr., "The First Federal In-Service Internship Program," *Personnel Administration,* VII (December, 1944), 8.

[74] Jean Coman, "Internship Program for Federal Employees," *Personnel Administration,* VI (February, 1944), 5-6.

[75] Reining, "The First Federal In-Service Internship Program," *loc. cit.,* 10.

[76] *Ibid.,* 18.

vision, orientation arranged by NIPA, weekly group discussions, conferences with advisers from NIPA, an educational program pursued through recommended courses at American University, and participation in the activities of Washington professional societies.[77]

The next step was the adoption of the in-service internship program by the government. The small steering committee which had helped to start the program studied and evaluated its effectiveness as a training medium in June, 1944, and recommended its continuance by the Federal government to the Council of Personnel Administration.[78] The Council, therefore, recommended that it be conducted on an interdepartmental basis under the guidance of a committee on administrative interns made up like the committee on appointments for the first program but serving as a board of directors. The administration of the program was located in the Civil Service Commission under its Federal Work Improvement Program. Some thirty agencies co-operated. Franklin G. Connor from the War Department personnel staff was appointed director. Interns were selected between January 15 and February 12, 1945, and commenced their two weeks of orientation at the latter time.

Interns were selected in much the same way as the previous year under the NIPA program. After the co-operating agency had screened applicants, the committee administered to 112 nominees the American Council of Education psychological test. Only those above the 85 percentile rank were selected. OPA had done the best screening by means of a test followed by an interview of the top quarter of those who had taken the test. Every OPA nominee, of whom there were five, qualified with the committee administering the internship program, but only two became interns after OPA decided it could not forego the services of more than that number for six months. The interns were released from their position responsibilities for the six-month period of the internship. When the second group of interns was ready for selection in midsummer, 1945, it was given a battery of tests lasting the entire day, some standardized and some constructed by the Test Construction Unit of the Civil Service Commission. After

[77] See Dr. Reining's article for a full explanation.
[78] Interview with Franklin G. Connor, Civil Service Commission, Federal Work Improvement Program, Director of Administrative Intern Program, July 2, 1945.

the preliminary test had been given in January, 1945, the committee scheduled interviews which, in fact, confirmed the results of the test. Final selections were made by the committee after consultation with the personnel directors of the interns' agencies. Thirty interns were selected, with the division exactly even between the sexes. The average age was twenty-nine years, with a range from twenty-three to thirty-eight years. The NIPA age limitation of thirty was discarded. CAF-4 happened to be the lowest grade held by both nominees and selectees while a top limit had been set for nominees at CAF-9 or P-3. There were no Negroes nominated for the first group of interns. Two were, however, nominated by agencies for the second group.

The orientation program of the second internship program was designed to provide a uniform frame of reference in the field of public administration for a group characterized by a wide range in age and experience. Lectures were utilized to explain administration as exemplified in the varied operations of a large department, in a specific function (for example, planning), in service and control agencies, in a highly technical scientific agency, and in a large holding company type of organization. The lectures were followed by visits to relevant agencies: Agriculture, the Civil Service Commission, the Bureau of the Budget, the Weather Bureau, and the National Housing Agency. One technique was introduced to the interns and studied during orientation, namely, the conduct of conferences. During this period they were asked to write a statement of their objectives in the government service and their plan to attain them; copies went to the committee of directors and the agency adviser of the intern. The orientation period was also utilized as a time for the completion of assigned readings in the "classics" of public administration and the testing of knowledge acquired through reading assignments. Finally each intern had to prepare with his agency adviser a schedule of work assignments for the six-month internship as a time budget for planning in order to achieve the specific objectives of the internship. Educational counseling was done by American University.

The heart of the program consisted of the rotating work assignments under supervision. Progress reports were submitted to the committee frequently; they had to be approved by the agency in which the intern was stationed for training. Criticism of the quality of supervision was permissible to the committee if the agency was willing to accept it in the reports. The Monday night meetings, characteristic of NIPA internships, were utilized for acquiring information from outside speakers, panel discussions, and evaluation of the program. The speakers and subjects for these meetings were determined by the interns themselves through their own organization.

That the participating agencies themselves set a high value on administrative training of the kind described was attested by the fact that as the first program drew to a close, 50 per cent of the interns were offered better positions. Others received added duties, but departmental budgets prevented an immediate grade increase. Other agencies, too, wanted them but were estopped for a period of six months by an agreement on the part of all interns to return to their employing agencies for at least that period. The committee believed a manifest improvement in the individuals had been accomplished through their training. Also important was the fact that the presence of the interns in any office had served as a stimulus to improve the quality of supervision.

The program was so small, however, that promising as it seemed to be, it was a mere drop in an ocean of need for administrative talent. It actually devolved upon the larger departments to follow the pattern of this pilot course with agency-conducted internship programs to make the training widespread enough to help noticeably. The central course could then be continued for the benefit of the smaller agencies. In addition, the larger departments could draw their field services within the orbit of administrative training.

There were a few other instances during the war of sporadic attempts to provide administrative training. The Department of Agriculture was sufficiently motivated by the in-service internship program to appoint a committee early in 1945 to explore the problem of providing administrative training within the department.[79] The Forest Service had long had a systematic scheme for transferring capable technical employees to administrative positions in the field and Washington for training purposes before sending them out as regional executives. But a planned program for a career service of that type was exceptional. In the War De-

---

[79] Interview with Dr. Eisele, July 11, 1945.

partment the major training device for executive officers, personnel, and control officers was through manuals published on virtually all aspects of management and specialized administrative functions. The manuals were, however, designed primarily for military officers placed in administrative work at an installation. During the spring of 1942 two courses were sponsored by George Washington University and given at the War Department, one on principles of War Department administration and supervision and the other on personnel management in the department. Instructors were selected from War Department military and civilian personnel. Costs were borne by the Office of Education through the Engineering Science Management War Training Service. By June, 1942, 176 War Department supervisors had completed one of the two courses.[80] The Navy co-operated with George Washington University in the establishment of a similar type of course, given, however, at the university. The instructors were Navy supervisors. The class met in the evenings for a total of thirty-five hours. Tuition costs were met by the Office of Education. The Navy adjudged the course to be poorly organized and managed and disappointing in its results.[81]

Conclusions

Developments in the training field were spectacular during the war primarily because the field had been little explored. Many agencies like the War Department entered a new frontier in personnel administration. That they entered this new field was due not to a pioneering spirit but to the exigencies of the times, particularly the state of the labor market and the production demands of total war. If they consolidate their wartime gains in but two fields, supervisory and administrative training, the Federal service will be the richer for all the wartime exploration and experimentation in training.

The operating departments had provided the leadership in attacking the training problem. Postwar progress in the field of in-service training would continue to rest on the employing agencies for several reasons. On-the-job skills training and su-

[80] CSC, *Departmental Circular No. 349*, June 30, 1942.
[81] Unpublished report on Navy departmental service training, 1939-1942.

pervisory training could not be effectively centralized. Administrative training, to make any real headway, had to expand through departmental programs. Further it was always easier for the departments to obtain funds than for the Commission to do so. Faced with a drastic cut in appropriations immediately after V-J Day, coupled with congressional antipathy to training, the Commission was compelled to curtail its programs. Eventually the Federal Work Improvement Program was entirely liquidated. The departments were in a stronger position to press their needs before Appropriations subcommittees and keep some momentum in the training movement.

CHAPTER NINE

Increased Mobility Within the Service

THE PROLIFERATION of new defense and war agencies as well as the expansion of old ones opened new vistas for transfer and promotion to able and ambitious Federal employees. The new mobility of employees horizontally, that is, by transfer across organizational lines, and vertically, by promotion up the hierarchy, was aided and abetted by two factors. One was the view taken by the Civil Service Commission that recruitment should be intragovernmental as well as extragovernmental. Only thus could persons possessed of essential skills engaged in work of less than first-rate importance be assisted in making a direct contribution to the war effort. Another factor of importance contributing to the use of transfers, in particular, was the desire among heads of new agencies to secure experienced government personnel versed in the intricacies of government procedures. Those employees who wished to change positions in the service and who had ability and experience to offer were faced by a plethora of opportunities.

Transfer and promotion from within were, of course, economical and expedient wherever possible. The expense of recruitment and of training was materially reduced when experienced employees could be located for critical work within the service. Savings were not merely to be measured in terms of dollars, for both transfer and promotion were invaluable to morale. By creating vacancies for a whole chain of promotions for other employees they have always been regarded as stimuli to increased work productivity, and, indeed, have been considered a necessary ingredient for a career service.

Once the service began to expand rapidly, it was natural that agencies resorted to raiding other government establishments for some of their best employees. Raids for personnel were simple to execute when the new war agencies or new units in old agencies could offer positions carrying more responsibility and higher salaries. Ambitious employees dissatisfied with their salaries or promotional opportunities in static departments were scarcely to be blamed for "shopping around" to seize the best opportunities available. Only the phlegmatic were immunized by long experience in a relatively static agency from grasping what the war agencies eagerly offered.

Attempts to guide transfers through the Civil Service Commission and make it the central procurement agency for shifting government personnel were doomed to failure. Shortly after the beginning of the defense period the Commission conceived a plan to effect centralization of information for transfer by coding the qualifications of government employees to facilitate the search by the appointing agencies for scarce skills. Known as the Interdepartmental Placement Service, the plan was a dismal failure. After the war service regulations were adopted and the Commission was delegated control over transfers by the War Manpower Commission, a War Transfer Unit was established in the Civil Service Commission to assist both appointing officers and employees seeking each other informally and often blindly. Nevertheless, many transfers continued to be negotiated outside the channels of the War Transfer Unit.

Interagency transfers required approximately the same types of manpower controls as were placed upon original recruitment. Raiding within the government was essentially the same as piracy in the labor market. Without control and limitation there was no guarantee that manpower available for transfer would be channeled to agencies of critical importance in the war effort. Priorities were, therefore, established among agencies for transfer purposes. They were, however, the cause of some dissatisfaction and wrangling inasmuch as it was difficult to distinguish between the essentiality of programs or the directness of their relationship to the war. The Civil Service Commission, as the representative of the War Manpower Commission, became arbiter for approving transfers within the frame of reference of priorities. Thereby it occupied for government a position analogous to that of USES in the labor market generally.

With the problem of transfers came that of re-employment rights. Moving about was profitable endeavor while the war lasted, but employees with civil service status were not ready to sacrifice the security of a hard-won place in the permanent service for a pleasant ride up the hierarchy in a temporary establishment.

The only way they could be induced to transfer was to guarantee their right to return to their old positions after the emergency.

Expansion within any organization, old or new, creates promotional opportunities all the way through the agency. Promotion from within was both logical and desirable. But rapid expansion accelerated promotions at a rate that seemed to endanger qualifications standards unless the brakes were applied. Promotions following too rapidly one upon the other or the leaping of several grades by relatively inexperienced employees were not calculated to inspire confidence on the part of the legislative branch or to improve morale in the executive branch.

The application of time limits to promotions and the promulgation of standardized qualifications schedules by the Commission were the methods of control employed. Any mode of standardization increases rigidity, but in the matter of promotion, rigidity was the price exacted for the controls deemed essential. Otherwise the agencies with more flexible wartime budgets would have nullified *in toto* the theory of the Classification Act. But lest the impression be conveyed that rigidity was excessive, the fact should be noted that the Commission allowed some circumvention of its own regulations. It was still possible by the end of the war to move upward in most agencies at a rate that seemed dizzy in comparison with that for prewar advancement.

Agency Competition for Trained Personnel

Experienced persons were sought eagerly and sedulously wherever they could be found in the tight wartime labor market. Government employees in all brackets were regarded by new agencies as a reservoir of talent they could not afford to overlook. Typists, stenographers, and clerks, as well as personnel technicians, budget officers, and administrators, were vital cogs to keep the wheels of every organization turning. The more difficult became the recruitment of capable personnel in those categories in the contracting labor market, the more appointing officers turned to the "old line" agencies to meet their needs.

Urgency was so pressing that inducements in the form of higher grade positions and higher salaries were in many cases a logical result of the desire to recruit skilled employees within the service. Added to the opportunity to transfer to a more responsible position were opportunities for rapid promotion in organizations growing visibly by the minute. The original lure was, therefore, compounded by future considerations. In the field service the attraction of higher classification could be made even more dazzling because the departments themselves, not the Commission, possess discretion to allocate positions and fix salary rates.

Adventurous individuals who had been attracted to the service by the social welfare programs of the New Deal found the challenge of the war agencies irresistible. Once a satisfactory transfer had been effected, it often set in motion a veritable chain of movement out of the old and into the new agencies. Friends were recommended, and word of similar opportunities was passed along the "grapevine." Ambitious employees not invited to move had only to remind acquaintances and former fellow workers who had already transferred of their availability in order to receive suitable offers.

The lot of administrators in low priority agencies was not a happy one as they faced depletion of experienced staffs for the benefit of higher priority agencies.[1] Comptroller Warren expressed their disgruntlement in these words:

> We have an acute and critical personnel problem. Our turnover has been terrific. When they were classing and giving priorities to the different agencies for personnel, the General Accounting Office was placed in class No. 5 and, as a result, we were raided, plundered, and pillaged by every other agency in the government. . . .
>
> Up until a few months ago, they took our very best men, many of whom did not wish to leave us. That has been corrected now because I had personally taken the matter up and secured our classification right under the war agencies in class No. 2. We are certainly more of a war agency than almost any other agency of the Government. . . .
>
> I want to say that I have never acquiesced in these raids. I have protested and, of course, they are stopped now but it is like locking the stable after the horse is gone.[2]

Congress took alarm in 1942 at the unwonted movement within the service because of fear that payrolls were rising unduly to the negation of the Classification Act. Although the Senate wished to

[1] See below for description of priorities system.
[2] *Investigation of Civilian Employment,* Part II, Hearing on June 3, 1943, pp. 453-54.

attach an amendment to an appropriation bill[3] to bar increases in compensation to transferees, the House requested a report from the Civil Service Commission on transfers before considering such action.[4] The resultant report was the only comprehensive wartime study on transfers.[5] In pointing to the need for such a report, Chairman Cannon of the House Appropriations Committee declared:

> The amendment aims at some abuse that has grown up during the development of the recruitment of personnel for the war agencies in taking many of the necessary personnel with experience from other agencies. This is a natural operation in a period of shortage of experienced manpower and the war agencies in taking present personnel in other agencies are drawing upon the only reservoir of trained Government employees that exists.
>
> There has also been an insistence on the part of some that instead of bringing new personnel into Washington that use should be made as far as possible of the personnel that is already here in other agencies. This has been done to a large degree and much of the personnel going to the war agencies from regular agencies has gone at higher salaries. This is a proper procedure and is mandatory under the classification laws which are in effect if the employee goes to the performance of more responsible duties and a higher grade of work which calls for a higher pay.
>
> There is, however, undoubtedly, a practice being pursued in some of the war agencies to raid other agencies wherever possible and this without any substantial change in duties. Such practices ought to be stopped.[6]

The Commission found no cause for concern in 19,062 transfers made between March 1, 1942, and June 30, 1942, the period under scrutiny in its report. Of 17,137 salaried employees transferred during that period, 64.2 per cent moved to positions in the

---

[3] The first supplemental national defense appropriation bill of 1943.

[4] 88 *Cong. Record* 6408, July 20, 1942. The House was influenced by letters from the Commission, the Liaison Officer for Personnel Management in the President's Office, the chairman of the War Production Board, and various other war agency administrators. The House discarded the Senate amendment and substituted its own requesting a report within sixty days from the Civil Service Commission on the transfer problem.

[5] Letter from the CSC to Congress and the President, *Personnel Transfers Between Departments and Agencies in the Executive Branch,* House Committee Print, 77th Cong., 2nd Sess., pursuant to Sec. 204, P. L. 678, September 24, 1942.

[6] 88 *Cong. Record* 6408, July 20, 1942.

same salary bracket, 28.2 per cent to the next higher salary grade, 3.9 per cent to positions in lower grades, 3.2 per cent two grades higher, 0.4 per cent to positions three grades higher, and 0.1 per cent four or five grades higher.[7] Nevertheless the Commission admitted that departments had taken advantage of their discretion over salaries of field service employees to engage in competitive bidding for desired personnel to perform work of the same difficulty and responsibility as that in which they had been previously employed.[8] The movement of transferees was, as expected, into the war agencies, although some few moved out of those agencies into others. Priorities among agencies, of which more will be mentioned shortly, had been established at the time of the study, and the Commission discovered that four-fifths of all transfers had been made to agencies in the first three priority classifications, about half to first priority agencies, and nearly 45 per cent from lowest priority agencies to those in a higher class.[9] Of the last group half were made to first priority agencies. The great majority of the transfers, in the opinion of the Commission, had been "definitely beneficial to the Government service as a whole and to the war program in particular."[10]

The Commission pointed out several causes for transfer, all of which were directly connected with wartime administrative problems. For example, removal of some agencies from Washington to other cities gave rise to exchanges of personnel even from higher to lower priority agencies. Reorganizations of units to arrange for the assumption of new wartime duties and the termination or tapering off of older programs accounted for other transfers. Rapid recruiting accompanied by poor original placement helped to swell the total. Significantly the Commission added:

> Unsatisfactory working conditions have resulted in considerable flux. It is natural in rapidly expanding governmental agencies for working conditions not always to be under the most satisfactory administrative control. These conditions led to a number of workers shopping around for other jobs, selling themselves to employers in other agencies—even in lower priority agencies—and prevailing upon the agencies to requisition their services.[11]

---

[7] Letter from the CSC to Congress and the President, *Personnel Transfers Between Departments and Agencies in the Executive Branch*, 3.
[8] *Ibid.*, 2.   [9] *Ibid.*, 3   [10] *Ibid.*, 2.   [11] *Ibid.*, 8.

Even in cases where through transfer employees advanced several grades the Commission concluded that the service had benefited "because through transfers, the Government was able to utilize to the fullest extent the skills, abilities, and experience of employees who were in positions definitely below the level of qualifications they actually possessed."[12] This finding was substantiated in the hearings before the Ramspeck Committee the next year, when the Commission reported that justifiable reasons usually existed for transfers that involved promotion.[13]

But approximately 20 to 25 per cent of all transfers did not promote the war effort and had to be disapproved, according to Commission reports. In March, 1943, the Commission reported to the Ramspeck Committee that of a total of 67,935 transfers made from February 27, 1942, until March 1, 1943, it had disapproved 13,000.[14] By November, 1943, the total number of transfers had reached 114,278; of that number 29,383 had been disapproved by the Civil Service Commission or canceled by the requesting agency after the Commission had made findings that the transfer would not promote the war effort.[15]

Commissioner Flemming reported on May 14, 1945, at House hearings on the pay bills for 1945 that 177,000 transfers had been approved by the Commission from March, 1942, until the end of December, 1944.[16] Only 25.9 per cent were transferred to higher salary levels while 74.1 per cent were moved to the same or lower salary levels out of the total number transferred from positions under the Classification Act to other positions similarly controlled.

A subcommittee of the Senate Appropriations Committee, in studying the removal of nonwar agencies from Washington in 1943, expressed dissatisfaction at the large number of employees content to remain in their positions in "unnecessary or overstaffed organizations."[17] In addition, it held inadequate Commission machinery to effect their transfer. Commission efforts to assist the

---

[12] *Ibid.*, 10.
[13] *Investigation of Civilian Employment*, Part I, Hearing on March 25, 1943, p. 181.
[14] *Ibid.*   [15] CSC, *Sixtieth Annual Report*, 23.
[16] U.S. Congress, House, Committee on Civil Service, Hearings on *A Bill to Improve Salary and Wage Administration in the Federal Service, etc.*, 79th Cong., 1st Sess., May 14, 15, 16, 17, and 18, 1945, pp. 35-36.
[17] U.S. Congress, Senate, *Transfer of Employees, Conserving Office Space, Relief in Housing Conditions, and Promotion of Economy and Efficiency*, Sen. Report 1554, 77th Cong., 2nd Sess., 12.

war agencies were thwarted by a tendency of many employees to demand an unreasonable increase in salary as the price of transfer. To alleviate this problem it proposed mandatory transfer, which, as will be indicated shortly, was soon adopted.

Indubitably there were raids upon many nonwar agencies for their abler employees. Recruitment within the service was, nevertheless, natural and, on the whole, desirable even though fraught with some danger to the Classification Act. But unchanneled and unsupervised interagency transfers were quite another matter, and had they continued beyond 1942 the manpower situation within government might well have become chaotic. This is not the place to examine the effect on the Classification Act since that subject will be discussed in a subsequent chapter. Suffice it to say at this time that the dangers inherent in random transfers for salary or promotional opportunities alone were far greater to the maintenance of equitable manpower allocations within the Federal service than to grade allocations and salaries. The Commission had the statutory authority to "hold down the lid," so to speak, on classification if it desired. Without a further delegation of power from the War Manpower Commission it was weak in the allocation of manpower already employed in the service.

Attempts to Guide Transfers

The Civil Service Commission tried to assist in the channeling of employees to government employers from the beginning of the defense period. Poor organization led to failure. The first attempt was through the establishment of the Interdepartmental Placement Service, the second through the creation of a War Transfer Unit.

1. THE INTERDEPARTMENTAL PLACEMENT SERVICE

The inauguration of the defense program in May, 1940, led the Civil Service Commission to undertake an ambitious project on July 23, 1940, known as the Interdepartmental Placement Service, to assist the defense agencies in locating skilled Federal employees expeditiously. There had never been any inventory of personnel resources within the Federal government to facilitate transfer, and the new project was revolutionary. The plan was to code and tabulate on punch cards all qualifications information for each employee in a master file from which it would have been possible by mechanical sorting equipment to discover within a few minutes whether and where in the service employees with particular skills and experience could be located. The Commission, therefore, immediately circularized all Federal employees to have them complete a qualifications and experience questionnaire to bring all personnel information up to date. Data respecting new employees were added as they were appointed. The Interdepartmental Placement Service was conceived as an instrument to maximize positive service by the central personnel agency to the employing agencies.

A false start in 1940 caused initial delays at the very time the qualifications questionnaires began to pour into the Commission from both increasing numbers of new accessions and old employees. Instead of calling in expert consultants to construct a new code inclusive of the refined categories of skills existent in the Federal service, those in charge of the project attempted to utilize the USES *Dictionary of Job Titles* code. The latter was defective in that it was designed for an entirely different type of clientele: the unemployed registrants of USES, many of whom were unskilled. This code soon proved inadequate. Therefore, time was consumed in designing a new code based in general on that of USES but providing more minute occupational classification. By the time the new code was ready for use, the number of new employees was increasing to such proportions that the employees in the Interdepartmental Placement Service were buried under a mounting avalanche from which they found it impossible to extricate themselves. The longer the delay persisted in disposing of the backlog of work on old employees, the more promotions and transfers among them had outmoded the data on the original questionnaires.[18]

Departments were not under compulsion to utilize the Interdepartmental Placement Service, for it was simply a service offered by the Commission. That question, however, was purely academic. The file was never brought up to date to render the service for which it was conceived.

Despite renewed efforts in 1942 to make data on Federal em-

---

[18] There were minor flaws in the coding process. For one thing, it was necessary to attach trailer cards to the master punch card, a device which delayed the sorting procedure. Instead of the three principal categories planned for classification of employees, six major groups had to be developed.

ployees current and place the system into effective operation, the final denouement was a sad commentary on this enterprise. It was impossible to overcome the backlog of work, and the questionnaires, thousands upon thousands never coded, were finally disposed of in 1943 as waste paper in the salvage drives current at that time. Coding of current applications coming into the Commission's Examining Division was placed in an Applicant Supply Section in that division. Thus ended one failure.

2. WAR TRANSFER UNIT

Another approach to the problem of trying to guide transfer, namely, to provide the medium for supplying agencies with the names of persons desirous of transfer, was attempted by the Commission in 1942 through the establishment of the War Transfer Unit. It was located in the Applicant Supply Section of the Examining Division. A precedent for the new organization was found in the Central Placement Section established by the Commission in August, 1941, to promote transfer in Washington of employees of agencies moved to other cities who were unable or unwilling to leave the capital. In a few months the latter was superseded by a Decentralization Service to offer two-way transfer facilities for employees of such agencies to the majority remaining in the capital as well as for employees of the latter to the former.[19] The War Transfer Unit was created, however, to assist in a simple one-way personnel movement into the war program by a co-ordination of the Decentralization Service with the War Transfer Service, a new Commission activity. The War Transfer Unit was established to determine eligibility for transfer and to obtain releases; employees desiring transfer, therefore, were requested to register with it. That co-ordination was needed was attested by the subcommittee of the Senate Appropriations Committee, which described Commission facilities in the transfer field as "in a highly chaotic state of organization which undoubtedly contributed greatly to the inefficiency and time-consuming redtape then existing regarding the transfer of personnel between departments and agencies."[20]

Nevertheless, the War Transfer Unit fell short of expectations. For one thing, the Commission later regarded it as mistaken

[19] CSC, *Departmental Circular No. 299,* December 19, 1941.
[20] U.S. Congress, Senate, *Transfer of Employees,* 11.

policy to have established a separate unit for transfer transactions. Commissioner Flemming declared in 1943 that transfer should have been regarded as a part of the regular recruitment and placement "assembly line" instead of having been handled through a separate entity.[21] Lack of advertising of the transfer program also left many employees without any knowledge of existent facilities to help them, according to the Byrd Committee.[22] The report of that committee seems, in addition, to support the conclusion that the Commission by a process of attrition was attempting to prevent transfer:

> The Committee's investigation showed that from an organizational standpoint that unit functioned well and its procedure was modernized in every way possible. However, for some reason not entirely clear, the Commission changed the procedure and instead of 6 actions being required to effect a transfer under the previous set-up, now 10 major and 35 minor actions by employees are necessary. The investigation showed also that war transfer files are not consulted before a new employee is certified to an agency. . . . A responsible official of the Civil Service Commission admitted that the Commission had not really tried to make the program as effective as it should be.[23]

The departments were, however, also censured by the Byrd Committee for failure to survey their own organizations in order to promote transfer of excess personnel. The Commission commented obliquely on their attitude:

> In the effort both to meet the problem of a declining supply of applications and to give emphasis to placement of Federal employees, the Administrative and Management Placement Section has placed with the War Transfer Unit a number of requests for recruitment of Federal employees in certain critical occupations from low priority agencies. Such requests have not, however, been productive in terms of usefulness in the placement process.[24]

The Commission tried, however, to facilitate transfer of higher grade administrative personnel in every way it could conceive. It

---

[21] *Investigation of Civilian Employment*, Part I, Hearing of March 24, 1943, p. 173.
[22] U.S. Congress, Joint Committee on Reduction of Nonessential Federal Expenditures, *Federal Personnel*, Sen. Doc. 66, 78th Cong., 1st Sess., 15.
[23] *Ibid.*
[24] Report on Transfer Operations by the Administrative and Management Placement Section, CSC, December 1, 1942 (unpublished).

adopted almost immediately one of the first suggestions made by the Committee on Administrative Personnel, namely, to appoint high-level employees to negotiate with the appointing agencies for the release of competent administrators to the war agencies.[25] A number of successful transfers were negotiated by the staff assigned to that task. The difficulty was that their efforts constituted only a small part of the total transfer program.

Many transfers continued to be negotiated between employees desirous of making a change in positions and the agencies eager to secure their services. Not only were mutually satisfactory arrangements more often secured through these informal negotiations than through reliance on the War Transfer Unit, but many employees were under the impression that the Commission's transfer machinery was painfully slow and uncertain as compared with their own efforts. At least many employees voiced the feeling that if they desired a transfer, they would turn only in desperation to the War Transfer Unit.[26] Instead they preferred to rely on information about openings furnished by friends in other agencies and upon the assistance those friends could render in effecting placement.

Establishment of Controls Over Transfer

Controls for transfer were postulated on the need for a delicate balance between necessary and excessive mobility. Federal employees had to be encouraged and even compelled to transfer to those parts of the government where their services were critically needed. But in so doing, the Commission had to exercise care to discourage transfer for the sake of monetary gain or change for the sake of change. "Shopping around" indiscriminately and leaving essential tasks for nonessential work could have created manpower shifts detrimental to the war effort. The effort to distinguish between the essential and the nonessential programs on the basis of their relation to prosecution of the war led to the establishment of priorities among agencies by the Bureau of the Budget. With the authority of the War Manpower Commission over the movement of government personnel delegated to it by

---

[25] Summary of the Meeting of the Committee on Administrative Personnel, December 20, 1941, February 14, 1942, and March 21, 1942.

[26] Opinions expressed to the author by numerous Federal employees during 1944 and 1945.

WMC Directive X, the Commission was in a strong position to discourage transfers deemed harmful to the service. The Commission thus gained the same type of control over the intragovernmental movement of employees as it had possessed with respect to the control of recruitment into the service. While transfer was slowed down, it was still a simple matter to effect an essential transfer to a higher priority agency or unit.

1. BUREAU OF THE BUDGET PRIORITIES

Before a definite system of agency priorities for transfer was evolved and while the defense program was in its initial phase, William H. McReynolds, administrative assistant to President Roosevelt and Liaison Officer for Personnel Management, had suggested to the Commission on July 1, 1940, that urgency of program might require retention of employees in their positions.[27] He proposed that the policy adopted should facilitate shifts of personnel from nondefense to defense agencies. But with respect to shifts in the opposite direction he recommended that defense agencies have the right to lodge objections with finality unless the Commission found for the particular needs of the nondefense agency. The same right of protest was suggested respecting movement between two defense agencies. To McReynolds' suggestions the Commission added in tentative manner that it might wish to identify agencies or organizational units as defense agencies in order to administer the policy. In these proposals, in short, came to be found the germ of the system of controls over transfers.

The first control, a requirement of approval in writing by defense agencies of transfers from them to nondefense establishments, was adopted at the very time relaxations were made in the form of allowing transfers during the probational period to defense positions and from the field services of the War and Navy departments to their departmental services subject only to Commission postaudit.[28] By 1941 employees were required to obtain written consent of their departments for permission to take examinations for other positions.[29]

[27] CSC, *Departmental Circular No. 225*, July 10, 1940.
[28] CSC, *ibid., Supp. No. 1*, July 29, 1940, and Executive Order 8514, August 13, 1940. After the first thirty days of probation transfer could be effected to any position for which the probationer was qualified. *Departmental Circular No. 243*, November 25, 1940. See also CSC, Letter of February 15, 1941, to War Department.
[29] Executive Order 8760, May 27, 1941.

The next step was to authorize the Commission to arrange transfers of employees to defense programs suffering from critical labor shortages, a step ordered shortly after Pearl Harbor.[30] The same order established re-employment rights of transferees. But consent of both the employee and the employing agency was still essential for transfer. The Commission, in effect, had merely the right of appeal to departments to release employees to the war agencies. The Commission directed such an appeal to all department heads and bureau chiefs on January 8, 1942, and followed up this appeal with the appointment of negotiators for transfer, mentioned above.

Along with the executive order for the war service regulations was another to provide for priority classification among agencies or their organizational units.[31] Before this order the division into defense and nondefense agencies had been on a rough basis. Executive Order 9067 authorized the Director of the Budget to establish priorities according to the relative importance of agencies in the war effort in order to facilitate transfers. Each agency or major part of an agency was ranked in one of five priority classes, and transfers were, as a rule, limited to movement from lower to higher priority classes. The Commission, on the other hand, was required to obtain information respecting competent employees who could do higher priority work to which it could transfer them with their consent. Employing agencies' objections to transfer could be overruled, but they were allowed to present a case for the retention of the employee to the Commission acting as final arbiter. To stop the change that had been ordered, agencies had to prove that their work would be jeopardized by the proposed transfer.

Transfer under the war service regulations was to some extent a part of the recruitment program.[32] Transfers had to be included in personnel requisitions for new employees, but particular employees could be requested as transferees. Employees desirous of transfer had to file applications for that purpose with the Commission, not with the employing departments. The Commission, of course, had been empowered under Executive Order 8973 of December, 1941, to initiate inter- and intra-agency transfers.[33]

[30] Executive Order 8973, December 12, 1941.
[31] Executive Order 9067, February 20, 1942.
[32] CSC, *Departmental Circular No. 323*, February 28, 1942.
[33] Apportionment no longer applied to any transfers from lower to higher priority

Commission approval was requisite for all interagency transfers but not for intra-agency transfers. Significantly, those to the same or lower priority agencies required consent of both the employing agency and of the employee.[34] The edict against competition in civil service examinations without consent of the employing agencies was withdrawn.[35] The term "war transfer" was applied to persons moved about either from one agency to another or within an agency under the new regulations, and their rights to the new positions were analogous to those of any war service appointee, that is, for the duration only. Commission jurisdiction over war transfers was not limited to positions under the Civil Service Act but extended to transfers to and from excepted positions and excepted agencies.[36]

Subsequently the transfer of employees within the Federal service and to private enterprise was placed under the WMC directives and regulations by Executive Order 9243 of September 12, 1942. The priority classifications of the Director of the Budget had to conform to the policies of the War Manpower Commission chairman. From time to time agencies were shifted from one priority class to another, depending upon the changing needs of the war program. The priority classifications endured until July 1, 1944, when they were revoked by Executive Order 9451 of June 20, 1944.

2. WAR MANPOWER CONTROLS OVER TRANSFERS

Following hard on the heels of Executive Order 9243, which placed transfer of Federal employees under WMC controls, the War Manpower Commission issued its Directive X to tighten the transfer system by extending manpower controls over the movement of Federal employees from agency to agency.[37] Through this directive the Commission could transfer employees within the Federal government without their consent. Furthermore, it could transfer them to private enterprise or state or local government whenever it found they could perform work in a critical

---

classifications or even to the same or lower priority classes if the Commission found that transfer would provide better utilization of skills in the war program. Forty-eight hours were allowed for agency protest and ten days for Commission decision on the protest.

[34] CSC, *Departmental Circular No. 322,* February 27, 1942.
[35] CSC, *Circular Letter No. 3608,* February 28, 1942.
[36] *Ibid., No. 3625,* March 24, 1942.   [37] 7 FR 7298, September 16, 1942.

occupation and thus make a more effective contribution to the war effort, but consent of the transferee was still required for transfer outside the Federal service. Both losing agencies and employees had a right of protest.[38] The Civil Service Commission was the enforcing agency for WMC transfer policy as for other manpower controls over the Federal government.

The Commission soon proceeded to issue more drastic controls under Directive X. Mention has already been made in Chapter II of the requirement of thirty days' unemployment as a penalty for an unauthorized change of positions under the war manpower program. This penalty was later raised to sixty days. The Commission applied the penalty to transfers effected within the Federal service without its express prior approval.[39] After controlled referral was effected by WMC in the spring of 1943, Federal transfers required an affirmative finding by the Commission that the projected transfer would make possible a more effective contribution to the war program by the employee.[40] This new ruling was more rigorous than the former one that transfers were prohibited only when the Commission found that the transfer was detrimental to the war effort. Transfers were forbidden when an increase in salary was the sole reason for a change in positions. Agencies reluctant to accept transfers with considerable accumulated leave were reprimanded by the Commission.[41]

The Commission tried to keep agency appeals against transfers to a minimum by requests to the agencies that they realize that appeal merely resulted in a loss of time and manpower unless they could prove that the proposed transfer would not be in the best interests of the government as a whole.[42] The Commission also

---

[38] No employee could be transferred to a position at a lower salary or beyond reasonable commuting distance from his home unless the agency securing his services paid the costs of transporting him, his family, and household goods. Private industrial establishments applied for transfer of Federal personnel by application to the Commission through USES. CSC, *Circular Letter No. 3135*, October 10, 1942.

[39] CSC, *Departmental Circular No. 323, Revised, Supp. No. 15*, April 2, 1943. Movement out of Washington was restricted unless based on urgent health or family reasons or the possibility of rendering a greater contribution to the war effort elsewhere. *Circular Letter No. 3949*, January 26, 1943.

[40] CSC, *Departmental Circular No. 420*, April 23, 1943.

[41] *Ibid., No. 413*, March 10, 1943.

[42] For fair procedure in these appeals the Commission created *ad hoc* committees, consisting of one employee representative and an administrative officer of a department not involved in the case, to hear the matter and report findings to the Com-

discouraged the approval of transfers retroactively to the date an employee entered on duty unless the Commission had committed unintentional error in withholding approval or in approving the appointment under the wrong regulation.[43]

3. THE PROBLEM OF RE-EMPLOYMENT RIGHTS

Since, during the war, mobility within the service had to be augmented, as well as controlled, the problem of re-employment rights was inescapable. The transfer of employees from positions in which they possessed civil service status to duration positions would have been inequitable without provision for opportunity to return at the end of the war. The question arose, of course, of how far the guarantees should extend in cases where transferees themselves had undertaken to effect their transfer.

The provision respecting re-employment rights was contained in Executive Order 8973 on December 12, 1941. Inasmuch as transfer could be requested by the Commission under that order, all transferees other than temporary employees were declared to be entitled to re-employment rights in their old positions or an equivalent position of the same seniority, status, and pay. They had to apply for reinstatement within forty days of the termination of their services or of the national emergency and had to be reinstated within thirty days of their application. If reinstatement proved impossible, their names had to be entered on the re-employment list. No reinstated employee could be discharged without cause within one year of reinstatement. These rights, however, were limited to transfers initiated by the Commission under the executive order.[44] War service appointees had no re-employment rights but merely had their names entered on a re-employment list.

---

mission's Legal Adviser or to the Regional Director for the field service. Appeal might be carried to the Commission for final decision if the committee found it impossible to agree. 8 *FR* 6387, May 18, 1943.

[43] CSC, *Circular Letter No. 3835, Supp. No. 6,* May 21, 1943.

[44] CSC, *Departmental Circular No. 303,* January 2, 1942. In cases of certification of Federal employees as a result of additional examinations taken, re-employment rights did not apply unless the Commission specifically invoked the order in certifying. Employees eligible to acquire status under the Ramspeck Act did not lose eligibility in cases of Commission-sponsored transfers, and *status quo* employees, that is, those not classified under the Ramspeck Act for any reason other than failure of a qualifying examination, could retain their re-employment rights to a *status quo* position. *Ibid., No. 527,* July 17, 1945.

Under WMC Directive X substantially the same re-employment benefits were conferred, for this order, as previously indicated, authorized the Commission to transfer employees with or without their consent.[45] In addition, authorized transferees under WMC regulations retained the right to be considered for promotion in their original agency.[46] If they were unable to return to take immediate advantage of the promotional opportunity, the position was to be filled only for the duration of their re-employment benefits.[47]

By the end of the war as critical manpower needs were somewhat eased, re-employment rights of transferees could be exercised at any time agreement was reached by the original agency, the agency presently employing them, and the employees.[48] Up to July, 1945, re-employment rights could be exercised only after an employee had been involuntarily separated without prejudice from the enterprise to which he had been transferred.[49] Intra-agency return to a former position had always been a matter of internal departmental administration as far as the time of return was concerned.[50] Those who had separated themselves voluntarily from their later positions could return to the original one to which they held re-employment rights only with Civil Service Commission approval. The later ruling to permit voluntary agreements for return indicated that the stage was being set for rapid mobility in the reverse direction to that of 1941 to 1943: namely, back to the original agencies.

THE CONTROL AND STANDARDIZATION OF PROMOTIONS

Promotion in the service was closely related to transfer and was as serious a problem during the war years. The lowering of qualifications standards for entrance into the service was accompanied by the necessity to promote rapidly the abler, experienced

[45] Likewise in the case of transfers effected under the Bureau of the Budget reductions-in-force authorized by the first and second War Overtime Pay Acts similar re-employment rights were attached. *Ibid., No. 412*, March 1, 1943.

[46] 8 *FR* 6387, May 18, 1943.

[47] Employees could present compelling personal reasons involving undue hardship or the best interests of the service to obtain Commission authorization for transfer but without re-employment rights. CSC, *Departmental Circular 323, Revised, Supp. No. 20*, July 16, 1943.

[48] *Ibid., No. 493, Supp. No. 14,* July 24, 1945.

[49] *Ibid., No. 397, Supp. No. 1,* January 6, 1943.

[50] *Ibid., No. 397,* December 19, 1942.

employees to positions of more responsibility. The Commission felt impelled by labor market conditions to delegate a wide latitude to defense agencies and then to all agencies in 1941, a latitude which was in some respects abused. Congressional concern over certain extraordinarily rapid ascensions in the service led to the application of brakes on agency freedom by the Commission in April, 1943. The process of slowing down agency zeal took the form of establishing promotion standards chiefly in the form of minimum time to be served in the various grades before promotion could be approved. Postauditing of promotions by the Commission was employed to check agency action, and threats of withdrawal of the delegation to act within the range of freedom granted by the Commission were held over the heads of agencies abusing their privileges. No privileges were in practice withdrawn. The standards, however, still permitted a rapidity of promotion foreign to the prewar civil service.

Employing agencies had actually enjoyed complete freedom with respect to promotions before the war so long as they could establish the fact that position qualifications had been met by the person recommended. Standards had not been developed in this field with respect to the time an employee had to remain within a grade before he was eligible to be moved up. Ordinarily, however, opportunities to go up the ladder were not frequent in any but the newer and expanding agencies. The static nature of the service and lack of funds for a promotional program helped to prevent abuse of freedom.

1. LATITUDE ENJOYED BY EMPLOYING AGENCIES IN 1940-1941

Although standards for promotion had not been published before the war, certain classes of employees, such as probational and temporary employees, could not be promoted. Experience and training qualifications in class specifications often served as a check on rapid promotion. Promotion from one type of work to another completely different type was not permitted.

The Commission began relaxing the foregoing restrictions in 1940. First it allowed promotion of probational employees in the War Department, soon after in the Navy Department, and within six months in all defense agencies.[51] From that step it

---

[51] CSC, *Minute No. 2,* June 4, 1940, and *ibid., National Defense Series No. 9,* December 6, 1940.

moved on in 1941 to permit promotion of either permanent or temporary employees into other occupational fields in which they had training or experience.[52] Again the War Department received this delegation of power first, then the Navy Department, and finally the Maritime Commission. Promotion was permissible after the first thirty days of service subject to Commission postaudit.

The Commission in April, 1941, delegated authority to the directors of personnel in all agencies to give advance approval to promotions or transfers within their own departments if they adhered to definite time standards established by the Commission.[53] These standards were a requirement of six months' service in a nondefense position and thirty days' service in a defense position. This authority was subject, of course, to Commission postaudit and could be exercised only with respect to employees with classified civil service status and to positions in the same line of work. The Commission announced the first standards for promotion in connection with a schedule of positions in the typing and stenography, clerical, and machine-operating series. Other series followed from time to time. Six months later this delegation was extended to cover probational-indefinite employees and all except temporaries and unclassified laborers.[54] By 1942 promotion of all except temporaries was permitted within an agency to positions classified under the Ramspeck Act if the employee had been in service on June 30, 1941.[55] By the end of the year all employees subject to the Ramspeck Act but not recommended for status and *status quo* employees could be promoted to any position for which they could qualify.[56]

2. ABUSES BY THE AGENCIES

Under the broad delegation to the employing agencies in 1941, the departments failed to enforce the time standards for promotion.[57] As a consequence they were taken to task later in the year. Promotions made in violation of the standards were allowed to

---

[52] CSC, *Letter to the War Department,* February 15, 1941, *Minute No. 1,* June 11, 1941, and *Letter to the Maritime Commission,* October 6, 1941.
[53] CSC, *Departmental Circular No. 257,* April 26, 1941.
[54] CSC, *Letter to All Departments,* October 6, 1941.
[55] CSC, *Departmental Circular No. 314,* January 30, 1942.
[56] *Ibid.,* No. 291, Supp. No. 11, December 18, 1942.
[57] CSC, *Letter to All Departments,* December 19, 1941.

stand if the employees met the requirements of intervening instructions, between April and December, 1941, but all future promotions had to meet the liberal standards of the earlier date.[58] The war service regulations did not change the 1941 authority delegated with respect to promotions.[59] After WMC Directive X on transfer had been issued in September, 1942, employees in indefinite positions in all departments could be promoted within their agencies in the same manner and on the same conditions as employees having status.[60] Even with that liberalization permitting promotion to all at the end of the first thirty days in a position, departments were promoting before the expiration of the thirty-day period and had to be reminded such actions were not legitimate.[61]

Commissioner Flemming admitted in December, 1943, to the House Appropriations Committee that the promotion problem had become so serious by early 1943 that the Commission had been forced to impose a "time brake."[62] The Byrd Committee found that from December 1, 1942, until May 30, 1943, out of 580,822 classified and per annum employees, 120,227 or 20.7 per cent received full grade promotions.[63] The distribution revealed that the war agencies were leaders in the institution of a liberal promotion policy. For example, 40 per cent of the employees in four agencies had received promotions: Central Administrative Services of the Office of Emergency Management, Liaison Office of OEM, the Office of Strategic Services, and the Railroad Retirement Board.[64] Nine agencies had promoted 30 to 40 per cent of their employees: National Labor Relations Board, Office of Lend Lease Administration, Office of Scientific Research and Development, Government Printing Office, the Administrative Office of the United States Courts, the National War Labor Board, Office

---

[58] *Ibid.* [59] CSC, *Departmental Circular No. 323*, February 28, 1942.

[60] *Ibid., No. 323, Revised, Supp. No. 8*, September 30, 1942.

[61] *Ibid., No. 388*, November 11, 1942. The Navy Department was exempted from the thirty-day requirement with respect to certain supervisory positions in the Navy yards which were impossible to fill by transfer. *Circular Letter No. 3916*, December 26, 1942.

[62] U.S. Congress, House, Hearing on *Independent Offices Appropriation Bill, 1945*, 78th Cong., 2nd Sess., December 9, 1943, p. 1055.

[63] U.S. Congress, Joint Committee on the Reduction of Nonessential Federal Expenditures, *Federal Personnel* (Additional Report), 78th Cong., 1st Sess., Sen. Doc. 131, p. 13.

[64] *Ibid.*, 14.

of War Information, National Capital Park and Planning Commission, and the Office of Censorship. Others almost as high were National Youth Administration with 29 per cent, WPB with 28 per cent, WMC and Office of Civilian Defense with 27 per cent, and the Selective Service System with 26 per cent. The "old line" agencies, other than War and Navy, averaged 19 per cent of their employees promoted during the same period studied by the committee, from December 1, 1942, to May 30, 1943. There were, of course, many employees who had received several promotions during the period.

3. RESTRICTIONS BY THE COMMISSION ON AGENCY PROMOTIONS

Taking cognizance of abuses, the Commission began in 1943 to establish more rigid promotion standards, gearing the time limits for promotion to the salary schedules. The following schedule was established for promotion early in 1943:

1. At least thirty days' service in cases which involved an increment in salary of less than $300 above the original salary.
2. Six months' service in a position when the increment was at least $300 per year and less than $600 above the original salary.
3. One year's service in a position when the increment was more than $600 per annum above the original salary.[65]

The foregoing limitations applied only to per annum employees. Where specific standards of training and experience had already been published, they were applicable. Exceptions were permitted only where justification was found in an employee's entire work experience, training, and demonstrated capacity to carry on the duties of the position to which promotion was proposed.[66] Exceptions had to be reported to the Commission immediately for post-audit.[67] The departments were still free of any requirement of prior approval of promotions so long as they adhered to the standards. The delegation could be revoked for flagrant violations or deviations.

A yet more drastic tightening of the reins on promotion in April, 1943, covered reallocations of positions which involved promotions for incumbents.[68] Prior to that time reallocations to

---

[65] CSC, *Departmental Circular No. 257, Supp. No. 4,* January 26, 1943, and *ibid., Revised,* March 22, 1943.
[66] *Ibid., Supp. No. 5,* February 2, 1943.   [67] *Ibid., Supp. No. 6,* March 10, 1943.
[68] *Ibid., Revision No. 2,* April 13, 1943.

a higher grade had been excepted from the limitations on promotions when the incumbent had benefited by the grade rise. The Commission gave authority to departmental personnel directors to approve promotion of unusually meritorious employees who did not meet the length of service requirements. When a promotion or reassignment involved a jump of more than one classification grade, it had to be reported to the Commission immediately, as was required also in cases where employees failed to meet the minimum qualifications in a published schedule. For promotional purposes movements from CAF-5 to CAF-7 or from CAF-7 to CAF-9 were considered one classification grade.

The Commission soon announced specific positions which required its prior approval for departmental promotions, namely, to those of personnel, budget, or finance director positions.[69] For all others the Commission simply retained a postaudit control although submission of other cases was permissive. Schedules of promotional standards were issued to cover grades CAF-1 through CAF-12, the entire subprofessional series, and grades P-1 through P-5. For positions above CAF-12 or P-5 the older stipulation of the time requirement of one year's service was retained.

Finally, in September, 1943, the promotion standards for the remainder of the war took shape and were announced.[70] One important change was the withdrawal of authority to promote temporary employees without prior Commission approval. Authority was delegated to make promotions without advance approval among classified employees, those serving in war service indefinite appointments, or *status quo* employees under the Ramspeck Act. The time limits announced were:

1. At least thirty days' Federal service in cases where the entrance salary for the grade of the proposed position was $2,000 or less per annum.
2. At least ninety days' Federal service in cases where the entrance rate was higher than $2,000 but did not exceed $2,600 per annum.
3. At least six months' Federal service in cases where the entrance salary was higher than $2,600 per annum and the increment was at least $300 and less than $600 per year over the entrance rate of the employee's present position.
4. At least twelve months' Federal service in cases where the entrance rate was higher than $2,600 and the increment was

[69] *Ibid., Supp. No. 1,* June 23, 1943. [70] *Ibid., Revision No. 3,* September 20, 1943.

$600 or more per year over the entrance rate of the employee's present position.

Personnel directors continued to exercise authority to make exceptions to the requirements in the published schedules for cases where time requirements had been met and actual experience had been gained in the work for which promotion was proposed. But cases which did not meet the time requirements had to be submitted to the Commission for advance approval. The Commission decision was based on a finding that the employee involved had met in full the recruiting standards for the position in question and that he was among the best qualified persons available. Promotions in ungraded positions, that is, wage board positions, merely had to meet the thirty-day requirement. Promotions from trainee positions were covered in individual training agreements between the agencies and the Commission. Advance Commission approval was still mandatory for promotions to personnel, budget, or finance director positions.

The immediate result of the more precise delegation made to the departments in September, 1943, seems to have been an improved degree of compliance. The Administrative Examining Unit handled 548 preaudit cases and 792 postaudits of promotions in the three months subsequent to the new rules. Of the former group 67 per cent were approved, and of the latter 86 per cent were approved.[71] Comparison of approvals in the two kinds of cases seems to indicate that the departments were giving more careful consideration to promotions where the burden of decision initially fell upon them.

Training agreements between employing agencies and the Civil Service Commission were permitted in 1944 to authorize training followed by promotion for recruits not fully qualified for the positions for which appointment was planned.[72] The central office of the Commission negotiated those for the departmental service, the regional directors for the field service and for units of the departmental service removed from Washington. Standards for the evaluation of such training programs were established in order that promotional standards would not be vitiated. The contract-

[71] CSC, *Report of Administrative and Management Placement Section to the Committee on Administrative Personnel,* January 19, 1944 (unpublished).
[72] CSC, *Circular Letter No. 4187,* July 19, 1944.

ing agency, of course, assumed full responsibility for the conduct of training whether on or off the job.

One of the difficult problems in determining promotions to administrative positions was the evaluation of experience. The Commission admitted that the evaluation was primarily a matter of individual judgment.[73] It went along with the stand of the war agencies that experience gained within their organizations should receive more credit than experience gained elsewhere. Experience offered from other agencies had to be rated on competitive standards, and only that type rated as qualifying in open competition was acceptable. Thus interagency transfers involving promotion were scrutinized and checked more carefully, but the standards came late in the war, in the summer of 1944.

Lest the promotion standards seem too harsh, the Commission provided two loopholes. One was the statement that the expressed policy did not prevent personnel directors or regional directors of any agency from effecting placements contrary to the general promotion policy when they were required by the "dictates of good administration or common sense."[74] The latter element could be interpreted individually to allow great or little latitude. The other loophole was the procedure whereby an individual who did not meet the time requirements could be assigned for no more than eight months to the duties of a position to which he might eventually be promoted. In the meantime, the latter position was allowed to remain vacant until his time had been served.[75] The artifice involved in this device is at once apparent. Either an individual was or was not capable of assuming the responsibilities of a higher position. If he was capable of performing its duties adequately, the adherence to arbitrary time limits which had to be served seems fatuous. One might well question the purpose served by standards for which such a loophole had to be provided in order to get assigned work produced. The sole purpose of promotion standards should have been to keep incompetent and unqualified persons from advancing to positions for which they were unfitted, not to delay arbitrarily the promotion of the competent. The responsibility of keeping out the unfit by tradition

[73] *Ibid., No. 4183,* July 18, 1944.
[74] CSC, *Manual of Instructions,* B3.03.07, April 13, 1945.
[75] CSC, Personnel Classification Division, *Field Memorandum No. 19,* August 8, 1944.

rested on the Commission, that for promotion of the competent on the operating agencies. Here the Commission forced its responsibility to supersede that of the agency. But another purpose may have been implicit in the Commission's policy, that is, the desire to allay the fears of Congress that upgrading was occurring with excessive rapidity. Time-serving devices at least slowed down the rate of advance.

4. CONGRESSIONAL CONCERN OVER THE PROBLEM OF PROMOTIONS

The two committees of Congress which investigated civilian employment during the war were both distressed at the general rapidity of promotion typical of the period. The Ramspeck Committee called on Commissioner Flemming for an elucidation of the broad delegation granted by the Commission in 1941 and delved into instances of what the Congressmen considered abuses of authority. These observations were made at a Ramspeck Committee hearing in March, 1943:

> *Mr. Flemming.* During the present fiscal year, that is, from July 1, 1942, to February 28, 1943, we have examined 193,841 intra-agency promotions in both Washington and the field.
>
> If those cases had been submitted to us for pre-audit, how many of them would we have questioned? Three thousand one hundred and fifty-seven or 1.6 per cent of the total.
>
> Now, would we have disapproved of all 3,157? No, because conferences with appointing officers would have brought to light additional facts on the basis of which we would have approved the proposed action; and in other instances the appointing officer would have said, "All right, let us assume that he isn't fully qualified; where are you going to get a better qualified person?" Our answer would have to be, in many cases, "We don't know."
>
> And therefore we would have had to let the promotion stand. . . .
>
> Are we satisfied with the manner in which we have handled this problem? No, not completely; and why?
>
> 1. We were too slow in getting out standards to the departments after delegating authority to act to them. I will be frank about that, and say that we were entirely too slow in getting out those standards. . . .
>
> 2. Although by our post-audits we were checking on qualifications, our standards had not been worked out in such a manner as to prevent rapid promotions for "90-day wonders." . . .

3. Finally, where we have found something wrong, I am not at all sure that our follow through has been vigorous enough, otherwise we would have withdrawn the authority in at least a few cases.

The Chairman. What have you done about the cases you disapproved? . . .

Mr. Flemming. Those that were not justified and where we were not able to present any better solution to the situation than the appointing officer had worked out, we let the transaction stand.

In other instances, out in the field, the field appointing officers—and this was in just a few instances, and I don't want to overstate this—we forced them to move the person back down to where he was in the first instance.

Now, my point is that I do not think that we have done enough of the latter. Also, I don't think we have moved enough in the direction of taking authority away from the appointing officers who may have abused their authority. But I would like to say that where we have found mistakes existing on the part of appointing officers, we have found that they were not concentrated in any one spot. They may have been scattered cases so it was pretty hard to come to a man and say, "Look here, you made this one mistake, and here's another and here's another, three, four, five mistakes, and, therefore, we are going to take away from you the authority we have delegated to you." . . .[76]

"Youthful personnel officers" were one class of employees who received intensive attention from the Ramspeck Committee because of what the committee deemed to have been phenomenal promotions. Examples were cited from fifty so-called "representative case histories" to prove that promotion policy had been unintelligent in advancing immature individuals, deficient in both tact and experience, to positions of responsibility. Their incompetence was cited as a bottleneck in the war program. But the committee offered no evidence that the persons whom they derided lacked the essential personal qualities and technical training to perform their duties competently, nor did the committee cite actual instances of failure on the job.[77]

The Byrd Committee's investigation of promotion led it to con-

[76] *Investigation of Civilian Employment,* Part I, Hearing on March 24, 1943, pp. 176-78.

[77] U.S. Congress, House, Committee on Civil Service, *Investigation of Civilian Employment,* House Report 766, 78th Cong., 1st Sess., 5-6.

clude that the Civil Service Commission had not exercised sufficient care in placing employees, in restricting promotions in certain agencies, and in educating operating officials on their responsibilities.[78] They decried the power in operating officials to waive the very liberal promotion standards prescribed by the Commission in 1943. The relaxation of length of service and qualifications standards, too, they felt was wrong. Their conclusion was: "From the committee's investigations and analyses it is believed that a promotion rate above $600 per annum for any Federal employee in the same twelve months is extravagant and conducive to poor morale among the rest of the employees."[79]

The answers received by congressional committees were never wholly satisfactory to them on the subject of transfers and promotions, both inter- and intra-agency. Serious trouble was narrowly averted by the Civil Service Commission when Congress was considering the Pay Act of 1945 only by the timely suppression of a report to the Committee on the Civil Service. The report by Colonel Edward J. McCormack, staff director of the House Civil Service Committee, was alleged to have within it damaging material on agency practices, but not even a determined fight on the floor of the House to release it pried it out of the committee's secret archives.[80] Chairman Ramspeck defended the action of the committee on the ground that the report was inaccurate by implication and had delved into personalities rather than the issues involved. There the matter rested so far as the whole House was concerned.[81]

Conclusions

Just as defense and war encouraged an uprooting and movement of the nation's labor force around the country, so the war years stimulated more rapid mobility within the Federal service. The new organizational units and agencies were attractive for transfer purposes and liberal promotion policies. Moreover, in order to retain their employees "old line" agencies had to compete with relaxed promotion standards. Rapid ascent through the ranks

---

[78] U.S. Congress, Joint Committee on the Reduction of Nonessential Federal Expenditures, *Federal Personnel* (Additional Report), Sen. Doc. 131, 78th Cong., 1st Sess., 14.

[79] *Ibid.*, 15. [80] 91 *Cong. Record* 7098, 7101, June 30, 1945. [81] *Ibid.*, 7100-101.

was, therefore, a phenomenon not limited to the war agencies alone.

Movement around the service threatened to disrupt vital agency programs unless curbs were applied. The controls for transfer fulfilled their original purpose of providing a balance between necessary and excessive mobility. Indiscriminate "shopping around" for jobs was slowed down both by priority classifications among the agencies and by WMC directives, but it was at all times possible for employees to negotiate highly profitable transfers into war agency positions.

Because promotion from within appeared in part to be a solution to recruitment difficulties from the lowest to the highest grades, the Commission granted the utmost freedom for promotion to appointing officers at first and only in 1943 checked its delegation by the development of definite standards. Employing agencies exercised a generous attitude toward promotion throughout the war. Labor market conditions made any other attitude unrealistic. When competent employees could leave the government service for industrial, commercial, or professional positions in equally vital tasks at any moment they desired, incentives were needed to retain them. Generosity in pushing up the ladder the young and ambitious who were able to assume added duties and responsibilities seemed to be the only solution to the problem of staffing positions above the trainee or junior level.

Dismay in the legislative branch was not wholly unjustified, but it was tinged with a degree of impracticality. Guardians of the purse strings were needed in the war years, it was true, but legislators who were not faced with operating responsibilities for critical objectives could ill appreciate turnover and morale problems in the executive branch. Had they but taken the trouble to view the problem comparatively, they would have realized that rapid promotion characterized the armed forces and industry as well as civilian government establishments.

The war afforded phenomenal opportunities to gain a breadth of experience through horizontal movement and to reap rewards for ability through rapid advancement in rank. The difficulties implicit in such opportunities, however, arose from the fact of their temporary duration. Re-employment rights, where they existed, were usually to mediocre prewar positions. Able, ambitious persons who had tasted the delights of variety, added authority, and prestige could scarcely be expected to return in a happy frame of mind, if at all, to a lesser role at a markedly reduced salary scale. Wartime mobility, which met the need for flexibility in time of crisis, could not but give birth to a postwar morale problem of serious proportions within the Federal service. This would be especially true when postwar reductions-in-force struck the service with a vengeance.

CHAPTER TEN

Intensification of Pressures for Higher Pay: Statutory Adjustments

THE PRESSURES for increased compensation made themselves felt in demands for statutory changes early in the war. Congress, however, chose to ignore those demands for the most part until the price level was altered to the point where basic amendments in the law were almost inescapable. Makeshift arrangements in the form of overtime pay were urged on Congress as temporary expedients by the executive branch on the ground that an increased workweek would necessitate fewer new recruits.

A study of the hearings and debates on the various pay bills from 1942 to 1945 reveals no attempt to construct a pay policy as such. Lack of consistency between the higher and lower levels of the service was continued in more aggravated form, if anything, by a sliding scale of increases for employees in the classified service from bottom to top. Provision for overtime pay showed the same inconsistency. To the fact that pressures for recruiting were more acute, quantitatively at least, in the lower levels of the service, may be attributed the persistence of discrepancies in pay. All that was done in the Pay Act of 1945, as in the overtime pay acts, was to add a percentage increase to the base scales provided in the Welch Act of 1928, as amended in 1930, on the assumption that the earlier scales were substantially correct or at least adequate for their time.

OVERTIME PAY LEGISLATION

Overtime pay for overtime work!
Hey, Mr. Congressman, hey!
We'll never quit and we'll never shirk,
Hey, Mr. Congressman, raise our pay.

Chorus: Pay, pay, overtime pay,
We'll work all night, and we'll work all day,
We'll work 'till we chase all the fascists away,
Hey, Mr. Congressman, raise our pay.

Overtime pay for overtime work,
Hey, Mr. Congressman, hey!
Don't stuff reaction inside your shirt,
Hey, Mr. Congressman, raise our pay.
Overtime pay for overtime work,
Hey, Mr. Congressman, hey!
We wanna work the American way,
Time and a half's the American way.
Overtime pay for overtime work,
Hey, Mr. Congressman, hey!
We'll work like horses, but we can't eat hay,
Hey, Mr. Congressman, raise our pay.
I looked over Jordan, and what did I see?
Hey, Mr. Congressman, hey!
Twenty-nine creditors a-chasin' after me,
Hey, Mr. Congressman, hey!
Overtime pay for overtime work,
Hey, Mr. Congressman, hey!
The cost of living's rising like the temperature in May—
It's gettin' hot, Mr. Congressman—it's gettin' awful hot, ain't it?
Overtime pay for overtime work,
Hey, Mr. Congressman, hey!
You can ration our rubber, you can ration our sugar,
You can ration our gas, you can ration our girdles,
But you can't ration morale in the OPA.[1]

This ditty gave the view Federal employees held of overtime pay. To them it was a means of adjusting government salaries to the rising cost of living in wartime in order to bring them into line with the increases industrial employees and some Federal workers had enjoyed through the adoption of the forty-eight hour week. So long as revision in basic salary schedules seemed unattainable, overtime pay was eagerly sought.

The provisions enacted for overtime pay from 1940 to 1942 were lacking in uniformity and represented a series of makeshift adjustments. Overtime pay was first permitted by Congress for per annum employees in the field services of the Navy and Coast Guard.[2] The discrepancy appeared that persisted all through the war between wage board employees and Classification Act employees as to overtime pay. The former group were paid at the

---

[1] Original words and music composed by Tom Glazer of the Priority Ramblers, reproduced in a collection of American folksongs by the Library of Congress.
[2] 54 *U.S. Statutes* 676 (1940).

rate of straight time and one-half for time over forty hours; the latter received daily overtime pay computed at the rate of time and one-half times 1/360 of their per annum salaries. Thus the first set of employees received 30 per cent additional pay in contrast to the 21 per cent paid to the second group. A few months after the first measure Congress enacted a similar statute for War Department field service and Panama Canal employees.[3] Measures for the two large departments, War and Navy, were not identical, in that the War Department and National Advisory Committee on Aeronautics could pay overtime only to certain field service employees, but the Navy and Maritime Commission were permitted to pay overtime to certain limited groups of departmental service employees in addition to field employees.[4]

1. THE FIRST GENERAL OVERTIME PAY PROVISION IN 1942

Serious morale problems and recruiting difficulties for the lower grades of classified employees resulted from the lack of uniformity in overtime pay provisions throughout the service by 1942. Employees working side by side on identical work suffered from gross pay inequities. One person might receive overtime pay as a wage board or per annum employee covered by the foregoing statutes. Another as a Classification Act employee was denied overtime pay or received a lesser amount than that paid to the wage board employee. Commissioner Flemming testified that a "milling around" from one job to another had resulted in the Federal government. In addition, the cost of living had risen by about 15.9 per cent between August, 1939, and March, 1942, without any concomitant pay adjustments.[5]

Chairman Ramspeck of the House Civil Service Committee, therefore, introduced bills to provide overtime compensation generally throughout the service. One of these bills, H. R. 7144, would have permitted agency heads to establish a work week exceeding forty hours for per annum and other employees not covered by existing legislation. The fraction used to compute one day of overtime was 1/360 of the per annum salary, but the over-

[3] 54 *U.S. Statutes* 1205 (1940). Both acts terminated June 30, 1942, but were extended for three months in July and October of 1942.
[4] 55 *U.S. Statutes* 148 (1941).
[5] U.S. Congress, House, Committee on Civil Service, Hearings on *Temporary Additional Compensation for Civilian Employees for the Duration of the War*, 77th Cong., 2nd Sess., June 3, 4, 5, 9, 10, 11, 1942, pp. 10-11.

time pay was not to bring any employee's aggregate salary beyond $3,800 per annum. The other bill, H. R. 7071, proposed a straight bonus of $300 per annum to all civilian employees and had been introduced by Ramspeck at the request of certain employee organizations. To the bonus bill Commissioner Flemming stated administration opposition on the ground that out-and-out bonuses would simply perpetuate existing inequities by giving all grades of employees an equal amount.[6]

The Senate bills, both introduced by Senator Mead, differed slightly from the House bills. The first one presented, S. 2666, authorized heads of departments to establish a work week of not less than forty-four hours and provided overtime pay for hours exceeding forty under the same formula as that used by the House but not on any portion of an employee's salary over $2,900 per annum. Employees who could not receive overtime were allowed 10 per cent additional of their earned basic pay or no more than $300 per year maximum.[7] The second bill, S. 2674, was almost identical except for granting additional pay specifically to the field service employees of the Post Office Department, a point to which the Commission objected.[8] The issue of the formula for computing a daily overtime by using 1/360 of per annum salaries was laid before the committee for the first time by the Bureau of the Budget, which reminded the committee that hourly employees received straight time and one-half, or 30 per cent more than their basic pay, in contradistinction to the 21.6 per cent resulting from time and one-half times 1/360 for each overtime day in a forty-eight hour week. The administration was not opposed to the more generous formula of 1/260, which would give a 30 per cent increase, in that it represented the actual number of days worked by per annum employees.[9] Both the War and Navy departments also supported the more generous formula.[10] Both agencies believed their recruitment difficulties for the departmental service might be partially solved by elimination of the existing inequities between wage board and per annum employees

---

[6] Ibid., 15.

[7] U.S. Congress, Senate, Committee on Civil Service, Hearings on *War Overtime Pay Act of 1942*, 77th Cong., 2nd Sess., September 22 and 23, 1942, pp. 1-2.

[8] Ibid., 3-5. The Commission objected to granting the postal employees an advantage in additional pay as well as the overtime they were already entitled to receive.

[9] Ibid., 20. [10] Ibid., 20-27.

in the field and the clerical employees in Washington.

The Senate committee waited for over a month after it had completed its hearings before it reported S. 2666, and the House committee failed to report any bills.[11] Significantly the Senate was liberal in its report for overtime, proposing time and one-half times 1/2080 of the base pay for each hour of overtime up to $2,900, the ceiling it adopted for computation of overtime pay.[12] The fraction 1/2080 represented the conversion of 1/260, the fraction representing one day's pay, into hours of work scheduled and actually worked per annum in a forty-hour week. To the original bill the committee added a provision requiring the Director of the Bureau of the Budget to certify that the number of employees in each agency was necessary and to order reductions in personnel when he thought agencies had too many persons on the pay roll. This provision will be discussed in more detail in Chapter XII.

The problem of overtime pay paled into insignificance in Congress in the face of elections in November, 1942, and not until Congress was prodded by President Roosevelt in December, 1942, was action forthcoming. Letters from the President to the two houses called attention to the "grossly unfair" condition Congress had allowed to develop among Federal employees which was a major cause of turnover.[13] The President requested immediate action or, alternatively, legislation to delegate power to the Chief Executive to act. Senator Byrd thereupon immediately introduced Senate Joint Resolution 169 to continue existing overtime compensation, which Congress had, incidentally, allowed to expire on November 30, 1942.

Spurred now to rapid action, the Senate and House civil service committees reported out Senate Joint Resolution 170 as a compromise, with amendments on personnel ceilings added by Senators Byrd and Langer, on December 15, 1942.[14] This measure passed both houses without a record vote. Some grumbling in the House came from Representative Rees of Kansas, the ranking

---

[11] U.S. Congress, Senate, Committee on Civil Service, *War Overtime Pay Act of 1942*, Sen. Report 1663, 77th Cong., 2nd Sess.

[12] *Ibid.*, 3.   [13] 88 *Cong. Record* 9469, December 11, 1942.

[14] *Ibid.*, 9548, December 15, 1942. Also U.S. Congress, Senate, Committee on Civil Service, *Wartime Compensation for Government Employees*, Sen. Report 1847, 77th Cong., 2nd Sess.

minority member on the Civil Service Committee, for the reason that the resolution had never actually come before the House committee for action although it had had months to consider the problem. While conceding that Rees was correct, Ramspeck urged its passage as necessary. On December 22, 1942, the day the new law took effect, the President immediately acted by sending a memorandum to the heads of all departments ordering that Saturday become a full working day in a forty-eight hour, six-day week for both the departmental and field service and that overtime pay commence as of December 1, 1942.[15]

In actuality the joint resolution of December 22, 1942, was simply another stopgap measure until permanent legislation could be studied and passed at the next session. The authorization of overtime pay, for example, extended from December 1, 1942, through April 30, 1943.[16] But all civilian employees of the Federal government had finally been covered. The joint resolution did not cover wage board employees as such, because the principle of time and one-half for overtime had been established by law for them in 1934.[17] The amount of salary on which overtime was to be paid was not to exceed $2,900 per annum, but in no case was the overtime pay to bring any salary to a total exceeding $5,000. In other words, employees who received salaries of $5,000 or better were not entitled to any overtime pay whatsoever. The less generous basis of computation, the fraction 1/360, was employed in figuring each day of overtime. Legislative and judicial branch employees, piecework, intermittent, irregular, or less than full-time workers received 10 per cent of their earned basic compensation in lieu of established overtime rates.

2. THE WAR OVERTIME PAY ACT OF 1943

The Seventy-Eighth Congress undertook the problem of overtime pay along the general lines laid down in the joint resolution of December 22, 1942. A House bill provided for overtime pay on the first $2,900 of salary, but eliminated the $5,000 ceiling, on the basis of 1/260 of annual compensation.[18]

[15] Press release, December 24, 1942, of memorandum of the President to all departments and agencies of the Federal government, December 22, 1942. Followed by Executive Order 9289, December 26, 1942.
[16] 56 *U.S. Statutes* 1068 (1942).   [17] 48 *U.S. Statutes* 522 (1934).
[18] U.S. Congress, House, Committee on Civil Service, Hearings on *A Bill to Provide for the Payment of Overtime Compensation to Government Employees and for Other Purposes*, 78th Cong., 1st Sess., February 24, 25, and 26, 1943, p. 1.

Consideration of the makeshift overtime pay instead of a fundamental salary revision was urged by the White House itself in order that study might be devoted to base pay changes. When one of the Congressmen commented on the desirability of effecting a complete overhauling instead of adding patchwork provisions on pay matters, William H. McReynolds, presidential Liaison Officer for Personnel Management, declared it was not then a good time to undertake complete revision.[19]

On that point the military departments expressed themselves unequivocally in disagreement. Both Admiral Charles W. Fisher and William H. Kushnick, in charge of civilian personnel in the Navy and War departments respectively, declared the need for a simple, uniform, just, and flexible personnel law and ventured the hope that Congress would address itself to the problem of revising the entire personnel system.[20]

When the committees reported out the bills, they had brought them closer to the provisions of the 1942 resolution. For example, in the House bill the $5,000 ceiling for pay including overtime was reinserted and the usual 1/360 as the basis for computing overtime had supplanted the fraction of 1/260.[21] But the committee accepted the recommendation of the Civil Service Commission that hiring be permitted at any rate within a range of pay for a grade instead of at the grade minimum when gross inequities were found between wage board and Classification Act positions side by side in the same establishment. The Senate committee remained firm in eliminating the $5,000 ceiling.

The House bill met little effective opposition and passed by a vote of 224 to 107.[22] An attempt was made on the Senate floor by Senator Thomas of Utah to amend the bill to allow true time and one-half for overtime by using the fraction 1/260, an amendment which was rejected.[23] Another amendment, of an entirely different nature, however, was passed to ban overtime pay to Classification Act employees who were members of unions that practiced racial discrimination. Senator Langer's amendment

---

[19] *Ibid.*, 10

[20] U.S. Congress, Senate, Committee on Civil Service, Hearings on *A Bill to Provide for the Payment of Overtime Compensation to Government Employees and for Other Purposes*, 78th Cong., 1st Sess., February 25, 26, and March 2, 1943, pp. 68-69.

[21] U.S. Congress, House, Committee on Civil Service, *War Overtime Pay Act of 1943*, House Report 339, 78th Cong., 1st Sess.

[22] 89 *Cong. Record* 2922, April 5, 1943.   [23] *Ibid.*, 3175, April 9, 1943.

for a similar ban affecting wage board employees was rejected, perhaps because it was in unions of wage board employees that racial discrimination was really practiced. After two conferences had been held on the bill, the House finally yielded on Senate elimination of the $5,000 ceiling on overtime pay, but struck out the antidiscrimination section.

In short, as finally enacted the War Overtime Pay Act of 1943 provided for overtime pay to per annum and monthly employees on the same basis as the joint resolution of 1942: time and one-half times 1/360 for each day of overtime work in excess of the basic forty hours per week.[24] Overtime pay was computed on the first $2,900 of annual salary only, but it was paid in all salary brackets. Legislative and judicial employees and those with irregular or intermittent hours of duty or for whom overtime work was not feasible were granted additional pay at the rate of $300 per year if their basic pay was less than $2,000 per year or at the rate of 15 per cent of all basic pay not exceeding $2,900 per year. Employees hired for less than full time or whose pay had some basis other than a time period received 15 per cent additional pay rather than the former 10 per cent granted in 1942. No employee could receive overtime pay amounting to more than 25 per cent of his basic pay for the period. The Civil Service Commission was empowered to correct inequities existing between Classification Act employees and wage board employees within the same government establishment by fixing any rate within a grade range as the entrance salary of that grade for the former group. This was the first notable relaxation of Classification Act salary schedules. The 1942 provision for personnel reports to the Bureau of the Budget for the latter's reductions of excess personnel was continued on a quarterly basis. The act terminated June 30, 1945.

The act of 1943 did not fully settle the issue of overtime pay. Per annum employees were still receiving 21.67 per cent salary increases through overtime as compared with the 30 per cent or straight time and one-half earned by wage board employees. But because it seemed apparent that Congress was not friendly to the higher rate, having twice rejected it, the issue was allowed to wait on a yet more fundamental request: revision of the entire compensation schedules of the Classification Act.

[24] 57 *U.S. Statutes* 75 (1943).

Increases in Basic Pay

As early as 1941 some Congressmen, particularly members of the two civil service committees, saw clearly that salary levels of the Classification Act were out of line with 1941 recruiting conditions in certain occupational groups. Another four years were required before the realization became widespread that salaries for all services and grades were no longer consonant with labor market conditions and general wage and price levels. General revision of salary schedules was simpler to obtain in 1945 than the partial revision had been to effect in 1942. But one attitude of mind was common at both times, a reluctance to make any fundamental adjustments for the higher administrative and professional grades.

1. THE 1942 REVISION OF CUSTODIAL AND SUBPROFESSIONAL SALARIES

The move initiated in 1941, to raise the salaries in the lowest grades of the custodial and subprofessional services, was combined with an attempt to revise the higher grades of the CAF and professional services. A bill (H. R. 6217) was introduced into the Seventy-Seventh Congress to effect changes by instituting five new CAF and professional grades to replace the existent top three.[25] Starting at a slightly lower salary and ending with a somewhat higher one, the ranges were somewhat narrower for each grade. The theory involved was that position-classification in the ranges affected could be made a closer approximation of actual ranges in responsibility, especially as between the existing $6,500 and $8,000 levels. Represented schematically these were the existing and proposed grades and salaries:

Existing Grades and Salary Ranges

P-6 and CAF-13	$5,600	$5,800	$6,000	$6,200	$6,400
P-7 and CAF-14	6,500	6,750	7,000	7,250	7,500
P-8 and CAF-15	8,000	8,250	8,500	8,750	9,000

Proposed Grades and Salary Ranges

P-6 and CAF-13	$5,400	$5,600	$5,800	$6,000	$6,200
P-7 and CAF-14	6,200	6,400	6,600	6,800	7,000
P-8 and CAF-15	7,000	7,250	7,500	7,750	8,000
P-9 and CAF-16	8,000	8,250	8,500	8,750	9,000
P-10 and CAF-17	9,000	9,250	9,500	9,750	10,000

[25] U.S. Congress, House, Committee on Civil Service, Hearings on *A Bill to Amend Sec. 13 of the Classification Act of 1923, as Amended*, 77th Cong., 1st Sess., December 16, 17, 18, 1941, pp. 1-3.

Proposals for the other services affected raised the entrance salaries and pay steps correlatively. The bill introduced a $1,200 minimum entrance salary for adult workers in the new crafts, protective, and custodial service, which replaced the former custodial service, and the subprofessional service. Former entrance salaries had been $1,080 and $1,020 per annum in the two services respectively.[26] Salaries for all grades in the CPC and subprofessional services were increased to correspond to the increment in the lowest grades in order to meet recruitment and turnover pressures.

By and large, several principles of pay policy emerged from the arguments presented by William H. McReynolds of the President's Executive Office and Edgar B. Young of the Bureau of the Budget in giving backing to the bill. In actuality these principles could have been conflicting. Mr. McReynolds pointed to the need for the government to adjust its lowest salaries to conform to generally accepted minimum living standards,[27] a view confirmed by Ismar Baruch of the Civil Service Commission, who ascribed to the proposed $1,200 minimum salaries a "social flavor."[28] While adhering to that idea, Edgar B. Young also presented two additional principles: internal consistency allied with adherence to the ideal of equal pay for equal work and, on the other hand, the desirability of government using as its major criterion for setting pay rates the prevailing rates for similar types of work outside government.[29] Of course, no witness took the trouble to define minimum standards of living. In the actual application of its two theories the Bureau of the Budget fell short; it could support neither internal consistency nor the prevailing rate idea because of fiscal considerations. Mr. Young admitted that pay rates for journeyman mechanics in classified positions could not be adjusted to match those of Washington Navy Yard wage board employees doing similar work because the amount of money involved in a precedent-making change of that kind was too great.[30] The spending of additional funds for such changes was not contemplated by those shaping fiscal policy.

[26] The entering rate for grade 1 in the new CPC service, which was the junior messenger grade, was also raised from $600 per annum to $720. To meet recruiting and turnover problems guards were reallocated from grade CPC-3 to CPC-4.

[27] U.S. Congress, House, Committee on Civil Service, Hearings on *A Bill to Amend Sec. 13 of the Classification Act*, 8.

[28] *Ibid.*, 39.   [29] *Ibid.*, 13.   [30] *Ibid.*

Rejecting all ideas but that of internal consistency between positions under the Classification Act and similar government positions outside the statute, the committee recommended the bill unqualifiedly, apparently oblivious to the lack of consistency shown up in committee hearings.[31] In short, there was no real philosophy back of the bill. Congress still labored under the misconception that it could achieve through the bill what the Bureau of the Budget had admitted it was not feasible to do from the standpoint of fiscal policy. But under its misconception, the committee was willing to liberalize the Classification Act in a way the rest of Congress found impossible to accept. It said:

> It is the duty of the Government at all times to recruit and endeavor to retain in the public service the very best available administrative talent, particularly in the higher posts. . . . In times like these, the necessity of attracting and retaining able administrators to manage the new and critical civilian activities of our war effort accentuates the relative lowness of the highest entrance salary, $8,000, for positions of the highest responsibility under the present standard pay scales of the Classification Act.[32]

The estimated cost of increasing the number of the upper grades in the CAF and professional services was virtually infinitesimal in terms of modern Federal finance: $300,000 out of an estimated cost of $19,898,000 for the entire bill.[33] Yet the significance of the recommendation far outweighed the low cost according to the testimony of McReynolds, Young, Baruch, and Herbert Emmerich, executive secretary of OPM. The committee agreed with their conclusions.

However generously Chairman Ramspeck chose to view the problem of recruiting for important administrative and professional posts, his colleagues in the House scarcely shared his enthusiasm. By July of 1942, when the bill finally came up for consideration, adjustments for the lower grades seemed more pressing than for the higher levels. First by opposing the creation of a new grade at the top, the $9,000 to $10,000 bracket, the House prevailed on Ramspeck to withdraw that proposal.[34] Having

---

[31] U.S. Congress, House, Committee on Civil Service, *Amending Further the Classification Act of 1923, as Amended*, House Report 1557, 77th Cong., 1st Sess., 2.
[32] *Ibid.*, 3.
[33] U.S. Congress, House, Committee on Civil Service, Hearings on *A Bill to Amend Sec. 13 of the Classification Act*, 17.
[34] 88 *Cong. Record* 5876-78, 5892, July 1, 1942.

forced a retreat on that point, Representative Rees, ranking Republican member of the Civil Service Committee, joined by his own party and southern Democrats, pressed his tactical advantage further by raising the hue and cry against a pay increase to the "bureaucrats."[35] Rees proposed an amendment to strike out the provision for the four remaining new CAF and professional grades. Representative Moser, a Democratic member of the Civil Service Committee, joined him, declaring, "We have a tendency on the part of different agencies of the Government to jump aboard and take a free ride for a group of bureaucrats through the help that they get from the Bureau of the Budget."[36] He and Representative Robsion of Kentucky denounced pay increases to the "bureaucrats" as unfair to the Congressmen who were under heavier expenses by reason of their biennial elections.[37] Once again Congress displayed a "dog in the manger" attitude toward allowing mere civil servants to approach the salary the legislative branch received. Backed up by this barrage, the Rees amendment, of course, carried.[38] At the other end of the scale Congress displayed more liberality, for the charwomen were granted an increase to sixty cents an hour, five cents over the committee's recommendation. With that change, the bill passed the House by a vote of 109 to 7 on July 1, 1942.[39]

The Senate Civil Service Committee quickly substituted the House bill for a similar one it had recommended. Senator Mead fought off such weak objections as those of Senator George, who opposed raising government wages because it was impossible to obtain agricultural labor,[40] with the statement, "When some poor devil is looking for an increase of fifteen or twenty cents a day, it is implied by some that all-out inflation will result if we grant this small increase."[41] The bill passed the Senate with an amendment raising charwomen's rates to sixty-five cents an hour.[42]

In short, the 1942 amendment to the Classification Act provided merely for an adjustment upward of salaries in the crafts, protective, and custodial service and subprofessional service in line with the new minimum entrance rate it established at $1,200 for adult workers in the two services.[43] The name of the former custodial service was changed by the act to crafts, protective, and custodial service.

[35] *Ibid.*, 5881-83, July 1, 1942.   [36] *Ibid.*, 5893.   [37] *Ibid.*, 5894.
[38] *Ibid.*, 5895.   [39] *Ibid.*, 5896.   [40] *Ibid.*, 6526, July 23, 1942.
[41] *Ibid.*, 6534.   [42] *Ibid.*, 6646, July 27, 1942.   [43] 56 *U.S. Statutes* 733 (1942).

2. THE FEDERAL EMPLOYEES' PAY ACT OF 1945

The Civil Service Commission was by no means satisfied with the pay structure of the Federal service during the war. In its *Sixtieth Annual Report* in 1943, the Commission recommended changes in the Ramspeck-Mead Act of 1941 to accelerate automatic increments and to use intermediate within-grade entrance rates to recruit for top management and technical positions at grades between CAF-12 and 15 and P-5 and 8 since the wide ranges between grades often forced unwise allocations.[44] The same kind of authority to recruit at intermediate salary rates was also urged generally to alleviate wartime recruitment difficulties at other levels.[45] In addition, the Commission sought authority to coordinate the schedules for wage board positions and to make a comprehensive study of all pay legislation affecting the executive branch to point out the need for correction of an increasing number of differentials between agencies.[46]

By 1944 the Commission became more specific in recommending upward revision of the basic rates of pay to compensate for the rising cost of living.[47] In addition, it urged a permanent overtime pay law for salaried employees at straight time and one-half for overtime beyond forty hours per week based on the formula of 1/2080 to convert annual rates to hourly rates.[48] Again it urged more freedom to determine minimum rates of pay.[49]

Not until President Roosevelt in his budget message for fiscal 1946 reminded Congress that permanent overtime legislation was needed and that the time had come for revision of basic salary rates did Congress begin to act. Bills were introduced in both the Senate and House, and the staff of the House Committee on the Civil Service prepared a comprehensive report on the Federal pay structure.[50] Hearings were held in both houses.[51]

---

[44] CSC, *Sixtieth Annual Report*, 36-38.   [45] *Ibid.*, 40-41.
[46] *Ibid.*, 42-43.   [47] CSC, *Sixty-First Annual Report*, 1.
[48] *Ibid.*, 3.   [49] *Ibid.*, 4.
[50] *Special Report Concerning Pay Structure of the Executive Branch of the Federal Government* (Confidential Committee Print), Staff Report to the Committee on Civil Service, March 24, 1945. Another report by the same committee was U.S. Congress, House, *Investigation of Civilian Employment*, House Report 514, 79th Cong., 1st Sess.
[51] U.S. Congress, House, Committee on Civil Service, Hearings on *Salary and Wage Administration in the Federal Service*, 79th Cong., 1st Sess., May 14, 15, 16, 17, and 18, 1945; and Senate, Committee on Civil Service, Hearings (same title), April 25, 26, 27, 30, and May 2, 1945.

The Commission endorsed both bills, but especially did it support enthusiastically the straight 15 per cent pay raise proposed in a third bill, H. R. 2703.[52] But in the Senate hearings the idea of increasing salaries for all grades up to the top ran into the customary difficulty, namely, that $9,000 employees by a straight percentage increase plus overtime would receive more than the Senators themselves. The following exchange expressed that feeling:

> *Senator Langer.* I want to say to Commissioner Flemming that he is getting into the same fix that we got into in the post office bill two months ago, by increasing the $9,000 salaries $1,350. That comes to $10,350, which is $350 more than Senator Byrd is drawing today as his salary for being a United States Senator. . . .
>
> I do not believe that you can ever get the Congress to pass a bill that is going to increase the $9,000 man $1,350. Do you think so, Mr. Chairman? Purely as a practical proposition, they will not vote for it.
>
> I agree with Senator Byrd in that the Congressmen want to increase the fellows in the lower brackets, but you are never going to get it through if you increase these higher fellows.
>
> *The Chairman* [Senator Downey]. Senator, I appreciate your compliment in asking me what Congress may do.
>
> *Senator Langer.* Do you believe, Senator, that any of these employees are worth more than Senator Byrd?
>
> *The Chairman.* My answer is immediately and very strongly in the negative.
>
> *Senator Langer.* Yes; and that is the way the other Senators feel about it.[53]

In contrast, the House hearings brought out the fact that some Congressmen at least regarded as unfair the overtime scales which reduced overtime pay for higher level employees. Congressman Herter deplored the idea of paying the higher-ranking Federal employees who ought to be worth considerably more than those far down the line only half as much for overtime as employees in

---

[52] *Salary and Wage Administration in the Federal Service*, Senate hearings, 6 and House hearings, 13.
[53] *Ibid.*, Senate hearings, 89.

the lower grades received.⁵⁴ He felt this was not a desirable principle for permanent legislation.

Increases in the cost of living and in the gross weekly earnings of employees in private industry showed that the Federal government by 1945 faced severe recruitment problems as a result of pay policies. Testimony by the Bureau of Labor Statistics in the hearings showed that the cost of living had risen about 30 per cent since January, 1941.⁵⁵ Federal employees in the same period had received 25.7 per cent more in average gross weekly earnings. But in comparison with gross weekly earnings outside government, Federal earning contrasted unfavorably. Increases in gross weekly earnings had been 78 per cent in manufacturing, 53 per cent in brokerage, 45 per cent in street railways. Only in retail trade had the percentage increase been smaller than that for Federal employees, but the Bureau of Labor Statistics explained the cause as the widespread employment of part-time workers in retail trade during the war.⁵⁶

Taking into consideration the impact of increased living costs on the lower-grade employees and consequent recruitment difficulties, the Senate committee discarded a straight 15 per cent increase in favor of sliding scale increases in base pay.⁵⁷ The proposed scale in the Senate bill granted a 20 per cent increase on the first $1,200, 10 per cent on the difference between $1,200 to $4,600, and 5 per cent on all salary above $4,600. A minimum salary of $1,440 was thus proposed for all adult Federal per annum employees. In so far as overtime was concerned, the committee clung to the old formula based on 1/2880, primarily because it considered overtime pay an issue of declining importance in the postwar period. The bill passed the Senate, as recommended by the committee, on May 17, 1945.

The House subcommittee studying this bill not only recommended true time and one-half based on 1/2080 of annual salary for the hourly rate but also made it clear that the sliding scale

---

⁵⁴ *Salary and Wage Administration in the Federal Service,* House hearings, 48-49.
⁵⁵ *Ibid.,* hearing on May 16, 1945. This figure included the hidden rise of 3 or 4 per cent pointed out by the President's Cost of Living Committee.
⁵⁶ *Ibid.*
⁵⁷ U.S. Congress, Senate, Committee on Civil Service, *Pay Increases for Government Employees,* Sen. Report 265, 79th Cong., 1st Sess., 3.

increases were not wholly adequate. It declared, with some prescience:

> In the postwar period, the problems of Government, the inevitable complexities of administration, and the importance of effective service to the people will justify unusual emphasis upon high standards in selecting, promoting and retaining personnel. This is particularly true of middle and higher brackets. But with high qualification standards must be associated rates of compensation that are reasonably attractive to persons who meet those standards. . . . At an appropriate time, the Congress can and should make the gap between private salaries and public salaries less disadvantageous to the Government than it is now and will still be under the plan of increases recommended in the bill.[58]

A determined opposition presented itself against the bill on the floor of the House when it was called up for debate on June 11, 1945. Representative Rees, ranking minority member of the Civil Service Committee, launched into an attack on the bill on the basis of allegedly excessive numbers in the Federal service, the impermanence of any pay legislation in 1945 to align salaries with living costs, and the stupendous cost of the bill.[59] He was joined by Representative Rankin, an avowed enemy of the Civil Service Commission, who alleged that a "kind of Civil Service fascisti" was being built up in the country.[60]

But amid the clamor against the bill there were a few tributes to the Federal employee, rare phenomena in the halls of Congress. One came from Representative Gearhart of California, who said:

> These men and women have done a wonderful wartime job. They have worked at top speed and for long hours and they have given the utmost of their skill and earnestness to the job. . . . The War Overtime Act by no means granted them justice. . . .
>
> This remedial measure is long, long overdue, so much so, in fact, that considerable sentiment has been expressed to the effect that it should have been made retroactive. . . .
>
> It is time for a basic revision of Classification Act salaries. If the tremendously increased cost of living alone did not justify it, the glorious services of these employees during the

[58] Report of the Subcommittee of the Committee on the Civil Service on the *Federal Employees' Pay Act of 1945*, 79th Cong., 1st Sess., June 4, 1945, p. 4.
[59] 91 *Cong. Record* 5901-902, June 11, 1945.   [60] *Ibid.*, 5902.

STATUTORY PAY ADJUSTMENTS   231

war would entitle them to recognition; and, finally, the American view that there should be a constantly rising standard of living in this country, and that its people should benefit from improved methods and techniques, gives them a further just claim.[61]

Opposition amendments were beaten off and the bill passed the House by a vote of 317 to 36 on June 13, 1945, which set the stage for early enactment.[62] It was then substituted for the Senate bill, and the main point cleared in the conference was that the Senate managers were won to the advocacy of the House proposal of true time and one-half for overtime based on the fraction of 1/2080.[63] The conference report was adopted by the House on June 25 and by the Senate on June 26, 1945.

Aside from adjusting basic annual salary rates upward for Classification Act employees by the sliding scale formula, as shown below, the Pay Act of 1945 was a landmark in other respects. Not only did it establish as a permanent policy the forty-hour week, introduced by the War Overtime Pay Acts for salaried employees, but it provided overtime compensation at true time and one-half for regular salaried employees receiving up to $2,980 per annum.[64] For those paid at a rate above that figure, a sliding scale was introduced for overtime based on 416 hours of overtime per year, or eight hours a week for fifty-two weeks. The amount of $628.33 per year previously paid under the overtime legislation of 1943 was the point at which the scale stabilized for all employees receiving $6,440 or more per year. In addition, the new law gave more scope to the Civil Service Commission in establishing as entrance rates any within-grade rates up to the middle of the grade range for positions when the Commission found such action necessary by reason of comparative duties and responsibilities or to eliminate pay inequities between Classification Act and wage board employees in the same government establishment. Not only were the waiting periods shortened for within-grade salary increments from eighteen to twelve and from thirty to eighteen months respectively, but employees with efficiency ratings of "good" could advance beyond the middle rate. The granting of

---

[61] *Ibid.*, 5913-14.   [62] *Ibid.*, 6068, June 13, 1945.
[63] U.S. Congress, House, Conference Committee report, *Federal Employees Pay Act of 1945*, House Report 784, 79th Cong., 1st Sess., 2-3.
[64] 59 *U.S. Statutes* 295 (1945).

meritorious pay increases was liberalized to permit such an increase, in addition to any regular periodic pay increase within a waiting period, for sustained work performance, a beneficial suggestion, or a special service. Departments were permitted to grant merit increases under standards set by the Commission and post-audited by it for compliance. The Commission was required to report to Congress each year the kinds and numbers of merit increases. A night pay differential of 10 per cent was granted to salaried employees working between 6 P.M. and 6 A.M. on a regularly scheduled tour of duty. Overtime pay was mandatory for scheduled work performed on any of eight statutory holidays, in contrast to the wartime practice of scheduling as regular working days without special premium pay all days but Christmas.[65]

President Truman directed that work be scheduled as nearly as possible on the first five days of the week with Saturday left for any overtime regularly required in a work week.[66] Comprehensive new overtime pay regulations were issued in Executive Order 9578 of June 30, 1945, incorporating the statutory changes. In addition, the President placed all departments except War, Navy, Treasury, the Veterans Administration, TVA, and the Panama Canal on a forty-four hour week beginning July 1, 1945.[67]

The nearest clue to any basic policy underlying the 1945 Pay Act was the idea expressed in Congress of the desirability of not decreasing the "take home" pay of Federal employees when the government service would abandon overtime work and compensation. No comprehensive studies were made of industrial or commercial scales to determine how closely the old or new Federal pay rates approximated prevailing rates for similar occupations. No one knew how wide the discrepancies were between salaries paid to middle and higher bracket administrators and those paid for positions of corresponding responsibilities outside. Furthermore, although there was mention of a minimum standard of decency pay of at least $1,900 per year required in Washington, no one proposed that figure as minimum pay for Federal employees. The conclusion seems inescapable from the testimony and debate that, instead of formulating a pay policy, Congress

---

[65] For a useful summary of this new legislation see Ismar Baruch, "The Federal Employees Pay Act of 1945," *Public Personnel Review*, VI (October, 1945), 201-12.
[66] CSC, *Departmental Circular No. 529*, June 30, 1945.
[67] Press release of President Truman, July 3, 1945.

simply found it convenient to add a percentage which the War Labor Board and the Bureau of the Budget approved as within the economic stabilization and fiscal policies and which could get through Congress with a minimum of outcry and denunciation. If the nation had a pay policy for the Federal employees, it seemed to have resolved itself into the rate feasible in a legislative body antipathetic to the "bureaucrats."

TABLE 12

INCREASES IN SELECTED SALARY RATES UNDER THE PAY ACT OF 1945 AS COMPARED WITH RATES EFFECTIVE THROUGH JUNE 30, 1945[a]

Basic Rates June 30, 1945	Increase Amount	Per Cent	Basic Rates July 1, 1945
$1,200.00	$240.00	20.0	$1,440.00
1,440.00	264.00	18.3	1,704.00
1,620.00	282.00	17.4	1,902.00
1,800.00	300.00	16.7	2,100.00
2,000.00	320.00	16.0	2,320.00
2,300.00	350.00	15.2	2,650.00
2,600.00	380.00	14.6	2,980.00
2,900.00	410.00	14.1	3,310.00
3,200.00	440.00	13.8	3,640.00
3,500.00	470.00	13.4	3,970.00
3,800.00	500.00	13.2	4,300.00
4,600.00	580.00	12.6	5,180.00
5,600.00	630.00	11.3	6,230.00
6,500.00	675.00	10.4	7,175.00
8,000.00	750.00	9.4	8,750.00
9,000.00	800.00	8.9	9,800.00

[a] Ismar Baruch, "The Federal Employees Pay Act of 1945," *Public Personnel Review*, VI (October, 1945), 203, Table 1.

Conclusions

Surprisingly little resistance, on the whole, was manifested in Congress to pay adjustments requested by the executive during the war years. That Congress was laggard in bringing basic pay rates into some consonance with those paid by private employers for similar types of work seems to have been due to reluctance of the executive branch to address itself firmly to the pay problem. The argument may be advanced that Congress itself should have realized the need for salary modification without waiting for instructions and prodding from the executive. But the fact remains that Congress usually waits for executive proposals on matters respecting the Federal personnel system. As for executive procrastination on this subject, a guess may be hazarded that it was not politically feasible to urge adjustments in basic compensation rates when the administration was trying to enforce an economic stabilization policy.

Congress might have explored the idea of delegating to the executive branch the task of fixing and adjusting pay scales in time of crisis, subject to a legislative review. Thus flexibility and more intensity of study of the problems might have been obtained. The former is especially important in a period of fluctuating living costs. Congress might have utilized the procedure it developed in the Reorganization Act of 1939 of a legislative veto within sixty days of executive orders it disapproved. But such a delegation would have entailed the surrender of a prerogative jealously guarded by the legislative branch, that of controlling in detail all aspects of Federal expenditures. In any event, by adherence to the idea of statutory revision as the sole method of salary readjustment, Congress preserved the rigidity of the Federal salary system and forced a warping of position-classification standards.

CHAPTER ELEVEN

Intensification of Pressures for Higher Pay: On the Classification Act and Wage Administration

BECAUSE the exigencies of recruitment, including transfer, could not wait for retarded congressional revision of salaries, a more readily accessible method to secure necessary salary adjustments had to be found. The solution was in the generous allocation or reallocation of positions covered by the Classification Act. Only through the liberalization of position allocation could flexibility be introduced into an otherwise inflexible salary structure. Once adjustments were made in a few agencies at any grade level, it was inevitable that almost all agencies would seek to make similar grade allocations and that reallocations became quite general for most positions.

The liberalization of allocations soon gave rise to inequities and anomalies between positions, and the inequities were compounded across organizational lines. This was especially true in the field service where agencies had more control over allocation. Because promotion standards had been liberalized, it was difficult to ascertain at first glance whether the relaxation had occurred in position allocation or merely in the qualifying of the individual incumbents of positions examined.

The Civil Service Commission, guardian of the Classification Act, could not impede critical war work by lengthy investigations and surveys of positions. The word of administrators had to be accepted at face value with respect to the level of responsibilities and duties in new positions or reallocations of existent jobs. Any attempt to keep the power of preliminary decision over the allocation of critical positions in its hands alone would soon have stripped the Commission of all controls. This result would have been especially true with respect to classification of civilian positions in both the military branches, for the War and Navy departments had sufficient prestige in the legislative halls to rid themselves expeditiously of any delaying influences. The Commission thus seems to have been faced with the kind of dilemma that confronted Lincoln during the Civil War, when he had to violate the Constitution in order to save it. In order to preserve the Classification Act for the future and conserve its own authority under it, the Civil Service Commission had to acquiesce in many allocations it could scarcely have countenanced before the war.

Because the Civil Service Commission had never possessed final authority over position allocation in the field service, wide disparities had always existed among similar positions from one region to another and even from one establishment to another within a region. Discrepancies of that kind took on a serious aspect in impeding recruitment during wartime, and the need for standards to guide allocations in the field service had to be faced by the Commission. Indeed, by executive order and War Manpower Commission directive the Commission was compelled to institute publication of standards in 1943. By that time the great expansion in the field service had already taken place, and the significance of the new standards seemed to be for realignment during the postwar period rather than for eradicating wartime inequities.

Getting Around the Classification Act

The departure from rigid adherence to the Classification Act was not premeditated but constituted a convenience too simple to overlook. Furthermore, decentralization of the administration of classification in both the departmental and field services allowed discrepancies to creep in as between establishments and bureaus, both within and across departmental lines. Few administrators, in both war and "old line" agencies, failed to avail themselves of the advantages of decentralization and the emergency procedures. Failure by the Commission in the years from 1923 to 1939 to publish the standards for position allocation was a factor militating against any kind of firm central control. Had standards been developed and published, a few guide-lines would have existed for new wartime positions reasonably similar to many already found in the service. As it was, standards were developed too late to be of much assistance for anything but postwar demobilization and reconversion.

1. CLASSIFICATION IN THE DEPARTMENTAL SERVICE

When the liaison service of the Commission was established in 1940, as described in Chapter II, classifiers were stationed in the defense agencies as part of the decentralization program to expedite position allocations. The classifiers were representatives of the Personnel Classification Division detailed to complete allocations the same day the agency's recommendation was transmitted to them, if possible.[1] Owing to the fact that recruitment could not proceed until allocation had been completed, the element of speed in classification assumed primary importance. By 1941, when recruitment assumed an aspect of greater urgency, the Commission established a priority list for classification actions, placing at the head of the list newly created positions and all cases involved in a chain of actions which affected recruiting.[2] By 1943, 75 per cent of all classification allocations were made in the departments and merely postaudited by the Commission.[3]

By way of accelerating procedures in classification the Commission established a means whereby departments could merely report the creation of identical additional positions to those already allocated whenever possible.[4] Combined position descriptions covering several complete descriptions of positions across a bureau or an agency, with different duties and responsibilities but allocable to the same service, grade, series, and class, were issued in 1942 as an extension of the use of identical additional positions.[5] The device represented by combined position descriptions was to be used either for broad organizational coverage or high numerical coverage or both. In this way, the volume of paper work in both the agency and the Commission was materially reduced. Appeals from allocations were transferred from the Board of Appeals and Review to the Personnel Classification Division because of the pressure of loyalty cases on the former.[6]

Without recognized standards decentralization and expediting of procedures cast each classifier and each agency adrift on an uncharted sea. Departmental personnel officers had themselves stated the case for publication of classification standards by the Commission many times, most recently in 1942.[7] In fact, the de-

[1] CSC, *Fifty-Seventh Annual Report,* 42.
[2] CSC, *Circular Letter No. 3485,* November 26, 1941.
[3] CSC, *Sixtieth Annual Report,* 35.
[4] CSC, *Departmental Circular No. 317,* February 16, 1942.
[5] *Ibid., No. 381,* October 13, 1942, and *ibid., Revised,* June 26, 1943.
[6] *Ibid., No. 339,* May 18, 1942.
[7] See Roy F. Hendrickson, "If I Could Remake the Classification System," *Personnel Administration,* IV (June, 1942), 10-12; Edgar B. Young, "If I Could Remake the Classification System," *Personnel Administration,* V (October, 1942), 10-12;

sirability of developing standards and publishing class specifications had been pointed out in the original Personnel Classification Board as early as 1924 by Guy Moffett.[8] But for one reason or another, action by the old Personnel Classification Board and by the Commission, which took over classification work in 1932, was not forthcoming. This failure left classifiers in the war years susceptible to the "cross organizational fallacy," the temptation to allocate positions that seemed similar in a superficial way to others in different organization units to the same grade. When a premium was placed on speed, it was virtually impossible to resist the preliminary work done by administrators in writing specifications to secure a desired grade. Neither in the agencies nor in the Personnel Classification Division of the Commission was there time to train the classification analysts properly in the techniques of their work to avoid even the more egregious blunders.

OPA offered an example of the "cross organizational fallacy" employed to obtain high allocations for its attorney staff. For example, in 1942 in the Legal Department were found under an Associate General Counsel in charge of legal aspects of price control various divisions exactly parallel to similar ones in the Price Department, each with a chief whose title corresponded to the title of the chief of the co-ordinate Price division. This pattern was repeated throughout the Legal Department with respect to the Rationing Legal Division and the Rationing Department.[9] The purpose was apparent on its face: by creating a parallel legal hierarchy to that of the main operating division it was possible to obtain the same grade and salary for attorneys serving as legal section chiefs as their "opposite numbers" among the operating section chiefs.

Administrators urged high allocations on the ground that the novelty of work in the war program required more initiative and leadership on the part of the incumbent than in an older agency which operated under a set of well-established precedents and

---

Theodore F. Wilson and Albert J. Faulstich, "If We Could Remake the Classification System," *Personnel Administration*, V (November, 1942), 10-12.

[8] U.S. Congress, House, Committee on Civil Service, Hearings on *The Law and the Personnel Classification Board*, 68th Cong., 1st Sess., March 1, 1924, p. 100.

[9] See OPA, *Administrative Order No. 14 (Second Revision)*, November 2, 1942.

rules.¹⁰ The Commission took the stand that in doubtful cases it could ill afford to contest the factor of novelty with the agency. "In cases of doubt the Commission had to be generous with both old and new agencies," declared Ismar Baruch, Chief of the Personnel Classification Division.¹¹ But it was hard to tell how far this added responsibility went in a new agency. The best that any classifier could do in any agency to which he was detailed was to make position-to-position comparisons within the particular agency. Without standards he was estopped from service-wide comparisons.

Attributing inequities to Commission failure in not publishing standards, the Byrd Committee stated: "Investigation has revealed that thousands of employees all through the Federal service performing identical duties have been placed in different classifications and are receiving various salaries for the same work. This not only is a reprehensible situation unfair to the Federal employees, but wastes thousands of dollars of Federal funds."¹²

The pressures from the war agencies on classification can perhaps best be summarized in the words of a former regional classification chief:

> Within the Division (Personnel Classification) itself it was a recognized fact that according to the previous background and ability of the classifier detailed to a particular agency his allocations would reflect existing standards (standards in the sense of position-to-position comparisons), or be determined by the pressure of operating officials. You can appreciate the impact of some of this pressure if you realize that much of it came from high officials, especially in the War Department, who would not hesitate to make rather serious threats about the use of their authority and prestige to obtain from higher officials within the Division the allocations which were being demanded.
>
> Because of the lack of standards, allocations came to be made on a position-to-position comparison basis when such comparisons became known. For instance, in certain bureaus of the War Department, programs would be better described or "promoted" and classifiers being sincerely impressed by the

---

[10] Interview with Ismar Baruch, Chief, Personnel Classification Division, CSC, July 23, 1945. [11] *Ibid.*

[12] U.S. Congress, Joint Committee on Reduction of Nonessential Federal Expenditures, *Federal Personnel*, Sen. Doc. 66, 78th Cong., 1st Sess., 13-14.

scope and significance of the program would grant higher allocations. Often the proposed facts were never realized. Subsequently, other bureaus would become aware of these allocations and demand the same for their positions. Failure of PCD to reduce erroneous allocations in most cases made it almost necessary to recognize the pressure of later demands. However, PCD usually stood off this type of pressure for as long as it possibly could. . . .

While it might be true that there was in the "old line" agencies no counterpart of the War Production Board position of Priority Analyst; yet there were positions in other agencies involving a comparable knowledge of rules and regulations, although different in subject matter which would have made acceptable allocation possible. Positions of Wage Rate Analyst in the War Labor Board could be compared to positions of Income Tax Specialists or Research Analysts in the Labor Department. . . . Many positions in the war agencies, such as engineers, accountants and information specialists were directly comparable to those in the "old line" agencies.

Clerical positions, such as stenographers, file clerks, bookkeepers and others, would of course be directly comparable. Here also the war agencies began to break over the line in order to meet the recruiting pressures. The shift would usually begin by the allocation of borderline positions to the higher grades, such as CAF-3, Clerk-steno, to CAF-4. By continued reference to these borderline positions which were only somewhat less equal in content, the war agencies continually deteriorated the content of higher grade positions. "Old line" agencies did not follow this practice immediately because they knew they would be faced with administrative and morale problems resulting from the post-war downgradings which would be required.[13]

Tardily the Commission started the publication of standards for classification during the summer of 1943, both for the departmental service and the field.[14] During fiscal 1944, 147 standards were published for the departmental service, covering 35,000 departmental positions and 70,000 field positions.[15] This step came, however, after the new defense and war agencies and programs had been organized, so that it could scarcely be conceived as an

[13] Letter to the writer from Miss Thadene Hayworth, former Chief, Regional Classification Section, San Francisco Regional Office, CSC, October 19, 1945.

[14] CSC, Personnel Classification Division, *History of Position-Classification and Salary Standardization in the Federal Service 1941-1944*, PCD Manual A-2-Supp. 1, February 1, 1945, p. 109 (mimeographed).

[15] U.S. Congress, House, Hearing on *Independent Offices Appropriation Bill, 1946*, 79th Cong., 1st Sess., January 17, 1945, 1172.

instrument to bring into line the wartime discrepancies on a wide scale. Rather standards were of future value in helping to effect the postwar downgradings mentioned above.

The extent to which the war agencies weakened the application of the Classification Act is hard to determine. For one thing, few, if any, Federal administrators felt free to commit themselves on that subject, for the power of retaliation in the hands of the central personnel agency, like the mills of the gods, grinds slowly but surely. Persons in responsible positions in the war agencies were not ready to admit what had transpired in their agencies. On the other hand, the Commission itself steadfastly maintained that there had been no discrepancies between war agencies and "old line" agencies. Indeed, it was a poor administrator in one of the older departments who could not and did not eventually eradicate classification disparities, in so far as feasible, between his own and the new agencies. The impression was common among Federal employees—and persistently so—that allocations had been originally higher in the war agencies, a fact which had eventually affected many of the older agencies confronted by the same recruitment problems. Without a comprehensive survey by an independent group, such as a congressional committee, it would be impossible to establish the facts throughout the service.[16] As matters stand, one can only find bits and pieces of evidence, as represented by the OPA organization and classification of legal positions.

2. CLASSIFICATION IN THE FIELD SERVICE

The classification of field positions presented a somewhat different problem from that of the departmental service because the allocation of field positions was made by the departments and agencies and merely postaudited by the Commission. Under the Classification Act of 1923 the Commission's authority to allocate was limited to the departmental service. Disparities, therefore, had long persisted in the field between agencies and within agencies. The Commission in 1944 called attention in its *Sixty-First Annual Report* to the chaotic salary conditions in the field service resulting from competitive bidding by agencies because of the wartime manpower shortage.[17]

[16] Neither the Byrd nor Ramspeck committee delved into the classification problem in a comprehensive way.
[17] CSC, *Sixty-First Annual Report*, 4.

Lack of standards for the allocation of field service positions had, therefore, been even more serious than for the departmental service in the prewar years, since the agencies which had authority to allocate had no guide-lines. To remedy that defect War Manpower Directive XII was issued on September 24, 1942, to implement transfer policies by attempting to bring about greater uniformity in field service allocations. The Civil Service Commission was given authority to survey field positions and prepare and promulgate standards. The conditions under which it was to prepare standards occurred when field service allocations (1) interfered with the manpower program or Federal transfer policies under WMC Directive X, (2) created undesirable interdepartmental competition for employees, or (3) provided an impediment to effective manpower utilization. After standards had been issued, departments were to classify their field positions properly and report the classification to the Commission, which made postaudits to determine compliance. Reports of noncompliance with standards went to the Bureau of the Budget.

The Commission postaudited several thousand positions of guards and patrolmen under the authority of WMC Directive XII. Although some evidence of noncompliance was revealed, all agencies co-operated well in the long run in adjusting allocations properly. No cases, therefore, were reported to the Bureau of the Budget.[18]

Executive Order 9330 of April 16, 1943, which transferred some functions of the Division of Central Administrative Services of the Office of Emergency Management to constituent agencies, as ODT and WPB, transferred the classification of field positions in all constituent agencies to the Civil Service Commission. The latter was responsible for promulgation of standards, postaudits of allocations by the constituent agencies, and the reporting of erroneous allocations to the head of the war agency concerned for correction or explanation. Ismar Baruch, Chief of the Personnel Classification Division of the Commission, reported:

> Under Executive Order 9330 we post-audited several thousand positions in the Office of Emergency Management agencies (WPB, ODT, WLB, OWI, etc.) and OPA. Considering

[18] Letter to the writer from Ismar Baruch, Chief, Personnel Classification Division, CSC, March 28, 1946.

each agency as a whole we found an honest attempt to apply the standards promulgated by the Commission, and a marked degree of cooperation in adjusting erroneous allocations. There were a few cases where we could not reach an agreement with the agency concerned but the number of these was negligible—much less than one percent of the positions audited.

We found that the agencies subject to E.O. 9330 welcomed our post-audits and made every effort to facilitate them.

Before Executive Order 9330 was issued there were numerous complaints from the "old line" government establishments that the emergency agencies were pirating their employees and that the emergency agencies were pirating employees from each other. After the program provided by the Order had been in operation for a few months these complaints ceased.

Very few reductions in salary were required through the application of standards because of the overlapping salary schedules provided in the Classification Act of 1923, as amended. Except in the higher grades, an employee's position would have to be reduced more than two grades before a salary reduction would be required. Then, too, since the programs of the emergency agencies were expanding during the period E.O. 9330 was in effect, it was usually possible to transfer an employee to more responsible or more difficult work and thereby avoid reduction in both grade and pay.[19]

Executive Order 9512 of January 16, 1945, conferred a more comprehensive authority on the Civil Service Commission. The Commission was empowered to prepare and publish allocation standards for all field service positions under the Classification Act. In addition, it was to co-ordinate field standards with those for the departmental service. Agency heads had to comply with the standards in the allocation of individual positions. The Commission received authority to investigate the degree of compliance and to report noncompliance to the President through the Liaison Officer for Personnel Management. Commission authority thus extended over the greater part of the field service on a standards and postaudit basis.[20] Commission efforts up to the end of hostilities were wholly concentrated on the publication of standards under Executive Order 9512, and no postaudits were made.[21]

[19] *Ibid.*
[20] CSC, Personnel Classification Division, *Circular Letter, Position Classification Series No. 3*, January 29, 1945.
[21] Letter from Ismar Baruch, March 28, 1946. No postaudits were planned until after July 1, 1946.

Individual allocations were of no more concern to the Commission under WMC Directive XII and the two executive orders than they had been earlier. Their sole significance was as they occurred in classes of positions showing the determination or application of standards.[22] Appeals to the Commission through the departments were, however, permitted from individual employees whose salaries had to be reduced by application of the standards.[23] Although the pertinent department made a preliminary review of the appeal, the Personnel Classification Division of the Commission had final jurisdiction over all cases of adverse departmental action on employee appeals and made the ultimate decision.[24]

Regional classification sections were established in the Commission regional offices early in 1943 as local representatives of the Personnel Classification Division.[25] Only through this extension of the classification staff into the Commission's own field offices could adequate information be supplied to the employing agencies' field offices, especially those of the war agencies, and to the Commission in Washington. Part of the work in Commission regional offices was that of training classification analysts in their own offices, Commission representatives in the employing departments, and representatives of other field offices in the principles and practices of position-classification and of postauditing work.[26] By the spring of 1944, Commission regional directors, through their regional classification chiefs, could give final advisory allocations to OPA field positions up through grades CAF-12 and P-5;[27] by summer of that year similar authority was extended over WBP field positions.[28] Controversies between regional classification staffs and the regional offices of OPA and WPB, regardless of the grade level of the position involved, were forwarded to the Commission in Washington for resolution, as always.

[22] CSC, *Departmental Circular No. 382*, October 15, 1942.

[23] Objections had to be submitted in writing and appeal made within thirty days of notice of prospective reduction in pay. *Ibid., No. 422*, May 1, 1943.

[24] The employing department had to review the appeal within twenty days of its receipt.

[25] CSC, *Circular Letter No. 3989*, April 6, 1943.

[26] *Ibid., No. 4109*, January 31, 1944.

[27] CSC, *Personnel Classification Division Field Memorandum No. 5, Supp. No. 1*, April 10, 1944.

[28] *Ibid., No. 3, Supp. No. 1*, July 21, 1944.

PRESSURES ON CLASSIFICATION 245

Standards for field service allocations began to appear in greater number by 1945. Commissioner Flemming testified to the House Appropriations Committee that of the 5,200 needed for the field service, 210 had already been issued by the beginning of the calendar year 1945 and a total of 300 would be promulgated by the end of fiscal 1945. Additional funds were requested in order that the Commission might complete 1,200 standards in fiscal 1946.[29]

Congress, however, showed its inconsistency with respect to the whole problem of classification. The criticism made by the Byrd Committee of disparities in classification has already been cited.[30] Nevertheless, Chairman Woodrum of the Appropriations Subcommittee questioned the need for the Commission's program of issuing allocations standards in wartime.[31] Antagonism and misunderstanding led the committee to lop off $229,810 from the funds requested for the work of the Personnel Classification Division in preparing and issuing standards, a crippling blow to the whole program.[32] The Appropriations Subcommittee was unable to evaluate needs outside the limited field of recruitment activities and was incapable of perceiving the relationship of allocation standards to recruitment. Its negative action followed shortly after the President by Executive Order 9512 had placed in the Commission responsibility for the work of developing standards for all departments, a task formerly in the hands of the departments themselves when exercised at all, and for co-ordinating and combining standards of the field service with those of the departmental service.

How did the war agencies compare with the nonwar agencies in classification of field service positions in view of the general disparity found between agencies in field service allocations? Again, one classification officer has described the situation in these terms:

> Because the War Department field establishments enjoyed a degree of autonomy almost no other agency had, the classifi-

[29] U.S. Congress, House, Hearing on *Independent Offices Appropriation Bill, 1946*, 79th Cong., 1st Sess., January 17, 1945, p. 1206.
[30] *See above*, p. 239.
[31] U.S. Congress, House, Hearings on *Independent Offices Appropriation Bill, 1946*, p. 1210.
[32] U.S. Congress, House, Committee on Appropriations, *Independent Offices Appropriation Bill, 1946*, House Report 54, 79th Cong., 1st Sess., 5.

cation practices reflected much more than ordinarily would be true the recruiting pressures of the area. For this reason, the War Department allocations in the Pacific coast area, a notoriously high wage area, were one or two grades above the recognized standards of the Commission and the War Department. In the Middle West the allocations were fairly consistent with the standards, and in the South they were often one or two grades below the standards. . . .

Most Federal agencies, including the Navy Department, until the last year or so were subject to a highly centralized system of classification control. For this reason they reflected far less accurately the recruiting and wage pressures of the areas in which they operated. However, it was recognized practice of the Pacific Coast agency administrators in the pre-war agencies to "write up" facts about jobs in presenting them to their Washington offices. By allocating the position on the Pacific coast on the basis of fictitious facts their Washington offices were able to maintain, if challenge were made, that they had acted properly and in good faith.

The situation with respect to the OEM agencies was a particularly extraordinary one, as the standards which the Commission's Regional Classification Division were [sic] using in approving positions were initially written by the Washington offices of the agencies and approved by the PCD (Personnel Classification Division). These standards reflected the emergency level of allocations of the Washington administration of classification and seemed particularly distorted at the field level where comparison with the pre-war allocations was easily made. The OEM agency personnel officers complained, however, that while standards for professional and technical positions were usually liberal enough, those for clerical positions were usually not. They insisted, and to some degree were able to prove, that their own Washington offices had received higher allocations for clerical positions than the Commission was willing to approve for field standards.[33]

Moreover, among War Department administrators, facing the realities of recruiting and turnover in high wage and tight labor market areas, a feeling existed that the Classification Act should have permitted field salaries to vary according to community wage levels. James P. Mitchell, Director, Industrial Personnel Division, Headquarters, ASF, expressed his views on that point to the Ramspeck Committee in 1943:

[33] Letter to the writer from Miss Thadene Hayworth, October 19, 1945.

PRESSURES ON CLASSIFICATION 247

Mr. Mitchell. In Seattle, Wash., it was necessary to recruit certain checkers and stock clerks for depot operations. This type of position pays $1,440 per annum. Continuing difficulty has been experienced in keeping these positions filled, since Boeing Aircraft Co. in that locality pays its checkers $2,160, which is a fair measure of the local wage market. The So-Tac Co. pays its stock clerks $1,976 a year, as opposed $1,440 [*sic*], which is the rank set by the Classification Act.

On the other hand, local conditions are disrupted by the activation of a Federal establishment when, as in the Huntsville area, the stenographers in our arsenal received $1,440 per annum, while the same type of position in private companies will pay $960 to approximately $1200. . . . Teachers in lower grades which require only two years of college experience are hired as low as $594 per annum—and we pay a stenographer $1,440. . . .

Mr. Rees. . . . Do you suggest then that it might be well if the War Department were given authority to pay a little less wages, we will say, for a stenographer in Tennessee or Kentucky, or Kansas, or wherever it may be if the prevailing rates for stenographers and typists is a little lower than the going rate under the Classification Act?

Mr. Mitchell. I would like to say that if the War Department and other agencies of government were permitted to pay for services rendered at the going market rate—

Mr. Rees (interposing). Whatever it is.

Mr. Mitchell (continuing). Whatever it is, that many of our recruitment and turn-over problems would be lessened.[34]

An implied recognition that the War Department had upgraded where necessary to bring salaries into line with the going local rates came shortly after the Pay Act of 1945 took effect on July 1, 1945. Since basic rates were increased under the Pay Act a little better than the equivalent of one grade in the lower CAF grades, the subsequent War Department action is comprehensible. Circular No. 77 of the War Department, issued on July 7, 1945, provided that revisions in grade could be made either upward or downward, with corresponding salary adjustments.[35] Downward revision was permissible on a re-evaluation of positions in which

---

[34] *Investigation of Civilian Employment,* Part III, Hearing on June 17, 1943, pp. 599-601.
[35] War Department, *Civilian Personnel Circular No. 77,* July 7, 1945.

there had been no change of duties, but it was painlessly inflicted after the new salary legislation allowed a virtual continuance at the old amount. The regulation, coming when it did, was almost an admission that grades had been governed by the salaries attached rather than by duties and responsibilities.

3. DIFFICULTIES INHERENT IN THE CLASSIFICATION ACT

However much one may deplore the circumvention of the Classification Act for salary purposes during the war years, the rigidity of the Act made any other course unrealistic and impracticable. The statute provided fixed and immutable salary schedules attached to each grade in the services. The minimum entrance salary was mandatory for the initial hiring of employees at each grade until the War Overtime Pay Act of 1943 allowed the first departure from that principle, namely, the hiring at rates within grades to eliminate inequities between wage board and Classification Act employees. Furthermore, the rates applied universally throughout the nation to all positions covered by the statute.

Although the rationale of the act was that the government should provide equal pay for equal work, that idea was difficult to honor when administrators were conscious of the salaries attached to the grades and of the fact that salaries could not be adjusted. So long as salaries could not be altered, allocations had to be adjusted to meet the stresses and strains. Edgar B. Young, then of the Bureau of the Budget, put it succinctly in 1942: "It is no wonder that during a time of manpower shortage such as the present, all kinds of reasons, excuses, and subterfuges are employed in order to get classification grades which carry rates realistically in keeping with current labor-market conditions. Flexibility has to be forced into an inflexible system."[36]

Even during the period when the act was being enforced for the first time, the fact was made clear at congressional hearings that positions were allocated with an eye to salary rates rather than duties and levels of responsibility.[37] Individual employees were identified with salary ranges, which were determinative of the grades and classes into which the positions fell. Existing inequities

---

[36] Young, "If I Could Remake the Classification System," *loc cit.*, 10.

[37] U.S. Congress, House, Committee on Civil Service, Hearings on *The Law and the Personnel Classification Board*, 108-11.

which the Classification Act was designed to correct were thereby perpetuated for some years longer and eliminated only by the slow process of appeals in the departmental service and administrative decisions in the field service. For example, in the Veterans Administration it took three and one-half years of wartime labor shortages to effect reclassification from subprofessional to professional status of nurses, social workers, dietitians, and librarians.[38]

William H. Kushnick, Director of Civilian Personnel and Training in the War Department, told the Senate Civil Service Committee bluntly the effect of the Classification Act on the War Department:

> Moreover, these inequities often lead to iniquities. An operating official in the War Department who has to obtain employees to get his job done so that plans, supplies, or troops reach the fighting front won't be excused for failing to accomplish his mission by an explanation of the antiquated salaries of the Classification Act which prevented him from getting and keeping the people he needed to execute his important assignment. Instead he dreams up a lot of extra duties and responsibilities so as to get higher grades and the Government pays the price anyway.[39]

Successful operation of the Classification Act was postulated on the existence of "normal" conditions, particularly in the labor market. No provisions for flexibility existed to meet the urgencies of crisis administration or regional labor market dislocations and distortions. Administrators in other war agencies were under the same compulsion as those in the War Department to secure higher allocations so long as they could not adjust salary scales to meet local competition with private industry. Eventually the older agencies were forced to go along in order to obtain any employees at all.

The Personnel Classification Division of the Civil Service Commission held steadfastly to the view that critics of wartime classification had confused the abilities and qualifications of incumbents with the position requirements.[40] Because the caliber of those

---

[38] Veterans Administration, *Advance Releases*, June 16, 1945, OWI-4533 and 4534. Apparently the reclassification applied to all such positions in both the field and departmental service of the VA.

[39] U.S. Congress, Senate, Committee on Civil Service, Hearing on *Salary and Wage Administration in the Federal Service*, 79th Cong., 1st Sess., April 30, 1945, p. 125.

[40] Interview with Ismar Baruch, July 23, 1945.

promoted was so often inferior to that of prewar personnel promoted, many failed to realize that positions themselves had not changed during the war, the Personnel Classification Division held. In other words, the relaxed promotion policy described in Chapter IX was held accountable for the discrepancies alleged to exist. Although the point cannot be minimized that many persons not quite good enough to promote before the war in the older agencies obtained higher grade positions during the war because of the manpower shortage, that reason alone does not explain such anomalies as War Department Circular No. 77, described above. Under the War Department order positions were to be reallocated downward. It did not provide for a mere shifting or reassignment of incumbents. As the largest employer in the Federal government, the War Department could not be held to have had an insignificant effect on Federal classification policies.

Wage Administration

The problem of wage administration for almost 1,000,000 Federal employees under wage board procedures was, on the whole, much simpler than that of the Classification Act. The basic principle for setting wage rates was conformance to the local prevailing rate in each community paid by private employers for similar types of work. Labor force or mechanical trades employees were covered by this procedure in the Federal government. Since 1862, the prevailing rate principle had been applied by Congress to Navy yard employees and subsequently to other categories in the labor force.

The wartime wage stabilization policy expressed in executive orders and significant decisions by the National War Labor Board had a noticeable effect on Federal wage administration, for it applied to all employers. One of the earliest controls in the field of wage stabilization was the "Little Steel formula," the decision made by the War Labor Board on July 16, 1942, in the Little Steel case that a maximum increase adjustment of 15 per cent was permissible for workers whose straight-time hourly earnings had not been increased at all since January 1, 1941. Early in October, 1942, President Roosevelt issued the so-called "wage freeze" order establishing the Office of Economic Stabilization in the Office of Emergency Management.[41] Broad powers for the stabilization of

[41] Executive Order 9250, October 3, 1942.

the cost of living were coupled with an injunction against wage rate increases granted without the approval of the National War Labor Board. The latter body was forbidden by the terms of the "wage freeze" order from approving any increases over wage rates prevailing on September 15, 1942, unless such increases were to correct inequities or maladjustments or to eliminate substandard living conditions. The "hold the line" order in April, 1943, directed the War Labor Board to authorize no further increases in wages or salaries except when clearly required to correct "substandards of living."[42] But it did, nevertheless, preserve the opportunity for wage adjustments in accordance with the terms of the "Little Steel formula," and allow for promotions, reclassifications, merit increases, and incentive wages to the extent that production costs were not increased appreciably or a basis furnished to justify price increases or to resist justifiable price reductions. Through the second order "fringe" adjustments for vacation pay, incentives, bonuses, and the like were legalized. Federal agencies which were the larger employers of labor force workers were delegated power by the War Labor Board to make wage adjustments subject to WLB review.[43]

The need for wage rate surveys preliminary to fixing local Federal rates was materially lessened for government establishments by the existence of schedules of rates in the hands of the War Labor Board.[44] WLB schedules were frequently based on surveys conducted by the Bureau of Labor Statistics of the Labor Department, and it was thus more efficient to utilize existing informational facilities than to make new surveys in many cases.

The war highlighted the need for central departmental supervision over wage rate procedures and determinations in order to maintain local consistency among establishments of the same department. The Navy had long provided for a review by a national wage board of local board determinations,[45] but within the War Department rates had been fixed independently by each technical service.[46] In September, 1942, War Department wage procedures

---

[42] Executive Order 9328, April 8, 1943.
[43] "Determination of Wage Rates for Mechanical and Laboring Positions in the Federal Service," *Monthly Labor Review,* LIX (November, 1944), 1065.
[44] *Ibid.*   [45] *Ibid.,* 1066.
[46] C. Canby Balderston, "Wartime Lessons in Wage Administration," *Advanced Management,* X (January-March, 1945), 23.

and determinations were made uniform and centralized in ASF immediately under the director of the Industrial Personnel Division, Civilian Personnel Branch. A little over a year later, in November, 1943, the department centralized wage determinations for the whole War Department except for a few branches. The procedures were installed in about 2,000 War Department establishments in continental United States and Hawaii. The Industrial Personnel Division headquarters staff on wage administration reviewed the assignment of jobs to grades and the determination of the level of pay for each locality.[47] Although the Navy Department determined wage rates administratively—that is, by officers within the department—the War Department combined wage board procedures with administrative determination. Local wage boards made up of representatives of each War Department establishment within an area secured the essential data on private positions common to those in War Department installations. On the basis of their information they formulated schedules for approval.

War Department experience in setting wage rates emphasized the importance of accurate job descriptions, rather than mere reliance on job titles, in order to achieve internal consistency within an establishment and within an area.[48] Once a rate schedule was developed on the basis of a survey of the principal relevant occupations in the area, it was not too difficult to match jobs, properly aligned, with prevailing rates. In that way external consistency was achieved along with internal consistency.

Marked fluctuations in wage rates nationally or locally could be met for wage board employees by open administrative determinations openly arrived at, made expeditiously as the various departments felt impelled to face recruiting problems. There were no tricks or devious actions by way of "blowing up" jobs or faulty allocations required to meet pressures. For example, the War Department wage rates for common labor on the Pacific Coast were approximately double the rates in Mississippi and a few other low-wage areas in response to different labor conditions.[49] The difference in meeting pressures as between classified and unclassified employees was found, of course, in the fact that legislative action through statutory amendments was needed for the former and administrative action alone for the latter.

[47] *Ibid.*, 25. [48] *Ibid.*, 24. [49] *Ibid.*, 23-30.

Conclusions

The war period revealed the intrinsic weakness of the Classification Act: its rigidity of salary scales which tempted administrators to adjust position allocations. Commission failure in the prewar years to develop allocations standards permitted wide discrepancies between agencies and from locality to locality. Since the Commission as enforcing agent of the Classification Act faced the realities of recruitment, its generosity in allowing flexibility in grade allocations during the war is comprehensible. No other course was open. But that very generosity, unless applied with evenhanded justice and absolute consistency, weakened the laudable purpose of the statute in providing equal pay for equal work. The evidence scarcely supports the conviction that reallocations in either the departmental or the field service were made consistently or uniformly.

It is impossible to say what faulty position allocation cost the Federal government during the war years, as compared with an outright salary increase that might have been granted as early as 1942. It would be fair to conclude that the government probably saved money by following the course it did and allowing individual administrators to use pressure to inflate jobs for allocation purposes. But in the larger sense what was the loss? The student of personnel administration is tempted to ponder the many practices in administrative deceit and trickery that were encouraged, which cannot be reformed overnight by mere paper standards, and the many able employees ultimately lost to the Federal government through disparities between positions.

CHAPTER TWELVE

Controls On Federal Employment

THE PHENOMENAL expansion in Federal employment during the war years gave rise to a new awareness in Congress and in the press of the problem of size in the Federal government. The expansion of our armed forces and the rise of the nation's labor force were both comprehensible. The presentation of sixty billion dollar budgets for armaments became a commonplace, taken in stride. But the employment of three million persons by the Federal government as civilian employees was baffling to the average legislator and citizen. It was Leviathan running wild.

Congress grew genuinely alarmed at what had happened in Federal employment. On the one hand, this concern was based on a desire for economy in civilian activities to offset in some small degree the waste that war itself entailed. On the other hand, the legislative branch had long chafed at the growth of the executive branch in power and prestige and decried its own powerlessness to halt this trend. Wartime developments both increased its feeling of impotence and fanned the desire to overcome that feeling by making a show of authority to halt what it disliked and could not understand.

Congress employed two diverse means in its attempt to check the expansion of Federal personnel. First, it turned to that instrument of indirect control always ready to the hand of the zealous legislator, the congressional investigation. Both houses participated through the Joint Committee on the Reduction of Nonessential Federal Expenditures under the chairmanship of Senator Harry Flood Byrd, from whom it took the more common name of the Byrd Committee. In addition, the House of Representatives authorized its own Civil Service Committee under Chairman Ramspeck to conduct a separate investigation of civilian employment. Secondly, through statutory enactment Congress undertook to exercise direct control over numbers by delegating power to the Director of the Budget through the two War Overtime Pay Acts to establish personnel ceilings and order reductions. So impressed was the legislative branch with this technique that it attached similar controls to the Pay Act of 1945, a piece of permanent legislation.

But the problem of numbers was allied to that of manpower utilization. It was foolhardy to denounce vast increases in mere numbers if all employees were needed in essential tasks and each was utilized at his highest skill. Concomitantly it was foolhardy to recruit hordes of new workers if those already in the service were not employed to best advantage for the war effort. But the employing agencies did little on their own initiative to investigate or improve utilization of staff. The Civil Service Commission, therefore, sponsored a program of personnel utilization by encouraging agencies to make surveys to discover underutilization and to adopt corrective measures. The Commission, of course, hoped thereby to reduce its own recruiting load, and, in addition, it served as the agent of the War Manpower Commission, which was interested in the utilization as well as the allocation of the nation's manpower resources.

If the test of numbers alone is taken—the test Congress seemed to have chosen for its own criterion of the effectiveness of controls—the legislative attempts at checkmate clearly were on a par with King Canute's attempts to halt the tide. By February, 1945, both the War and Navy departments had gone beyond the levels of employment which had disturbed Congress in 1942 and 1943. There were reasons, of course, for the ineffectiveness of the controls, reasons Congress did not probe intensively in its inquisitorial excursions into the problem. The only conclusion it could reach was that the overstaffing it found was due to lack of over-all management control. Though that reason gave an incomplete answer, it pointed to a grave weakness in Federal administration.

Congressional Investigations of Overstaffing

Interest in economy in government operations, of which reduction in personnel was merely one aspect, led to the creation in 1941 of the Byrd Committee, or the Joint Committee on the Reduction of Nonessential Federal Expenditures. Federal personnel practices were but one of the formidable list of subjects investigated with more or less intensity by that committee to determine where reductions in cost might be effected. Although the committee's original interest manifested itself in eliminating as many as possible of the "normal" and "depression" functions as seemed frivolous or superfluous in wartime, its orientation was soon changed to a questioning of numerous wartime phenomena, as, for example, the charges of overstaffing and underutilization.

It was left to the House of Representatives to authorize an investigation solely of civilian personnel practices in wartime. The House passed H.R. 550 in October, 1942, to authorize an investigation by the House Committee on the Civil Service to undertake the following tasks: (1) a study of the effect of Federal policies and practices in civilian employment on the conduct of the war to determine whether they were efficient and economical; (2) an inquiry into the number of employees in each agency to ascertain their necessity and utilization; (3) an investigation of the recruitment and efficient and economical use of employees.[1] Thereby, under the chairmanship of Robert Ramspeck, was launched the Investigation of Civilian Employment, which contributed an extensive amount of testimony on employment practices, not the least of which was a consideration of overstaffing. The House quickly passed the resolution because it shared the respect Representative Sabath, chairman of the Rules Committee, expressed that "under his [Ramspeck's] direction this will be a fair, unbiased investigation."[2] The investigation was undertaken under the aegis of the House alone because the Rules Committee, which sponsored the resolution, felt time was of the essence in an investigation of the kind desired and a special joint investigating committee would consume too much of that precious commodity.

1. THE BYRD COMMITTEE

Primarily concerned with the problem of economy and through that with overstaffing, the Byrd Committee was especially troubled by the rise in numbers of clerical and office workers in both the War and Navy departments as well as in the new war agencies. Its first personnel report in June, 1943, drew attention to the increase in the number of CAF's in the Navy Department from 10,437 in September, 1939, to 94,390 in January, 1943.[3] In addi-

---

[1] 88 *Cong. Record* 8227, October 15, 1942.   [2] *Ibid.*, 8228.
[3] U.S. Congress, Joint Committee on the Reduction of Nonessential Federal Expenditures, *Federal Personnel*, Sen. Doc. 66, 78th Cong., 1st Sess., 7.

tion, the Navy Department, it pointed out, utilized 25,510 Waves, Spars, members of the Marine Corps Women's Reserve, and male enlisted and commissioned personnel in similar types of routine clerical duties. War Department CAF's had risen from approximately 300,000 in July, 1942, to 425,048 by January, 1943, with the result that they constituted one-third of all War Department civilian personnel. Comparing the proportions of CAF's to mechanical workers in the two departments, Senator Byrd confessed that he was at a loss to understand why the War Department had one clerical employee to every two so-called war workers whereas the Navy Department had one in five in the respective categories.[4] "The number of clerical workers in the War Department," he declared, "is very much in excess of what is necessary for the government."[5] Although Undersecretary of War Patterson tried to explain that the Navy had nothing corresponding to the Army service commands, his explanations fell on deaf ears. No attention was given to the vast amount of record-keeping involved in transportation, storage, and handling activities in waging global war in the machine age. Objectivity would have required an extensive study of modern military administration and technology, to say nothing of logistics, before arriving at the Senator's sweeping generalization. Instead the committee reminded itself of the fact that World War I was successfully waged with one civilian employee to every five soldiers instead of two and one-half to one as in World War II.[6]

Along the same line, the committee criticized the doubling of the number of employees in OPA and an increase from 528 to 3,670 employees in the War Manpower Commission from July 1, 1942, to April 1, 1943.[7] The committee overlooked the problems faced by OPA in developing and enforcing maximum price ceilings and extending rent control during that period. Similarly it failed to appreciate the fact that the WMC had only begun to swing into effective operation after September, 1942. The Civil Service Commission likewise was criticized as was the General

[4] U.S. Congress, Joint Select Committee, Hearings on *Reduction of Nonessential Federal Expenditures,* 78th Cong., 1st Sess., Part VIII, October 8, 1943, p. 2405.
[5] *Ibid.,* 2428.
[6] U.S. Congress, Joint Committee on the Reduction of Nonessential Federal Expenditures, *Federal Personnel,* 5.
[7] *Ibid.,* 6.

Accounting Office, among other agencies, for failing to "redirect their recruiting to reasonable levels," despite the fact that both carried an increased work load with each new appropriation for war.

In similar vein the Byrd Committee accused twenty-eight agencies of "wasteful spending" because in each 15 per cent or more of its classified employees received salaries of $3,800 or more per annum.[8] The list included the Interstate Commerce Commission, Securities and Exchange Commission, Federal Trade Commission, National Labor Relations Board, Board of Economic Warfare, Office of the Co-ordinator of Inter-American Affairs, War Production Board, National Housing Agency, and the Reconstruction Finance Corporation. A charge of this kind is shocking from a responsible committee in view of the fact that anyone familiar with the functions and responsibilities of the various agencies in Washington could have pointed out quickly the highly specialized economic and regulatory functions carried on by the enumerated agencies, requiring the employment of large numbers of attorneys, economists, and experts of various types.

Ignoring the labor market prevailing in 1943, the committee said:

> For a long time the committee has been aware that the departments and agencies are solving the problem of inefficient personnel by the recruitment of scores of additional employees. This policy of making up in quantity what is lacking in quality is tacit admission that an effective personnel administration is absent and a dilatory and more expensive solution is being used. The committee believes that in the future attempts should be made to recruit for and employ in key positions only those who are fully qualified and are capable administrators, and those who are more concerned with winning the war than with personal aggrandizement.[9]

Perusal of the hearings held by the Byrd Committee on personnel problems does not contribute to one's enlightenment as to the basis for the indictment of the last sentence above. The committee was barely conscious of the problem of personnel utilization and dealt it only a glancing blow. In the absence of supporting evidence for many of their generalizations and in the light of their failure to analyze the personnel problems before them, one

[8] *Ibid.*, 10.   [9] *Ibid.*, 14.

can but conclude that the Byrd Committee was not "on the main track" in quarreling over mere numbers as such. At no time did it introduce the problem of employee productivity, nor did it investigate the training of employees for improved utilization. Therefore, its conclusion that a reduction of 300,000 in personnel could be effected at once in June, 1943, seems highly questionable.[10]

Moreover, when the Byrd Committee found that its recommendation of reduction of 300,000 had not been followed, it held four hearings and issued an additional report, the tenor of which was in a querulous vein. It found, for example, that the Bureau of the Budget had issued reduction orders covering only 25 per cent of the Federal employees instead of 70 per cent as authorized by the first Overtime Pay Act,[11] while in the meantime Federal employment had risen to 191,941 additional persons in agencies not covered by the Bureau of the Budget orders. In looking back over the year prior to its second report, it found the trend toward increase in numbers had been steady. Therefore, with more particularity this time, the committee recommended reductions of 150,000 in the War Department alone and 35,951 in other agencies whose appropriations had been reduced or curtailed entirely by Congress.[12] With some vagueness it reiterated that the rest could be eliminated by abolishing overlapping and duplicating activities and improving work procedures. In a very real sense, the committee was striking at a serious problem when it touched on work methods, but it had barely referred to it before it dismissed it. The committee simply repeated its old refrain that a reduction of 300,000 should be made forthwith.

One point the committee made with cogency was the fact that the Civil Service Commission had neglected to take any positive steps to initiate personnel utilization surveys for a year after it had been delegated authority to do so by WMC Directive X.[13] Commission neglect had been due to "fear of offending departments and agencies which might then refuse to cooperate entirely in manpower-utilization surveys." Therefore, the committee

[10] *Ibid.*, 18.
[11] U.S. Congress, Joint Committee on the Reduction of Nonessential Federal Expenditures, *Federal Personnel* (Additional Report), Sen. Doc. 131, 78th Cong., 1st Sess., 1-2.
[12] *Ibid.*, 8-9.   [13] *Ibid.*, 12.

urged the Commission to institute surveys immediately throughout the government service, but, laboring under a misconception, urged the use of the Investigations Division for this work.[14]

With the refrain of a 300,000 reduction the Director of the Budget refused to agree. His reply was:

> Reduction of personnel on the basis of an arbitrary quota would necessarily impair services which the Congress through legislation and appropriations has declared essential.
>
> The staffing of Government agencies must be related to the specific functions and work load of each agency as established by law or imposed by the exigencies of world-wide war. Personnel needs can be determined only by systematic investigation on the basis of comprehensive and detailed knowledge of each operation and establishment. The Bureau of the Budget endeavors constantly to reduce personnel by suggesting improvements in organization and procedure.[15]

2. THE RAMSPECK COMMITTEE

Not only did the Ramspeck Committee conduct many more hearings than did the Byrd Committee, since it had a singleness of interest in the personnel problem which the former had not, but it also touched on a wider range of problems of personnel management. However, although it covered more aspects of personnel administration, it failed to get into the heart of any of the problems. Thus it gave no definite answers to any of the problems of wartime personnel management. One of the methods of investigation the committee employed was to make a few visits to field establishments, reported to be both well and ill managed.

In the course of the many hearings held in 1943, the Ramspeck Committee elicited the fact that there was no central authority, even in the War Department, to compel reductions in personnel. Although Undersecretary Patterson expressed the expectation in June, 1943, that the War Department would soon reduce its rolls by 100,000, it soon developed through his testimony that every commanding officer at a local establishment was in final control of the volume of employment at his installation.[16] All that the personnel officers, even in the Office of the Secretary of War, were able to do was to bring pressure by persuasion on the top command level to effect reductions and to rely on the top echelon to

---

[14] *Ibid.*, 20. [15] *Ibid.*

[16] *Investigation of Civilian Employment,* Part III, Hearing on June 8, 1943, pp. 486-87.

bring corresponding pressure down the line of command. The Secretary of War delegated management responsibility to the three commanding generals of Ground Forces, Service Forces, and Air Forces. Their authority covered the field of personnel utilization.[17] With that placement of authority Chairman Ramspeck disagreed categorically because he believed that the military was untrained in economical operation and interested only in achieving results regardless of cost. But whether or not that point was significant, the fact was made clear by General Somervell's testimony a few days after that of Undersecretary Patterson that 30 per cent more munitions were required and that personnel needs in ordnance had not reached their peak.[18] Thus, Patterson had to return to the committee two weeks after his original hope of reduction had been expressed and try to explain paradoxically how additional work was being assumed by the War Department, requiring 200,000 more employees at the same time that their existing work load could be discharged with 100,000 fewer persons.[19] A new increase of 100,000 employees ensued, therefore, instead of a net decrease in the War Department, an increase which had been planned in the service for some time before any testimony had been given to the committee.[20] Patterson did not seem to have been informed of those plans.

Confusion of responsibility was what Chairman Ramspeck held as the cause of the above reversal of testimony as well as of other incidents in the War Department unearthed by the committee. For example, the committee learned that the officer in charge of the Dependency Benefit Division in moving that office to Newark had failed to inform the Personnel Director's office of the transfer of some four hundred employees to the War Bond Division until after the transfer had been consummated.[21] In the meantime, the transferees had stood around idle for a week until work was found for them. Actually the Personnel Director's office was never informed of the transfer but had simply learned about it on its own initiative. In the same way, it learned indirectly that eight hundred employees had been separated when the Dependency Benefit Office was moved although the Civil Service Commission

[17] *Ibid.*, Hearing on June 11, 1943, p. 532.
[18] *Ibid.*, Hearing on June 16, 1943, p. 579.
[19] *Ibid.*, Hearing on June 22, 1943, pp. 644-45.   [20] *Ibid.*, 648.
[21] *Ibid.*, Hearing on June 10, 1943, pp. 517-18.

simultaneously was engaged in recruiting for other units of the War Department.

In another case, that of the transfer of the Bond Deduction Unit to Chicago, employees who were not transferred were allowed fourteen days of idleness though still on the payroll, since they had been earlier ordered not to look for other positions.[22] The Interservice Placement Committee of the War Department had promised to effect their transfer, for which task it and the various personnel placement branches of the War Department had twenty days. At the end of that period the War Department came forward with places for only 322 employees and then had to call on the Civil Service Commission hastily two weeks before the release of the affected employees to obtain transfer of the rest. The Commission placed 414 persons within the ensuing three weeks.[23] Some seven to eight hundred persons the Commission was still unable to place. Personnel Director Kushnick took the view that the Commission needed no earlier notice than had been given it, for its liaison representatives in the War Department should have learned what was transpiring.[24] Both examples pointed to the lack of an adequate reporting system to the highest echelons, and especially to the highest personnel office, that in the Office of the Secretary of War. The result of this deficiency was that the Commission was left to grope in the dark with respect to recruitment activities because no one War Department office assumed the responsibility for channeling to it accurate up-to-date information on organizational changes in the department.

The failure of the Ramspeck Committee as an investigating body was due primarily to the weakness of its staff. The committee unfortunately selected as staff directors men whose chief qualifications were political rather than administrative experience. The first of these directors, Dillard B. Lasseter, who was with the committee during the 1943 hearings, guided the committee in its probes of some individual abuses in the War Department, but he did not see or understand the typical problems involved in manpower utilization. The committee, therefore, never understood the training problem in 1943 nor the bearing of placement and classification on utilization. A later director, Colonel Edward J. McCormack, proved weaker, and the report he prepared on pro-

[22] *Ibid.*, Hearing on June 11, 1943, p. 523. [23] *Ibid.*, 524. [24] *Ibid.*, 525.

motions in 1945 had to be suppressed by the committee because of inaccuracies and concentration on personalities rather than on principles.

Time as well as staff served to limit the Ramspeck Committee. The Navy Department, for example, escaped virtually unscathed, only one installation having been subjected to committee scrutiny.[25] Outside the War Department few other agencies, particularly the new war agencies, received any attention. Thus the conclusions of the Ramspeck Committee seem startling:

> Your committee is of the opinion that its very establishment saved the taxpayers countless millions of dollars. If it accomplished nothing else, the committee set up a danger signal against further useless hiring of Government employees. It served notice on personnel officers that Congress and the people were aware of what threatened to be an inherently dangerous situation. . . . The committee's investigation has been a wholesome, psychological deterrent to further needless hiring. . . . The employment decline and the establishment of the committee appear to be more than a coincidence. . . . If the pre-investigation rate of employment had continued to the present we would have had an additional 350,000 workers on the Government pay roll today. Thus the committee believes its activities have been an important factor in preventing the hiring of some 350,000 employees, the additional annual cost of which would have been $700,000,000.[26]

A clearer example of the *post hoc ergo propter hoc* fallacy would be hard to locate. The committee chose to ignore the fact that by November, 1942, the first fine frenzy of hiring for new agencies and programs had passed its post-Pearl Harbor peak. It also overlooked the controls over employment that had been given the Bureau of the Budget in the War Overtime Pay Act of 1942, passed shortly after the committee had started work. Thus the committee arbitrarily crowned its own efforts with the laurels of achievement. It blandly assumed that its very existence had created an awe-inspiring force to the many departments and agencies never called before it.

Without minimizing the Ramspeck Committee's efforts to learn the truth of the charges of overstaffing the War Department and

[25] U.S. Congress, House, Committee on Civil Service, *Investigation of Civilian Employment*, House Report 2084, 78th Cong., 2nd Sess., 6.
[26] U.S. Congress, House, Committee of Civil Service, *Investigation of Civilian Employment*, House Report 766, 78th Cong., 1st Sess., 2-3.

its study of many ramifications of the Federal merit system, the reader of Ramspeck Committee testimony is forced to the conclusion that the size of the Federal government could not be checked by an investigating committee. At least a poorly staffed committee was at a hopeless disadvantage. Before the gargantuan size of the executive branch in wartime the committee assumed the proportions of a gadfly. So far as controlling numbers was concerned, the net effect of the committee seems to have been nugatory, for even the War Department, investigated as it was, grew despite the committee. So long as Congress heaped new tasks on the various agencies by swollen wartime appropriations and new regulatory measures and at the same time the Commission was unable to produce the caliber of recruits needed to complete assignments within a minimum of time, the number of Federal employees was destined to grow. A mere investigating committee probing into the activities of one part of the executive branch could scarcely be expected to have a markedly restrictive effect on untouched departments.

STATUTORY CONTROLS

Not content with after-the-fact investigation, Senators Byrd and Langer offered a new mode of attack, of a direct type, on the problem of controlling multiplication of Federal personnel. The essence of their control was a requirement that each department report on the number of employees to the Bureau of the Budget with a justification for the number reported. The Director of the Budget was empowered to order reductions when he found the number reported unjustified by supporting data. Thereby the first legal control on numbers short of curtailment of appropriations was instituted in 1942 and continued permanently in 1945.

1. THE FIRST WAR OVERTIME PAY ACT OF 1942

After President Roosevelt had called on Congress for expeditious action on the overtime pay question in December, 1942, and Senate Joint Resolution 169 had been placed before the Senate Civil Service Committee, Senators Byrd and Langer came forward with their amendment for personnel ceilings to be ordered by the Director of the Bureau of the Budget. The significance of their amendment was to render compulsory the reporting by agency

CONTROLS ON FEDERAL EMPLOYMENT 265

heads to the Bureau of the Budget of the numbers employed.[27] On enactment of Senate Joint Resolution 170, the first general overtime pay law, on December 22, 1942, the heads of all departments and agencies were allowed thirty days to present their reports and justifications to the Director of the Budget.[28] If they did not comply with the latter's reduction orders within thirty days after their notification, the provisions for overtime pay were inapplicable to their agency. In the meantime, the Civil Service Commission effected the transfer of excess personnel released under the reduction orders issued by the Bureau of the Budget in so far as possible.

Following hard on the heels of enactment, the President requested a forty-eight hour, six-day week and stressed the need for more effective manpower utilization within government in these words:

> The legislation places an added responsibility on the executive departments and agencies to make full use of manpower, to dispense with every surplus employee, and to reduce personnel wherever possible. We will accept that responsibility and act accordingly.
>
> The Federal Government must concentrate on one task— the winning of the war. At this time we must measure all Government activities against the grim standards of total war. Many activities, desirable in peace times, must be eliminated, provided only that such eliminations do not result in permanent harm to the future health and security of our individual citizens; many services must be provided at a reduced standard; all agencies—military and civilian—must take all necessary measures to organize their work for maximum efficiency. Although we have made great strides in converting the government to an all-out war basis, I am not satisfied that we have exhausted all the possibilities.
>
> I wish to be certain that we have stripped government activities of every non-essential, that work in one agency is not being duplicated in another, that we are carrying on our work in the war and so-called nonwar agencies with an irreducible minimum of personnel fully employed, and that we are doing our job in the most effective and quickest way possible with only the absolute minimum of paper work or "red tape."
>
> I am expecting you, with the help of your employees from

[27] U.S. Congress, Senate, Committee on Civil Service, *War Overtime Pay Act of 1942,* Sen. Report 1847, 77th Cong., 2nd Sess., 2.
[28] 56 *U.S. Statutes* 1068 (1942).

the top to the bottom of your agency, to begin immediately a continuing review of your activities, to eliminate every nonvital service, to seize every opportunity for improving the speed and efficiency of your operations, and to conserve manpower, materials and money.

The Director of the Bureau of the Budget and the Civil Service Commission have been instructed to assist you in every way possible. I desire that you report quarterly through the Director of the Bureau of the Budget the results of your efforts. The Civil Service Commission, acting under the authority of Directive No. X of the Chairman of the War Manpower Commission, will transfer personnel who are not effectively utilized to positions where their services are needed.[29]

The Bureau of the Budget soon implemented the President's message with a budget circular requesting the statutory information and justifications.[30] Besides presenting personnel justifications, agency heads had to cover fifteen subjects in their reports due on January 31, 1943. Among the subjects were data respecting backlogs of work which had to be cleared up, recommendations of activities which could be eliminated, duplications of work within and among agencies, specific economies already effected since Pearl Harbor or planned for the remainder of the 1943 fiscal year, hours of work as of October 31, 1942, names of overstaffed units and reasons therefor, agency turnover, and the effect of increased hours of work. Although the first Overtime Pay Act had required only one report to the Bureau of the Budget, the President had made this a regular quarterly requirement by his memorandum.

Because only one-fourth of the Federal agencies received reduction orders from the Bureau of the Budget under the first Overtime Pay Act and Federal employment actually rose, the Byrd Committee was dissatisfied with the results of the bureau's enforcement. It described the legislation as having had "little salutary effect."[31] The committee alleged that while reductions were being effected in a few agencies, others were recruiting as intensively as before the Overtime Pay Act. Of course, there was no gainsaying the fact that over-all Federal employment had been

[29] Press Release of President's Memorandum to the Heads of All Departments and Agencies, December 22, 1942.
[30] Bureau of the Budget, *Circular No. 408*, December 24, 1942.
[31] U.S. Congress, Joint Committee on Reduction of Nonessential Expenditures, *Federal Personnel* (Additional Report), 1-2.

moving upward despite legal control. The law did not apply to wage board employees, thus removing at least one-third from ceiling controls. The Bureau of the Budget had ordered a reduction of 27,726 up to April 30, 1943, and had ordered a further reduction of 13,905 after that date.[32] The "old line" agencies, not the war agencies, were the ones hit by these orders. This was especially true of the Post Office Department. But actually a net increase in employment had occurred in April, 1943.[33]

2. THE WAR OVERTIME PAY ACT OF 1943

Not only was the provision for budgetary reduction orders continued in the War Overtime Pay Act of 1943, but the new law required regular quarterly reports from agency heads.[34] Many Congressmen shared the misgivings of Representative Harness that the rise in Federal employment stemmed from a kind of Machiavellian design of "social planners teaming with political opportunists and bureaucrats."[35] To them as well as to others the idea of control through personnel ceilings appeared as the one continuing instrument to halt the trend toward expansion of the service.

The Bureau of the Budget employed virtually the same process to review and evaluate the quarterly personnel reports from agencies as had long been developed for regular budgetary review.[36] The necessity of programs conducted by each agency was questioned, work was measured and expressed in terms of man years of employees, and the entire result was sent to a special review committee of the bureau. The latter committee was especially appointed by the Director of the Budget to provide uniform consideration of all personnel estimates, regardless of the agency of origin. The results of their deliberations were issued to the various departments and agencies as personnel ceilings.

The effectiveness of the personnel ceilings under the War Overtime Pay Act of 1943 cannot be easily determined. Although the ceilings showed a steady quantitative decrease from September 30, 1943, when the total was 1,786,000, to March 31, 1945, when it

[32] U.S. Congress, House, Hearings on *Urgent Deficiency Appropriation Bill, 1943*, 78th Cong., 1st Sess., May 7, 1943, pp. 67-68.
[33] *Investigation of Civilian Employment*, Part II, Hearing of May 21, 1943, p. 342.
[34] 57 *U.S. Statutes* 75 (1943).   [35] 89 *Cong. Record* 135, January 12, 1943.
[36] Edgar B. Young, "The Control of Government Employment," in *Civil Service in Wartime*, 170-71.

stood at 1,597,000, other developments require consideration.[37] Air Force mechanics were transferred from a per annum salary to the wage board category of employment, outside the jurisdiction of the Bureau of the Budget ceilings. In fact, the transference of employees to positions outside the bureau's authority reduced the coverage of the personnel ceiling limitations from a total of 60 per cent in 1943 to 53 per cent of Federal employment in 1945.[38] Simultaneously turnover and impediments to recruiting had increased to the point where recruiting activities had to be geared to the maintenance of replacement of the working force rather than to effecting increases. Some programs also tapered off with the beginning of fiscal 1944, when Congress terminated WPA, CCC, NYA, and other depression agencies and reduced appropriations drastically for others. Whatever the cause for reductions, a Byrd Committee report in March, 1945, acknowledged that the Bureau of the Budget had "worked diligently in reducing excessive Federal personnel in overstaffed agencies and in curtailing Federal expenditures."[39]

The value of establishing personnel ceilings was apparent and real, at least to Congress, for provisions similar to those in the overtime pay acts of 1942 and 1943 found their way into the pay bills reported by the Senate and House civil service committees in 1945.[40] The Pay Act of 1945 continued the requirement that departments report their employment data quarterly at least to the Director of the Budget. The act also temporarily excluded wage board employees of the War and Navy departments and War Shipping Administration employees from personnel ceiling limitations until after the cessation of hostilities, but their eventual inclusion was an innovation. In addition, the Director of the Budget was given additional authority to establish reserves from salary savings arising from the enforcement of personnel ceiling orders.[41] Thus the establishment of personnel ceilings by

---

[37] *Ibid.*, 172.   [38] *Ibid.*, 173.

[39] U.S. Congress, Joint Committee on the Reduction of Nonessential Federal Expenditures, *Economy Progress Report of 1945* (Additional Report), Sen. Doc. 31, 79th Cong., 1st Sess., 1.

[40] U.S. Congress, Senate, Committee on Civil Service, *Pay Increases for Government Employees,* Sen. Report 265, 79th Cong., 1st Sess., 6. Also House, Committee on Civil Service, *Federal Employees Pay Act of 1945,* House Report 726, 79th Cong., 1st Sess., 22.

[41] 59 *U.S. Statutes* 295 (1945).

the Bureau of the Budget became a permanent directive in the struggle to control the volume of Federal employment.

The Need for Personnel Utilization Under Ceiling Controls and the Development of Surveys

The expansion in Federal employment, coupled with the decline in quality of recruits, drew attention to a new area of personnel administration, that of manpower utilization. Continued demands for recruits in a progressively more restricted labor market inevitably raised questions as to use of employees already furnished to employers. Similarly the personnel ceilings set by the Bureau of the Budget stimulated agency heads to devote some thought to securing the best service possible from a limited contingent of employees. The Bureau of the Budget, as a matter of fact, asked for information in its first reports under the War Overtime Pay Act of 1942 on the use of organizational facilities or special staffs, studies, projects, "drives," surveys, or other programs to effect savings in the use of manpower.[42] But agency heads, pressed by other wartime problems, showed few results in the way of organizing definite programs for improved manpower utilization until the Civil Service Commission started its surveys.

1. CIVIL SERVICE COMMISSION PROGRAM OF PERSONNEL UTILIZATION

Although the Civil Service Commission did not launch a government-wide program for personnel utilization until 1943, after the War Overtime Pay Acts had instituted the establishment of personnel ceilings, it had devoted passing attention to the subject as early as 1941. It began by requesting reassignment of clerks with training in stenography to regular stenographic positions.[43] In 1942, the Commission declared that although the main emphasis in its war activities had been recruitment, it believed the time had come to stress proper utilization of personnel already employed.[44] Refusal by the employing agencies to follow the suggestions for improved utilization made by the Commission was to be brought to the President's attention through the Liaison Officer for Personnel Management. Whenever the Commission questioned personnel requisitions on the ground of revealing

[42] Bureau of the Budget, *Circular No. 408*, December 24, 1942.
[43] CSC, *Departmental Circular No. 292*, November 25, 1941.
[44] CSC, *Fifty-Ninth Annual Report*, Letter of Transmittal, iv.

duplication of similar work in other agencies, it referred the matter to the Bureau of the Budget for study, but it was obliged in the meantime to fill the requests. Of course, by order of the Bureau of the Budget recruiting could later be halted.[45]

Regional directors of the Commission were directed to attempt to prevent manpower hoarding in government establishments. They could negotiate with agencies to obtain modification of personnel requisitions which might result in labor hoarding or constitute a contravention of the WMC program.[46] In cases of actual underutilization of personnel or of failure to utilize skills in either a critical war occupation or an essential activity, Commission representatives could require a transfer under WMC Directive X.

The change of name from Examining Division to Examining and Personnel Utilization Division in the Commission in 1943 betokened the new stress the Commission had given to the development of a personnel utilization program. The section concerned with the latter function had the responsibility of planning and developing the methods for conducting personnel utilization surveys and for making recommendations to the departments on the basis of information revealed by the surveys.[47] It could also exercise authority to order interagency transfers wherever necessary. In the field, regional offices had the same functions and authority with respect to field service establishments. The sections in Washington and in the field were considered a part of the WMC organization on manpower utilization as well as that of the Commission, as was shown in the chart in Chapter II.

Both in Washington and the field the personnel utilization sections were charged with the duty of arranging transfers for employees separated under Bureau of the Budget ceiling orders.[48] Agencies ordered by the Bureau of the Budget to reduce personnel had to prepare lists of all employees in the organizational units affected by reduction orders within five days of the receipt of the orders. The Commission received the lists and used them with the agency as the basis for decisions on transfers. Although the agencies affected by reduction orders retained final authority

[45] CSC, *Memorandum to the Heads of All Departments from the Three Commissioners as to Federal Recruiting Policies,* February 8, 1943.
[46] CSC, *Circular Letter No. 3842,* October 13, 1942.
[47] CSC, *Manual of Instructions,* A7.03.03, July 17, 1943.
[48] CSC, *Departmental Circular No. 412,* March 1, 1943.

to decide the occupational groups or organizational units in which transfers could be effected, the Commission alone determined what persons could be transferred. It tempered this authority, however, by consultation with the agency and by permitting employees willing to transfer to indicate the agency of their preference, the type of position desired, and the lowest acceptable salary. There were no guaranties that transfer could be arranged to preferred agencies, but the Commission promised to comply with the wishes of employees in so far as possible.[49] The usual re-employment rights associated with transfers under WMC Directive X were attached to those resulting from personnel ceiling orders.

The Commission recommended six steps for the development of a personnel utilization program.[50] The first step was for informational purposes: to conduct an agency-wide survey to discover neglected and unused employee skills. The Commission recommended the type of questionnaires already used in some agencies, which, when filled out by employees, described their skills, uses to which they were put, training received and additional training required, quality of supervision, and time wasted waiting for work assignments. On the basis of an analysis of the data accumulated through the survey, in the second place, training programs were to be organized by agencies and placed in operation to supply employee needs for training. Third, supervision had to be improved all through an organization. Fourth, a system of periodic review by supervisors with their employees of work assignments and responsibilities was recommended. In the fifth place, a planned, progressive employee-relations program was deemed essential. Similarly, as the final recommendation, the Commission proposed medical, health, and safety programs within employing agencies under the terms of existing authorizations and law. The entire program was voluntary on the part of the agencies and the Commission merely rendered advisory service at the time this program was proposed in 1943.

As employees became aware of the drive for more effective manpower utilization in 1943, provision was made to handle their complaints of underutilization. The Commission suggested to departmental personnel directors that when employees requested

---

[49] Agencies were allowed to receive transfer applications directly from employees about to be separated under Budget Orders. CSC, *ibid., No. 417*, March 31, 1943.
[50] CSC, *Sixtieth Annual Report*, 16.

release to non-Federal employment because of employment at less than full time or failure to utilize their highest recognized skill needed in the war effort, the directors should investigate the allegations of underutilization thoroughly.[51] If the personnel director decided that the employees' charges were not correct, no further action was necessary. The employee, however, had the right to appeal the director's decision to the Commission. If the charges proved to be true, then the personnel director was obliged to exert effort to reassign the employee to another position in the same agency which would utilize his skills more adequately. Failing to place him in the same agency, the personnel director had to send the employee's Form 57, together with a statement of agency inability to utilize the employee fully, to the Commission. Within fourteen days the latter had to make a placement, or, failing to do so, to refer the person to USES. It is hard to imagine any employee willing to wait for these procedures except for the necessity of obtaining a release to comply with WMC requirements.

Criticism by the Byrd Committee of failure to institute a more effective personnel utilization program[52] stung the Commission to action in 1944 to obtain agency co-operation in instituting personnel utilization surveys and programs. True, agency co-operation was voluntary, but the three commissioners wrote on January 3, 1944, to urge the six steps for personnel utilization, heretofore listed, on every agency head.[53] Not only were employing agencies urged to co-operate, but they were in addition requested to report quarterly, beginning on March 31, 1944, the results of their surveys. Information was desired in the reports on such subjects as the number of surveys conducted during the quarter and a description of their type, the total number of employees and of women employees at the beginning and end of the quarter in each organizational unit surveyed, estimates of personnel savings realized from action taken as a result of each personnel utilization survey, the number of employees reassigned for more effective use of their skills as a result of each survey, and a comparison of monthly turnover and absenteeism rates at the beginning and end

[51] CSC, *Departmental Circular No. 442*, October 19, 1943.
[52] U.S. Congress, Joint Committee on the Reduction of Nonessential Federal Expenditures, *Federal Personnel* (Additional Report), 12.
[53] CSC, *Departmental Circular No. 476*, March 20, 1944.

of the quarter. From the Commission reports went to the President. In short, while personnel utilization surveys were not compulsory, there was an incentive to co-operate in the fact that they were submitted to the White House.

In connection with the first quarterly reports initiated during 1944, the Commission issued a pamphlet entitled *Better Use of Personnel,* outlining the scope of a typical agency program to conserve manpower, with emphasis on personnel practices.[54] The Commission offered an outline and checklist to which it called the attention of agency heads. This outline was really a comprehensive summary of modern personnel practices to be followed.

The Bureau of the Budget attacked the complementary problem of improvement of management by its own checklist contained in the pamphlet *An Agency Management Program,* subtitled *A Guide for Self-Appraisal and Planning Economies in Operation.*[55] Pertinent questions were propounded and space left for "notes for action" under these subjects: (1) What's our attitude toward management? (2) Are all our activities essential? (3) Are we well organized? (4) What have we done to conserve men, money and materials? The Bureau of the Budget checklist, of course, did not duplicate the Commission's list because it concentrated on management practices rather than on personnel practices.

Lack of common understanding of what constituted a "survey" forced the Commission to undertake a definition of terms. A survey was described as "an organized appraisal of personnel utilization (other than that which is exercised by day-to-day management control) from which a report of findings and recommendations is required by management."[56] At least eight different kinds of surveys had been conducted by agencies during the first quarter of 1944, some of which sounded vague. For example, one type reported an "attitude survey," another a "survey of value of total personnel program." Most agencies gave no "results of surveys" in their first reports because of a feeling that no reliable figures could be cited as "estimated savings in personnel." What the Commission sought was information on positions filled at the time

---

[54] CSC, *Better Use of Personnel,* February, 1944.
[55] Executive Office of the President, Bureau of the Budget, *An Agency Management Program,* March, 1944.
[56] CSC, *Circular Letter No. 4140, Revision No. 1,* June 7, 1944.

of a survey but eliminated as a result of it, savings in measurable work load, over-all reduction in civilian personnel during a quarter traced at least partially to improvements resulting from a survey, cancellation of personnel requisitions, abolition of established vacancies, downgrading of positions, or findings indicating the need for corrective action, all as a result of having conducted a personnel utilization survey. A manual, *How to Conduct Personnel Utilization Surveys,* accompanied by a supplement, *Notes on Better Use of Personnel,* was issued in 1944 to clarify survey procedures, techniques, legal authority, and other questions. By 1945 the Commission had participated in 188 surveys covering approximately 350,000 civilian employees in thirteen different agencies.[57] But it never assembled the data from the surveys to show concrete results achieved in manpower savings or positions eliminated.

Because the recruitment of stenographers and typists had reached the "desperate" stage in 1944, with 6,600 more requisitions for these workers than there were persons available, the Commission underlined the need for better utilization of employees in possession of typing and stenographic skills.[58] It issued a pamphlet in the form of concrete proposals and a checklist to improve procedures for utilization of stenographers.[59] In fact, from early in March, 1944, the Commission required proof by agencies that they had made a recent survey on the utilization of their present staff of stenographers and typists and had made an effective follow-up, based on the survey, to reassign personnel, combine resources, and reschedule work as it was found necessary to bring about the maximum utilization of stenographers and typists.[60] Both these steps were required before the Commission would attempt to fill outstanding or new orders for stenographers or typists in Washington, authorize joint recruiting agreements, or honor or extend existing agreements. To insure concrete data on surveys, the Commission issued standards for minimum acceptable evidence. Initial surveys such as the Com-

[57] U.S. Congress, House, Hearings on *Independent Offices Appropriation Bill, 1946,* 79th Cong., 1st Sess., January 17, 1945, p. 1194.
[58] CSC, *Departmental Circular No. 467,* February 3, 1944.
[59] CSC, *Better Utilization of Stenographers and Typists, A Handbook for Supervisors,* May, 1944.
[60] CSC, *Departmental Circular No. 467.*

mission had ordered in February, 1944, were merely a first step in the utilization of stenographers and typists. The Commission called for a continuing review in each agency of stenographic and typist positions and of the use of relevant skills.

The entire personnel utilization program undertaken by the Civil Service Commission had a broad scope, inclusive of more than mere sponsorship of utilization surveys. It embraced the encouragement of training activities by agencies themselves and the promotion of supervision improvement through the "J" courses. Indeed, the Commission itself, as indicated in Chapter VIII, performed actual training activities in "training the trainers" for the "J" courses.[61]

The Commission's program had several weaknesses. Inasmuch as agency co-operation in conducting surveys was voluntary, there were virtually no sanctions in the hands of the Commission for failure to co-operate except the threat of refusal to recruit. Reports were to be made to the President of agency failure to co-operate. No such reports were ever made by the Civil Service Commission. Another weakness was the tendency of agencies to request more personnel than they needed in some cases in order to hoard labor because of fear of a shortage later. This had been common in 1943 and was difficult to stop.[62] An additional shortcoming was the Commission's failure to follow up after surveys had been made to insure that the employing agencies actually carried out their promises.[63] Therefore, it was difficult to employ the sole sanction in Commission hands so long as the Commission was unable to ascertain whether co-operation was real or merely verbal.

One of the serious difficulties in promoting better manpower utilization was the absence of standards of performance for the vast majority of government positions. Determination of the use of skills and decisions in underutilization were difficult in many instances, especially for stenographic and typist positions, without some guidance as to what qualitative and quantitative output was expected of incumbents within particular agencies. Admittedly

[61] *See above,* pp. 168-71.
[62] *Investigation of Civilian Employment,* Part I, Hearing on March 18, 1943, pp. 90-91.
[63] Interview with Dr. John McDiarmid, Chief, Personnel Utilization Section, CSC, August 7, 1944.

standards to be valid could not apply across agency lines because of variations in agency work. But within agencies, and particularly within their smaller organizational units, for routine positions where activities were standardized it was possible to develop performance standards. Neither the agencies themselves, which had the primary responsibility for such a step, nor the Bureau of the Budget had entered the field.

Despite the lack of standards, the entrance of the Civil Service Commission into the field of personnel utilization was a significant step in expanding the Commission's part in personnel administration into a positive role. The fact that personnel ceilings became a permanent feature of administration through the Pay Act of 1945, coupled with Commission responsibility for recruitment, compelled continuing attention to the problem of utilization of employees. In itself that study had forced the Commission to direct agency attention to other phases of personnel management, particularly training, placement, and employee relations. Eventually perhaps in a more settled and normal period attention could be devoted to performance standards by the agencies to increase the effectiveness of utilization.

More than simply expanding the Commission's role in personnel administration, the institution of personnel utilization surveys pushed the Commission into an invasion of management functions. The utilization of employees after recruitment is in actuality a responsibility of management. Because management overlooked or neglected its responsibility in that area during the war, the Commission in its role of conserving manpower resources within the government was forced to undertake the unpopular task of compelling agency heads to attend to the problem.

2. PERSONNEL UTILIZATION IN THE WAR AND NAVY DEPARTMENTS

a. *The War Department.*—As early as 1942 the Secretary of War created a War Department Manpower Board under Major General L. D. Gasser, which in 1943 instituted surveys on duplication of work and overstaffing and developed "yardsticks" for the number of persons required to perform specific activities.[64] This board came to be known as the Gasser Board, and at the Army service commands in the field "little Gasser boards" were appointed. The Gasser Board had the continuing aid of Griffen-

[64] *Investigation of Civilian Employment*, Part III, Hearing on June 8, 1943, p. 476.

hagen and Associates, management consultants, in making its surveys. Because military and civilian work were both part of an integral whole and not easily separated in War Department establishments, the scope of authority of the Gasser Board, originally limited to military personnel, was extended to include civilian personnel in March, 1943.[65] Indeed, its authority covered both wage board and Classification Act civilian employees in contradistinction to the authority of the Bureau of the Budget over personnel ceilings. The Bureau of the Budget, however, gained the right by agreement with the War Department to participate in the final review and determinations by the Gasser Board.[66] The determinations of the Gasser Board could be subjected to final review in so far as salaried employees were concerned by the Director of the Budget under the latter's power to set personnel ceilings. The Gasser Board made a continuing review of manpower utilization.

Within each service command the little Gasser board was headed by a general officer who reported directly to the Gasser Board in Washington.[67] The ten field boards undertook surveys and studies to eliminate or scale down activities of decreasing importance to the war effort, to analyze work loads, and to determine the number of persons necessary to perform each activity. Their attention was not directed to such matters as the quality of civilian personnel administration or the classification of civilian personnel. The scope of their jurisdiction differed from that of the manpower survey teams of the Army Service Forces, which were similar to those in other government agencies. The Gasser boards developed yardsticks on personnel requirements from work measurement data secured locally by observing installation activities considered reasonably typical and economical.[68] The only reported results of the Gasser board surveys indicate a decrease of personnel by 400,000 from June, 1943, to the end of the war.[69] This figure was not broken down to show savings in civilian and in military personnel. Furthermore, it applied only to the "zone of the interior," that is, continental United States.

[65] George W. Peak, "The War Department Manpower Board," *American Political Science Review*, XL (February, 1946), 3-4.
[66] Young in *Civil Service in Wartime*, 175.
[67] CSC, *Circular Letter No. 4211*, September 25, 1944.
[68] Young in *Civil Service in Wartime*, 175.
[69] Peak, "The War Department Manpower Board," *loc. cit.*, 25.

Agreement was reached in June, 1944, between the Civil Service Commission and the Army Service Forces that the manpower utilization factor could not be permitted to impede recruitment.[70] Allegations of poor utilization or the fact that a utilization survey was in progress were not allowed to interfere with ASF and Commission representations to WMC Area or Regional Manpower Priorities committees for employment ceilings for recruiting. However, when allegations of poor utilization of employees had been made, the Commission could request an investigation by the War Department. If the charges were supported by the investigation, the ASF representative on the Area Manpower Priorities Committee had to institute corrective measures immediately as a condition precedent to securing the maintenance of employment ceilings, future manpower allowances, or priority assistance in recruitment. The need for personnel utilization surveys was determined by the War Department alone, and surveys were conducted under the responsibility of the War Department. The area or regional ASF representatives on manpower priorities committees were responsible for suggesting surveys to local commanding officers at installations and for evaluating the progress of the utilization program. ASF area or regional manpower representatives had been delegated power to suggest surveys on their own.

ASF surveys used questionnaires to locate neglected skills and followed up the questionnaires with interviews and reassignments for better utilization.[71] Questions on the quality of supervision, on undertime and overtime work, and complaints or suggestions for improved management and utilization could not be included in the signed questionnaire. Instead ASF developed an anonymous attitude survey which was designed to elicit frank employee reactions and was circulated as a companion piece with the signed questionnaire on skills and their use. The unsigned questionnaires were deemed useful to provide bases for comparative investigations across organizational lines, for follow-up and diagnostic investigations on particular trouble spots, and for analysis of steps taken by units to secure more favorable reactions. No Washington clearance was necessary for an ASF installation commander to order a personnel utilization survey, as was required by Army Air Forces when a non-War Department agency suggested a survey

[70] CSC, *Circular Letter No. 4173,* June 23, 1944.
[71] *Ibid.,* No. *4100,* January 13, 1944.

to AAF.[72] No reports have been made available of the results of ASF surveys.

b. *Navy Department.*—Although the Navy Department felt itself under fire in 1942 from other government agencies for its hoarding of labor and for overmanning its shore activities in high skills,[73] it did not undertake a comprehensive utilization survey until early in 1944. The Navy had late in 1942 called on all shore activities to put their "houses in order," primarily to meet the demands and inroads of Selective Service. But, in addition to the preparation of "manning tables,"[74] the Navy proposed to inquire into existent training programs, skills already possessed by employees, their present use and probable future uses, and procurement possibilities by way of recruitment, transfer, or upgrading and training. The Commission could not undertake a personnel utilization survey at a Navy shore establishment without approval first by the local commandant and ultimately by the Assistant Secretary of the Navy.[75]

The only comprehensive manpower utilization survey conducted by the Navy Department was early in 1944 after the so-called "Andrews Board," the Navy Manpower Survey Board, had been created for that purpose late in 1943.[76] The Andrews Board employed the services of a firm of management consultants to assist it with the survey. It made only one survey in contrast to the continuous work of the Gasser Board in the War Department. The procedure employed by the Navy Department was to make each bureau and installation responsible for the conduct of its own survey under the direction of a program director, who coordinated all teams sent out within the bureau.[77] A bureau advisory committee consisting of bureau executive officers helped the director. Two-man teams, made up of a personnel analyst and a methods or procedures analyst in each case, conducted the survey and reported to the program director. The objectives of all teams were to review and evaluate job classification, personnel

---

[72] *Ibid., No. 4217,* October 6, 1944.
[73] *Ibid., No. 3835, Supp. No. 2,* November 7, 1942.
[74] Manning tables showed the draft status, draft deferment, expiration of deferment of each male employee, and listed those who would be called over a period of three to six months and the plans made for their replacement.
[75] CSC, *Circular Letter No. 4053,* August 12, 1943.
[76] Young in *Civil Service in Wartime,* 175.
[77] CSC, *Circular Letter No. 4147,* April 15, 1944.

placement, staff requirements, and work methods. The personnel analyst on each team presented the program to the supervisors and employees. Questionnaires had to be filled out by every employee and all military personnel up to lieutenant commander; in the questionnaires such subjects were covered as a description of the job, the employee's qualifications, his comments on his placement, job classification, and working conditions. Together with the methods analyst, the personnel analyst interviewed selected employees to obtain additional information and prepared a final analysis of data with recommendations for reassignments and reclassification. The methods analyst was held responsible for recommendations respecting organization, work methods, and staff requirements based on work load. Although the two analysts on each team made up separate recommendations, they consulted each other to determine how each set accorded with the other.

Personnel utilization surveys organized in the same way as the Navy surveys were conducted in the Coast Guard and Marine Corps.[78] Of 4,000 Coast Guard positions in the departmental service surveyed by June, 1944, 15 per cent were eliminated, while 41 per cent of all the employees interviewed were reassigned and only 7 per cent of the positions reclassified. The survey, on its face, seemed to take care of a large number of cases of misassignment. One recommendation for the transfer of 85,000 male officers and enlisted men to different assignments, with their replacement by civilians or Waves, and another that there be an increase of 40,000 or 3 per cent in the total personnel of naval shore establishments were the notable features of the Andrews Board report in the Navy Department.[79] The Marine Corps eliminated 20 per cent of all positions surveyed.

The principal achievement in the manpower surveys conducted in the military departments was the development by the War Department of yardsticks for the number of persons required to perform a typical operation. Because much of the work in the War Department establishments was industrial in nature, work measurement on which the yardsticks were based was by no means alien. But yardsticks were established for nonindustrial types of

[78] Lt. Commander James M. Mitchell, Chief, Administrative Management Division, USCG, in talk to personnel utilization conference at National Housing Agency, July 3, 1944.
[79] Young in *Civil Service in Wartime,* 175.

activities as well, as, for example, the number of persons required in a civilian personnel office at installations of various sizes. Although the establishment of personnel yardsticks ran the risk of fostering inflexibility in organization, nevertheless in a large organization they seemed essential to assure some uniformity and keep personnel requirements at far-flung establishments within reasonable bounds. By continuous central review and comparisons of requirements and results achieved a degree of flexibility was introduced. For "big democracy" the yardstick idea presents one means of keeping personnel requisitions within reasonable limits and offers a starting point from which to explore the field of standards.

Conclusions

Although Congress held extensive investigations to probe into the reasons for growth of the Federal service, its efforts to frighten the executive branch into a pruning of the rolls were not eminently successful. The Ramspeck Committee never faced, as the Byrd Committee never faced, the fact that big government was traceable to decisions made by Congress with respect to legislative policy and appropriations and that the waging of global war created an imperative to production and performance unprecedented in world history. Nor did Congress seem to realize that controversial new programs could not be administered by newborn agencies with the same efficiency as were older projects in the more mature agencies that had "shaken down" over the years.

A direct approach to the problem of halting expansion was adopted through statutory requirements that the Bureau of the Budget establish personnel ceilings and order reductions within agencies. Originally adopted in the first War Overtime Pay Act of 1942, the delegation of this power to the Bureau of the Budget was continued in 1943 and adopted permanently in 1945. Reports had to be made to the Bureau of the Budget quarterly on all salaried employees. The limitation of coverage in the legislation, restricting ceiling orders to salaried employees, robbed this device of some of its potential effectiveness. While it is difficult to establish the efficacy of this control, nevertheless, because it required continuous re-examination into the volume of employment and continuous justification for that volume, it was a useful technique as a means of future control of numbers.

For the first time during the war, the Civil Service Commission devoted attention to the manner of utilization of the working force in the Federal government after recruitment. Actually the Commission surveys were an intrusion on the responsibility of agency heads, required primarily because utilization had been been overlooked by them. Because these constituted an intrusion, they were resented. Although agencies supposedly co-operated voluntarily in conducting personnel utilization surveys, the Commission could, of course, report their failure to co-operate to the President and the Bureau of the Budget. This sanction was never exercised. Utilization surveys were synchronized with reports to the Bureau of the Budget.

Both the War and Navy departments employed their own utilization surveys among uniformed personnel as well as civilian employees. The War Department attacked the problem of utilization continuously, the Navy only once, in 1944. The War Department made the closest approximation in the government service to the establishment of performance standards by the development of yardsticks for personnel requirements at its various installations.

War had created a consciousness of the size of the Federal government. For the first time controls were attempted, all of which directed attention to the quality of management, including personnel administration. The controls were qualitatively unequal in effectiveness; but at least two, the setting of personnel ceilings by the Bureau of the Budget and the sponsorship of personnel utilization surveys by the Civil Service Commission, were instruments far from perfect but capable, after some study, of serving the cause of improved management and economy in the future.

CHAPTER THIRTEEN

Broadening Employee Relations Programs

THAT INCREASED compensation alone does not provide the answer to problems of employee morale has been pointed out in studies of industrial workers' problems and their motivations. Increasingly during the war years it became apparent that a sound employee relations program, with increased employee services, was indispensable to assist management in meeting the many new war-born pressures, such as housing shortages, poor supervision, incomplete recreational facilities, and lack of credit arrangements. The influx of inexperienced, undisciplined persons away from home for the first time, of course, aggravated these difficulties in the milieu in which the worker had to live and labor. Concentration on manpower utilization required the direction of attention to the nonfinancial conditions and incentives that would stimulate employees to devote their full energy and ability to increased production.

The discovery of areas of tension and trouble became vital as turnover mounted. Several means, new in government, were adopted to supply this information to management. One was the adoption of the exit interview, which furnished employing agencies with the reasons for departure from the service. Another was employee counseling, which probed into reasons for maladjustment to the working environment. Still another was the provision for regular channels for presentation of grievances in many agencies without regularized grievance procedures before the war.

Rewards to employees for especially meritorious services and for beneficial suggestions were recognized as important morale builders. Both required attention. Departmental disparities in awarding salary increments for meritorious services caused congressional uneasiness and Commission directives to achieve uniformity. On the other hand, Congress itself allowed a lack of uniformity for rewarding suggestions for work improvement by permitting cash awards in some departments but not in others.

Employee health and safety programs also engaged the attention both of personnel administrators and of a few members of Congress. Although sick and annual leave regulations were liberalized, little could be done to provide the minimum of adequate emergency treatment in most government agencies under existing statutes and the Comptroller General's interpretation. The War Department and some of the new war agencies alone were able to move ahead unhampered with a program for health service more nearly parallel to that in private industry.

Inasmuch as the development of an employee relations program rested with the individual employing agencies, not with the central personnel agency, the same approach will be adopted in this discussion as in the explanation of training activities. Four agencies have been selected as typical of their kind in the war years: the War and Navy departments, unique for their phenomenal expansion and preoccupation with direct mechanical production for war purposes; OPA, a new war agency, unrestricted by a line of precedents and traditions; and the Department of Agriculture, one of the "old line" agencies, which had developed a comprehensive program of employee relations before the war and which made but slight alterations in that program during the war.

The New Stress on Employee Relations

Responsibility for the improvement of employee relations rested in the hands of the employing agencies. One source of inspiration for improvement arose from the impact of vitalized personnel offices on top management, which in turn stimulated an entire organization down to the first-line supervisors. It seemed obvious, therefore, that both staff and services of departmental personnel offices required expansion to enter what was for many a new area.

But Congress did not adopt a friendly attitude to the idea of providing funds for expansion of departmental personnel offices. Instead, it slashed the estimates for that purpose both in 1939 and 1940, rejecting proposed expenditures of $750,000 in 1939 and $108,730 in 1940.[1] The House Appropriations Committee

---

[1] U.S. Congress, House, *Independent Offices Appropriation Bill, 1941*, House Report 1515, 76th Cong., 3d Sess., 4-5.

declared without elucidation that it was not in sympathy with some of the programs outlined. This attitude made it difficult to launch employee relations programs of any scope in most agencies in time to anticipate the problems and troubles of sudden expansion.

At the same time the Council of Personnel Administration conducted a survey among the departments that revealed the absence of any written policy governing employee relations.[2] In many cases the absence of a written policy betrayed the absence of all thought on the subject. With what resources it had the Council sponsored a study of existing policies in government and industry in order to stimulate departmental action, especially with respect to the problem of handling grievances and complaints equitably. Eventually the Council produced a significant statement on employee counseling and another on grievances.[3]

As turnover rates increased in all agencies, causes were sought, both in deficient compensation and in abnormal working conditions. The year which revealed the greatest difference from prewar levels in turnover was, as might be expected, 1942. The annual turnover rate rose from 18.42 per cent in fiscal 1941 to 44.35 per cent in fiscal 1942.[4] For the departmental service it jumped in the same period from 27 per cent to 76 per cent. For fiscal 1943, turnover averaged 5.4 per cent per month, although at times, as in November, 1942, it reached 7.3 per cent per month.[5]

Realizing that the co-operation of employees must be won if production goals were to be met, the Navy took two significant steps in 1942. One was the calling of a conference in Washington with representatives of labor from all the Navy yards and industrial shore establishments on October 1, 1942.[6] The other step was the employment of a firm of industrial relations consultants, Industrial Relations Counselors, Inc., to survey some of the larger

[2] CSC, *Fifty-Seventh Annual Report*, 26.

[3] CSC, *Departmental Circular No. 439*, October 27, 1943, and *Statement on Counseling in the Federal Service*, June 11, 1943. For statement on grievances see *Departmental Circular No. 251*, February 24, 1941.

[4] U.S. Congress, House, Committee on Civil Service, Hearings on *Temporary Additional Compensation for Civilian Employees*, 77th Cong., 2nd Sess., June 2, 3, 4, 5, 9, 10, 11, 1942, p. 12.

[5] U.S. Congress, House, Hearing on *Independent Offices Appropriation Bill, 1945*, 78th Cong., 2nd Sess., December 9, 1943, p. 1029. *See* Table 2.

[6] Navy Civilian Personnel Instructions, *Instruction 60*, June 23, 1945, Inclosure of letter of August 6, 1942, pp. 9-10.

Navy yards to discover existing conditions and recommend needed changes.[7] The Navy Department confessed the need for the conference with labor in these terms:

> It is apparent that we have not yet attained that measure of cooperation which is possible and vital in this all out war, and we in the management end of the Navy admit our share of the responsibility for this lack of unity and express our determination with the cooperation of labor to rectify this situation in every way possible.
>
> We expect all representatives of Navy management to meet at all times representatives of labor on an all out basis of openmindedness, friendship, tolerance and mutual good will. We believe such a working policy carried on by all concerned will further enhance the morale of our Naval Establishments and we call upon all in authority, in all levels of management, and upon labor spokesmen and labor itself, to adapt its thinking, its actions, and its sentiments, to the end that the utmost cooperation may exist in all of the relationships within the Navy family; all of whom should be engaged now in helping to make the Navy the most effective and powerful weapon possible for the service of our country in this, the most difficult hour of its history.[8]

On the basis of the survey and recommendations by Industrial Relations Counselors, Inc., the Navy established its personnel relations organization for industrial employees, both per diem and per annum.[9] The survey had recommended an organization in shore establishments similar to that in private industrial plants because of the nature of Navy industrial operations. Under a personnel relations officer directly responsible to the commanding officer of the establishment six sections were usually created: (1) a labor board, which was a recruiting and examining adjunct of the Civil Service Commission; (2) a labor relations section, which worked on group relationships with shop committees, unions, and employee organizations and assisted in handling employee grievances; (3) an employment section, which dealt with problems of employment and separation, such as placement, exit interviews,

---

[7] Naval Shore Establishments, *Conference of Personnel Relations Officers*, August 18, 19, 20, 1943, Shore Establishments Division, Office of the Assistant Secretary of the Navy, NAVEXOS, P-7, p. 7.

[8] Navy Civilian Personnel Instructions, *Instruction 60*, p. 9.

[9] Interview with Lieut. H. A. Heimbach, Chief, Employee Policy Section, Employee Relations Branch, SECP, Navy Department, July 9, 1945.

efficiency ratings, transfer, promotion, manpower problems, records and statistics, job analysis and classification, and the administration of annual and sick leave; (4) a training section; (5) a safety section, which dealt with safety engineering, safety education, accident analysis data, compensation, health and sanitation; and (6) an employee services section which assumed responsibility for employee publications as well as the usual combination of service activities. In so far as possible, the Navy recruited as commissioned officers to head these sections men with industrial experience. The foregoing organization superseded the traditional old-fashioned reliance in the Navy on the chief clerk, whose primary role was merely the enforcement of civil service regulations and keeping of records.

The Council of Personnel Administration in Washington appointed a committee on employee relations to explore the problem of formulating a policy for the Federal government. In explaining the relationship of employee relations to management, the committee said:

> Progressive management is becoming aware of the fact that in performing its primary functions there are two inseparable, inescapable responsibilities: the organization and control of operations related directly to its production requirements, and the adequate management of the personnel involved in meeting production requirements. It is recognized that in planning for the first full consideration should be given the second. Personnel administration, therefore, assumes importance equal to that of operating responsibilities. Employee relations, as an integral part of personnel administration, contributes to the fulfillment of those responsibilities by promoting means whereby the fullest use of the human resources of the agency may be effectuated.[10]

The War Department, like others, felt the need to develop the employee relations function in civilian personnel administration. Before 1942 it had done little but sponsor a few welfare services which were primarily in the fields of nursing service in an emergence room and organization of emergency financial assistance to employees.[11] In consequence, the first problem facing the War

[10] CSC, Council of Personnel Administration, *Employee Relations in the Federal Service*, May 25, 1944, p. 6.
[11] Interview with J. H. Mason, Chief, Employee Relations Branch, Civilian Personnel Division, Office of the Secretary of War, July 19, 1945.

Department was the formulation of an employee relations policy. Various private consultants were employed from time to time. The first policy statement was made on January 31, 1943, followed by lesser specific statements from time to time, respecting commitments by management to the employees and establishing procedures to implement the commitments. Still, despite its slow start, the War Department was the first agency other than the Tennessee Valley Authority to go on record with a statement of principles defining its relationships with employee organizations.

OPA commenced its life cycle with a recognition of the importance of employee relations work, which was combined with the other work of the first personnel officer.[12] Originally in OPA a dichotomy existed between employee services and employee relations, but as the relationship between the two became clearer a merger was effected. Both came to be viewed as essentially one one function.

Agriculture was in a fortunate position, having recognized the existence of employee relations problems some time before the war. For example, it had promulgated a regularized grievance procedure on May 4, 1938, even before the famous Executive Order 7916 of June 24, 1938, which called on all agencies to address themselves to the task of formulating such policies.[13] In addition, the Department of Agriculture was among the first government agencies to employ a counselor, as early as 1938. As a result of its early progress, few changes were made in the wartime personnel relations program.

The Development of Employee Services

> I think the people that the Personnel Relations Division are [sic] dealing with are more than the 4 per cent—who are the problem children. And you take our own section—across the road and two miles down—is a large shipyard that is operated by the Maritime Commission. At the Maritime Commission shipyard, the rationing problems are solved for the employees; the recreational activities are planned and promoted for them; the housing is taken care of; credit facilities are arranged; transportation is handled; it is all done for the entire organiza-

[12] Interview with Miss Jeanne Erlanger, Employee Relations Branch, OPA, July 19, 1945.
[13] Interview with Harry Jarrett, Chief, Personnel Relations and Safety Division, Department of Agriculture, July 12, 1945.

tion. As a result of that, they can afford to employ high-caliber people to look out for that. If we don't provide the same sort of service for our employees, they would quit and go over there where they could get those services, even though they were intensely loyal to the Navy and to their job and to their supervisors.[14]

Succinctly the officer who uttered the foregoing words summarized the reason for the multiplication of employee services during the war: competition in the contracting labor market forced the least progressive employers to "keep up with the Joneses." Government agencies had commonly manifested no official interest before the war in such problems as housing, transportation, or recreational facilities, especially in the War and Navy departments. Within a year after Pearl Harbor competition for manpower reversed their indifference.

The Navy Department, like all other government agencies, relied on community facilities in so far as they met employee needs. The task of employee services officers was, therefore, to present needs, win co-operation, and plan concrete programs with local organizations. Often, however, housing and transportation facilities were nonexistent in overcrowded or remote and newly developed defense centers. In such instances the mere listing of desirable housing had to be discarded for direct appeals to the National Housing Agency to get expeditious construction of an adequate number of housing units.[15] At times the Navy had to buy buses to transport workers from neighboring towns and the countryside to shore establishments. The need for community nurseries and child day-care facilities financed by the Federal government under the Lanham Act had to be presented to local governments when women workers were sought for Navy yards. At last the problem of feeding employees properly on the job was recognized; thus the old-fashioned dinner bucket gave way to modern cafeterias serving hot meals, especially making meat dishes available to those performing hard physical labor.[16] Shore establish-

[14] Statement made at the *Naval Shore Establishments Conference of Personnel Relations Officers*, August 18, 19, and 20, 1943, Washington, D. C., Shore Establishments Division, Office of the Asst. Secretary of the Navy, 16.

[15] Interview with Lieut. Heimbach, July 9, 1945.

[16] Recreational programs in Navy yards varied. For example, at Quonset Point, Rhode Island, eighteen miles from Providence, workers relied largely on car pools for transportation, arranged by the personnel office, and, therefore, were unable to remain for after-hours recreation.

290   IMPACT OF WAR ON FEDERAL PERSONNEL

ments naturally showed great variation in the type of employee services promoted, depending largely on the environment in which the yard was located.

The War Department, like the Navy, had been traditionally concerned only for the welfare of military personnel, not at all for civilian employees. But after some pressure from the Employee Relations Branch, the War Department adopted a policy statement setting forth the principle of parity treatment in recreational and welfare activities as between military and civilian personnel.[17] Fearing dependency on the part of the workers, ASF followed a policy of keeping services to a minimum consistent with actual employee needs that workers could not satisfy through their own efforts. "Employee activities sponsored as part of the personnel program of the installation and which are intended to develop morale, must be viewed with some sophistication," stated the *Civilian Personnel Officers' Handbook*.[18] Sound advice was given by ASF to determine the degree and extent of employee interest before the organization of recreational activities.

The official War Department policy in providing recreational facilities for Negroes was that the department "could not innovate sociological custom."[19] When Negroes complained of being barred from participation, the department canceled activities for all employees. This policy was defended by the Employee Relations Branch on the ground that the aim of recreational activities sponsored by the department was greater productivity from the individual worker through equity, fairness, and good working conditions. The aim was not just the worker's individual happiness.

OPA tried to draw employees into the administration of employee services. At first that agency placed the responsibility for employee services in the Employee Relations Branch, but by 1945 it tended to minimize the centralized handling of that function in an effort to enlist employee participation in the administration of those activities or at least to decentralize them to the administrative officers of the divisions.[20] Employee unions assisted in directing blood donor campaigns and clothing drives for European

[17] Interview with Mason, July 19, 1945.
[18] ASF, *Civilian Personnel Officers' Handbook*, 39.
[19] Interview with Mason, July 19, 1945.
[20] Interview with Miss Erlanger, July 19, 1945.

refugees. In connection with recreational activities OPA encouraged the use of community facilities as much as possible, supplying information to employees. The agency policy, unique on racial participation in recreation, was to publicize and plan only activities available to all employees, including Negro workers. In consequence, no agency-wide dances were sponsored in the departmental service because of local hotel and club restrictions against Negro attendance. The only alternative was to encourage supervisors to stimulate section parties or office parties and to assist employees in arranging activities in which others in the agency were interested. A recreation room in the departmental service was open daily during the lunch hour. From each division a representative was selected to an Employee Recreation Advisory Council to assist and advise the Employee Services Section.[21]

The Department of Agriculture, in order to reach more employees through their own organizational units, in April, 1942, had each bureau designate an employee as a bureau contact officer.[22] The latter worked with the Office of Personnel on welfare services and related activities, including housing, transportation, recreation, voluntary war services, and drives for funds, such as Red Cross and Community War Chest. Bureau contact officers had monthly meetings and among their number organized committees on housing, transportation, nutrition, welfare, recreation, information, child care, and health.[23] Department-wide dances and boat rides were regularly sponsored for departmental service employees. In the field service USDA clubs were promoted to bring together in social gatherings all Department of Agriculture employees in each important field service center. Because Negroes could not attend dances in Washington hotels, the department declared itself ready to sponsor similar activities for its Negro

[21] OPA, Memorandum to the White House, *General Evaluation of OPA Recreational Program,* February 9, 1945, and *OPA Recreation Program and Policy,* May, 1944.

[22] Memorandum for Heads of Administrations, Bureaus, and Offices, *Bureau Contact Officers,* June 21, 1944, Department of Agriculture.

[23] Interview with Miss Lois E. Monie, Employee Counselor, Personnel Relations and Safety Division, Department of Agriculture, July 12, 1945. The Personnel Relations and Safety Division sent out a questionnaire to departmental service employees in April, 1945, to discover their interests in services offered both by the department and the community. Department of Agriculture, Memorandum for Heads of Administrations, Bureaus, and Offices, *Morale Building Program,* March 30, 1945.

employees in centers open to them. Through the counselor's office, budget information was prepared by the Bureau of Human Nutrition and Home Economics for the benefit of the many young girls coming into Washington at low salaries and living away from home for the first time.[24] Agriculture, as was true of other departments, provided not merely information but actual housing arrangements for girls recruited directly from school. Personnel relations officers met and chaperoned these girls their first day in Washington.

Many employee activities in the Department of Agriculture were subsidized by the Welfare Association, which derived its income from the operation of all USDA cafeterias, lunch rooms, and lunch counters in the departmental service. Agency operation of food dispensing facilities was unique and was found in no other department. The arrangement dated back to World War I days. Various recreational activities recommended by the personnel office were supported by the Welfare Association during wartime. For example, it sponsored an art show of departmental talent and a victory garden show.[25] Emergency loans to employees were also negotiated from the reserve funds of the Welfare Association through the help of a welfare committeeman in each bureau.

In all departments the successful conduct of employee services required a thorough knowledge of the community in which the establishment was located: its services; organizations, governmental, religious, and philanthropic; and its social attitudes. Knowledge of that kind was desirable in peacetime, indispensable in wartime. In addition, the administration of employee services required individuals possessed of initiative and resourcefulness to discover employee needs and organize to meet them. In many instances services had to be planned in anticipation of needs; for example, housing accommodations and transportation had to be arranged for recruits brought in from distant areas by the time of their arrival. To have waited until a problem appeared or to make a survey would have been disastrous. Agencies under the greatest recruiting pressure naturally developed employee services earlier than most "old-line" departments, but even in the State Department a services program was instituted by 1944.

[24] U.S. Department of Agriculture, *Living on Your Salary in Wartime Washington*, March, 1943 (mimeographed).
[25] Interview with Miss Monie, July 12, 1945.

Employee Counseling

1. THE DEVELOPMENT OF COUNSELING

Employee counseling was one of the newer services which was widely adopted in employee relations programs in the government service during the war years. The more progressive private employers, such as Western Electric Company at its Hawthorne plant, had utilized counseling services for some time. The Federal government, therefore, was not pioneering in a new field. The first agency to recognize counseling as an integral and distinct part of its personnel relations program had been the Social Security Board, which appointed an employee counselor in November, 1938.[26] Although counseling has usually been associated with the handling of "problem cases," it embraces a much wider range of activities than listening to the woes of the abnormal employee and persuading him to go to a psychiatrist. In fact, employee counseling is primarily supplying services, information, and advice to the normal employee who may be seeking data about educational resources, vocational opportunities, agencies for financial assistance, recreation, housing, churches, budgeting, and kindred subjects. Many of the wartime services described in the foregoing paragraphs were centered in the counselor's office.

So apparent was the need for counseling in wartime that the Civil Service Commission appointed a committee to explore the duties and qualifications requisite for counseling positions in order that standards might be evolved for recruiting and placement. In its report in 1942 the committee established as basic considerations in the creation of counseling programs the following postulates: (1) counseling must be done on an individual and confidential basis, with the number of counselors sufficient to handle the work load; (2) supervisors could substantially reduce the number of persons seeking counseling services by establishing satisfactory working relationships; (3) counseling services could not take the place of healthy working conditions; (4) most employees sought the help of a counselor primarily for information and the problems were of short duration; (5) the resources and experts of the community should be known and utilized by counselors; (6) the counseling services should not be combined with

[26] Margaret E. Barron, "Employee Counseling in a Federal Agency," *Personnel Administration*, IV (March, 1942), 1.

those dealing with grievances related to promotions, grade allocations, and misassignments; (7) employee activities must not be allowed to consume time that should be spent in individual counseling; (8) the services of counselors should not be confused with those of nurses or follow-up workers who check absenteeism.[27] Counselors, of course, had little worth to management unless they passed along information respecting unfavorable working conditions or factors causing a deterioration of workers' morale in order that corrective steps could be taken by the line officers responsible for operations. The committee eschewed the use of such terms as "welfare workers" or "social service worker" to describe the newly created counselor positions.[28]

Nearly a year later the Interdepartmental Conference on Employee Counseling, organized under the aegis of the Council of Personnel Administration, prepared a second statement on counseling, defining it and describing the work.[29] The conference defined counseling as "an organized approach to the solution of individual employee problems which affect general morale, efficiency, and productivity, the purpose being to assist management in maintaining a degree of stability in its working force necessary for the fulfillment of its operating responsibilities."[30] The conference reiterated the need for counseling both because of the difficulty of adjusting to wartime living and working conditions and because of the large number of untrained and inexperienced supervisors in the enlarged Federal service. Even trained supervisors were said to have had less time than formerly to concern themselves with the personal difficulties of individual employees because of increased responsibilities in organizing and planning

[27] CSC, *Departmental Circular No. 356,* July 10, 1942.

[28] Desirable qualifications were four years of college study and at least two years of qualifying experience for junior counselor positions at the $2,600 salary level. Alternatively one year of graduate study and one year of experience were accepted. Qualifying experience included industrial or vocational counseling, certain aspects of personnel administration such as placement and interviewing, social group work or leadership of recreational groups, and social case work. The committee recommended that counselors be of the same sex as the employees seeking help. Therefore, agencies were advised to employ the same proportion of male and female counselors as existed among their workers.

[29] CSC, *Departmental Circular No. 439,* October 27, 1943, and *Statement on Counseling in the Federal Service,* June 11, 1943. Reprinted in *Personnel Administration,* V (August, 1943), 10-13.

[30] CSC, *Departmental Circular No. 439,* October 27, 1943.

work programs. A warning was sounded that counselors must not try to assume the responsibility for placement, improper classification, or physical conditions which belonged either to other sections of the personnel office or to the supervisor. Rather, the counselor's role lay in interpreting the employee's needs to management and to the community and relaying management's reasons for certain operations and conditions of work to the employee. The counselor was not a psychiatrist, but on the contrary referred employees suffering from mental or emotional disturbances to a psychiatrist or physician for assistance.

Necessarily the relationship between employee and counselor was of a confidential nature similar to that between physician and patient or lawyer and client. Many employees needed merely an opportunity to "think out loud" in order to analyze their problems and themselves to formulate their own solution. If specialized attention was needed for solution, the counselor's function was to win employee acceptance of the idea of seeking and receiving help from a competent person outside the line of command prepared to give it. Counseling clearly required balanced, well-adjusted, experienced, and mature individuals who understood the action and reaction of environment on human nature and the extent to which human beings could adjust to the conditions around them or to which those conditions could be changed. Those who had merely a juvenile "love of people" or the ability to get along well with others to offer as background and equipment were not fitted for the tasks facing a counselor.

3. *Exit interviews.*—The task of conducting exit interviews fell usually to employee counselors. The exit interview was really a pre-exit interview with employees who had given notice of their impending departure from the service or who had received separation notices. The purpose was to ascertain and record the real reasons for employee dissatisfaction or failure and report to management so that correction of remediable conditions could be undertaken. Another purpose was served in that the exit interview also provided a means to retain the services of able employees by presenting to them possibilities for transfer or reassignment. Beginning in October, 1942, all agencies were asked by the Commission, following the recommendation of the Council of Personnel Administration, to conduct exit interviews and report the results monthly in order to help ascertain the causes for turn-

over.[31] Reasons for turnover are shown below. Of those employees given exit interviews in the first few months of the program 16.5 per cent were persuaded to remain. So great was the interest of the Commission in salvaging employees who resigned that a special interviewing unit was created to deal with them if the counselor's efforts to retain them had proved unavailing.[32] In March, 1944, the Commission discontinued the order for monthly reporting of exit interview summaries, although it requested agencies to continue the interview system and retain the information for their own use.[33]

TABLE 13

REASONS FOR TURNOVER, FEDERAL DEPARTMENTAL SERVICE, OCTOBER THROUGH DECEMBER, 1942[a]

Reasons Given for Leaving Agency	Percentage of Total
To enter military service	25.0
Interagency transfer	17.0
Inadequate salary	11.1
Poor health	11.1
Family reasons	10.4
Poor living conditions	8.6
Lack of opportunity for promotion	8.3
Return to school	6.8
Involuntary (separation notice)	5.0
Marriage	3.6
Lack of belief in usefulness of work	3.2
Inability to use highest skills	2.9
Working conditions within agency	2.3
Insufficient work	2.1
Retirement or death	2.0
Maternity leave	1.6
Transportation difficulties	1.4
Poor housing facilities	0.8

[a] Total separations in period shown were 16,667. Data given in U.S. Congress, Senate, Hearings on *Overtime Compensation to Government Employees*, Committee on Civil Service, 78th Cong., 1st Sess., February 25, 26, March 2, 1943, pp. 14-15.

b. *The Interdepartmental Conference on Counseling.*—The number of counselors in the Federal service grew from the pioneer position in the Social Security Board in 1938 to approxi-

[31] *Ibid.*, No. 377, September 30, 1942. [32] *Ibid.*, Supp. No. 1, October 27, 1942.
[33] *Ibid.*, Supp. No. 3, March 21, 1944.

mately 350 positions in at least twenty-five agencies in Washington by 1945, to say nothing of the counselor positions in agencies temporarily moved from the national capital and in the War and Navy field establishments.[34] A natural result of the growth in number of these positions was the establishment of the Interdepartmental Conference on Counseling in the summer of 1942, on the recommendation of the Employee Relations Committee of the Council of Personnel Administration. The conference brought together monthly the chief counselors to share ideas and ways of meeting their common problems.[35] The first task before it was to assist in securing the solution to emergency wartime problems by enlisting community help and informing the counselors themselves of available local resources. From that base the conference moved on to attack the problem of retaining employees to reduce turnover. At first interested in recreation, it dropped that problem after a Federal Recreation Committee had been established to assume the responsibility. Instead the conference worked on in-service training of counselors, such as training in interviewing and counseling techniques, referral methods, standards, the place of counseling in an agency program, and methods of evaluating counseling programs.

2. OPERATION OF COUNSELING PROGRAMS IN TYPICAL AGENCIES

There was naturally considerable variance in interests and attitudes toward employee counseling among even the four agencies with which this chapter is primarily concerned. The Navy Department, for example, had little counseling as such and disclaimed any interest in "social case work."[36] Instead, it relied in its industrial work, which, of course, overshadowed all other Navy civilian work, on the shop masters and shop personnel supervisors to carry on counseling as a part of their duties. The shop personnel supervisors were of either sex, depending upon the relative number of men and women in the organizational unit. They had come up from the ranks and were trained for the personnel aspects of supervisory work by the section heads from the personnel relations office.

[34] Margaret E. Barron, "The Emerging Role of Employee Counseling," *Public Personnel Review*, VI (January, 1945), 11.
[35] Interview with Mrs. Mildred Clarkson, War Department, Chairman of the Interdepartmental Conference on Employee Counseling, July 25, 1945.
[36] Interview with Lieut. Heimbach, July 9, 1945.

The War Department, on the other hand, employing many more office workers, utilized counselors to a much greater degree. A quota of one counselor to every five hundred employees was considered desirable by the War Department.[37] Their work was viewed primarily as a training task, to help supervisors do as much counseling as was needed and within their abilities.[38] In any event, the counselor had a fact-finding assignment, not one of decision, according to War Department policy. Since the counselor as a staff officer could never be permitted to supersede the supervisor and line officers, the responsibility for decisions had to remain in the line. Counseling was regarded as a useful listening post for management to discover employee attitudes, to make comparative studies of units for analysis, to learn its own mistakes, and to know whether remedial steps were required. Thus the War Department believed that supervisors alone could not perform all the counseling necessary and that counseling was a supplemental mechanism to assist the supervisors. It was a means to help employees help themselves, not to solve their problems for them.[39]

ASF in outlining counseling services for its industrial installations declared that the counselor had no right to handle on-the-job problems, which were within the exclusive province of the supervisor.[40] Warning was sounded against allowing a situation to develop in which an employee received a more sympathetic hearing from a counselor than from his supervisor on problems within the orbit of working relationships. The supervisor's responsibility was absolute; he had the right to be wrong. In contrast, the counselor's function was limited to off-the-job problems. By a sympathetic reception of those problems ASF felt that the employee would acquire the feeling that he had the support of a strong organization which was interested in its employees and their place in the community.

OPA had an approach somewhat analogous to that of the Navy Department, viewing counseling as the primary responsibility of the supervisor rather than of a specialist.[41] In consequence, no

---

[37] War Department, *Personnel Counseling*, Civilian Personnel Pamphlet No. 1, July 23, 1943, p. 4.
[38] Interview with Mason, July 19, 1945.
[39] War Department, *Personnel Counseling*, 2.
[40] ASF Manual, *Civilian Personnel Officers' Handbook*, 38.
[41] Interview with Miss Erlanger, July 19, 1945.

professional social workers were appointed to OPA counseling positions. In fact, all personnel officers were regarded as counselors. Supervisors were trained to handle exit interviews as well as induction interviews. By means of interviewing supervisors, personnel officers taught them the techniques of interviewing. A radical difference between OPA and other agencies was the disposition in OPA to use employee unions for counseling activities, but agency officers admitted that this could by no means be adopted as a universal technique. It required mutual confidence built up over some period of time to operate satisfactorily.

The definition OPA gave to counseling was broad:

> A counseling interview is one which takes place between two persons when one is unsure of the proper course of action and the other is in a position to advise. It occurs because a problem exists; its purpose is to clarify the factors causing the situation and help the person involved in the problem to correct it.[42]

The personnel staff regarded it as a part of their function to explain and demonstrate counseling to the supervisors, and, in so far as the conduct of counseling was concerned, to make their services available to both supervisors and employees alike. The personnel officer was always, however, regarded as an impartial middleman, useful for fact finding and the discovery of the relative importance of contributing factors in the creation of any problem studies.

The Department of Agriculture placed less stress on counseling by the supervisors, but employed a degree of decentralization of counseling services in that bureau contact officers were expected to carry some of the counseling work. In bureaus of at least 3,000 employees a full-time counselor was employed.[43] The counselor in the personnel relations and safety office was responsible for interviewing problem cases sent in by supervisors as well as talking with the average employee facing personnel problems who came in for assistance. In addition, the counselor gave central direction to the departmental activities and services program.

3. CRITICISM OF COUNSELING ACTIVITIES

The stress that some counselors drawn from the field of professional social work gave to psychiatric analysis of employee prob-

---

[42] OPA, *Draft Statement on Counseling,* May 22, 1945.
[43] Interview with Miss Monie, July 12, 1945.

lems lent an unfortunate tone to counseling in the Federal service. Congress, quick to get repercussions, adopted a hostile view of all employee counseling as a type of valueless folderol, foisted on the government in wartime, which possessed potentialities of harm if not used with moderation. The Ramspeck Committee issued this blast against the social work orientation of much counseling:

> Members of the Congress and this Committee are deluged by employee complaints, who resent the type of assistance offered by the employee counseling program in the Government. The following is an excerpt from the job description of CAF-12 counselor:
>
> . . . "provides for competent psychiatric assistance to employees requiring this type of aid. . . ."
>
> Of 30 counselors ranging in grade from CAF-9 to CAF-12 the majority have been drawn from colleges or social work. Usually these persons have university training showing courses in social work or consultant and welfare work, personnel and counseling, or psychiatry and teaching.
>
> The Committee observes a tendency on the part of employees with real grievances to generally avoid contact with employee counselors. With rare exceptions the position of the employee counselor in the Federal structure is innocuous. It is not established that this expanding and expansive program has resulted in an appreciable improvement in employee-employer relations. There is basis for the feeling on the part of many employees that the most simple grievance, when reported to the employee counselor, may be translated into a major problem.
>
> The employee who took a few days out for no good reason except plain cussedness may find that he has a psychosis. Hangovers, resulting from a series of nights out, are authoritatively diagnosed as some form of neurosis. A complainant who visits his Congressman is amazed by the discovery that the counselor's report reveals a persecution complex.
>
> The influence of this type of counselor is infecting administrative and supervisory attitudes. In several agencies it is noted that supervisors were inclined to label aggressive or complainant employees with psychiatric terms detrimental [*sic*] to the employee and the implications of which were unappreciated by the supervisor.
>
> Experience in dealing with gainfully employed persons is seldom the main qualification for employee counselors.
>
> Usually no complaints were heard from agencies where prac-

tical employee-employer relations experience is prerequisite to counseling.[44]

Congressman Wigglesworth of the House Appropriations Committee lost no time in seizing the above criticism to attack counseling in the hearing on Civil Service Commission estimates for 1946. He made an oblique attack on counseling, actually an agency responsibility, by attacking the Council of Personnel Administration. He asked: "Could we not get rid of those constantly expanding set-ups for personnel and some of this social work and psychiatric work if we just drop out this item for the Council of Personnel Administration?"[45]

The distaste for emphasis on psychiatric interpretations and terminology was well founded, however sound may have been analyses given in psychiatric terms to certain employee difficulties. Certain it is that any institution as large as most Federal agencies would employ many misfits and maladjusted individuals, especially in wartime. But no one appreciates being labeled as a "case study," as was learned in connection with medically discharged veterans. Nor was psychiatric analysis of problems the whole story in employee counseling. Much trouble unquestionably could be attributed to poor supervision, which, as was mentioned in the chapters on training, was one of the most serious weaknesses in the Federal government.

Many supervisors also resented the new counseling activities, either because of a misunderstanding of their purpose or because the counselors themselves did not perform properly.[46] Occasionally supervisors felt that counselors undermined their standing with the employees supervised by listening sympathetically to unfounded tales of woe. One small, unofficial study of employee attitudes indicated that the predominant causes of dissatisfaction lay in overrecruitment, poor placement, poor supervision, and inadequate opportunities for advancement.[47] If these causes had validity, then the counseling program, with its emphasis on off-the-

[44] U.S. Congress, House, Committee on Civil Service, *Investigation of Civilian Employment*, House Report 2084, 78th Cong., 2nd Sess., 13.

[45] U.S. Congress, House, Hearing on *Independent Offices Appropriation Bill, 1946*, 79th Cong., 1st Sess., January 17, 1945, p. 1239.

[46] Based on information from a number of Federal employees elicited during 1944 and 1945.

[47] Charles N. Cofer and Eleanor B. Cohen, "Job Attitudes of a Hundred and One Federal Employees," *Public Personnel Review*, IV (April, 1943), 101.

job problems, was able to do little to correct them. Counseling could, however, serve in a diagnostic capacity to discover causes of dissatisfaction and low morale in order to report them to management for correction.

The counseling function which flowered in the war years and was so closely associated with employee services and activities was still too new to evaluate at the end of the war. Its permanent place in the Federal personnel program can be ascertained only now after the re-establishment of approximately normal working conditions, as the services aspect of personnel relations fades into a secondary role. The worth of the counselor to management in assisting in reporting general employee attitudes, causes of dissatisfaction, and conditions which need correction can today be assessed. It is entirely possible that the counselor should become primarily an agency trainer, as the OPA conceived the role. The counselor's worth may well depend on how he strengthens the supervisor.

Rewards for Meritorious Services and Suggestions

1. WITHIN-GRADE PAY INCREASES FOR MERITORIOUS SERVICES

Employee morale is a product not merely of good working conditions and adequate compensation, but of recognition for work well done. Not until 1941 was there any statutory provision to permit an extra salary increment for especially meritorious services. Interestingly enough, the suggestion for such a provision came from the Bureau of the Budget when the House Committee on the Civil Service was considering bills providing for uniform and regular salary increases for Federal employees.[48] The bill enacted, the Mead-Ramspeck Act, besides providing for regular salary increments, permitted agency heads to recognize especially meritorious services by making additional one-step salary increases.[49] The law failed to define "especially meritorious services," but did limit them to one salary step within any grade and one award within a waiting period between regular incre-

---

[48] U.S. Congress, House, Committee on Civil Service, Hearings on *Bills Proposing a Salary Advancement Plan for Federal Employees*, 77th Cong., 1st Sess., March 11, 12, 13, and 14, 1941, p. 19.

[49] 55 *U.S. Statutes* 613 (1941).

ments.[50] Agencies had to report their actions with respect to such increases to the Civil Service Commission, which, in turn, reported the numbers and types of actions taken to Congress. The law applied only to Classification Act employees.

After a full year and one-half of operation under the Mead-Ramspeck Act, it seemed clear that wide variation existed among agencies in the standards on which meritorious increases were granted. The House Appropriations Committee observed this fact and commented that the "privilege is one that should be exercised sparingly and in the unusual circumstance."[51] Both the Commission and the Council of Personnel Administration were convinced that meritorious increases possessed a strong incentive value that should not be restricted to any occupational group or salary level, nor should the honor be given lightly and considered easily obtained.[52] High efficiency alone was not sufficient. The five essentials outlined by the Commission and approved by the Council were (1) an act or service in the public interest; (2) an act related to the employee's position or employment; (3) one over and above normal job requirements; (4) one of unusual or distinctive character; and (5) one that served as an incentive to others. In order to achieve the desired uniformity, at least between bureaus of the same agency, each department was asked to establish a committee to pass on recommendations which the Commission then reviewed. Publicity was recommended by the Commission to increase the incentive value of such increases.

The Ramspeck Committee regarded the establishment of standards in 1943 as "locking the barn door after the horse had been stolen."[53] It was especially irate at Department of Justice awards to 126 employees in the first year in contrast to seven in Agriculture and three in Labor. Chairman Ramspeck fulminated, "I cannot use any parliamentary language strong enough to describe my disgust with what has happened in the Department of Justice in this situation."[54]

The Commission desired a liberalization of the Mead-Ramspeck

[50] The waiting periods between regular increments were eighteen months for grades in which the regular increments were $60 or $100 and thirty months when the regular increments were $200 or $250.
[51] *Investigation of Civilian Employment*, Part I, Hearing on March 25, 1943, p. 185.
[52] CSC, *Departmental Circular No. 321, Supp. No. 1*, March 30, 1943.
[53] *Investigation of Civilian Employment*, Part I, Hearing on March 25, 1943, p. 187.
[54] *Ibid.*, 186.

Act not merely with regard to shortening the waiting periods but also with respect to the increases for meritorious services. It sought authority to establish standards for such increases and to postaudit them as a part of central administration. More important, however, it desired abandonment of the limitation to one meritorious pay increase in any pay increment period, for the Commission reasoned that such a limitation destroyed the incentive value.[55] The relaxation sought was not achieved except in one minor measure in that the Pay Act of 1945 changed the expression "especially meritorious services" to "superior accomplishment."[56]

2. REWARDS FOR BENEFICIAL SUGGESTIONS

Suggestion systems which paid monetary awards for ideas of demonstrable worth had long been accepted in industry but were a wartime innovation in the Federal government. Beginning in 1940, Congress permitted the War Department's Ordnance Department to make cash awards to its employees for suggestions resulting in improvements or economy in the operation of any department plant.[57] Similar authority was extended to the entire War Department early in 1943.[58]

The War Department organized a suggestion plan for the entire department after Congressional authorization had been received. The plan provided for a continuous channeling of suggestions for improved procedures to suggestion committees in each establishment. The anonymity of the employee making the suggestions was protected when the committee adjudged the merits of each proposal. The amount of estimated savings determined the sum of money recommended as an award by the committee when the proposal was approved and sent up to the commanding officer for adoption. Commanding officers gave recognition in the installation to those whose ideas had been adopted, and the Secretary of War gave suitable commendation in calling department attention to those whose ideas had been considered worthy of adoption in divisions outside their own establishment.[59] Table 14 shows the extent of participation and rate of adoption in the prin-

[55] CSC, *Sixtieth Annual Report*, 65.   [56] 59 *U.S. Statutes* 265 (1945).
[57] 54 *U.S. Statutes* 350 (1940).
[58] *Investigation of Civilian Employment*, Part III, Hearing on June 11, 1943, p. 528.   [59] *Ibid.*, 529-30.

cipal branches of the War Department in 1944 and 1945.

The War Department estimated that it had saved $126,000,000 in the first twenty months of operation of the suggestion system.[60] Over one thousand suggestion committees were at work evaluating ideas. In addition to monetary awards, the War Department by 1945 conferred emblems and citations for distinguished or meritorious civilian service, analogous to campaign ribbons and medals for military personnel.

The Navy Department, like the War Department, was empowered to make cash awards for beneficial suggestions, the amount of the award to be based on estimated savings. A sum of $250 was the maximum award which could be given in any one Navy yard for an employee suggestion adopted there.[61] Of course, additional sums were paid by other yards if the suggestion was adopted elsewhere. In that case it had to be sent to the Washington headquarters before it was offered elsewhere. The highest award paid any Navy civilian employee was $3,000, given to a Chinese-American employee at the Mare Island yard for an idea which gained widespread acceptance. In addition, the Secretary of the Navy gave the Distinguished Civilian Service Award for outstanding employee contributions, while commandants at local establishments conferred meritorious civilian awards for lesser achievements.

Both OPA and Agriculture had suggestion systems but were limited to letters of commendation and public mention of those whose suggestions were adopted. No legislation had been passed enabling them to make cash awards from appropriations. The Commission favored uniform enabling legislation to permit all departments to make cash awards to their employees for suggestions that led to notable improvements.[61] However, Congress took no such step.

HEALTH PROGRAMS

The Commission stressed employee health and safety as subjects for agency concern in developing a sound personnel utilization program, but lethargy and the absence of legislation prevented extensive developments in these fields.[62] Serious neglect

---

[60] Interview with Mason, July 19, 1945.   [61] CSC, *Sixty-First Annual Report*, 4.
[62] CSC, *Departmental Circular No. 476,* March 20, 1943.

306   IMPACT OF WAR ON FEDERAL PERSONNEL

TABLE 14
PARTICIPATION IN WAR DEPARTMENT CIVILIAN SUGGESTION PROGRAM, APRIL, 1945[a]

Major Components	Average Strength - Current Month	Average Strength - Preceding Six Months	Average Strength - One Year Ago	Suggestions Received[b] - Current Month	Suggestions Received[b] - Preceding Six Months Average	Suggestions Received[b] - One Year Ago	Monthly Rate of Participation Per 1,000 Employees - Current Month	Monthly Rate of Participation Per 1,000 Employees - Preceding Six Months Average	Monthly Rate of Participation Per 1,000 Employees - One Year Ago
Office, Secretary of War	1,676	1,634	1,574	26	25.0	18	15.5	15.3	11.4
Office, Chief of Staff	1,844	1,689	1,837	9	18.2	5	4.9	10.8	2.7
Army Air Forces	398,041	409,598	428,152	4,130	3,262.8	3,054	10.4	8.0	7.1
Army Ground Forces	1,194	1,256	1,514	5	4.8	0	4.2	3.8	0.0
Army Service Forces	767,556	771,659	765,717	9,752	8,744.2	8,535	12.7	11.3	11.1
Total	1,170,311	1,185,836	1,198,794	13,922	12,055.0	11,612	11.9	10.2	9.7

[a] Table taken from War Department, *Civilian Personnel Statistics Bulletin*, April, 1945, p. 23.
[b] The total accumulated initiated savings from the beginning of the program in June, 1943, to date are $94,546,367.41. The number of suggestions received from June, 1943, to date totals 246,871. The total number of suggestions adopted from June, 1943, to date is 34,788.

of both programs was charged to the Federal government by the Commission, which cited the high accident rate of 12.3 accidents per 1,000,000 man hours worked during 1943 as compared with lower rates in representative industrial corporations.[63] Periodic physical examinations and the adjustment of working conditions affecting health, it held, might reduce absenteeism due to illness in a manner comparable to reductions in private industry.[64] The Commission urged the passage of the bill pending in the House in 1944 to authorize the establishment of health and medical programs.[65]

In Interdepartmental Safety Council of representatives appointed by each agency head was organized in 1939, but its accomplishments were negligible, as indicated by the results above. One of the difficulties which was pointed out by Congressman Randolph of the House Civil Service Committee was that responsibility for safety and accident prevention was never located within the agencies.[66] To compel agency heads to devote attention to the subject Congressman Randolph on July 9, 1945, introduced a bill to require agencies to ask for appropriations to defray the expenses of accident compensation.[67] By making each agency head justify his accident rate, Congressman Randolph hoped to achieve what committees and talk had not accomplished in an area which he felt the Commission and the Bureau of the Budget had hitherto neglected.

In the field of health services little had been done other than to provide for the establishment of emergency rooms operated by nurses. In May, 1942, there were approximately eighty-five such rooms employing 155 nurses.[68] The Council of Personnel Administration had deemed the matter of health programs worthy of study and had appointed a Health and Safety Committee in the autumn of 1941 for that task.

---

[63] CSC, *Sixtieth Annual Report*, 21. In 1943 the U.S. Steel rate was 3.2, General Motors Corporation 4.3, U.S. Rubber Company 3.3, and the DuPont Company 1.9 per 1,000,000 man hours worked. The Commission estimated the 1943 accident loss at 600 employees killed, 76,500 injured, and 1,800,000 working days lost to the Federal government, equivalent to 6,000 man years of work, or $10,000,000.

[64] *Ibid.*, 22.   [65] CSC, *Sixty-First Annual Report*, 7.

[66] Jennings Randolph, "Congress Looks at Civil Service," *Personnel Administration*, VII (September, 1944), 7.

[67] *H. R. 3731*, 79th Cong., 1st Sess.

[68] Memorandum of Dr. V. K. Harvey, Medical Director, CSC, to Commissioner Flemming, May 8, 1943.

The outcome of the appointment of the Health and Safety Committee was the drafting of a letter for signature by the President, calling on agency heads to establish medical divisions and to co-ordinate their medical services through the Public Health Service in consultation with the Commission.[69] The letter was not signed, and nothing came of it.

Some agencies in the meantime instituted limited health programs of their own. These agencies included OPA, WPB, the Bureau of the Census, the Bureau of Standards, the Bureau of Engraving and Printing, the Government Printing Office, and the Veterans Administration. Public Health Service physicians were assigned to WPB, Census, Treasury, and the Bureau of Engraving and Printing. Under that arrangement the doctors were guided in the development of employee health programs by Public Health Service but were administratively responsible to the personnel departments of the agencies in which they were stationed.[70]

The difficulty confronting other departments was a ruling by the Comptroller General in 1938 against the employment of a physician by the Department of Agriculture. The Bureau of the Budget stated informally in 1943 that the health programs then conducted would be declared illegal if a formal opinion were requested of the Bureau of the Budget.[71] Legislation was, therefore, held to be essential to legalize the newly instituted services. The Bureau of the Budget worked with the Public Health Service on a bill to legalize the program, but the Public Health Service was reluctant to sponsor it. In the end, sponsorship had to come from the House Civil Service Committee.

---

[69] The scope of the services contemplated by the Council of Personnel Administration included attention to health hazards in working conditions, study of worker reactions to the strain of wartime and other unusual demands, worker education on health hazards, first-aid and nutrition, counseling personnel officers on the placement and employment of the physically handicapped, warning workers of incipient illness for referral to private physicians, emergency treatment of injuries and minor illnesses during working hours, analysis of sick leave records, administration of periodic physical examinations, and attention to the reduction of respiratory infections and mental illness.

[70] Both War and Navy departments employed doctors at their field establishments. In addition, the War Department employed several doctors and nurses in the Pentagon Building, but the Navy Department refused its departmental medical service to civilian employees.

[71] Memorandum of Dr. Harvey.

EMPLOYEE RELATIONS PROGRAMS 309

Two bills to enable agencies to proceed with health programs for emergency treatment of injuries and minor illnesses, for educational and preventive medicine, and for alleviation of health hazards were introduced in 1944.[72] The House Civil Service Committee held hearings and issued a favorable report on Congressman Randolph's bill.[73] A similar bill was introduced in the Senate in 1944, permitting the inclusion of treatment of minor dental conditions, and reported favorably.[74] Congress took no action on either bill. Therefore, Congressman Randolph in 1945 introduced a bill similar to the Senate bill of 1944.[75] Once again a favorable report issued from the House Civil Service Committee, but no action was taken by Congress before the end of the war. Thus the health program, resting in part on a shaky legal foundation, had actually advanced little during the war if a government-wide view is taken of the problem.

GRIEVANCE PROCEDURES

Fair procedures for the settlement of employee grievances are basic to any employee relations program which can be labeled progressive. In the Federal government, concern for the establishment of regularized grievance procedures is of relatively recent origin. Only in 1938 through Executive Order 7916 did President Roosevelt require all agencies to formulate grievance procedures and submit them to the Civil Service Commission for approval. Two years later only a half dozen agencies had complied with that request.[76] The lack of machinery to handle grievances tended to channel many to Congress. Because the legislators did not have access to the facts of cases appealed to them, they were frequently unable to differentiate between the neurotic and frustrated employees without genuine grievances and those with legitimate complaints. For example, the reader of testimony taken by the Ellender Committee in 1939 and 1940 is forcibly impressed by the number of persons obviously verging

[72] U.S. Congress, House, Committee on Civil Service, Hearing on *Health Programs for Government Employees*, 78th Cong., 2nd Sess., August 21 and 22, 1944.

[73] *Ibid.*, House Report 1837.

[74] U.S. Congress, Senate, Committee on Civil Service, *Health Programs for Government Employees*, Sen. Report 1299, 78th Cong., 2nd Sess.

[75] *H. R. 2716*, Union Calendar No. 138, 79th Cong., 1st Sess.

[76] U.S. Congress, Senate, Hearing on *Investigation of Administration and Operation of Civil Service Laws*, 76th Cong., 1st Sess., Part II, May 10, 1940, p. 852.

on mental illness who paraded their woes before the Senators. Of course, it is possible to believe that wretched personnel administration and deficient supervision aggravated the neuroses of many of them. Still, Senator Ellender and his committee had little discernment in separating the wheat from the chaff with respect to grievances. Indeed, resort to a congressional committee for redress of grievances should not have been necessary. The question of grievances was suddenly of concern to Congress to the extent that in 1940 nine bills to establish an independent board of appeals were heard by the House Civil Service Committee.[77] None was enacted.

As emergency tensions mounted, the need for recognition of grievances and establishment of machinery to handle them became more pressing. The Commission and the Council of Personnel Administration gave careful consideration to the formulation of a policy statement on the establishment of grievance procedures. The Commission required for approval the observance of eight basic principles. In addition, it held that agencies must in their policies recognize the right of employees to join or refrain from joining unions freely and without fear of discrimination or reprisal and must also recognize the illegality of employee membership in subversive parties or organizations.[78] The principles were:

1. The right of employees and supervisors to an opportunity to participate in the formulation and development of a program to hear and settle grievances.
2. An opportunity for all employees, through a written statement, to be informed of the grievance plan established in their agency.
3. Recognition in the plan adopted of the administrative responsibility of supervisors at all levels to receive and act promptly and fairly on employee grievances; the delegation of authority to supervisory officers to execute their responsibility.
4. Simple, orderly procedures for the presentation of grievances, either by employees themselves or representatives of their own choosing with the right to appeal ultimately to the head of the department. Assurance that there would

[77] U.S. Congress, House, Committee on Civil Service, Hearings on *Bills Proposing the Establishment of Boards of Appeals for Civil Service Employees*, 76th Cong., 3d Sess., April 16, 17, and 18, 1940.
[78] CSC, *Departmental Circular No. 251*, February 24, 1941.

be no impediment in presenting the grievance and no restraint, interference, coercion, discrimination, or reprisal because of its presentation.
5. An opportunity before the final decision by the head of the department for the employee to present his case to a permanent or *ad hoc* committee or board of review acting in an advisory capacity to the head of the agency.
6. The right of the employee to designate a representative of his own choice to present his grievance.
7. Concentration of the responsibility for administering the grievance plan in the Director of Personnel in each department or in some other officer reporting directly to the head of the agency. Maintenance of an open door policy by the Director of Personnel for employee consultation, with appropriate consideration for supervisory responsibility.
8. Presentation of all the facts in writing by an employee as soon as the grievance has been appealed beyond the immediate supervisor, except for counsel with the Director of Personnel, and a corresponding presentation in writing by any individual against whom a grievance is lodged. The statements should contain the specific nature of the grievance.

1. THE WAR DEPARTMENT

The War Department did not produce a regular grievance policy until a memorandum was issued by the Secretary of War on March 26, 1943.[79] Military command at War Department establishments and the long failure to recognize the need for any civilian personnel administration had combined to retard that department. World War II effected a reorientation of thought on grievances as on other personnel problems.

The essence of the War Department plan was to preserve the line of appeal up to the commanding officer and to minimize the use of the personnel office.[80] An employee first presented his grievance orally to the immediate supervisor, or to the next higher supervisor if he could demonstrate that an interview with the immediate supervisor would be prejudicial to him. Only if he was dissatisfied with the first decision did he write out his grievance for presentation to the next higher supervisor, who had to acknowledge its receipt in writing. The first-line supervisor, of course, had an opportunity to comment in writing on the case.

---

[79] *Investigation of Civilian Employment*, Part III, Hearing on June 22, 1943, p. 631.
[80] Interview with Mason, July 19, 1945.

The counselor or any other officer in the personnel office could assist the employee in preparing his statement. Appeal could be carried up to the commanding officer at an installation, but before a final decision was made by him, the employee could request a hearing before an impartial committee. From the commanding officer the channel of appeal lay to the head of the technical service in Washington. Only if a violation of law, of a War Department regulation, or a discrimination prohibited by Executive Order were involved could the appeal be carried to the ultimate authority, the Secretary of War, whose decision was final. Prompt handling of all grievances was insured by a department rule that decisions had to be made within one week after the receipt of the grievance.[81] Grievance procedures were not applicable to reductions in force, classification allocations and evaluation of positions, actions to protect internal security, separation for disqualification, and efficiency ratings.[82] Nor did they apply to proposals and petitions made by employee groups or unions, inasmuch as grievances were considered individual complaints.

Because disciplinary actions were likely to lead to grievances, the War Department deemed it desirable to establish uniform penalties for various types of infractions of the rules. In an organization as large, complex, and far-flung as the War Department, that policy was probably well grounded. In addition, advice was given to supervisors on fair administration of disciplinary actions.[83]

2. THE NAVY DEPARTMENT

The Navy Department grievance procedure was on the whole similar to that of the War Department, except for certain minor variations. For example, no statements in writing were required until the appeal had been carried to the chief of the Navy bureau in the departmental service or to the department head concerned in the field service. If a hearing was held by the bureau chief, the latter could at his discretion order the employee to attend. The last stage of appeal for departmental service employees was to the

---

[81] *Investigation of Civilian Employment*, Part III, Hearing on June 22, 1943, p. 631.

[82] War Department, Civilian Personnel Regulation No. 105, *Employee Grievances*, February 23, 1945, p. 1. The Ramspeck Act provided for appeals of efficiency ratings before special boards created for that purpose.

[83] War Department, Civilian Personnel Pamphlet No. 12, *Common Sense in Disciplinary Actions*, October, 1944.

Undersecretary of the Navy for his final decision. In the field, appeal was open to the commanding officer, and from his decision there was a last stage to the Undersecretary. Employee organizations or unions were not per se barred from presenting grievances, as in the War Department. Matters affecting general working conditions were not of themselves grievances, but efficiency ratings appeals of ungraded employees could be so regarded. The determination of what constituted a grievance was made by the bureau chief or commanding officer.[84] As with the War Department, the Navy issued a schedule for uniform penalties for certain standard and common offenses.[85]

3. OPA

In contrast to the War and Navy departments, OPA had a more flexible approach toward grievances, as might be expected from their personnel policy. For one thing, OPA stressed informal procedure in the belief that once formal machinery was brought into play the main aim of preserving good relations within the agency had been lost.[86] In fact, use of the formal machinery was deemed an indication of management failure. The personnel office was "extremely skeptical of anything formal in personnel administration." OPA also drew no hard and fast line in defining grievances, but simply stated that a grievance was anything about which an employee wished to complain. The stress was placed on the personnel office getting the aggrieved employee and his supervisor together to talk matters over informally.[87]

All this was not to say that there was no formal machinery in OPA. On the contrary, the agency made provision for appeals up the regular line of authority from the first-line supervisor to the administrator.[88] Employees could select a union or another employee to represent them if they desired a hearing. If the first attempt at informal settlement failed between the immediate supervisor and the aggrieved employee, the grievance could be

[84] Navy Department, Civilian Personnel Instructions, Division of SECP, *Instruction 80*, Grievances and Complaints, March 9, 1945.

[85] Navy Department, *Suggested Uniform Schedule of Disciplinary Offenses and Penalties for Civilian Employees in Naval Shore Establishments*, August 5, 1943.

[86] Interview with Miss Erlanger, July 19, 1945.

[87] *OPA Manual*, Sec. 8-2605.03 (R: 6-30-45).

[88] Kenneth O. Warner, "Handling Employee Grievances," a paper read at the Office Management Conference of the American Management Association, New York City, October 29, 1943.

restated in writing. The employee could request that the director of personnel hold an informal hearing to define the issues in the case and to recommend terms of settlement. The personnel director had no authority to settle the case, however. A hearing before a board of three could be requested when the case was appealed to the administrator. The board consisted of one person designated by the employee, one by the supervisor, and one jointly by the two members. The purpose served by the board was to make recommendations to the administrator, who made the final decision.

4. THE DEPARTMENT OF AGRICULTURE

Notable for its initiation of a regularized grievance procedure on May 4, 1938, even before Executive Order 7916, the Department of Agriculture made only slight revisions in its policy during the war, the last one being in 1943. The chief differences between the procedure in Agriculture and those heretofore described were in Agriculture's emphasis on a judicial weighing of evidence and in bringing the director of personnel into the process of actual decision at one stage. Appeal beyond the regular supervisory channels to a bureau chief had to be in writing, but it was optional whether or not the grievance was in writing before that stage.[89] The bureau chief organized a board of three to investigate, report findings of fact, and make recommendations to him within thirty days.[90] Decision by the bureau chief had to come within ten days of the board's report. Appeal lay beyond the bureau chief to the director of personnel, who could decide the case on the basis of the written record or who could also organize another board on the same basis as the first. His decision had to be made within thirty-five days of the receipt of the appeal. The last stage for appeal was to the Secretary of Agriculture, within ten days of the decision by the director of personnel. Neither efficiency ratings nor classification allocations were within the meaning of grievances under the foregoing procedure. Neither

[89] U.S. Department of Agriculture, *Memorandum of the Secretary No. 753, Rev. No. 2, Personnel Relations Policy and Procedure,* March 5, 1943.

[90] The board consisted of a representative named by the employee, one by the bureau chief, and the third named by the first two members. If the first two named were unable to agree on the third member within fifteen days after the appeal had been received, the board was dissolved. A new board was then selected in the same way and, if still unable to agree on the third member, the Director of Personnel selected the third person.

OPA nor Agriculture made any attempt to standardize disciplinary actions, for such uniformity seemed to them incongruous in any but industrial operations.

Relations with Employee Organizations

Although the law with respect to the right of Federal employees to organize remained unchanged during the war years, a liberalization of policy was apparent in the handling of group relations, particularly in the War Department. The Navy had, of course, long dealt with unions in the Navy yards. Similarly employee unions had for years presented matters for consideration to the Department of Agriculture.

The War Department adopted the policy of extending "reasonable encouragement" to employee groups and organizations.[91] Apparently the department simply meant by that phrase that it placed no obstacles in the way of formation of unions. On the point of bargaining, however, the now famous letter of President Roosevelt to Luther Steward, president of the National Federation of Federal Employees, of August 16, 1937, was cited as basic. The letter enunciated the idea that collective bargaining as understood in private enterprise could not be transplanted into the public service. The War Department took pains to eliminate employee grievances from group negotiations and to restrict the latter to matters of strictly group interest. The freedom of all groups to organize was recognized, but no one group could secure exclusive recognition or exclusive dealing. The military commanders had to be educated through policy guidance and inspection by the Office of the Secretary of War to deal with organized employees.[92] Workers were free to join or refrain from joining any union, and no employee organization could be required to furnish a list of members as a basis of proof of organization. Employee organizations which wished to post notices on War Department bulletin boards had to secure approval of the posted material from the commanding officer on the ground of "security" before it could be posted, a strange type of censorship. Unions could distribute literature only before or after working hours and had to receive approval of it before circulation.[93] Both of these restrictions re-

[91] ASF, Manual, *Civilian Personnel Officers' Handbook*, 41.
[92] Interview with Mason, July 19, 1945.
[93] War Department, Civilian Personnel Circular No. 72, *Relationships with Employee Groups or Organizations in War Department Installations*, June 26, 1944.

vealed that the War Department still had a distance to travel before it could be said to have adopted an enlightened labor policy.

The Navy Department defined group dealing as "nothing more than a recognition of the rights of employees to present in group meetings recommendations and suggestions of general pertinent interest which will be courteously received and upon which the management will render decisions within its administrative discretion on the basis of full and fair consideration of facts."[94] The Navy, too, as this definition makes abundantly clear, rejected the idea of collective bargaining in the Federal service and relied on the policy enunciated by President Roosevelt in his 1937 letter. Organizations were recognized as speaking only for those employees whom they represented regardless of whether they represented a majority of the workers or not. In other words, no possibility of gaining exclusive representation rights existed since employee membership was purely voluntary. Supervisors could be union members but could not actively participate in union affairs.[95] As was true in the War Department, only approved employee notices could be posted on the unofficial bulletin boards.

The possibility of a commandant of a Navy establishment refusing to deal with a union was ruled out by the following declaration:

> A disposal to find out what employees think and feel by a medium through which they are willing to express themselves is a definite responsibility of the head of the activity. This is independent of whether the head of the activity approves or disapproves of the organization, and even with a reasonable allowance made for the manner of approach. The alternative is to ignore employees who are willing to express themselves only through collective representation and this alternative is impossible in this modern day and age.[96]

The Navy Department, in addition, organized shop committees to bring civilian employees and management together in somewhat the same fashion as was done through labor-management committees in private industry. On the initiation of management or of the employees, shop committees were established and representatives were elected by the employees to speak for the workers

---

[94] Navy Department, *Civilian Personnel Instruction 60, Employee Group Relations,* June 23, 1945, p. 1.
[95] *Ibid.*, 7.   [96] *Ibid.*, 4.

in a particular shop.[97] They were entirely independent of unions or other employee organizations. Similarly they had no connection with any craft, only with a shop. Nor were they grievance committees. Elections were held annually by secret ballot for the representatives in each shop.[98] The Navy recommended that meetings with the shop master or head be held at least semimonthly while monthly meetings of all shop committees be held with the head of the shore establishment.

OPA viewed unions in a friendly light, regarding them as partners with management.[99] In fact, the organization of employees appeared to OPA to serve as a help to management. OPA personnel officers felt that the fact that all employees were not organized was a handicap to management. This attitude was, of course, far more liberal than that of any other Washington office. In line with their expression of policy OPA allowed unions freedom in the uncensored use of the bulletin board and provided union representation on the Recreation, Transportation, and Reporter (for the *Employees' Calendar,* the agency newspaper) councils. Unions became useful educational instruments in OPA to inform employees of agency policies on such vital questions as impending reductions in force and to participate in such activities as counseling.

Agriculture had never formulated a statement on collective bargaining and had felt no impact on employee group relations as a result of the war. When any important matter of personnel policy was before the department for consideration, the chairmen of the unions in the department, who formed a council, were called on to comment on the proposed policy.[100] As a matter of fact, little impetus for organization existed among the clerical and stenographic force in the Department of Agriculture as compared with the mechanical employees of the War and Navy departments.

No department of the Federal government went so far as to suggest the establishment of formal negotiating machinery with union representatives on the pattern of the Whitley councils of Great Britain. Even OPA, which regarded its program as more friendly to employee unions than that of any other Washington agency, failed to suggest regularized channels by which manage-

[97] *Ibid.*   [98] *Ibid.,* 5.
[99] Interview with Miss Erlanger, July 19, 1945.
[100] Interview with Jarrett, July 12, 1945.

ment and union representatives could meet to discuss personnel policies. The result in the Federal service was a lack of stability in union-management relationships from department to department. Unions had no reason to feel secure in their position in the War Department, for example, once the war pressures were removed. War agencies like OPA, where unions had made some small gains, soon passed from the scene. The position of the unions in the various departments seemed to depend on the condition of the labor market which induced agencies to adopt a certain magnanimity in extending "reasonable encouragement" to their existence.

For the Federal service as a whole, however, the Civil Service Commission took a significant step in 1942, which carried within it the potentialities for permanent formal negotiating machinery. Within the office of the Civil Service Commissioners a Labor-Management Advisory Committee was appointed in November, 1942, to assist in recommending policies and expediting the government's part in the war program.[101] Commissioner Flemming served as chairman of this committee. From the ranks of labor two persons represented the American Federation of Labor, two the Congress of Industrial Organizations, and two the National Federation of Federal Employees on the Commission's Labor-Management Committee. Management was represented by the Assistant Secretary of the Navy, Ralph A. Bard, the administrative assistant to the Secretary of War, John W. Martyn, the Chief Post Office Inspector, Jesse M. Donaldson, administrator of the National Housing Agency, John B. Blandford, chairman of the National Mediation Board, William M. Leiserson, and Librarian of Congress, Archibald MacLeish. Ex officio members consisted of Dr. Frederick M. Davenport, chairman of the Council of Personnel Administration, and Edgar B. Young, Bureau of the Budget. The committee considered such problems as procedures for reduction in force, efficiency ratings, medical and health programs, deferment of Federal employees from military service, and placing of individual positions in their appropriate salary class on the basis of production standards.[102] That this committee, however, fell considerably short of providing a real instrumentality for getting labor and management together is evident.

[101] CSC, *Minute No. 2,* November 20, 1942.
[102] CSC, *Sixtieth Annual Report,* 52.

Conclusions

An awareness of the need for an employee relations program came late in many Federal agencies. Not until after Executive Order 7916 in 1938 did many agencies devote even passing attention to the development of policy in this field. Actually reminders from the Civil Service Commission and the Council of Personnel Administration during the war were necessary to secure effective execution of the order. Agencies confronted by the manpower shortage were forced to think in terms of providing positive services for their employees as well as of designing equitable means for settlement of grievances.

The chief point of difference among agencies in the development of employee relations programs was in the concept each held of the rule of the supervisor in personnel administration. One pattern of employee relations, characteristic of OPA, attempted to strengthen the relationship between supervisors and employees by training supervisors to handle both the positive and negative aspects of employee relations activities. The OPA personnel office tried to decentralize as many employee services as possible to the supervisor and to the employees. The War Department and to a lesser extent the Navy Department represented a contrasting view. The War Department centralized employee services in specialized officers, including the counseling force, in the personnel offices. The department exerted an effort to preserve the responsibility of the supervisor through such safeguards as definitions and manuals outlining his jurisdiction and that of the counselor. Nevertheless, the centralization of counseling and of the organization of services left the supervisor untrained to handle many types of problems he encountered. The pattern in employee relations in the War Department bore a marked resemblance to that in training. Both stressed uniformity; all supervisors were given an exactly standardized training; all were informed of the narrow limits of their authority in personnel relations. Any greater decentralization of authority and delegation of discretion when they were all given a brief "packaged" training course in so-called "job relations" might have entailed risks the War Department could not afford to assume under wartime pressures.

The Navy Department employee relations policy and organization placed somewhat more emphasis on strengthening the supervisor. The creation of the shop committees within the province of the shop masters constituted one of the principal ways in which the Navy attempted to broaden the authority and experience of the supervisors in handling group relations. The employment of shop personnel supervisors for Navy industrial personnel instead of counselors in the central office revealed the same preference for some decentralization in the handling of employee relations work. Possibly the Navy Department felt a little more confidence in its supervisors because of their more extensive training for their responsibilities.

In the same mold fell the Department of Agriculture with its centralized counseling, employee services program, and stress on formalized grievance machinery. It is true that some little decentralization was developed during the war years through the establishment of bureau contact officers, but still the individual supervisor was not of necessity given more discretion by decentralization to bureau administration of personnel programs. Again, in Agriculture supervisory training was "packaged" in the same manner as in the War Department, and supervisors may not yet have reached a stage of development to assume additional responsibility and discretion.

Among Washington agencies OPA developed a unique approach to employee relations. Starting afresh as a new agency and unhampered by the traditions of military authority or a line of precedents, it could experiment in a way few other departments were able to do. Further, its personnel office exercised a deliberate effort to think through personnel problems anew, an effort absent in some other new and older agencies. It pioneered among Federal agencies in pointing out one way that the problems of supervision, serious as they were, might be approached.

Wartime pressures for production forced the adoption of certain employee relations programs and services from industry without preliminary or subsequent study of their applicability to or effect on the government service. Indeed, time and staff were not available for such studies. The need still exists for studies of employee morale, turnover, the effect of incentives, overtime pay, and a long-run evaluation of counseling.

CHAPTER FOURTEEN

Administrative Changes and Reorganization of the Civil Service Commission

THE CIVIL Service Commission, with its loose and rambling organizational structure of 1939, could not have met the heavy wartime recruiting and placement program without a concentration of responsibility for direction of the war program. In addition, it needed an integration of related divisions and a simplification of structure. The old heterogeneous organization, starved for funds and staff, had been allowed to muddle along many months late in producing registers so long as there was no urgency in recruitment. But the promise made by Commissioner Flemming in 1940 to deliver all the recruits demanded at the time they were needed meant that from top to bottom the Commission had to take a new view of its organization. It had to consolidate units and functions into a few simple but essential divisions in which responsibility was placed clearly and unevasively. Because the Commission had to enlarge its own force, the need for clarification of responsibility and authority increased.

Procedures as well as organization merited attention. Shortened examinations did not alone provide an answer to the improvement of paper work. Lost motion from unnecessary forms, useless or outmoded reports, excessive handling of papers, all had to be questioned and re-examined both by administrators and by an expert on procedural analysis. The reporting and analysis of statistics demanded attention, for incomplete information or inability to discover results of programs carried possibilities of confusion and harm to the war effort.

The additional responsibilities for recruitment delegated to the field staff of the Commission required both additional field offices and staff and the clarification of functions and responsibility within each regional headquarters. New duties meant new divisions and more assistance for the regional directors. The larger grew the field service of the Federal government, the more authority had to be transferred to the regional directors to make decisions on the spot without reference to Washington. The volume of their work became so heavy and the pressure so great to supply workers in many establishments engaged in direct mechanical war production, that they could not be expected to fulfill Commission obligations without being granted a discretion that was far in excess of what many other Federal agencies were willing to extend to their field officers.

The wartime need for co-ordination of personnel programs and consultation among departmental personnel directors helped invigorate the reorganized Council of Personnel Administration. Any new organization requires concrete tasks in order to catch the breath of life. These tasks the Council found in abundance in the personnel problems facing the Federal government during the war. The expansion of the Federal field service and the need for continuing consultation between regional personnel directors and regional Civil Service Commission directors helped to bring into being field Councils of Personnel Administration.

Organization of the Civil Service Commission in 1939

When the war began in 1939, the Civil Service Commission was understaffed and ill organized to handle its normal work load. In fact, President Mitchell described its arrearages of work as "of such proportions as to undermine confidence in the practicability of selecting personnel on a merit basis."[1] Although he attributed the difficulties to lack of funds, which consequently meant lack of staff, a glance at Figure 5 will indicate that the Commission suffered from a diffusion of responsibility and an unmanageable span of control for the executive director and chief examiner. That unfortunate man had no less than seventeen division chiefs reporting directly to him on services and problems of unequal importance, ranging all the way from library maintenance to the examination process, the major function of the Commission. The arrearages of work, often running to nine months, were comprehensible in view of the multiplicity of independent units which handled applications from the time of initial correspondence to the moment of certification.

The diffusion of responsibility actually commenced in the high-

[1] U.S. Congress, House, Hearing on *Independent Offices Appropriation Bill, 1941*, 76th Cong., 3d Sess., December 12, 1939, p. 652.

FIGURE 5

ORGANIZATION OF THE CIVIL SERVICE COMMISSION IN 1939[1]

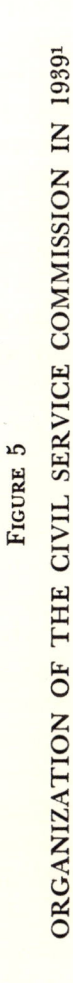

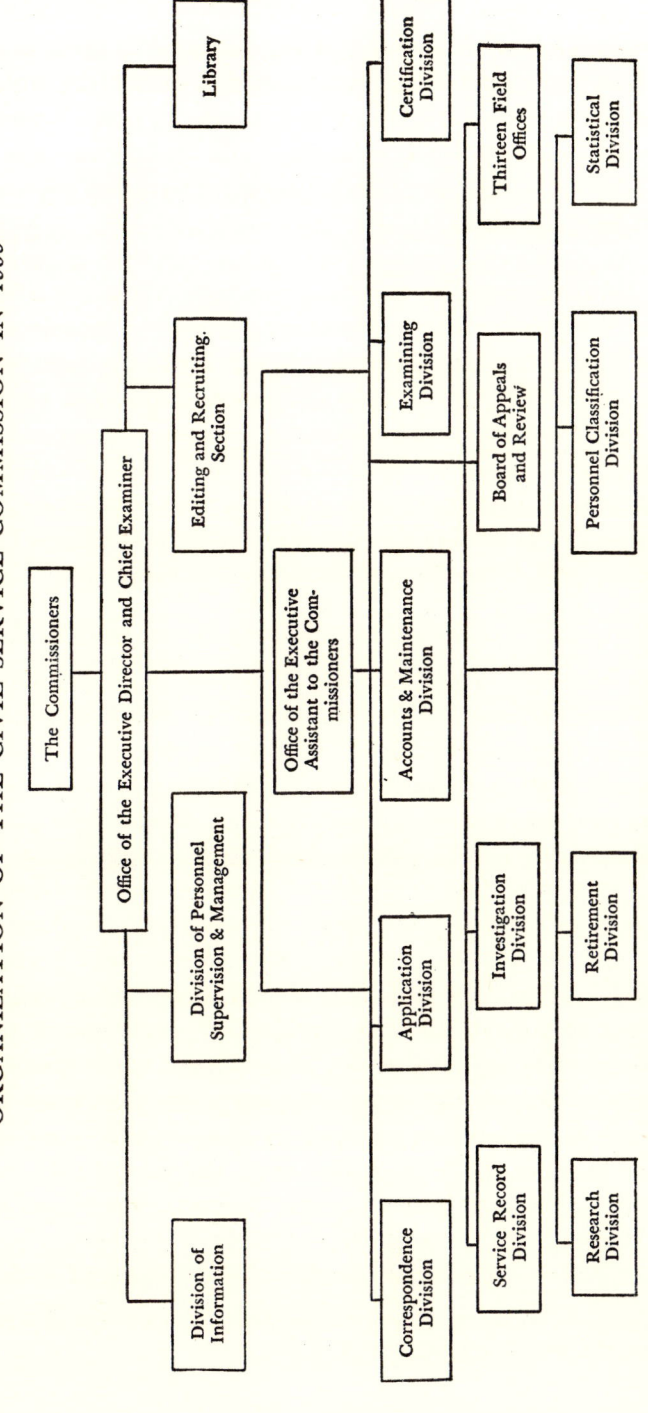

[1] Office of Government Reports, *United States Government Manual*, October, 1939, p. 505.

est level of Commission organization. In 1939 there was no differentiation of function among the three commissioners and hence no location of responsibility among them for management improvement. Differentiation of function should not, of course, exist among commissioners or board members. Management responsibility should reside in a general manager or executive director responsible to a board. But the experience and qualifications of the executive director and chief examiner of the Civil Service Commission precluded placement of that type of broad responsibility, along with the burden of carrying on wartime negotiations with the War and Navy departments, in his hands. Because all three commissioners were nominally responsible for the problem of management improvement, in actuality no one was. Auxiliary services were not differentiated from the operating divisions, and, in consequence, those services were not integrated into a cohesive unit. Direction of such services could not be placed on a unified and co-ordinated plan of operations. Lack of integration of auxiliary services was accompanied by a total absence of procedural analysis, which should have been one of the more important of those services. One of the auxiliary services to be found in the Commission at that time, the Statistical Division, was, on the other hand, distinguished by inadequate reporting and statistical analysis. The reports it issued at that time failed to show turnover rates, proportion of men and women in the service, number of employees in the various classification grades in the sundry agencies, and the number of Negro employees in the entire service and in each classification grade and department.

The purpose of the organizational changes in the Commission during the war years was to enable it to execute its responsibilities more efficiently in the tremendous Federal recruitment program. Organizational changes came gradually in the Commission from 1940 until 1943, when the final wartime pattern was determined. Procedures, especially in recruiting and examinations, changed slowly at first and then with increased acceleration until they were revolutionized by the war service regulations of 1942. Only as procedures were streamlined, especially in examinations, and new duties assumed by the Commission were any fundamental reorganizations consummated or was pressure built up of sufficient force to compel reorganization. Such reorganization at times induced adoption of new procedures.

Integration and Co-ordination Within the Commission

The single most important change for management improvement in the Civil Service Commission was the concentration of responsibility for directing war activities in the hands of one commissioner. About the time that Congress located responsibility for defense recruitment in the Commission in May, 1940, the two older commissioners, President Harry B. Mitchell and Lucille Foster McMillin, transferred to their younger and more vigorous colleague, Arthur S. Flemming, the task of directing the war program. Although the placement of this responsibility would seem to violate an important rule of administration with respect to the board type of organization, in practice the ability of Commissioner Flemming, as compared with that of the other two commissioners and the executive director, made the differentiation of function among the commissioners plausible and successful in operation. Inasmuch as almost all business of the Commission became an integral part of the defense and war program of that agency, the Commission to all intents and purposes functioned administratively as though under a single head. Thus by an internal delegation the Commission achieved to a major degree the reform urged by the President's Committee on Administrative Management in 1937. The delegation to one effective head was significant not merely for internal management but for external relations. Liaison with the War Manpower Commission, the War and Navy departments, largest clients of the Civil Service Commission, and the committees of Congress was more precisely and consistently accomplished thereby. Still the Commission retained whatever values resided in a multiple head for rule-making, judicial, and deliberative functions.

The number of divisions within the Commission had not been immediately lessened by the mere fact of the existence of an emergency. In November, 1939, an eighteenth division, that of Budget and Finance, had appeared.[2] The increased span of control was slightly reduced early in 1940 by merging the Editing and Recruiting Section with the Information Division to make a new unit called the Information and Recruiting Division.[3]

Not until April, 1941, when the recruitment pressures began

---

[2] CSC, *Minute No. 1*, November 1, 1939.
[3] CSC, *Minute No. 1*, February 23, 1940.

to intensify, did the first important consolidation of divisions take place. At that time the Examining Division integrated recruiting, testing, and placement activities by taking over the Application and Certification divisions in order to unify the various functions in the selection process under one division chief in order to improve service.[4]

More changes followed in 1942, hard on the heels of the adoption of the war service regulations. Most sweeping was the integration of auxiliary services. A new Chief of Administrative Services, appointed in June, 1942, co-ordinated the Budget and Finance Division, Personnel Supervision and Management Division, Office Services (which had superseded Accounts and Maintenance briefly), the Library, and a Planning staff.[5] Reorganization of auxiliary services was designed to help the operating activities meet their responsibilities more expeditiously and to relieve the executive director of maintaining separate contacts with the lesser services. In the same sweep the Statistical Division had disappeared in favor of a Statistical Section under Budget and Finance. Simultaneously the Communications Division was eliminated as a major entity. Earlier in 1942, a new division, Training, had appeared but was to survive for a year only.[6] Through these changes the span of control of the executive director and chief examiner had been reduced to thirteen separate divisions.

The next major reorganization was the conversion of the Examining Division into the Examining and Personnel Utilization Division in February, 1943.[7] Emphasis on manpower utilization and the need to co-ordinate Commission activities in that field with the total manpower program affecting recruitment motivated the new alignment. Because training was viewed as a part of manpower utilization, the Training Division was merged with the new division and dropped out as a separate unit. The same shift liquidated the Research Division, and those persons in the old Research Division who had been engaged in testing work were transferred to the Test Construction Unit in the new Examining and Personnel Utilization Division.

For the first time, the Commission instituted procedures

---

[4] CSC, *Minute No. 1*, April 11, 1941.   [5] CSC, *Minute No. 1*, June 13, 1942.
[6] Office of Government Reports, *United States Government Manual*, Spring, 1942, p. 600.
[7] CSC, *Minute No. 1*, February 15, 1943.

REORGANIZATION OF THE COMMISSION 327

analysis in April, 1943, through the creation of a new division under the Chief of Administrative Services called the Organization and Methods Staff.[8] The need for more rapid wartime service and streamlining of procedures clearly induced the change. The first flow charts showing each step in the processing of a particular item of work soon began to appear from this unit.

With slight changes the integration of auxiliary services remained much the same as it was in 1943 until the end of the war. One of the minor changes was to move the Personnel Division to an independent position from the units supervised by the Chief of Administrative Services.[9] Other changes added a Program Planning Staff and an Instruction and Manuals Staff to the divisions under the Chief of Administrative Services. The Federal Employment Statistics Staff became a separate division under the Chief of Administrative Services instead of remaining a section under the Budget and Finance Division. Thus there were seven divisions responsible to the Chief of Administrative Services. Figure 6 shows the organization of auxiliary services under staff activities as brought together in 1943 and 1944.

The Byrd Committee in 1943 had criticized the inadequacies of personnel reporting by the employing agencies and the Commission.[10] Even Commission staff members admitted that policies affecting turnover were made without complete data on the subject.[11] The Byrd Committee complained of the failure to break down personnel figures by classification grades, occupations, areas, sex, or age.[12] The committee, therefore, conferred with the Commission, Bureau of the Budget, War and Navy departments, and various other departments to plan improvements in the reporting and statistical compilations respecting Federal personnel. The monthly reports of the Commission became more comprehensive after the reorganization of statistical services, the conferences, and a change in staff in the Commission, but they still failed to fur-

---

[8] Interview with Mr. Allison B. Lowstutter, CSC, Organization and Methods Staff, August 12, 1944.

[9] See Figure 6 on p. 328.

[10] U.S. Congress, Joint Committee on Reduction of Nonessential Federal Expenditures, *Federal Personnel*, Sen. Doc. 66, 78th Cong., 1st Sess., 12.

[11] John W. Mitchell, "Personnel Turnover in the Federal Government," *Personnel Administration*, V (May, 1943), 12.

[12] U.S. Congress, Joint Committee on Reduction of Nonessential Federal Expenditures, *Federal Personnel* (Additional Report), Sen. Doc. 131, 78th Cong., 1st Sess., 16.

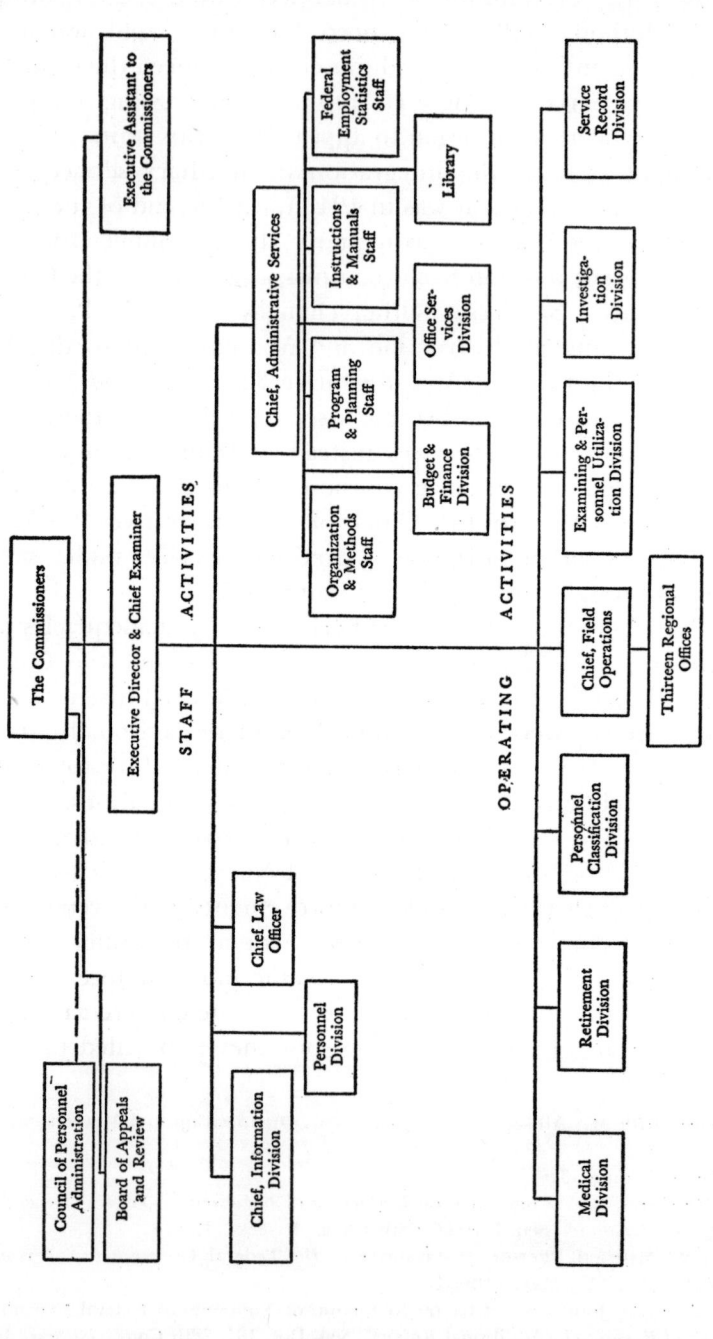

Fig. 6—Chart showing organization of the Civil Service Commission in 1944. Taken from Civil Service Commission, *Manual of Instructions, Policies and Procedures*, AG.02.01, Revised October 17, 1944.

nish data on numbers by classification grades in the service.

As for operating activities, the 1943 reorganization of the Commission left seven major divisions under the direction of the executive director and chief examiner. The span of control of the latter totaled eleven organizational units, very nearly reaching a minimum for a functional organization like that of the Civil Service Commission. The largest division, Examining and Personnel Utilization, showed a major division of work among its sections on the diverse bases of subject matter, function, and clientele. For example, its operating sections consisted of three examining sections divided according to the major fields of examinations, namely, an Administrative and Management Personnel Placement Section, a Social Science Placement Section, and a Physical Science and Clerical Placement Section.[13] There were, in addition to the three examining sections, the Test Development Section, Liaison Section,[14] the Personnel Utilization Section, and the Veterans Service Section.

The liquidation of research activities with the abolition of the Research Division in 1943 constituted a genuine loss to Federal personnel administration. An examination of the duties which had been assigned to the Research Division indicates how serious that loss was in a period of rapid and far-reaching change. The division had been directed before the war to analyze the duties of positions to determine the qualifications essential to their performance; to develop means of measuring those qualifications; to prepare model examinations and standardize examination material and methods; to survey the efficiency rating system and recommend needed changes; to engage in research in the theory and practice of classification; and to promote research in cooperation with universities, industries, other government agencies, and research foundations in the fields of selection, placement, promotion, and training.[15] The activities listed were, indeed, comprehensive in coverage, and yet wartime developments suggest other subjects which might have been probed by an active, well-staffed research division of a central personnel agency. Employee counseling, supervisory training, skills training, turnover and absenteeism, work incentives, the effect of overtime on morale

[13] CSC, *Manual of Instructions*, A6.13.01, Revised, August 28, 1944.
[14] For a full description of the work of the liaison officers, see Chapter II.
[15] CSC, *Division Organization Manual*, III, 3d edition, July, 1939, Part I, 1.

and work production, and the results of transfers and increased mobility were among the many problems which deserved analysis. It is by no means clear that the Research Division had ever manifested interest in any field except that of examination. Certainly, although training had been one field assigned to it for study, the Commission had entered the war period without any concrete plans in that area. Those plans it developed came primarily from the War Manpower Commission and the Council of Personnel Administration, as pointed out in the chapters on training. When the Director of Research transferred to another agency, the Commission chose to confine itself to mere validation and item and general examination analysis in the small Test Construction Unit. To anyone who conceives of the central personnel agency playing a positive role in discovering broad trends, results of past policies, and future needs, the demise of the Research Division can only appear as shortsighted policy. Above all, the action of the Commission indicated a lack of sense of direction for long-term usefulness and leadership. The negative concept of the Commission as a device to "keep the rascals out" was still struggling for ascendancy in Commission policy.

Without the facts relative to existent conditions it is difficult for the administrator to ascertain where he is standing in relation to the success or failure of present programs or to plan in which direction he should move. Without facts he is simply playing "hunches." Granting the difficulties of staffing and reorganizing a research office in wartime, still it is inconceivable that any modern administrative agency should attempt to operate without an analysis of data and forecasting of trends associated with its administrative program. Many of the Commission programs remained unevaluated, for the simple reason that there was no one unit responsible for collecting and analyzing the data and operating unit chiefs were too pressed with their management problems to direct any such studies. In 1941 Lawrence A. Appley pointed to research in the field of personnel policies and procedures as a basic function of modern personnel administration. Research he held no less essential in time of crisis than in normal periods because the "field most susceptible to altering practice is personnel administration."[16]

[16] Lawrence A. Appley, "Organizing for Personnel Administration," *Public Personnel Review*, III (April, 1942), 102.

To improve internal co-ordination and develop more adequate channels of information and communication within the Commission, the management conference system was instituted in the summer of 1939.[17] By means of management conferences, labelled "A," "B," "C," "D," and "E," depending on the level of the hierarchy in which they occurred, each supervisor of an organization unit met with the group of employees under his direct supervision to discuss, define, plan, and evaluate work assignments and organization. Conference chairmen met with the group of supervisors on their own level under the chairmanship of their immediate supervisor, while each of their subordinates acted as chairman of a conference held among the employees under his immediate supervision. Through the conferences ideas and policies traveled through the organization from top to bottom and back to the top. The "A" conference consisted of the division heads of the Commission meeting weekly with Commissioner Flemming. In turn, each division held a "B" conference between the division chief and his section heads; thus conferences were held until every first-line supervisor had met with his employees. The object was to attain participation by every employee in a management conference. Minutes were kept of all conferences, and those from each lower level were sent to the management conferences immediately above it.[18] The same conference system was extended to regional offices where the regional director acted as chairman of the "A" conference.

In the eyes of the Ramspeck Committee the management conference system was of doubtful efficacy. It had this to say of it:

> For some time the committee has expressed concern as to the amount of time spent by Government officials and employees "in conference." The Committee has made a brief survey and finds that conference activities in the Federal system are many and varied.
>
> In the Civil Service Commission committees and conferences reach surprising proportions. The Committee has found that 665 committee or conference groups hold upward of 15,000 sessions per year. Fifty-four hundred employees participate. Each year 242,000 man-hours, equivalent to more than 103 full-time employees, are consumed. It requires 24,000 pages of typing to record these proceedings. In Washington alone 13 rooms in six buildings comprising 4,748 square feet of floor

[17] CSC, *Manual of Instructions*, A7.01.01, July 17, 1943.
[18] *Ibid.*, A7.01.04, November 1, 1943.

space, equipped with 302 pieces of furniture are largely dedicated to conference use.[19]

The committee called for a justification of the conference system.

As has been mentioned in Chapter II, co-ordination with the War Manpower Commission was achieved through the functioning of two Commission organization heads, the Chief of Field Operations and the Chief of the Personnel Utilization Section, as WMC organization directors. In actual fact, the pertinent division and section in the Commission which each directed was the identical organization shown under each in the War Manpower Commission. In this way, duplication was avoided and planning simplified with other WMC division chiefs.

According to many Commission employees communication within the agency had long been one of the major administrative problems. Both the management conference system and the reorganizations of 1942 and 1943 to combine and consolidate hitherto independent divisions were designed to improve the flow of information from the bottom to the top and back again to the bottom of the organization. Many complaints directed against Commission delays in decisions requested by the employing agencies had arisen out of poor communication. Because individuals who had proved to be "bottlenecks" in communications in the past were left in positions where they could continue to delay the passage of information, many Commission employees looked upon the reorganizations skeptically. A general complaint was that although information was more readily passed up the hierarchy to Commissioner Flemming after reorganization, it was still blocked on the way down short of the employees who needed a knowledge of decisions in their negotiations with the departments.[20]

DELEGATION TO THE REGIONAL OFFICES OF THE CIVIL SERVICE COMMISSION

Mention has already been made in Chapters II and V of the authority delegated to the field staff of the Commission with respect to recruiting and examination because of the vastly in-

[19] U.S. Congress, House, Committee on Civil Service, *Investigation of Civilian Employment,* House Report 2084, 78th Cong., 2nd Sess., 15-16.

[20] Based upon statements made by a number of Commission employees in Washington in 1944-1945.

creased recruitment responsibilities in the field service. The Commission granted analogous authority over investigations for loyalty and suitability, transfer, promotion, and personnel utilization in the field service. Few areas of Commission authority over personnel administration remained in the hands of the central office alone. The natural result of the various delegations of authority was a systematic reorganization of the regional offices.[21]

The more important transfers of authority from the central office to the regional offices of the Commission covered a wide range. Beginning in the summer of 1940, regional directors gained the right to authorize noncompetitive appointments for the defense program under Executive Order 8257.[22] By 1941 they were permitted to decide examination requirements, including age limits, and to announce examinations for field positions in any defense agency.[23] No previous consultation with the central office was needed when a regional office had to meet an emergency situation. When eligibles could not be certified from the registers or assigned to duty in time to meet agency deadlines, regional directors could approve temporary appointments of qualified persons obtained from any source available to any position in any locality.[24] Regional directors also gained the right to adjudge the adequacy of objections to eligibles certified from central office Commission registers and rejected by field appointing officers.[25] After the adoption of the war service regulations the Commission delegated authority to the regional directors to approve war transfers in the field service under all the limitations on transfer existing under the WMC and Commission regulations.[26]

Regional directors had the same authority over appointments in agencies moved from Washington to other cities and temporarily located within their regions as over those in the field service.[27] Exceptions to this rule existed only with respect to allocations of positions under the Classification Act in those agencies which remained a part of the departmental service for classification purposes and hence under the jurisdiction of the Commission's central office.

[21] See Chapter II, tables 3 and 4, for figures on the growth of the field service of the Commission and the growth of a typical field office.
[22] CSC, *Circular Letter No. 3007*, August 26, 1940.
[23] *Ibid.*, No. 3156, February 6, 1941.   [24] *Ibid.*, No. 3180, February 19, 1941.
[25] *Ibid.*, No. 3232, April 23, 1941.   [26] *Ibid.*, No. 3625, March 24, 1942.
[27] CSC, *Departmental Circular No. 348*, August 26, 1942.

The entire work of suitability and loyalty investigations was moved to the field; the central Investigations Division of the Commission became a policy-making and review office. At first regional directors received authority merely to remove a bar or flag against the names of persons thus marked on Commission records,[28] but within a few months in 1941 they acquired the power to flag names as well as to remove the flag.[29] Likewise, the power to initiate investigations in disloyalty cases was granted to the regional directors in 1941.[30] Later, because an excessive number of persons had been flagged under what the Commission considered an unrealistic view of the labor market, the Commission enumerated specific grounds for flagging names as well as grounds too trivial for placing names under that disadvantage.[31]

The increase in the recruiting load in the field brought about an enlargement in the number of Commission field offices by the creation of branch regional offices in 1942. The new branch offices were located in Pittsburgh, Washington, D. C., Cleveland and Dayton, Ohio, Detroit, Kansas City, Dallas, Omaha, Los Angeles, and Salt Lake City.[32] In the last three cities the principal officer of the Commission was a special representative-in-charge; in the others he was an associate or assistant regional director. Later the Commission moved the tenth regional office to Dallas from New Orleans and made the latter city a branch regional office because of the increased volume of personnel transactions in Texas.[33] By 1942 another branch office was established in Portland, Oregon.[34] The old central ratings boards had been abolished in favor of branch offices. The designation of the thirteen principal field offices of the Commission had been changed from district offices to regional offices in September, 1942.[35]

The regional directors' conference in Chicago in October, 1943,

---

[28] CSC, *Circular Letter No. 3204*, March 14, 1941.

[29] *Ibid., No. 3383*, August 20, 1941, and *No. 3420*, September 19, 1941. A bar prohibits Federal employment of an individual so marked for a specific period of time or permanently; a flag is a warning to the Commission and appointing officers of the need for close investigation of the individual flagged in the case of future certification.

[30] *Ibid., No. 3308*, June 27, 1941.

[31] *Ibid., No. 3420, Supp. No. 2*, September 29, 1943.

[32] CSC, *Departmental Circular No. 323, Supp. No. 9*, October 1, 1942.

[33] CSC, *Minute No. 1*, April 13, 1943.

[34] CSC, *Departmental Circular No. 444*, November 3, 1943.

[35] *Ibid., No. 373*, September 1, 1942.

REORGANIZATION OF THE COMMISSION 335

helped shape the organization of regional offices into five divisions.[36] These divisions were an Examining and Personnel Utilization Division, Classification Division, Investigations Division, Service Division, and Medical Division, shown on Figure 7. By 1945 the Examining and Personnel Utilization Division was divided into two divisions, one for Recruitment and Placement and the other for Personnel Utilization.[37] In addition, regional committees on administrative personnel had been constituted to assist the regional offices in the formulation of recruitment policies in their areas. The creation of these six divisions reflected the emphasis on the major types of work which had developed in the regional offices during the war. For example, the institution of the separate division for personnel utilization was the outgrowth of the assistance regional offices were expected to give the employing agencies both in the conduct of personnel utilization surveys and the adoption of the supervision improvement program in the field service.

However great was the desire of the Commission to delegate increased authority to its own field service, it was limited by the degree to which the various departments and agencies were willing to carry the delegation of authority over personnel transactions to their own field officers. When approval of field appointments, promotions, or transfers remained in the Washington headquarters of any agency, the Commission was effectively estopped from granting the power of final approval of those transactions to its own regional directors. Therefore, in a move to hasten its own decentralization of duties and authority, the Commission appealed in August, 1943, to the heads of all agencies to decentralize to their field officers as much authority over personnel transactions as possible.[38] In cases wherein departments ruled that field positions had to be filled through central office authority, the Commission requested justifications for the decision. Moreover, it reserved the right to rule finally on exceptions to the policy of decentralization it was establishing. Once a position was placed under the jurisdiction of field service officers, both in the agency and in the Commission, the principle of exclusive jurisdiction applied. Under that rule, all personnel changes had to be referred

[36] CSC, *Circular Letter No. 4074*, October 23, 1943.
[37] CSC, *Manual of Instructions*, A6.23.01, April 27, 1945.
[38] CSC, *Departmental Circular No. 487*, July 15, 1944.

FIGURE 7

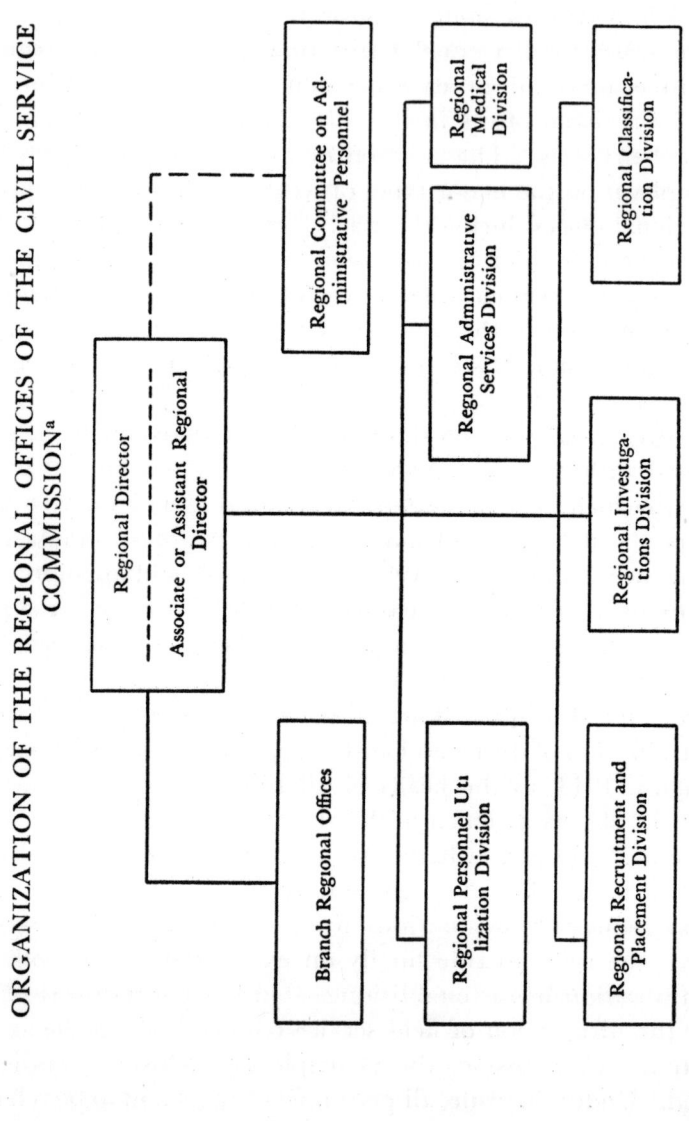

ORGANIZATION OF THE REGIONAL OFFICES OF THE CIVIL SERVICE COMMISSION[a]

[a] CSC, *Manual of Instructions*, A6.23.01, April 27, 1945.

to the Commission's regional office, never to the central office. The Commission tried to limit certification from central office examinations and registers to the departmental service except when special agreements were made with agencies to fill special field positions on a nation-wide basis through central office registers.[39]

The Commission, however, recognized the fact that complete delegation of authority over field positions to its own regional offices was unattainable.[40] It could not cope with the rigid insistence of some agencies upon keeping the reins over field positions in their Washington headquarters. The lack of agency personnel facilities in some departments in the field likewise impeded delegation. Nevertheless, the Commission pronounced delegation to its own regional staff a good long-run policy as well as a good wartime policy and declared:

> The long-term objective is that of working out procedures under which a) agencies will be encouraged to decentralize to the maximum extent possible their part of the work in recruiting for field duty positions, and b) regional offices will be in a position to fill, from their own resources, vacancies in all types of professional, scientific and administrative positions, as well as vacancies in trades, custodial, clerical and subprofessional positions which are now almost completely decentralized.[41]

THE COUNCIL OF PERSONNEL ADMINISTRATION

Although not a creature of the war emergency, the Council of Personnel Administration enjoyed a great opportunity to render valuable service to strengthen the merit system during the war years. Re-created by Executive Order 7916 in June, 1938, the council came to life on February 1, 1939, when a chairman was appointed, Dr. Frederick M. Davenport. The council consisted of the departmental personnel directors, a representative from the Bureau of the Budget, and one from the Civil Service Commission. A staff agency, the Council of Personnel Administration advised the President and the Commission in the formulation of personnel policy. It also had power to conduct special investigations and hearings at the direction of the President or the Commission. The council employed a small permanent staff.

[39] CSC, *Circular Letter No. 4258,* February 20, 1945.
[40] *Ibid.* [41] *Ibid.*

Because at first no funds had been appropriated for the council, that body was placed within the Commission for organization and budgetary purposes, and the staff was placed on the Commission payroll and detailed to the council. Later in fiscal 1939, after funds were appropriated to the council, it became an independent entity for one year. Funds were cut off in 1940 by the House Appropriations Committee,[42] but the Senate Appropriations Committee recommended that the sum cut by the House be made available to the Commission.[43] Thus the council came back into the fold of the Commission and remained there throughout the war period.

The Council of Personnel Administration played an important part in wartime personnel administration. The close and regular contacts effected between departmental personnel directors brought into the open through discussion the common problems facing agencies, attempts at solution, and vagaries and disparities in policy and program. When manpower requirements made it imperative to view the Federal government as one employer and to prevent interagency raids, unity of approach was essential in the solution of personnel problems. A common solution was often achieved through the pooling of ideas and experiences in the council.[44] Committees were created to probe more deeply into significant difficulties and proposals which required intensive study.

The council contributed thoughtful reports which led to adoption of new personnel policies in a number of areas. It was a council committee study at the request of President Roosevelt which led to the adoption of the in-service internship plan of training administrators late in 1943,[45] described in Chapter VIII. The council gave its hearty approval also to the "J" courses for supervisory training. Assistance was given the Commission in designing the standard application, Form 57, combining other forms, and eliminating employee personal-history statements and notices of personnel action, formerly required by the Commission

[42] U.S. Congress, House, *Independent Offices Appropriation Bill, 1941*, House Report 1515, 76th Cong., 3d Sess., 9.

[43] U.S. Congress, Senate, *Independent Offices Appropriation Bill, 1941*, Sen. Report 1177, 76th Cong., 3d Sess., 2.

[44] Frederick M. Davenport, "Let's Look at the Record," *Personnel Administration*, VI (January, 1944), 5.

[45] *Ibid.*, 6.

of the departments.[46] Standard leave regulations and procedures were drawn up, and by 1945 standard forms for leave records were designed.[47] Changes were effected also in the efficiency rating system.[48] The report of the council committee on counseling helped to promote the adoption of employee counseling programs in the service after 1942 and later led to the sponsorship of the Interdepartmental Conference on Counseling. Another study by the council on employee health and safety programs has been mentioned in Chapter XIII. Reporting of turnover data for uniform comparisons across agency lines was recommended to the Commission.[49] A committee on employee relations studied grievance procedures and helped develop the standards adopted by the Commission. Before the passage of the Mead-Ramspeck Act in 1941 for uniform salary increments, the existing disparate practices and the problems involved in effecting legislation for uniformity were considered by a council committee at the request of the Bureau of the Budget.[50] The scope and variety of committee studies and reports indicate the value of council deliberations to the Commission, the Bureau of the Budget, and the President in assisting all three to achieve reasonable co-ordination in personnel management.

The growth of the Federal field service to the point where it included more than 90 per cent of all Federal employees, a phenomenal growth in and near many large urban centers in the country, induced the next logical development: Regional Councils of Personnel Administration. The first regional council was organized in New York City, December 17, 1942, at a conference of personnel officers from the various Federal agencies in the second civil service region.[51] Chicago soon followed with a second regional council early in 1943. The parent council in Washington officially endorsed these new field councils on September 2, 1943, and the Commission gave its approval on September 6, 1943.[52] The regional directors of the Commission were, therefore, asked to assist in the organization and operation of other councils.

[46] CSC, *Departmental Circulars No. 399,* January 5, 1943, *No. 402,* January 5, 1943, and *No. 409,* February 17, 1943.
[47] *Ibid., No. 504,* October 20, 1944.
[48] Davenport, "Let's Look at the Record," *loc. cit.,* 8.
[49] *Ibid.,* 9-10.   [50] *Ibid.,* 9.
[51] CSC, *Circular Letter No. 4038,* July 13, 1943.
[52] CSC, *Minute No. 1,* September 6, 1943.

Before the end of 1943 twenty-one field personnel councils had been added to the original two. On each sat a Commission regional director or his representative together with the area personnel officers of each Federal agency located in the region served by the council.[53] The agency representatives were designated by the departmental directors of personnel. The regional councils communicated with Washington through the regional Commission directors.

The regional councils represented the first concrete step in bringing together for regular exchange the Federal personnel representatives in many different areas who had previously had only sporadic, if any, contact with each other. The council was a means of strengthening the common bonds of professional interest and aiding in the solution of the common problems that beset them all. Indeed, the councils had a value for reconversion and for times of peace as well as for the pressures of the war period. They were a necessary complement to the parent council in Washington, for at all times in recent decades the field service has far outnumbered the departmental service. Without some regularized channels by which policy could be assessed within the frame of reference of field operations and evaluated by those who had to administer it and their reactions relayed to Washington, the deliberations of the parent council remained unrealistic and gave a distorted view of Federal personnel administration as it affected a small minority of Federal employees. The regional councils actually augmented the limited resources of the Commission for gathering and weighing facts.

Conclusions

The wartime pressures for attaining levels of performance beyond the wildest peacetime dreams of the Civil Service Commission compelled more attention to organization and modernization of methods and procedures than that agency had ever devoted. The Commission entered the defense period with an organization based on so many trivial functions that the task of direction from the top was extremely difficult. Inasmuch as the Commission had viewed its role in personnel administration as essentially that of recruiting and the wartime demands for personnel emphasized

---

[53] CSC, *Manual of Instructions*, A6.20.03, December 17, 1943.

that function, many of the organizational changes were directed at consolidation of responsibility for all processes in that field.

In many respects the Commission emerged from the war with a strengthened organization. Administrative responsibility and authority in a single head were proved of value in achieving speed and efficiency in transactions. Delegation of authority to the regional directors had been established as the only way to get the work of the Commission done quickly on the spot. Consultation with the employing agencies through their personnel directors was valuable at the highest policy level in meeting new problems. Commission reorganizations made sense if a short-run view is taken of them. Whether all reorganizational changes it underwent, as, for example, the liquidation of the Research Division, made sense for long-term policy might well be open to question.

The question naturally arises whether the Civil Service Commission was an effective administrative agency. Did the various reorganizations assist the Commission in fulfilling its responsibilities more efficiently? Since the clearest and most pressing responsibilities in wartime were for recruitment and the record of the Commission was, on the whole, one of impressive success in recruitment, the answer would seem to be in the affirmative. No consideration of Commission administration, however, could overlook the weaknesses in Commission organization which were manifested by various minor failures from time to time. Nor could such consideration neglect the point that Commission service was sometimes impeded by poor intra-agency communication, as mentioned before. But if the Commission is judged on its entire wartime record and the speed as well as the degree to which it fulfilled its commitments, then the conclusion must be sustained that, on the whole, it functioned effectively.

CHAPTER FIFTEEN

An Evaluation of Wartime Personnel Administration

WARTIME Federal personnel administration viewed in retrospect made several permanent contributions to the improvement of the Federal service. The achievements were five in number, namely, the survival of merit system principles through the adaptability and flexibility of the personnel system, success in recruitment for staffing the expanded Federal service, progress in the building of training programs, realization of the importance of employee relations in the public service, and a new recognition of personnel administration itself. The wartime achievements represented concrete gains which could be consolidated for the permanent improvement of the service. Indeed, as will be pointed out briefly, the forward-looking steps taken to improve Federal personnel administration in the postwar years came as a direct result of wartime experience.

As is also inevitable in any prolonged crisis, certain problems arose which remained unsolved during the war. The latter group included the handling of transfer and promotion, the handicaps of an inadequate Federal salary structure, the control of numbers in wartime, and the control of subversive elements in the public service. In connection with both the achievements and the problems of the public service the role of the Civil Service Commission in relation to the agencies it served and in the execution of the goals it set for itself must be assayed.

WARTIME ACHIEVEMENTS IN PERSONNEL ADMINISTRATION

1. SURVIVAL OF THE MERIT SYSTEM

The merit system survived the wartime collapse of standards and deterioration in the quality of Federal recruits. Paradoxical as the foregoing statement may seem, a decline in qualifications standards does not denote abandonment of selection on the basis of merit provided standards are geared to the necessities of the labor market and not subordinated to political considerations.

The adoption of new recruitment and selection procedures consonant with the changed wartime labor market indicated an innate flexibility in the merit system which enabled it to meet the crisis. The adaptability of the system to the demands for speed and quantity in recruitment was a powerful factor in the preservation of the merit system. Neither breakdown nor scandal marred the process of adjustment.

The Federal war service regulations which were adopted early in 1942, although radically different from the rules which had grown up over the years since 1883, stressed speed and service to the employing agencies. Moreover, they were possible within the framework of the Pendleton Act of 1883, for nothing in the statute impeded a general application of positive recruitment procedures, the use of open continuous examinations, or the development of new sources of personnel. The sacrosanct "rule of three" could and did fall into the discard for over two years.

Positive recruitment and direct recruitment served to widen the area of selection during the war as Civil Service Commission and operating agency recruiters traveled around the country on regular recruiting campaigns. The Commission lent force to President Roosevelt's policy of affording wartime employment opportunities to all Americans by urging appointing officers to consider women, Nisei certified from Relocation Centers, and the physically handicapped. In addition, Negroes found new opportunities in clerical, administrative, and professional positions, especially in the new war agencies. Thousands of persons not previously interested in government employment because not apprised of the opportunities for it were enlisted for the duration. Many were, of course, from the ranks of marginal unemployment of the years preceding the war. But it would be a serious mistake to assume that all new Federal recruits came from that group. Many were persons of ability who left private employment to enter the Federal service, as, for example, the scientists and professional persons reached through the National Roster for Scientific and Specialized Personnel. Many patriotic individuals preferred government employment in wartime as the one means open to them to assist directly in the war effort.

Federal selection standards were geared to the state of the labor market for the most part. As labor shortages developed during the defense period and the war, the Commission, in order to fulfill its pledges to supply personnel in the numbers and by the "deadlines" demanded, had gradually to lower standards until in some critical occupations all who could prove availability under War Manpower Commission regulations could establish eligibility. No need existed, therefore, to rank eligibles in certification if all who could meet the diluted qualifications standards could obtain jobs. Recruitment, examination, and certification were frequently telescoped into one procedure: the interview. By a delegation from the appointing agencies the Commission exercised the power of appointment for many positions while agency employees by a delegation from the Commission were frequently engaged in joint recruitment activities.

The fall in Federal employment standards during the war was not colored by political considerations. What had changed was the minimum quality or degree of fitness for a position measured in terms of training and experience. In other words, the concept of fitness changed in degree, but it was not abrogated or subverted. Further, this concept was a flexible one which could be raised or lowered depending on the state of the labor market for specific occupations in particular regions of the country. By shifting the emphasis from a demand for specialized skills for discrete tasks to a judgment of the probability of the ultimate development of recruits in any of several positions, the Federal civil service approached more closely to the traditional British view of recruitment and selection.

The mere fact that both rules and standards could be and were changed suggested that greater flexibility and adaptation to agency needs are possible for normal operation of our personnel system. For one thing, the Commission during the years from 1940 to 1944 had gained a control over the staffing of the Federal government unique in our history, but a control so great as to be replete with possibilities of "bottlenecks." The Ramspeck Act of 1940, the congressional delegation of responsibility for staffing the defense and war agencies made in 1940, the delegation of control over government employment by the War Manpower Commission, and the transfer under the Starnes Act of increased responsibility for protecting veterans' preference, even in unclassified positions, all combined to make a power too great to hold tight within the Commission if the personnel function were to be exercised efficiently and expeditiously. Further, the Commission itself had urged the operating agencies to delegate more power over personnel transactions to their field officers. Underscoring its own philosophy, the Commission had built up in its field offices an experienced staff progressively schooled in the exercise of discretion and independent judgment by the delegation of central office functions and authority to them.

Within less than one year after the end of hostilities the cooperative relationship of the war years between the Commission and the operating agencies was institutionalized by Executive Order 9691.[1] This was followed up by a similar but stronger executive order in 1947 directing delegation of power by the Commission to the agencies in a variety of personnel matters and making the latter responsible for personnel management.[2] Through the first order the Commission was given the right to establish boards of examiners in both field establishments and the departmental service consisting of agency employees to draft and administer examinations and certify eligibles. The Hoover Commission in 1949 pointed up the need for a greater delegation of primary responsibility for recruitment and examination to the operating agencies. Indeed, it felt that the Commission should become essentially a staff agency.[3]

If, indeed, commitment to the merit system survived in full force and effect, as no one today can doubt, still a great chorus of dissatisfaction with the merit system as it has operated began to swell in the postwar years. Thousands of articulate men and women left the Federal service shortly after the end of hostilities convinced that the country deserved a better personnel system. Their dissatisfaction found official expression in the Hoover Commission report on personnel management. In the committees of Congress concerned with civil service legislation the theme was the discovery of ways and means to build a real career service. Our war experience, therefore, strengthened rather than weakened national faith in the merit system principle at the same time that it created a discontent with "things as they are."

[1] 11 *FR* 1381-83, February 6, 1946. See John McDiarmid, "The Changing Role of the U.S. Civil Service Commission," *American Political Science Review*, XL (1946), 1067-96.

[2] Executive Order 9830, February 24, 1947, 3 *CFR, 1947 Supp.* 108.

[3] The Commission on the Organization of the Executive Branch of the Government, A Report to Congress, *Personnel Management* (February, 1949), 9-11.

2. SUCCESS IN RECRUITMENT

The Commission with the co-operation of many agencies handled successfully the task of wartime recruitment. Difficult as were the labor market conditions under which the Federal government competed with private enterprise for manpower, the most critical quotas were met. Despite the fact that under manpower controls the Federal government possessed no competitive advantages over private employers and for over half of all positions rigid salary scales placed it at a distinct disadvantage, Federal employment grew to more than three times its 1939 total during the critical year 1943. Up to the middle of 1943 the rate of growth was about at the speed and volume the operating agencies desired in order to meet their program requirements. By that time manpower shortages prevented the attainment of many recruitment quotas and acted as a brake on growth.

Although the Commission had a creditable record in the recruitment of workers in mechanical production and even of clerical and office workers, its inexperience in the mobilization of higher grade administrators prior to 1940 handicapped its wartime efforts in that field. Thus it had to delegate unusual freedom to the agencies to engage in recruitment activities for executive talent. Operating officers of the employing agencies deserve much credit for enlisting many able business and professional leaders as civil servants for the duration. Similarly, the recruitment of dollar-a-year men was an agency program, primarily that of WPB, and in no way to be attributed to the Commission. War agencies experienced difficulties in competing with the armed forces which offered commissions to attract the caliber of men they desired for what were really civilian administrative tasks. Credit for the effective mobilization of scientists belongs principally to the National Roster of Scientific and Specialized Personnel with which, it is true, the Commission co-operated.

Previous inexperience with large-scale expansion of government functions and the ensuing recruitment problems taught Federal administrators at least two lessons of permanent value. One was that government needs young persons with a broad background, especially in the social sciences, whose potentialities can be developed for future administrative responsibilities. The other lesson learned was that government also needs mature persons who have successfully held administrative positions in business, education, the professions, or labor. This lesson was pointed up recently by Patterson French in his analysis of wartime personnel problems.[4] To meet these needs two steps were taken in the postwar period. One was a broadening by the Civil Service Commission in 1948 of its junior professional assistant examination into a junior management assistant examination to provide a register of able young generalists who may be trained in managerial responsibilities. The second was the establishment by President Truman in 1950 of a committee of assistant secretaries from the departments to discover persons of exceptional administrative talent for presidential appointment and to prepare a national register of such persons.[5]

3. PROGRESS IN TRAINING

Wartime training programs embraced a variety of types of work and revealed an inventiveness in method and an intensity of activities that would have seemed incredible when the war started in 1939. As never before the employing agencies became aware of the value of in-service training in meeting production goals. Indeed, deterioration in the caliber of recruits under low qualifications standards scarcely allowed departments to overlook the need for training.

In the field of training the employing agencies were, for the most part, on their own. Few precedents or guide lines existed in the Federal government to help in charting the new wartime programs. The Civil Service Commission established a Training Division in 1942, too late to be of help to the departments suffering the most acute problems in training: the War and Navy departments and OPA. In some agencies virtually no training programs had existed before the war, and any development of training activities represented progress. Only a few, like Agriculture, had drawn up a training policy some time before the war which could serve as a foundation for emergency programs. No government-wide policy regarding the responsibility for training existed or was ever developed. Thus many agencies were loath to admit that a shortage of qualified workers had to be met by in-service training. But once labor market conditions were clearly under-

---

[4] Joseph E. McLean (ed.), *The Public Service and University Education* (Princeton, 1949), 33-48.
[5] New York *Times*, April 20, 1950.

stood, policy at the departmental level was determined. Organization for training varied, therefore, according to departmental needs and traditions.

Six types of training enjoyed phenomenal new development during the war. Three of these, preservice or contract training, training in basic mechanical skills, and that in stenographic and office skills, were the outgrowth of passing wartime deterioration in the quality of recruits. Normally Congress frowned upon these three types of training and did not provide funds to finance them. The technical nature of World War II, however, compelled the agencies, especially the War and Navy departments, to utilize private facilities, to analyze jobs into their component simpler skills, and to organize on-the-job instruction in those skills. Improved indoctrination of new employees, the inception of supervisory training, and the inauguration of administrative training represented wartime developments of permanent value to the Federal service.

The lessons learned about employee training have not been lost in the postwar years. The administrative training program has, for example, not only become an integral part of the Federal personnel system but it has led to the incorporation of the former National Institute of Public Affairs preservice internship program into the Federal system. Many departments and agencies have instituted their own administrative training programs for the young recruits they select from the junior management assistant register. Many agencies have also developed more advanced supervisory and administrative training courses modeled on the original "J" courses. Notable among these has been the work simplification programs sponsored by the Bureau of the Budget.

4. REALIZATION OF THE IMPORTANCE OF EMPLOYEE RELATIONS

As with training, wartime labor shortages forced personnel administrators to focus attention on employee relations. The problems inherent in human relations, both on-the-job and away from it when outside conditions affect work production, demanded attention during the war. Hordes of additional employees brought together into already overcrowded cities or raw new settlements to perform strange jobs experienced tensions in living and working. Many of the problems of the period which personnel offices had to handle were ephemeral, such as transportation and day care of children of working mothers. Others, however, were fundamental to any modern employer, public or private, and included recreational programs, statements of grievance policy and procedures, relations with organized employee groups, incentives to work improvement, attention to reasons for turnover, and employee counseling.

Because employee relations were closely related to, if not a part of, operating responsibilities, they rested in the hands of the employing agencies and not with the central personnel agency. The only responsibility the latter possessed in this field was one of recommending policies to the agencies for their consideration and developing standards for the evaluation of agency programs. During the war the Council of Personnel Administration rather than the Civil Service Commission undertook both tasks to a limited extent with respect to specific policies, particularly on counseling and grievances.

At no time did the Federal government or employee unions propose the establishment of any formal negotiating machinery comparable to the Whitley councils of Great Britain. The nearest approach to such a step was the creation of the Labor-Management Advisory Committee in the office of the Civil Service Commission, which brought union representatives together with selected agency heads to discuss wartime personnel problems. Agency-union relationships still varied widely throughout the service and had not attained stability during the war.

In this period the existence of the problem of employee relations had been recognized, even the admission of a responsibility for the welfare of employees had been made, but what government agencies did they performed for employees as individuals. The government employer did not find the majority of employees organized as yet and was far from subscribing to collective bargaining. The approach was paternalistic, for progress was scored briefly in supplying services correlated with the exigencies of wartime living and working conditions.

5. NEW RECOGNITION OF PERSONNEL ADMINISTRATION

World War II gave an impetus to personnel administration at the departmental level similar to that given by World War I to the personnel function in private industry. Not until June, 1938, were federal agencies required by Executive Order 7916 to establish the position of personnel director. The War Department even required additional pressure from the President to comply with the 1938 order. But by 1939 when the war started many agencies had barely established their personnel divisions and had little specialization of function within them. Regional personnel directors were almost nonexistent before the war.

The War Department experienced the most noticeable burgeoning of functions within its personnel organization. Moreover, this differentiation of functions was paralleled throughout the three highest echelons in Washington and down into the field installations. Somewhat the same multiplication of personnel activities occurred at naval shore establishments. In some of the older agencies, like the General Accounting Office, an attempt was made to build up the personnel office by reorganizing it and bringing in a new director from another agency recognized for his leadership in the personnel management field.

In the field the number of regional personnel officers had grown to proportions that made feasible the organization of Regional Councils of Personnel Administration. The Civil Service Commission regional offices organized the division of their functions to work with the new field personnel offices and their divisions.

As might be expected, some critics looked askance at the expansion of personnel activities, for every new function developed in any organization may appear to older divisions to be an invasion of authority traditionally theirs. Some spoke deridingly of a "cult of personnel administration" and an overemphasis of the importance and function of personnel administration. Indeed, the Society for Personnel Administration felt moved to answer these criticisms.[6]

As a matter of fact, most of the new programs in government had already been tried in American industry over a period of years and in principle had proved profitable. The practical application of employee counseling services, recognition of group relations, and the development of training may, however, have missed fire in some quarters when applied to government agencies by zealots or "administrative imperialists." Then, too, a tendency always exists in a new field to develop specialization of function to such a degree that a broad understanding of the field is soon lost. Personnel administration was no exception to this tendency, and it was not until the postwar years that an attempt was made to reverse the trend and to develop personnel "generalists" rather

[6] "Is Personnel Overemphasized?" *Personnel Administration,* V (February, 1943), 2.

than, for example, classification, training, test, or counseling specialists.

The Civil Service Commission was the focus of much antipathy because its controls grew most extensively during the war. The denial of recruits to one agency in favor of another under the manpower controls was an unprecedented power deeply resented by officials placed at a disadvantage. Restrictions on transfer and enforcement of promotion standards seemed to many employees and administrators arbitrary interferences with agency responsibilities. But most unpopular of all Commission controls were the personnel utilization surveys which delved into the prerogatives of management to place and use manpower as it deemed best.

One final point may be made in connection with the expansion of personnel activities in wartime. The programs borrowed from industry were seized quickly, sometimes scarcely adapted to nonmechanical operations, and put into operation on the assumption that they possessed universal validity. War with its pressures and haste allowed little time for research to test the value of the new programs or to measure their results. If new programs are to be built on a solid foundation for application to the public service, studies and research must be done. Otherwise they merely represent "rule of thumb" or guesswork which was characteristic of public administration in earlier years.

Unsolved Problems of the War Years

1. Transfer and Promotion

The rapid expansion of the Federal service and the induction of thousands of employees into the armed forces accelerated mobility of employees from one agency to another as well as up the promotional ladder. Many individuals were pushed into added responsibilities by a lack of any other qualified available persons and could not have met the prewar standards for transfer or promotion. Others, however, found in the war their first real opportunity to prove their innate capabilities.

Chaos in the government program as a whole might have ensued from unlimited transfer had not controls been devised. Opportunities for transfer to war agencies were in some instances converted by those agencies into raids on personnel in "old line" agencies. The President, therefore, conferred power upon the Bureau of the Budget to impose priority ratings for transfer purposes among the agencies based on the relationship of agency programs to the war effort. Under a War Manpower directive the Civil Service Commission was delegated power to order necessary transfers or stop those contrary to the manpower program and the priorities. Because of the war agencies' pressing need for experienced government employees the Commission was impelled to appoint special negotiating officers to expedite such transfers.

More opportunities for transfer might have developed for qualified persons in critical demand had the Commission not failed in establishing a qualifications file of all Federal employees. Many Federal employees, therefore, continued to negotiate their transfers privately despite the establishment of a War Transfer Unit in the Commission to bring employees desiring transfer together with agencies seeking their services. Private negotiation was more rapid and increased the certainty of securing a satisfactory position. Thus Commission efforts to guide transfer failed of their objective.

Promotion followed much the same development as transfer. At first the Commission encouraged the departments to promote rapidly by delegating to them broad authority to pass upon the qualifications of employees for higher-grade positions. Postaudits revealed abuse of the authority, and Congress was aroused by the number of younger persons advancing to responsible positions. The Commission, therefore, in 1943 fixed more rigid standards to retard the frequency of promotion by setting time limits which were geared to salary levels and the increments involved in promotions.

The wartime problem with respect to promotion and transfer was to conserve manpower resources within the service by prompt shifting of trained personnel into the positions where it was urgently needed. Mere checking of movement from agency to agency or from a lower grade to a higher one was not alone sufficient to insure full utilization of manpower. If the Federal service is to benefit from the education, training, and experience of any of its civilian employees, some means must be developed whereby individuals with skills to contribute can be discovered quickly by the central personnel agency. In a period of manpower shortage compromise is inevitable between qualifications standards for promotion and the need to push experienced employees up into increased responsibilities in expanding programs as rapidly as possible. The problem is not one of mere mechanics. By rigid formulae the purpose of promotion—rewarding the capable by utilizing their talents—was partially lost. Indeed, the formulae stimulated the invention of ways to evade them, a situation which suggests that the promotion problem was in actuality far from solution during the war.

2. HANDICAPS OF AN INADEQUATE FEDERAL SALARY STRUCTURE

The rigidity of Classification Act salaries, which were dependent on statutory revision, revealed a weakness in the Federal personnel system during the war. In any period of inflationary price rises and labor shortage wage or salary systems which are "sticky" contribute to high turnover, low morale, and manipulation of the salary system by unjustifiable upgrading of positions. Internal discrepancies appeared in field establishments where employees under flexible wage scales based on local prevailing rates worked side by side with Classification Act employees and supervisors. Congress failed to recognize the basic need for general revision of Classification Act salaries until the end of the war but resorted to overtime work and pay for per annum employees through two makeshift measures.[7]

Resort to overtime pay to meet the rising cost of living and nongovernmental pay increases could only partially solve the pay problem. Overtime work was limited to eight hours per week additional at most; true overtime at time and one-half times the hourly rate earned was not granted to salaried employees in any event.[8] Even at the lesser rate of time and one-twelfth, it was limited to the first $2,900 of salary. Overtime was tolerable only because industrial concerns were requested by the President to adopt a forty-eight hour week. But in industry and business offices the rate was higher and was in addition to base pay increases allowable under the "Little Steel formula."

Congress rejected the sole attempt to adjust higher grade administrative and professional salaries by increasing the number of grades and raising the top salary level to $10,000. Subterfuge in the form of upward adjustment of classification allocations was

[7] 56 *U.S. Stat.* 1068 (1942); 57 *U.S. Stat.* 75 (1943).

[8] Instead overtime was paid at the rate of time and one-half times 1/360 for each overtime day. In actual fact Federal employees worked 260 days per year. In hours the formula was 1/2880 instead of 1/2080.

the only escape left to the harried war agency administrators. The older agencies were thereby forced to safeguard their working force by corresponding reallocations wherever possible. The erosion of qualifications standards by circumvention of the Classification Act was complementary to the deterioration of examination standards. The fall in standards was inescapable by reason of the wartime labor market. The circumvention of the Classification Act was a direct result of statutory rigidity and hence not an inevitable result of the manpower shortage.

Not until four years after the Japanese surrender did Congress systematically grapple with the classification and pay problem when it passed a new Classification Act.[9] By that time it was more than apparent that a simplification of grades and services was essential to provide a real unity in the government service, and the consolidation of four services into one was just as important as the lifting of the $10,000 salary ceiling for the top level positions of the civil service. In addition, Congress at last permitted a system of cash awards for outstanding employee contributions to the improvement of management.

3. CONTROL OF NUMBERS IN THE FEDERAL SERVICE

Early in the war Congress took alarm at the amazing growth of the civil service. First it probed into the problem through two investigations, one by a joint select committee, that on the Reduction of Nonessential Federal Expenditures, under the chairmanship of Senator Byrd, and the other by the regular House Committee on the Civil Service, headed by Representative Ramspeck. The committees made stout claims of cutting down the service from what it might have been had they not intervened. Then the problem was handed over to the Bureau of the Budget to establish personnel ceilings within the agencies over most Classification Act employees. The Civil Service Commission instituted personnel utilization surveys as another type of attack on the problem. But the size of the service remained very close to the 1943 peak of over 3,000,000 and actually exceeded it if the hundreds of thousands of employees outside the continental United States were considered a part of the total Federal employment.

Several reasons may be found for the failure of the congres-

[9] 63 *U.S. Stat.* 954 (1949).

sional investigations to provide any answer to the problem of numbers and utilization of employees. In the first place, Congress itself had imposed wartime tasks and responsibilities on the Federal government. To have the Federal government manufacture munitions, build warships, allocate scarce materials and equipment, supervise wartime scientific research, administer rationing, rent, and price controls, and undertake the dozens of other new tasks without marked increases in staff was unrealistic. There is evidence of congressional ambivalence in electing to fight total war and desiring to reduce Federal personnel when two-thirds of the Federal employees were to be found in the War and Navy departments.

Secondly, the problem of size of the service was related to the quality of agency management. The hasty construction of the war agencies precluded good management, at least at first. As Paul Appleby has said, "New bureaus will have a lot of 'policy drive' but, on the whole, less efficient administration."[10] Many administrators were new to government, unfamiliar with the programs they directed, and had to learn as they went along. Then, too, programs shifted with the course of the war. Political considerations often entered into agency management, as they will in a democracy. The best example of political interference was in OPA with its change of administrators, congressional ill will, and harrying by pressure groups. For a brief period the War Manpower Commission found its appointments unreasonably delayed by the necessity of political clearance when Congress required senatorial confirmation of all WMC employees receiving $4,500 per annum or more.

Performance standards for routine tasks by which agencies might have measured the efficiency of their employees had never been developed by either the Division of Administrative Management in the Bureau of the Budget or by the agencies themselves. In fact, the service grew too rapidly for the small Division of Administrative Management to cope with all the problems of internal management. It is entirely possible that performance standards might have possessed little validity if based on prewar qualifications of employees. High turnover and deterioration in the quality of recruits and supervisors required more personnel to meet the work performance of prewar years.

[10] Paul H. Appleby, *Big Democracy* (New York, 1945), 105.

In the third place, Congress could not discover any answers to the problem of agency management and poor utilization of personnel without adequate staff assistance for its committees. Without a sizable staff, well trained in the field of public administration, on hand to assist the committee by gathering and analyzing relevant data for them, they could come to no sound conclusions.

The effectiveness of the Bureau of the Budget ceilings to control numbers was seriously limited by inadequate coverage and the manpower situation during the war. Wage board employees who constituted at least one-third of the Federal service were not included by Congress within the scope of its jurisdiction. Reductions ordered among salaried employees in mechanical work could be offset by moving some of the salaried positions in the group under wage board procedures. Then, too, poor caliber of recruits and high turnover were not matters for which the Bureau of the Budget possessed a nostrum. Ultimately, of course, the power to fix personnel ceilings became a significant budgetary control, but that is a story of the postwar period.

The personnel utilization surveys of the Civil Service Commission were designed to get into the problem of agency management. Ordinarily utilization should have remained a problem solely of agency heads, but neglect of that problem in many quarters forced the Commission to institute its surveys in 1944. No results of manpower savings through the surveys have been revealed, and it is impossible, therefore, to gauge their effectiveness.

The size of the service is a problem of management after the original statutory delegation has been made by Congress. The waging of total war, the tight wartime labor market, the newness of many war programs, and the deterioration in the caliber of recruits defined arbitrary concepts and limitations as well as prewar standards for the use of personnel.

The problem of numbers is as far from solution in 1950 as it was in 1945. As a matter of fact, Congress has turned to other aspects of the dilemma today, for the basic concern of the legislator is, after all, with the volume of government expenditures. It toyed, therefore, with the idea of ordering a flat cut of a fixed percentage of an entire appropriation, but finally it placed on the President the responsibility for making such a cut of $550,000,000 in the 1951 omnibus appropriation act.[11]

[11] *P. L. 759*, 81 Cong. (1950).

4. CONTROL OF SUBVERSIVE ELEMENTS

The United States has never passed through the heat of war without danger to civil liberties. World War II was no exception, but for the first time the hysteria was effectively directed against Federal employees. The attempt by Congress to remove named employees as disloyal through a rider to the 1943 Deficiency Appropriation Act was ultimately settled by the Supreme Court in June, 1946, in a decision which branded the congressional rider as constituting a "bill of attainder" and therefore unconstitutional.[12]

Through fear of foreign ideologies, particularly of Communism, Congress raised the loyalty issue by forbidding participation in subversive activities by Federal employees. The proscription applied to such activities or affiliations at any time prior or subsequent to Federal employment. Since "subversive" was undefined, the only limitation on arbitrary interference with employees' rights was the sense of moderation and respect for constitutional processes existent in Congress or the executive departments.

That a classified Federal employee suffered a curtailment in the exercise of some civil liberties had, of course, been apparent since 1883. The acceptance of Federal classified employment had proscribed political activity or public expression of political opinion. Forbidding political activity after appointment was a different matter, however, from banning "subversive" activity at any time in any employee's career. The rule against political activity required only even-handed justice in ascertaining the facts about active participation in the affairs of *any* political party. It did not mean raking through the embers of past statements or thoughtless associations to ferret out a particular social and economic slant. But the rule against "subversive" activities required investigation of past utterances, beliefs, and associations. Judicial sense of balance, self-restraint, and a conscientious desire to seek assiduously for the truth were necessary in that search. Unfortunately they were not always present.

Congressional failure to contain its actions within clearly defined limits in creating the loyalty qualification led that body into dangerous territory. That Congress had the constitutional right to demand loyalty of Federal employees was unquestioned. Its methods and assumption of what constituted loyalty were, how-

---

[12] *U.S.* vs. *Lovett,* 328 *U.S.* 303 (1946).

ever, open to doubt. Its sole attempt at definition of "subversive" activity was as vague and obscure as though no definition had been offered. Had the handling of the loyalty issue been confined to administrative hands alone, under strict definition of terms, the several opportunities for appeal and review accorded those under fire would have served to mitigate to a large extent the errors of original judgment or prejudice of an overzealous investigator. The judgment of a review board was made upon a record in an atmosphere which could be calmer than that accorded by legislators in the heat of partisan debate.

The congressional suspicion of "red" activity among Federal employees by no means abated after the war. In fact, the rapid deterioration of United States-Russian relations and the onset of the "cold war" only served to stimulate the launching of more bitter and more frequent verbal barrages by Congress against the executive branch. In order to keep the loyalty program within some reasonable bounds President Truman in 1947 established a Loyalty Review Board within the Civil Service Commission and ordered each department not only to create its own loyalty board but to assume the responsibility for investigating all employees then currently employed.[13] The Commission was ordered to investigate the loyalty of every person entering the Federal civil service. Regional loyalty review boards were soon organized by the Commission. Nevertheless the congressional attack reached a crescendo in the summer of 1948, when the House Un-American Activities Committee and the Senate Expenditures Committee vied with each other for weeks in conducting hearings based on accusations against past and current Federal employees. In 1950 Senator McCarthy indulged in almost daily tirades for a number of weeks accusing the State Department of harboring varying numbers of "reds" and "fellow travelers." Some of the accused persons demanded a hearing, and the busy Foreign Relations Committee had to appoint a special subcommittee and staff to sift the charges. One of the accused, who incidentally had never been a State Department employee, Owen Lattimore, described this kind of tactic in a book about his experiences as "ordeal by slander."

The nature of the Communist strategy of infiltrating into

[13] Executive Order 9835, March 21, 1947, 3 *CFR, 1947 Supp.* 129.

critical sectors of so-called "capitalist" governments, the appeal of their philosophy to many educated and otherwise respectable native Americans, their use of espionage, and their unremitting dedication to the cause of world revolution, have all combined to raise the issue of loyalty where it never existed before. World War II made the United States the dominant world power for democracy and thereby stimulated Communist efforts to capture government personnel in agencies important in the event of revolution. The unhappy Federal employee, whose thoughtless affiliation and in most cases innocent acts of the past may heap on his head bitter congressional vituperation, is the victim of an impasse in international relations. His problem remains unsolved so long as the Politburo follows a truculent and revolutionary policy.

An Evaluation of the Part Played by the Civil Service Commission

For much of the achievement and a little of the failure in wartime personnel administration the Civil Service Commission was responsible. In evaluating its contribution during the years from 1939 consideration must be devoted first to the concept the Commission held of the role of the central personnel agency. From that point it is possible to judge its performance in fulfilling that role. Thereby the way in which it contributed to both success and failure may become clearer.

Two views are possible of the function of the Civil Service Commission as the central personnel agency. One is that its function covers merely procurement of personnel and that its responsibility ends once recruits become employees. That was the traditional view of its work held by the Commission for many years. The other interpretation of its function holds that it is to provide service and leadership to the departments in the improvement of personnel management and to furnish guidance to Congress and to the President in the formulation of enlightened personnel policies for building a real career service. The second interpretation is the newer view advocated by the Commission, advanced with increasing vigor during the war years.[14]

[14] See the annual reports of the Commission from 1939 to 1945 for an indication of its concern for the improvement of the Federal service and adjustment to the problems of war administration.

The interests of the Commission during the war years covered training, pay policies, employee relations, transfer, promotion, personnel utilization, safety and health, and unemployment compensation, all in addition to the statutory responsibilities for recruitment, position classification, retirement, leave regulations, and efficiency ratings. Indeed, its interests had broadened during the war years, for one finds the first references to some of these within the later war years.

As a service agency the Commission overhauled its own procedures, decentralized its authority to the field to the maximum extent possible, and adopted the position that it must stand ready to alter its program to fit the needs of defense and war. The flexibility introduced into wartime personnel administration was the direct result of Commission determination and policy. The principal form in which this flexibility took shape was in the war service regulations. Most of the success in recruitment was the result of the Commission's own efforts and Commission stimulation of and co-operation with the employing agencies and the USES. The Commission willingly accepted all manpower controls and operated successfully within their ambit. It rationalized its invasion of management responsibility through the utilization surveys on the ground that they would minimize unnecessary recruitment. In the field of transfer and promotion the Commission at first permitted the maximum freedom to the employing agencies. In addition, it tried to organize two programs to facilitate transfer. In training it eventually initiated institutes to spread the "J" courses for supervisory training among the agencies, and it co-operated with the Council of Personnel Administration in the establishment of the administrative internship program. It also called attention to the need for improved employee relations and for safety measures. To Congress it directed recommendations for more equitable pay policies, both with respect to overtime pay and basic salary adjustments and for unemployment compensation.

Moreover, several of the unsolved problems of wartime personnel administration were due to failures in Congress, notably in the handling of the salary problem and the control of subversive elements. The inability to control numbers seemed to rest, if anywhere, upon agency management although primarily due to extraneous circumstances. In what sense, therefore, if at all, did the Commission fail during the war years?

The failures of the Civil Service Commission were primarily administrative in not always executing successfully the plans it projected in order to be of maximum service to the agencies. Such administrative failures were essentially a failure of some Commission employees to measure up to the qualifications necessary to carry out their new wartime responsibilities. In other words, if the Commission suffered any serious deficiency during the war years, it was a shortage in its own staff of top-flight administrators. The inexperience of the Commission in recruiting high caliber executives for the Federal service before the war was a boomerang upon its own wartime program to some extent. Instead of being broadly trained men and women skilled in management, Commission executives were too often specialists in all the ramifications of the Civil Service Act and rules. In all fairness to Commissioner Flemming, in charge of the wartime program of the Commission, however, it must be admitted that he did secure the services of a few able individuals who had acquired experience in the various employing agencies and could bring a new viewpoint into the Commission. It was difficult to get enough of these people during the war years.

To recapitulate the Commission's failures is merely to corroborate the defects of its staff. The failure of the Interdepartmental Placement Service was due to a breakdown in planning and administration. The inability of the short-lived Training Division to render much advisory service to the agencies was due to a failure on the part of the staff to acquaint itself with the training problems of the service in 1942-1943, incapacity to inform itself of what was already being done in training in various parts of the service and outside, and inability to sell itself because of widespread disregard of it in the employing departments. Unfortunately this feeling was never overcome after the Training Division was liquidated in favor of the more active Federal Work Improvement Program.

Reorganization of the agency in 1943 left the persons responsible for bottlenecks in communications and tardiness in decisions still in positions where they could retard administration. Such individuals partially nullified the steps taken in the rationalization of administrative services, procedures analysis, and the development of management conferences. To a certain extent they also nullified the streamlining of Commission organization under one effective head.

The liquidation of the Research Division in 1943 was in a sense a result of a personnel failure with unfortunate consequences. Although the Research Division had made many valuable studies in preceding years, it had confined its work almost entirely to tests and their validation, neglecting the wider field of studies of other major personnel problems. Because the work of the Research Division had been so limited, the Commission found it easy to dispense with it entirely when the director of the division left in 1943. After all, validation of tests seemed futile under the deteriorated war standards. But the chance to render a larger service to the cause of improved personnel management was lost when research became a wartime casualty in the Civil Service Commission.

In summary, in the crucible of war Federal personnel administration made more gains than it suffered losses. The flexibility of the merit system had been proved beyond all doubt by its satisfactory adjustment and operation in a prolonged crisis. Recruitment of the great civilian army of Federal employees in a period of acute labor shortage was the successful achievement of many agencies working together, the Civil Service Commission, the USES, the National Roster of Scientific and Specialized Personnel, and the employing agencies. The primary responsibility and the brunt of the task fell on the Commission, and this responsibility the Commission bore well. With little prewar experience to guide them, many agencies improvised and borrowed ideas from industry in establishing training and employee relations programs of impressive scope and quality. Personnel administration acquired a new prestige as one agency after another had to broaden its personnel program to meet the unfamiliar tensions of war. Not even the debits the war inflicted upon the civil service in the form of attenuated qualifications standards and congressional interference with employee rights could eradicate the credits of solid accomplishment. Many steps were not taken that might have been taken had time permitted advance planning. But the nature of our diplomatic policy in the years of defense obscured the need for planning and forced improvising later. Mistakes were inevitable under improvisation, but wartime experience in personnel administration also contained many lessons. It seems clear today that the merit system emerged stronger in 1945 than it was in 1939 by virtue of the way it was administered during the war.

Index

Advisory Commission to Council of National Defense, 3, 66.
Aged, employment in government, 58; re-employment of retired federal employees, 58.
Agriculture, Department of—
  Employee relations, policy on, 288; services for, 291-92; counseling, 299; suggestion system, 305; grievance procedures, 314-15; employee organizations, 315, 317.
  In-service training, organization and policy on, 149-50; orientation program, 158; Graduate School program for office skills, 167; supervisory program, 175-76; internship, 182.
Allen, Charles R., 169, 173.
Anderson, Clinton P., 130.
Andrews Board, 279-80.
Appleby, Paul H., 355.
Appley, Lawrence A., 141, 330.
Appointments, probational-indefinite, 89; temporary, 90; war-service, 91-94; apportionment 91, 103-4; veterans' preference, 106-8; standards, age and physical reduced, 108-10; character requirements relaxed, 110; skills dilution, 110-13; experience requirements, 113-15; education requirements, 113-15.
Apportionment, 91, 103-4.
Appropriations Committee, House, 14, 76, 112, 120, 122-23, 125-26, 128-29, 130-32, 138, 170, 189, 205, 245, 284-85, 301, 303, 338.
Appropriations Committee, Senate, 131, 191-92, 194, 338.
Attainder, Bill of, 131-33, 357.

Bard, Ralph A., 318.
Baruch, Bernard M., manpower report of, 34, 37.

Baruch, Ismar, 224, 239, 242-43.
Barkley, Alben W., 129.
Bethune, Mary McLeod, 129.
Biddle, Francis, 132.
Black, Hugo L., 132.
Blandford, John B., 318.
Bone, Homer T., 131.
Budget, Bureau of—
  Administrative Management Division, 275-76, 355.
  Health programs, opinion on, 308.
  Management improvement program, 273.
  Meritorious service pay increases, 302.
  Overtime pay formula, explanation of, 218.
  Personnel ceilings, controls on, 35, 219, 222, 259, 260, 264-70, 277, 354.
  Priority ratings for employee transfers and recruitment, 197-99, 351.
  Reports on position-classification to, 242.
  Salary, policy on basic changes, 224, 233.
  Work Simplification Program, 172, 176, 348.
Bureaucrats, attacks on, 75, 226, 230, 233; defense of, 230-31, 267.
Burton, Harold H., 72.
Byrd Committee, 195, 205, 211-12, 239, 254, 255-60, 266, 268, 272, 327, 354-56.
Byrd, Harry F., 219, 228, 257, 264, 354.
Byrnes, James F., 6, 34.

Cannon, Clarence, 130, 189.
Carmichael, Leonard, 77.
Certification, 91; selective certification, 94-95; subeligibles use of, 101; "rule of three" relaxed, 102-

106; retained for selected positions, 104; reinstituted, 106-108; rejection of eligibles by appointing officers, 104-105.

Civil Service Commission—

Accusations against by other agencies, 38, 351.

Applications to, 98, 338.

Appointments, probational-indefinite, 89; temporary, 90; war-service, 91-94; apportionment 91, 103-104; veterans' preference, 106-108; standards, age and physical reduced, 108-10; character requirements relaxed, 110; skills dilution, 110-13; experience requirements, 113-15; education requirements, 113-15.

Arrearages of work, 14.

Attitudes toward, 230, 351.

Board of Appeals and Review of, 101-102, 126.

Certification, 91; selective certification, 94-95; subeligibles use of, 101; "rule of three" relaxed, 102-106; retained for selected positions, 104; reinstituted, 106-108; rejection of eligibles by appointing officers, 104-105.

Compensation, recommendations on, 217, 218, 221, 227-28, 231; authority over rates, 222.

Conference system of, 331-32.

Council of Personnel Administration, relation to, 337-40.

Decentralization to regional offices of, 16, 18-20, 332-37.

Delegation to operating agencies, 40, 45, 203-204, 237, 344, 345, 346.

Employee relations, counseling program, 293-94, 301; exit interviews, 295-96; meritorious pay increases, 302-304; suggestion systems, 305; health programs, 305, 307; grievance policy, 309, 310-11; employee organizations, 318.

Evaluation of, 359-63.

Examinations, noncompetitive, 89; unassembled, 95-98, 112; qualifications investigations, 97, 111; interviews, 97; assembled tests, 98-102; open continuous, 99; abbreviated tests, 99-100; appeal of ratings, 101-102.

Jurisdiction of, 12-16, 29.

Liaison officers of, 20-22, 41, 236-37.

Loyalty investigations by, 118; policy on, 119, 122-26; staffing for, 119-22; procedures in, 126, 334; Loyalty Board, 119, 126; Loyalty Review Board of 1947, 358.

Manpower policies of, 25-27.

Methods analysis in, 326-27.

Organization of, 321-41.

Position-classification, administration of, 235-36; lack of standards for, 236-40; publication of standards, 240-41; Personnel Classification Division, authority of, 237-44; field service classification, 241-50.

Promotions, agency latitude in, 203-204; restrictions on, 206-10, 352; congressional attitude on, 210-12.

Racial discrimination, policy on, 52-53.

Recruitment program, representatives for, 21-22; responsibility centralized for, 14, 27, 29, 30, 31, 33; interregional recruitment, 29, 36; unauthorized agency recruiting, 39-40; joint recruiting programs, 40, 45; direct recruitment, 40, 45, 46, 95, 98, 110; positive recruitment, 45; salared executives recruited, 73-77; Committee on Administrative Personnel created, 73-77; recruitment by dollar-a-year men, 75; scientists and professional personnel recruited, 77-80; recruitment of stenographers and typists, 80-81, 99; labor force recruitment, 82-85, 274-75; lack of coordination in programs, 261-62.

Reporting by, 327-28.

Research Division of, 326, 328-30.

Staff expansion of, 16, 19, 20, 257.

Training program, responsibility for, 136-39, 178; Training Division, 138, 326; Federal Work Improvement Program, 138-39, 180; orientation programs, 157; women employees urged, 162; of-

INDEX

fice skills suggested, 165-66; "J" courses promoted, 170-71, 275; administrative training, 178-83; agreements with agencies, 208-209.

Transfer of employees, efforts to guide, 186, 192-96, 352; reports on, 189-91; controls over, 196-201, 270-71; re-employment rights of transferees, 201-202.

Utilization of personnel, 38-39, 255, 259, 261-62, 265, 326; surveys, 269-76, 354; War Department surveys, 278-79; Navy Department surveys, 279-81.

Veterans' placement representatives, 61.

Civil Service Committee, House, 76, 191, 212, 217, 219-20, 221, 224-26, 227, 228-30, 302, 308-9, 310.

Civil Service Committee, Senate, 219, 221, 226, 228, 229, 249.

Classification Act of 1949, 354.

Coast Guard, overtime compensation in, 216; personnel utilization in, 280.

Committee on Administrative Personnel, 73-77, 178-79, 196.

Committee on Fair Employment Practice, establishment of, 51; Civil Service Commission use of, 50-51.

Compensation—
Inequities for Classification Act employees, 216-17, 220, 221, 222, 224, 229, 353.
Overtime pay, demand for, 215; legislation for, 216, 217-22, 227-32, 353.
Salary, basic pay changes proposed, 223, 225-26; legislation for custodial and subprofessional employees, 223-27; legislation for higher administrative grades, 223, 225-26, 228; general revision of scales, 227-33; merit increases, 231-32; inadequacy of salaries, 353-54.

Wage administration, 250-52.

Connor, Franklin G., 180.

Consolidated List, 45.

Controlled referral. See War Manpower Commission.

Council of Personnel Administration, 13, 98, 136, 178, 179, 180, 285, 287, 294, 295, 301, 303, 307, 310, 322, organization and work, 337-40, 349.

Counseling, policy on, 285, 293-95, 339; Interdepartmental Conference on, 294-97, 339; operation of programs of, 297-99; criticisms of, 299-302.

Cushman, Frank, 169, 173.

Davenport, Frederick M., 318, 337.
Dies Committee. See UnAmerican Activities, House Committee.
Dodd, William E., Jr., 129-33.
Dollar-a-year men. See Recruitment of.
Donaldson, Jesse M., 318.
Downey, Sheridan, 228.
Draft. See Selective Service.

Ellender, Allen J., 167, 310.
Ellender Committee, 167-68, 309-10.
Emergency Relief Appropriation Act, 1941, 118.
Emergency Relief Appropriation Act, 1942, 128-29.
Emmerich, Herbert, 67, 69, 70, 73, 86, 87, 225.
Employee relations—
Cash awards, 304-305, 354.
Counseling, 293-302.
Employee organizations, 315-18.
Federal Recreation Committee, 297.
Grievance policies and procedures, 309-15, 339.
Meritorious service increases, 302-304.
Responsibility for programs in, 284-88.
Services for employees, 288-92.
Suggestion systems, 304-305.
Employment stabilization. See War Manpower Commission.
Evaluation of personnel administration, achievements in wartime, 342-51; problems, 351-59; Civil Service Commission effectiveness, 359-63.
Examinations—
Assembled tests, 98-102; open con-

tinuous, 99; abbreviated tests, 99-100; appeal of ratings, 101-102.
Noncompetitive tests, 89.
Unassembled tests, 95-98, 112; qualifications investigations for, 97, 111; interviews, 97.
Executive order agencies, 5, 41.
Expenditures, Senate Committee on, 358.

Federal Work Improvement Program, 138-39, 180.
Felons, certification of, 110.
Flemming, Arthur S., 13-15, 26, 43, 73, 108, 112, 120, 122-23, 125-26, 168-69, 170, 191, 205, 210-11, 217, 218, 228, 245, 318, 321, 325, 331, 332, 360.
Fisher, Admiral Charles W., 221.
Foreign Relations, Senate Committee on, 358.
Frankfurter, Felix, 133.
French, Patterson, 347.

Gasser Board, 276-77, 279.
Gasser, L. D., 276.
Gearhart, Bertrand W., 230-31.
Gellhorn, Walter, 129.
General Accounting Office, 38, 188, 257-58, 308.
George, Walter F., 226.
Gore, Albert, 130.
Grievances, policy on, 285, 309-11; procedures, 311-15.
Griffenhagen and Associates, 277.

Handicapped persons, as government employees, 58-59; joint committee on, 58; Civil Service Commission placement manual on, 59; placement of veterans, 59; physical standards adjusted for, 109.
Harness, Forest A., 267.
Hatch Act I, 70, 118.
Health services, 305-309.
Hendricks, Joe, 129-30.
Herter, Christian A., 228.
Hoover Commission, 345.

Ickes, Harold L., 131, 132.
Industrial Relations Counselors, Inc., 285-86.

Interdepartmental Committees on loyalty, 127-28.
Interdepartmental Conference on Counseling, 294-97.
Interdepartmental Placement Service, 186, 192-94.
Interdepartmental Safety Council, 307.
Internship, administrative, 177-83, 338.
Interviewing, examinations, 95, 96, 97-98, 111, 344; placement, 98, 105, 173; induction, 157-58; training, 173, 299; exit, 106, 282, 295-96; counseling, 299.

"J" courses, 82, 136, 138, 169-73, 175-77, 338.
Job dilution, 135-36, 160, 161-62, 164.
Justice, Department of, 303.

Keefe, Frank B., 130.
Kerr, John H., 130.
Knudsen, William S., 70.
Kushnick, William H., 142, 145-46, 221, 249, 262.

Labor force, 25; new sources of supply, 48-61.
Labor-Management Advisory Committee, 318, 349.
Labor pirating, 25, 30.
Langer, William, 219, 221, 228, 264.
Lasser, David, 128-29.
Lassiter, Dillard B., 262.
Lattimore, Owen, 358.
Legal Examiners, Board of, 8, 92.
Leiserson, William M., 318.
Limited national emergency, declaration of, 3.
"Little Steel formula," 5, 250-51, 353.
Lloyd-LaFollette Act, 119.
Lovett, Robert Morss, 129-33.
Loyalty—
Appeals on, 101.
Appropriations acts requirements for, 118.
Bill of attainder case, 131-33.
Civil Service Commission, policy on, 119, 122-26; procedures in investigations, 126.
Congressional investigations of, 128-31.
Hatch Act requirements for, 118.

INDEX

Interdepartmental Committees, of Attorney General, 127; of President, 127-28.
Loyalty Board, 119, 126.
Loyalty Review Board, 358.
Unsolved problems of, 357-59.
Lucas, Scott W., 72.

McCarthy, Joseph R., 358.
McCormack, Edward J., 212, 262-63.
McKellar, Kenneth, 75, 131, 132; riders of, 76.
MacLeish, Archibald, 318.
McMillen, Lucille Foster, 325.
McReynolds, William H., 13, 197, 221, 224, 225.
Maloney, Francis T., 75.
Manhattan District Project, 36.
Manning tables, 279.
Manpower priorities. See War Manpower Commission.
Marine Corps, 280.
Maritime Commission, 217.
Martyn, John W., 318.
Mead, James M., 218, 226.
Mead-Ramspeck Act, 8, 231-32, 302-304.
Military Affairs, House Committee on, 14.
Miller, William J., 41.
Mitchell, Harry B., 322, 325.
Mitchell, James P., 246-47.
Moffett, Guy, 238.
Moser, Guy L., 226.

National Advisory Committee on Aeronautics, 217.
National Civil Service League, 47.
National emergency, declaration of, 4. See also Limited National Emergency.
National Institute of Public Affairs, 177, 179-80, 348.
National Roster of Scientific and Specialized Personnel, 74, 77, 343.
Navy, Department of—
  Compensation, overtime, 216, 217, 218; salary structure, 221; wage administration, 250-52.
  Employee relations, organization for, 285-87; employee services, 288-90; counseling, 297; suggestion system, 305; grievance procedures, 312-13; employee organizations, 315-17.
  Employment volume, 15-17, 84-85, 90, 256-57, 263, 268.
  Manpower controls, 25-26.
  Negro employees in, 53.
  Personnel utilization program, 279-81.
  Position-classification by, 235, 246.
  Promotions, freedom in, 203-204.
  Recruitment of labor by, 83.
  Standards for appointment reduced, 109, 111.
  Temporary employees, use of, 90.
  Training of employees, 136, 139; organization for, 146-49; policy on, 147-48; pre-service, 155-56; orientation programs, 158-59; apprentice program, 159-61; mechanical skills, 164-65; office skills, 166; supervisory, 173-75; administrative, 183.
  Transfers, intra-agency, 197.
  Travel funds for civilian employee recruits, 47.
  Waves, use of, 81.
  Women employees, use of, 48-49, 159, 165.
Negroes in government employment, 50-57; agencies' proportion of total in service, 54, 56; certification after discrimination proved, 52; Civil Service Commission nondiscrimination policy, 52-53; classification grades held by, 53-54; discrimination in hiring of, 57; union discrimination problem, 221-22.
Nelson, Donald M., 5, 70, 72.

Office of Economic Stabilization, 250.
Office of Emergency Management, 3, 242-43, 250.
Office of Price Administration—
  Economists criticized by Congress, 114.
  Employee relations, organization for, 288; services, 290-91; counseling, 298-99; suggestion system, 305; grievance procedures, 313-14; employee organization, 317-18.

Employment volume, 257.
Fallacies in position-classification, 238.
Training, policy and organization for, 150-52; supervisory program, 176.
Office of Production Management, 4, 5, 66.
Organization of employees, 315-18.
Overstaffing. See Utilization of Personnel.
Overtime work, 220. See Compensation.
Orientals in government employment, 59-60; Filipinos, 59; Japanese, 59-60; Navy and War Department objections to, 60.

Panama Canal, 217.
Part-time employees, 60-61.
Patterson, Robert P., 257, 260-61.
Personnel ceilings. See Budget, Bureau of.
Pickens, William, 129-30.
Piozet, Charles, 168.
Plumley, Charles A., 129.
Political activity, 70, 118, 357.
Porter, Paul R., 129.
Position-classification—
 Administration of, departmental service, 236-41; field service, 241-48.
 Appeals, 237.
 Classification Act of 1923, 248-50.
 Custodial and subprofessional services grades changed, 223-227.
 Inequities between Classification Act employees and wage board employees, 235, 239-41.
 New grades proposed, 223, 225-26.
 Personnel Classification Board, 238, 248-49.
 Personnel Classification Division, 239-44, 249-50.
 Pressures on, 234, 238-41, 245-48, 249, 353-54.
 Standards, lack of, 236-40; publication of, 240-43.
Priority ratings. See Budget, Bureau of.
Powers, D. Lane, 130.
Probationary period, 92, 105.
Production Urgency Committees. See War Manpower Commission.
Promotions, latitude of agencies in, 203-204; abuses by agencies, 204-206; restrictions by Civil Service Commission on, 206-10; congressional concern over, 210-12; volume of, 210.

Ramspeck Act, 13, 16, 112-13, 204, 207, 334.
Ramspeck Committee, 38, 39, 114, 145-46, 191, 210-11, 246-47, 254, 256, 260-64, 300-301, 303, 331-32, 354.
Ramspeck, Robert, 13, 73, 145-46, 168-69, 212, 217-18, 220, 225, 256, 260-64, 354.
Randolph, Jennings, 307, 309.
Rankin, John E., 230.
Recruitment—
 Difficulties resulting from pay policies, 217, 218-19, 227, 229.
 Direct recruiting, 40, 45, 46, 61, 83, 95, 98, 110.
 Dollar-a-year men, 65-73.
 Joint programs of agencies and Civil Service Commission, 40, 45.
 Labor force, 82-85.
 Positive recruitment, 45.
 Publicity devices for, 45-47, 79-81.
 Salaried executives, 73-77, 225.
 Scientists and specialists, 77-80.
 Stenographers and typists, 80-81, 99.
 Travel funds for recruits, 47-48, 80, 83.
 Unauthorized recruiting by operating agencies, 39-40.
Reduction of Nonessential Federal Expenditures, Committee on. See Byrd Committee.
Reed, Stanley F., 133.
Rees, Edward H., 219, 226, 230, 247.
Reeves, Floyd W., 108, 121.
Robsion, John M., 226.
Rogers, William C., 122.
Roosevelt, Franklin D., 3, 5, 12, 13, 16, 26, 50-51, 61, 71, 127, 132, 140, 219, 220, 221, 227, 265-66, 309, 315, 338, 343.

Sabath, Adolph J., 256.
Saposs, David J., 129.

INDEX

Scamping. See labor pirating.
Schuman, Frederick L., 129.
Selective certification. See Certification.
Selective Service, passage of act, 3, 22; age limits for registration, 4; ages for induction, 5; threat of induction for job-jumping, 37-38; data on IVFs for job placement, 46, 110.
Short, Oliver C., 168.
Snapper, 165.
Society for Personnel Administration, 350.
Spencer, W. H., 122.
Stanres Act for veterans' preference in employment, 61, 106-108, 114, 115, 344.
Starnes, Joe, 125.
State, Department of, 50, 358.
Stimson, Henry L., 141.
Subversives. See Loyalty.

Taber, John, 129, 132.
Temporary employees, 90.
Thomas, Elbert H., 221.
Training—
  Inservice, administrative, 177-83; apprentice programs, 159-61; contract type, 143, 155-56; "J" courses, 138, 169-73, 175-77; mechanical skills, 161-65; office skills, 165-67; organization for, 140-52; orientation programs, 157-59; policy on, 136-41, 147-52; responsibility for, 136-39; supervisory programs, 138-39, 167-77; Training Within Industry Program, 82; women workers' needs for, 49, 159, 162, 164, 165.
  Preservice, 155-56.
Transfer of employees—
  Commission efforts to guide, 186, 192-96.
  Competition, inter-agency, for employees, 187.
  Controls over, by Bureau of Budget, 197-99; by War Manpower Commission, 199-201, 202.
  Interdepartmental Placement Service, 186, 192-94.
  Priorities for, 186, 196-99.
  Volume of, 189-91.

Truman Committee, 65, 71-72.
Truman, Harry S., 65, 72, 232, 347, 358.
Turnover, 15, 18, 105, 106, 285, 295-96.

UnAmerican Activities, House Committee on, 120, 127, 128, 133, 134, 358.
United States Employment Service—
  Controlled referral plan of, 32-34.
  Employee availability statements, 37.
  Employment ceilings, 34.
  Employment stabilization plans, 31-33.
  Government recruiting, 33, 34, 36.
  Transfer to War Manpower Commission, 5, 16, 29.
  Use of, in recruitment, 30, 80, 82-87.
Urgent Deficiency Apporpriation Bill, 1943, 131-33, 357.
Utilization of personnel, program of, 38-39, 257-60; Civil Service Commission surveys, 269-76; War Department program, 276-79; Navy Department program, 279-81.

Veterans, Army release for civilian employment, 61; preference in government employment, 61, 106-108.
Veterans Administration, 249.
Volume of employment, statistics, 9, 10, 17, 84-85; size attacked, 230, 266-68, 354-56.

Wage administration, 250-52.
Wage-freeze order, 6, 250-51.
War, Department of—
  Compensation, overtime, 217, 218; salary structure, 221; wage administration, 251-52.
  Employee relations, policy on, 287-88; services, 290; counseling, 298; suggestion systems, 304-305; grievance procedures, 311-312; employee organizations, 315-16; 318.
  Employment volume, 15-17, 84-85, 90, 256-57, 259, 260-63, 268, 277.
  Personnel utilization, 276-79.

Position-classification by, 235, 239, 245-48, 249-50.
Promotions, freedom in, 203-204.
Recruitment of labor, 83.
Standards for appointment reduced, 109.
Temporary employees, 90.
Training programs, 136-39; organization for, 140-46; authorization of funds for, 143; contract training, 143, 155-56; pre-service programs, 155-56; orientation programs, 158-59; Air Force apprentice program, 161; mechanical skills, 162-64; office skills, 166; supervisory, 171-73; administrative, 182-83.
Transfers, intra-agency, 197.
Travel funds for civilian employee recruits, 48.
Wacs, non-use of, 81.
Women employees in, 48-49.
War Labor Board, creation of, 5; policies, 5, 27, 233, 250-51.
War Manpower Commission—
Authority of, 26.
Controlled referral plan of, 31-34, 37, 200.
Creation of, 5, 26.
Critical labor shortage areas, 32.
Critical occupations, 32.
Employee availability statements, 37.
Employment ceilings, 31, 34-35.
Employment stabilization areas, 33, 35.
Employment stabilization plans, 31-33.
Employment volume, 257.
Inter-agency transfer controls, 186, 196-97, 199-201.
Labor-Management Committees, 31.
Manpower controls, 30; rescission of, 36.
Manpower Priorities Committees, 35, 36.

Manpower priority ratings by, 31, 35, 278.
National Roster of Scientific and Specialized Personnel transferred to, 77.
Personnel utilization, 255, 259, 266, 270.
Position-classification directive, 242.
Production Urgency Committees, 35.
Relationship to Civil Service Commission, 26-27, 36, Figure 4.
Senatorial confirmation required for employees of, 75, 114, 355.
Training Within Industry Program, 82, 136, 169, 173.
USES transferred to, 29.
War Overtime Pay Act. See Compensation.
War Production Board, creation of, 5; recruitment of dollar-a-year men by, 65-73, 119.
War service regulations, 7, 91-93, 98-99, 343; transition procedures to, 93-94; certification under, 103-104; probation period changed, 105; age standards, 109; qualifications standards, 116; transfers under, 198-99.
War Transfer Unit, 186, 194-96.
Warren, Lindsay C., 38, 188.
Watson, Goodwin B., 129-33.
Weinberg, Sidney J., 68-69.
White, Leonard D., 120-21.
Wigglesworth, Richard B., 84, 125, 126, 139, 301.
Women, government employment 48-51, 79; training needs, 49, 159, 162, 164, 165.
Work Simplification Program. See Budget, Bureau of.

Young, Edgar B., 224, 225, 248, 318.
Youths, government employment, 55-58; minimum hiring age reduced, 57.